# RANDY TRAVIS

Music in American Life

*The Music in American Life series documents and celebrates the dynamic and multifaceted relationship between music and American culture. From its first publication in 1972 through its half-century mark and beyond, the series has embraced a wide variety of methodologies, from biography and memoir to history and musical analysis, and spans the full range of musical forms, from classical through all types of vernacular music. The series showcases the wealth of musical practice and expression that characterizes American music, as well as the rich diversity of its stylistic, regional, racial, ethnic, and gendered contexts. Characterized by a firm grounding in material culture, whether archival or ethnographic, and by work that honors the musical activities of ordinary people and their communities, Music in American Life continually redefines and expands the very definition of what constitutes music in American culture, whose voices are heard, and how music and musical practices are understood and valued.*

*For a list of books in the series, please see our website at www.press.uillinois.edu.*

# RANDY TRAVIS

## Storms of Life

DIANE DIEKMAN

Urbana, Chicago, and Springfield

© 2025 by Diane Diekman
All rights reserved
Manufactured in the United States of America
C 5 4 3 2 1
⊗ This book is printed on acid-free paper.

Library of Congress Cataloging-in-Publication Data
Names: Diekman, Diane, author.
Title: Randy Travis : storms of life / Diane Diekman.
Description: Urbana : University of Illinois Press, 2025. | Series: Music in American life | Includes bibliographical references and index. |
Identifiers: LCCN 2024054963 (print) | LCCN 2024054964 (ebook) | ISBN 9780252046667 (cloth) | ISBN 9780252047985 (ebook)
Subjects: LCSH: Travis, Randy. | Country musicians—United States—Biography. | Gospel singers—United States—Biography. | Singers—United States—Biography.
Classification: LCC ML420.T76 D54 2025 (print) | LCC ML420.T76 (ebook) | DDC 782.421642092 [B]—dc23/eng/20241118
LC record available at https://lccn.loc.gov/2024054963
LC ebook record available at https://lccn.loc.gov/2024054964

# CONTENTS

1 "Bring your toothbrush." 1

2 "It's too country." 9

3 "There was no way I could have not signed Randy." 26

4 "Don't record 'em if you don't love 'em." 46

5 "By this third album, he was a superstar." 59

6 "It's a tough job." 77

7 "Do you think he's as cute in person?" 89

8 "If you see what's wrong and you try to make it right, you will be a point of light." 103

9 "It's so competitive now. And this scares me." 118

10 "He signed autographs until the place was empty." 140

11 "We are proud to call Santa Fe our new home." 149

12 "We were both wrong." 164

13 "I am wearing what God gave me, and I am proud of it." 176

14 "In fact, I was feelin' mighty fine." 190

15 "Lord, please give him back to me." 200

16 "I think you would be the perfect person to manage Randy Travis." 210

Epilogue   223

Appendix A. Album Discography   229

Appendix B. List of Awards   241

Appendix C. Members of the Randy Travis Band   245

Acknowledgments   247

Notes   249

Index   275

*Photographs follow page 127*

# RANDY TRAVIS

# 1

## "BRING YOUR TOOTHBRUSH."

Randy Traywick stood in front of Judge Kenneth Honeycutt in Union County District Court. This May 1977 hearing wasn't the first for the eighteen-year-old Marshville resident. Since dropping out of high school in his freshman year, he had made numerous appearances at the courthouse in Monroe, North Carolina. He had been arrested and thrown in jail for larceny, driving while intoxicated, trying to outrun the police, assault, carrying concealed weapons, and other offenses. He didn't remember how many times he had been to court, but he knew he was going to prison this time.[1]

The felony probation violation bringing Traywick before Judge Honeycutt came from an arrest that had occurred the previous summer. In an interview years later, Judge Honeycutt summarized the events leading to that arrest: "He and some other fellows were out one night, and they stopped at some country store—it was in the middle of nowhere. Just out from Marshville, going to the Stanley County border. They had broken in the door and—like vicious hoodlums— they stole Lance crackers and Pepsis and Cokes. They sat there on the hood of their cars and drank their Cokes and ate their Lance crackers. I think a deputy sheriff drove by and saw them. It was felony larceny—anything you steal after breaking and entering is a felony." Traywick had been sentenced in September 1976 to a two-year suspended sentence and three years' probation.[2]

Then, in January 1977, he was arrested for attempted larceny. Left behind by his buddies and not wanting to walk home, he hot-wired a pickup truck in someone's driveway and drove it home. Before he could return it, the owner reported it stolen.³ Judge Honeycutt was meeting Traywick for the first time and was faced with revoking probation and putting the September sentence into effect. In the courtroom with Traywick that day were Elizabeth "Lib" Hatcher, his employer, and John Harper, a popular disc jockey. Traywick had recently won a talent contest at Hatcher's nightclub, Country City USA, in Charlotte, and she'd hired him to work part-time. Harper, the nightclub's announcer, assured Judge Honeycutt that Traywick was doing a good job at Country City USA. Hatcher promised to help keep the youth on a straight and narrow path.⁴ Traywick mumbled that he was sorry and it wouldn't happen again. Judge Honeycutt informed the young man, "I'm going to continue you on probation. But if you come back, bring your toothbrush and a change of underwear. We'll give you everything else you need."

Traywick's defense attorney then presented a guardianship request. A person under twenty-one and on probation could not work in an establishment that sold alcohol unless it was a parent or guardian's facility. To allow Traywick to work at Country City USA without violating the law, Judge Honeycutt designated Hatcher and her husband, Frank, as guardians.⁵ Traywick's parents had agreed to let their second-eldest son live with the Hatchers. They hoped the arrangement could further his music career and keep him out of jail. In June 1977, Traywick moved in with the Hatchers and started working full-time at Country City USA.⁶

Randy Bruce Traywick was born an eighth-generation North Carolinian, descended from a Quaker preacher who emigrated from England and settled in Stafford, Virginia, in 1699. Robarde Traweek's great-grandson, Berryman Traywick, was born during the American Revolution and moved to Anson County, North Carolina, in 1801.⁷ Traywicks still live in that area, which contains the towns of Peachland (Anson County) and Marshville (Union County). Several hundred family members are buried in the Fountain Hill United Methodist Church Cemetery near Peachland, beginning with Berryman in 1818.

Berryman's great-grandson (and Randy's great-grandfather), (William) Brownlow Traywick, was born in 1861 and lived through the Reconstruction period, past World War I, and into the Great Depression. He was one of many North Carolinians who experimented with making moonshine—illegal and untaxed whiskey distilled by the "light of the moon." When ratification of the Eighteenth Amendment in 1919 banned manufacture and sale of intoxicating liquor, daring drivers with fast cars delivered these illegal products. As moonshiners modified their vehicles to get the best possible smuggling space and driving performance, the North Carolina auto racing tradition was born. The still that Brownlow Traywick constructed from an old car sits today on the Traywick homestead, rusted out and hidden in the woods.[8]

One of Brownlow's sons, (Alexander) Bruce, married (Maud) Etta Davis in 1921, and they moved to Olive Branch Road, five miles northeast of Marshville. Bruce and Etta had three children, the youngest being Harold Bruce Traywick, Randy's father, who was born in Marshville in 1933. At age twenty-four, Harold married Bobbie Rose Tucker, age twenty-one, in 1957. Her parents and their ancestors were natives of Anson County. Harold built a house next door to that of his parents. The newlyweds would raise their family in this simple ranch-style house. Their firstborn, Ricky Harold, came along in 1958, followed by Randy Bruce on May 4, 1959.

In the 1960s, Harold owned Traywick Construction and built starter homes in nearby towns. Jerry Helms, who has lived his entire life on a neighboring farm, says his first paying job was painting Harold's new houses the summer before his senior year in high school. The day before Randy started the first grade in 1965, he and his grandfather rode along in Helms's 1956 Ford convertible to help paint. As they came to a little store about halfway between home and the construction site, Randy wanted to stop and get a drink. His grandfather told him he didn't need a drink. After a moment, Randy piped up from the backseat, "Ah, PawPaw, let's stop and get one. I'll pay for it." Helms recalls, "I'll never forget that. Randy knew his grandpa was tight with a dollar. We stopped and got one, and Bruce paid for it."

By then the Traywick family included five children. After Ricky and Randy, Rose Marie was born in 1961, David Brownlow in 1962, and Linda Sue in 1964. Harold built an addition onto the house, with a bedroom for Ricky and Randy and another for the girls. Dennis Erie completed the family in 1968. Each time Harold and Bobbie brought a baby home from the hospital, Harold put the infant on a horse to take a photograph. Dennis's first memory is of horses. "When school was out, in the summer," he recalls, "that's all we did, basically. We'd be gone all day, come back late in the afternoon."[9] On Sunday afternoons, Harold would saddle a dozen riding horses and tie them to the fence near the barn, available for friends who wanted to ride. That included the six children of cousins Curtis Traywick Jr. and his wife, Betty, who were the same ages as Bobbie and Harold's children. "Riding horses was a family affair for the Traywicks," Randy recalled, "and some of my best memories of my childhood are those times when our whole clan saddled up and rode together through the woods, fields, and trails around our home. At times I'd ride for miles with my friend Tim Griffin." The two boys did everything together—attend school, ride horses, get in trouble.[10]

Both Randy and Dennis shared Harold's passion for horses. They learned from him how to train horses to do tricks. Harold bought unbroken young colts at an auction, rode them for sixty days, and then sold them. Randy's favorite horse was named Buckshot. "When I had something on my mind, I'd ride for hours by myself—just Buckshot and me," he recalled. Buckshot served as a sanctuary to "escape the craziness" of Harold's drinking. Randy's father was an abusive alcoholic. "The trouble was that Daddy liked to drink—a lot—and when he did," Randy explained years later, "he turned violent, threatening people, fighting with others, breaking furniture, and shooting at anything that got in his way. Fortunately, he never actually shot any people, but he came close." Randy said, "For most of my early life, my siblings and I were afraid of Daddy, and I'm pretty sure Mama was too. He especially seemed to take out his anger on Ricky and me—knocking us around, beating us with leather horse reins, and screaming obscenities at us for the smallest thing we did or didn't do, anything that didn't meet his expectations."[11]

Harold had a decades-long rap sheet with the local police. "Everything from driving while intoxicated to public drunkenness, assaulting a law-enforcement officer, discharging a weapon in a restricted area, and threats and personal assaults," according to Randy, who called his father "a man of contradictions." But Harold enjoyed spending money on his children. "When he had money, Daddy bought us almost anything we wanted," Randy said. "All six of us kids had our own horses by the time we were five years old, as well as go-carts and, later, Honda motorcycles." Although the children were terrified of their father, they "had a saint for a mama," Helms says. Randy described her as "a quiet, brown-eyed, dark-haired beauty with an angel's heart." For many years, Bobbie worked in Monroe at the Barth & Dreyfuss textile mill, where she weighed and packed oven mitts and potholders for shipping. She also inspected finished textile work at Monroe Prints.[12]

At some point Harold decided to get into the turkey-raising business, a longtime income source in the mid-southern part of the state. By the mid-1970s North Carolina was the largest turkey producer in the nation. Harold, with the help of his sons, built four turkey houses across the road from the Traywick residence, along with others on a farm he owned several miles down the road. Feeding and watering turkeys, cleaning watering troughs, and removing excrement were added to the daily chores of the Traywick children.

They had to walk through the big houses and pick up dead turkeys while live ones roamed free. "It was nasty," Rose says. "It stunk. The turkeys would come after you." Dennis, at age seven or eight, was afraid of the big tom turkeys that almost knocked him down. "I hated it," he says. "I preferred the horses." Randy remembered turkeys as the dumbest animals he'd ever seen.[13]

The children attended Marshville Elementary School, graduating to East Union Middle School and then Forest Hills High School, all in Marshville. Randy dropped out at age fifteen, during his freshman year. "I hated school," he told an interviewer years later. "I would leave home, with Mama and Daddy thinking I was going to school. I'd get there and find somebody to leave with. I couldn't stand it. Just didn't like to be in school."[14]

Randy's first vehicle was a blue 1965 Chevrolet pickup truck. "I was a pretty good driver," he remembered, "but I tended to drive too fast and too recklessly." He talked about the night he drove off the road and rolled three times: "I said, 'Hmm, I'm in the ceiling. I'm in the floor. I'm back in the seat. I'm back on the floor.' If I died then, that would have been the last thoughts I had."[15] When Dennis was in elementary school, he would beg his mother not to let Randy pick him up from school. "I hated those days," Dennis says. "Although you got there quickly, it seemed like an eternity. When you're in second or third grade and he'd pick you up in his hot-rod truck, driving around curves and on the wrong side of the road. You laugh at it now, but it wasn't funny back then."[16] Randy once took Ricky's car for a joyride. When a police car appeared behind him, he tried to outrun it and was clocked at 135 miles per hour before losing control on a curve. The car spun around backward several times, and Randy crashed through a cornfield at seventy miles per hour. "They took me down and locked me up," he recalled. "It's hard to outrun police. I never had much luck doing it."[17]

Along with their passion for horses, Randy and his father shared a passion for traditional country music. Harold had all the records of his favorite singer, Hank Williams, along with those of Lefty Frizzell, Merle Haggard, George Jones, and other legends. Randy absorbed the music. The first songs he sang in public were those of Hank Williams. Harold insisted his children take music lessons. In 1967, when Randy was eight, he and Ricky began three years of guitar lessons with Kate Mangum, a well-known rhythm guitar player in the nearby town of Salem. She gave lessons to about sixty students in her small home, including all six Traywick children. Harold told Ricky and Randy, "Both of you will be guitar players, and one of you will be a singer. Which will it be?" Since Ricky didn't want to sing, that role went to Randy. Harold booked them into various regional venues for contests and benefit performances. In 1968 they played their first public performance as the Traywick Brothers duo; it was a contest at a fiddler's convention at Marshville Elementary School. Within two years, dressed in matching outfits of white pants with red shirts and red neckerchiefs, they were usually winning the contests they entered around the Carolinas. "I would pick the songs and tell them what to sing," Harold once told an interviewer. He described training Randy: "I've stopped him lots of time in practice when he'd hit a note wrong or do a song wrong and make him start over—right in the middle or wherever he was at."[18]

Harold added a twenty-by-forty-foot music room to the house, to give Ricky and Randy a place to play and sing. With a dance floor, stage, kitchen, bathroom, fully stocked bar, and two jukeboxes, it easily accommodated the forty-plus friends and business associates Harold frequently invited for private parties. He and Bobbie cooked steak dinners and treated everyone to an open bar. The stage contained a variety of instruments for guests to use.[19]

The Traywick Brothers expanded to include David, who played bass, and several cousins, eventually becoming a band that consisted of Ricky on electric guitar, Randy, cousin Mike Traywick on drums, and various bass players. The Traywick Brothers played a variety of music, including bluegrass conventions even though they weren't a bluegrass band. Randy fronted the country shows because he loved country music. Ricky preferred rock. When Harold lost his driver's license due to his drinking, neighbor Helms often drove Harold's Imperial station wagon and pulled the band trailer. "They'd go Friday nights or Saturday nights and play from eight o'clock to midnight, mostly beer joints in Charlotte," Helms recalls. "Where they hadn't oughta been playing, cuz they was underage." When Mike and Ricky turned seventeen, they sometimes drove to the venue and set up the equipment before Harold arrived. Cousin Ronnie, who occasionally played drums, remembers those evenings as "a good way to learn how to work a crowd—to hope to get them to appreciate what you're doing up there."[20]

As Ricky and Randy gained in popularity and success, they also increasingly got in trouble with the law. They once broke into the Nicey Grove Baptist Church in Wingate and held a beer party. They were charged with breaking and entering, public drunkenness, and parole violation. Another time, Randy threw a brick through the front window of Pruitt Phifer's country store so he and Ricky could steal pocketknives and Timex watches. This was the same store they'd visited as children on horseback, which Randy later recalled, saying, "We'd tie off the horses out back and go inside to get sandwiches and drinks or some snacks." Mr. Phifer, a family friend, did not press charges against the two teens. Dennis recalls his older brothers coming home on nights when they'd been drinking and carousing. He would quickly get to the other end of the house to avoid the inevitable confrontation. "Daddy was very quick-tempered," Dennis explains. "If you crossed him, he's gonna win, regardless. Or that belt would come off, and he would mark you up. Hand, belt, stick, whatever he had. And if he told you once, that's what he meant."[21]

Harold tried to get his sons to behave, but he couldn't change their behavior any more than he could change his own. He probably didn't realize the example he was setting. The American Addiction Center reports that children of alcoholics are three to four times more likely to develop alcohol use disorders than peers without alcoholic parents. They may begin in adolescence to abuse alcohol and engage in risk-taking behaviors. They may drink earlier because of access to alcohol or lack of supervision. Alcohol may help them cope with stress and deal with emotions they can't express.[22]

Music held the Traywicks together. Their house and car radios were always tuned to WSOC-FM in Charlotte. Radio manager John Harper had started the station's country format in 1971; he hosted a three-hour "Morning Drive" show. In early 1977, Harper announced a talent contest to be held at Country City USA, a nightclub in Charlotte. The Traywicks were listening.[23]

One Tuesday night in February, Harold and Bobbie took their sons to the first round of the eight-week competition. Ricky played lead, Randy sang and played rhythm, and they won that night's contest. Ricky's court appearance came the next week, and he was sentenced to a year in a minimum-security facility. Randy continued solo in the talent competition, even though he had never performed by himself. Helms usually drove him to and from Charlotte. Although Randy "had a really nice pickup," Helms remembers, he had no driver's license. Like his father, he had lost it as a result of drinking and driving.[24]

Another contestant was twelve-year-old Kevin Jonas, who routinely sang in churches while his mother played the piano. She brought him to the Country City USA competition, and he won the first night he performed. Jonas recalls, "This tall, skinny guy had this amazing deep voice, and he sang George Jones. His tone was unbelievable, rich and full. I was shocked that that kind of sound could come out of him. Even as a kid, I appreciated it." Over the remaining weeks of the contest, Randy and Jonas usually alternated winning. Each night's winner received fifty dollars. Jonas, who would later establish

Jonas Enterprises and is best known as the father and manager of the Jonas Brothers (a pop-rock trio that has sold more than seventeen million albums), calls Lib Hatcher "an encourager." He remembers "how encouraging she was to me as a young, talented kid."[25] A total of 120 contestants competed for the first prize of one hundred dollars in cash, a dinner at a steakhouse, and several hours in a recording studio. At the end of April, Randy won the overall contest because he won the most individual weeks. Jonas came in second. When the Marshville newspaper, the *Union News and Home*, announced Randy as the winner, he told the reporter he wanted to make singing a career. He said, "If I ever get to the stage of the Grand Ole Opry, I guess I'll know I made it." His buddies looked forward to being able to say they "knew him way back when," with one of them commenting, "He'll put Marshville on the map."

For Randy, the best reward was Lib Hatcher offering him a part-time job as a Country City USA handyman who could occasionally sing with the house band. When he told Hatcher he had an upcoming court date and was headed to jail, her reaction surprised him. "I believe in you, Randy," she said. "And we're going to do all we can to keep you out of prison."[26] Within a month, he was living with the Hatchers. His life had been changed forever, thanks in large part to Judge Honeycutt's decision.

## 2
## "IT'S TOO COUNTRY."

Elizabeth "Lib" Hatcher, along with her husband, Frank, purchased Country City USA in early 1977. It was one of several Charlotte nightclubs advertising a live country band and large dance floor. With years of experience working in and managing restaurants, Lib wanted to be in business for herself and make money by booking top acts in her own club. Born in 1941 in Kernersville, North Carolina, Mary Elizabeth Robertson grew up loving country music. While in high school, she worked at the restaurant her mother managed. She graduated from high school the month Randy Traywick was born in Marshville, 120 miles south. After taking a job as an office assistant, which bored her, Lib moved to Charlotte and worked for eight years at a restaurant whose owner later said, "She started out as a waitress, then I made her hostess, then head cashier. She ended up as manager." In 1967, at age twenty-six, she married Frank Hatcher, who built pipelines for Harrison-Wright Company.[1]

Talented in styling hair and applying makeup, Lib volunteered to assist country artists such as Loretta Lynn and Dottie West when they came to the Charlotte Coliseum for concerts. That gave her an opportunity to meet artists backstage. Energetic and persistent, she also made personalized ceramic ashtrays for the stars, using those as a way to get backstage and introduce herself. In 1976, upon hearing rumors that management at WSOC-FM, the popular country station, was considering firing its morning disc jockey, Lib started a fan club for sixty-three-year-old radio veteran John Harper. She and her friends at the beauty shop circulated petitions and brought 258 signatures of support to the radio station. Her group created and distributed a variety of T-shirts, bumper stickers, and stationery, emblazoned with the slogan, "Have a John Harper morning."[2]

Impressed by her zeal, the radio station not only retained Harper, it also hired Lib to sell ads. She promoted a concert by Gene Watson, a Texan who had gained national fame with hits like "Love in the Hot Afternoon" and "Paper Rosie." Being his fan, Lib volunteered to meet Watson at the airport. She took him to his hotel and to the venue. Watson recalls, years later, "The next thing I know, Lib had bought a club, and she booked me in there. She was extremely devoted to me and my music." One of the nightclubs Lib visited while selling ads was Country City USA. She had never been in a nightclub. "I had never had a drink, a cigarette, even a cup of coffee," she later told an interviewer. But she liked the club's commercial possibilities. Several months later, she owned it. One of her first actions in this new venture was to start an eight-week talent contest in February.[3]

When the Hatchers acquired Country City USA, one of their regulars was Larke Plyler, nineteen-year-old son of Lib's best friend, Janice Plyler. "Me being a young, broke kid, they would let me in for free," Larke remembers. "Lib and my mother did everything together, shopped and everything." They all knew that Lib would be a success. Plyler says, "There's not a smarter businesswoman in the country than Lib. That woman's a genius." Her husband, on the other hand, cared only about hunting, fishing, and working. "And that was pretty much it," Plyler says about Frank. With Frank working out of town most of the time, Lib focused on making the club a success. George Stoner and Country Lovin' provided dance music Wednesday through Saturday evenings. John Harper hosted a Wednesday talent night.

When Randy Traywick moved in with the Hatchers, he cooked at the club, cleaned, mowed the lawn, and did basic maintenance, as well as singing. Within two weeks, on June 24, 1977, the band was advertised as George Stoner, Randy Traywick, and Country Lovin'. Less than a year later, Stoner was gone and Traywick was leading the band. "When I started to sing, I was doing Hank Williams songs, Merle Haggard, George Jones, Lefty Frizzell, Ernest Tubb, people like that," he later told an interviewer. "I grew up with them, and those are some of my favorites still." His friends listened to rock 'n' roll, so he heard that music when at their houses or in their cars. It never appealed to him. "If I bought a record," he said, "if I was at home and turned on the radio, it was country."[4]

Traywick was content with his life of singing during the evening and cleaning and maintaining the club during the day. But Hatcher thought he could be a country music star. With no experience in managing an artist, she signed him to a contract that allowed her to manage his career. Gene Watson remembers playing his first gig at Country City USA, where Traywick opened the evening's show. "The guy had natural talent," Watson says. "You could tell, with the right management, he could probably amount to something." Hatcher asked Watson to produce a record by her protégé. "She was one of those types that if she really wanted something and had faith in it, she went after it," Watson says. He told her, "Lib, I'm not a producer, and I really don't have time to do it." He said Traywick deserved someone to really give some attention to him.[5]

Hatcher also regularly booked Joe Stampley, a Louisiana native who had three number one *Billboard* country hits: "Soul Song," "Roll On Big Mama," and "All These Things." She asked if he could help her young singer in any way. Stampley thought Traywick sounded a lot like George Jones and Merle Haggard. Hatcher and Traywick attended Stampley's shows throughout the Carolinas, driving long distances to see him onstage and discuss the possibility of making a record. When Stampley agreed to produce a recording session in Nashville, Hatcher and Traywick drove there. "He's the most humble, kind, good person," Stampley says. "I knew that when I recorded him." Stampley hired Nashville's A-team players for the session and recorded four songs. He took the recordings to the Nashville labels, who said, "No, he sounds too much like Jones and Haggard." Hatcher also pitched the recordings to major labels. The usual answer was, "It's too country."

Stampley then contacted Stan Lewis, the owner of Paula Records in Shreveport, Louisiana, the label where he had recorded in the 1960s. Lewis agreed to put out two singles on Randy Traywick. "She's My Woman" entered the *Billboard* chart on January 6, 1979, stayed four weeks, and reached number ninety-one. The second single did not chart. Lewis wouldn't let Stampley produce a Traywick album because he was afraid that first single might be the best they'd do. At nineteen Traywick was thrilled to have a record on the *Billboard* country chart, even if it didn't go far. He was encouraged that people had bought his music and radio deejays had played it. "I felt sure with enough time and effort I might be able to make a living playing and writing music," he said, reminiscing. He and Hatcher learned as they went. After watching the movie *Coal Miner's Daughter*, they followed the example set by Loretta Lynn and her husband. "We mailed our record to radio stations and then we got in the car and started going from one radio station to another, trying to talk them into playing our record," Traywick later said. "And people were pretty nice to us. A good portion of the people at the radio stations we visited did play the records."[6] The recordings surprised Gene Watson, who continued working shows at the club, with Traywick opening for him. "And the first thing you know," Watson says, "I heard that Joe Stampley had produced a record on him." He could see himself in Traywick onstage. "I kinda hid behind a guitar and a microphone," Watson explains. "If you liked singing, you might like me. If you liked a show, I wasn't the one to come and see. I didn't put on a show; I stood there and sung my songs. And that's the way Randy was. He was strictly an artist that sings, and he did it well."[7]

About this time, Hatcher became friends with Ann Tant, who had worked for Nashville record labels before returning to Atlanta, Georgia, to help run her mother's country nightclubs. Tant occasionally booked Traywick into those clubs. She sometimes traveled with the couple to their club dates. The women took turns driving while Traywick tried to sleep in the backseat. One night, as he adjusted his five-foot, nine-inch body in the cramped space, he kept thinking, *Please quit talking so I can go to sleep*. Eventually, they stopped at a convenience store, and Hatcher went inside. Traywick thought, *Finally, a little peace and quiet*. But no. Tant unfolded the road map and started talking to herself: "I could take this road here and follow this." Traywick wanted to reach up and choke her. During those trips, he ran into a problem with people being unable to pronounce or remember his name. They would say Trailways or Tire-wick or Treadway. One day, the travelers stopped at a radio station in South Carolina. The disc jockey introduced him for an on-air interview by saying, "Randy Tirewick we've got with us today."[8]

In addition to helping with road trips, Tant hosted parties for entertainers. Moe Bandy from Texas remembers Traywick sitting in the corner playing guitar and singing. Bandy was another artist Hatcher booked at Country City USA. With five years of his own hits, such as "Bandy the Rodeo Clown," he had recently collaborated with Joe Stampley on several comedy duets, including "Just Good Ole Boys." He considered Country City USA a typical honky tonk and a fun place to play. Hatcher told him she was trying to get Traywick a record deal in Nashville. "I thought he was a great singer then, and he improved as he went," Bandy recalls. "I thought he was that good that he should be famous."[9]

Traywick was gaining courage to sing his own songs. As a child, he'd tried writing songs to emulate the ones he heard on the radio. Growing older, he learned to express his thoughts in lyrics and chords. At Country City USA, he heard many stories about broken relationships and people struggling to get through tough times. "Sometimes I'd hear somebody say something," he recalled, "and think it's a good idea for a song. I'd take that line and build a story around it." He thought "Reasons I Cheat" would be a good idea for a song, and he wrote a story around that title. A teen who could listen to conversations and create lines like "A wife too demanding / With no understanding / Of why I stay dead on my feet" and "My children keep growin' / My age keeps on showin' / Like all of my old friends I meet" was showing great promise as a songwriter. The waltz ended with "The dreams that I've buried / the load that I carry / Are some of the reasons I cheat."

Another song that expressed older themes than expected of someone his age was "Send My Body (Home on a Freight Train)." He said, "Whenever I slipped in one of my own songs at Country City and the crowd responded positively, their support boosted my confidence to write more."[10]

◊ ♦ ◊

The suspiciously close relationship between the young singer and his manager bothered two men, in particular—Harold Traywick and Frank Hatcher.

When Harold came to Country City USA to see his son, he usually created a drunken scene. Randy explained years later, "He'd get in arguments with other customers or with Lib when she tried to calm him, or with me. Especially with me. He sometimes smashed beer bottles or turned over tables in the club, threatening people and brandishing his .38 caliber pistol." Harold and Lib were both headstrong people who thought they knew what was best for Randy and his career. Harold wanted his son to come home and out from under Lib's control. He worried about the type of influence this woman was exerting. Lib wanted Randy in Charlotte, away from his troublemaking Marshville friends.

One night Randy and Harold were arguing in the parking lot as the club's bouncer hovered nearby and monitored the confrontation. Harold got so angry and frustrated that he jumped in his car and rammed it into the side of the building. Lib banned him permanently from the club. Randy loved his dad and wanted to please him. He also wanted the life Lib offered. He trusted her and realized that was where his future lay. There was no future in Marshville. "Lib was one of the best things that happened to me in my young life, and I felt a strong allegiance to her," he said. "Although Daddy urged me to come back home, I decided to stay in Charlotte."

Frank had long been suspicious of the amount of time his wife spent with her young protégé. "He wasn't wrong," Traywick recalled years later. "So often as soon as Frank took off on another business trip, we hopped into bed."

Larke Plyler, who considered Lib "a powerhouse" who didn't let anything get in the way of what she wanted, recalls hearing about the evening that ended the marriage: "Frank traveled with my dad for work and did in fact leave one Sunday afternoon for work. But he stayed around till that night and went back and caught Randy and Lib together. Frank told Lib it's me or that goddamn guitar picker." Without hesitation, Lib chose the guitar picker. She emptied the house and moved herself and Randy into a mobile home. The Hatcher divorce was final by March 1980, with Lib becoming sole owner of Country City USA.[11]

Plyler maintained a lifelong friendship with all parties involved. At age twenty-three, in the summer of 1981, he began a twenty-one-year career with the Union County Sheriff's Office; he was the jail administrator for many years. Harold Traywick was incarcerated there from time to time. While in jail, he would cook for the others, making excellent catfish stew.[12]

The release of the movie *Urban Cowboy* in June 1980 fueled an urban cowboy craze across the nation. In the movie, Bud Davis (John Travolta) starts hanging out at Gilley's, a popular real-life nightclub in Pasadena, Texas, a suburb of Houston. Bud meets a cowgirl named Sissy (Debra Winger). They dance, fall in love, and get married. When con man Wes (Scott Glenn) entices Sissy away from Bud while teaching her to ride the mechanical bull, Bud signs up for a bull-riding contest to try to win her back. The movie's popularity brought cowboy culture and mechanical bulls into the mainstream. Mechanical bulls, also called bucking machines, were initially invented to help bull riders improve their rodeo performances. Although they buck and spin as a real bull does, an operator controls the intensity of movement and can instantly stop the machine. Sherwood Cryer, who owned Gilley's with country music star Mickey Gilley as a partner, had designed for his patrons' entertainment the machine that was used in the movie.[13]

Even before urban cowboys and cowgirls in hats and boots began flooding country nightclubs, Hatcher was on the move. She ordered a mechanical bull and had it shipped from Texas. When the three-horsepower, eight-hundred-pound mechanical bull arrived on a Saturday afternoon, Hatcher ordered two walls knocked down to get it through the front door. The ceiling had to be raised to keep riders from being tossed against it. Sixteen mattresses around the machine provided a bounce zone for those tossed from the bull. Fourteen bags of sand, totaling a thousand pounds, anchored the bull. By mid-August, "El Toro" was ready for operation. The debut of the first mechanical bull in Charlotte rated an article in the *Charlotte Observer*. The crowd at Country City USA numbered 271 that evening, with 129 riders forking over two dollars apiece for an attempt to stay on El Toro for ten seconds. According to the article, one of the observers that first evening was Randy Traywick, "lead singer in the club's band, Country Lovin'." Operating the machine became one of Traywick's duties. Plyler confirms, "He would jump all of us off that bull. He enjoyed doing that." Traywick would eventually establish a reputation as someone who could ride the bull at top speed and never get thrown off.[14]

Another beneficiary of the urban cowboy craze was Country Underground, a Charlotte nightclub similar to Country City USA. When Ronald Radford from South Carolina joined the Willow Creek Band there, the other band members told him he needed to go to Country City to hear this kid named Randy. After being urged several times, he went. "I was floored," he says. "He sounded the same at that young age as he did when he started making it big in the business. Had that deep baritone voice." He got to know Traywick and the other musicians and sat in with the band. He occasionally subbed as a guitarist and shot pool with Traywick. Radford remembers, "He'd sing the last part of the sets, and the rest of the time he was shooting pool. He loved doing Merle Haggard and Jones. And Hoyt Axton. He was country through and through." Radford sometimes visited with Hatcher while she ran the mechanical bull and Traywick sang onstage. "I got along great with Lib," Radford says. "She treated me very nice. Lib was considered a hard person, but I know of no woman at the time who accomplished so much for an artist. Whatever she said, she did."[15]

◇ ◆ ◇

The Iran hostage crisis ended on January 20, 1981. Militant Iranian students had seized the US embassy in November 1979, and Iran's political and religious leader, the Ayatollah Khomeini, imprisoned fifty-two US diplomats and citizens at the embassy in Tehran. They were held captive 444 days, despite continuous efforts to free them. A popular song called "Tie a Yellow Ribbon 'round the Ole Oak Tree," about a man returning home from prison, became a rallying cry for Americans. People all over the nation tied yellow ribbons on their trees. Negotiations failed, as did a military rescue attempt that ended in disaster. President Jimmy Carter's inability to end the crisis cost him the presidential election, giving a landslide victory to Ronald Reagan. Iran surprised the world by releasing the hostages only minutes after Reagan was inaugurated as the fortieth president of the United States. The nation erupted in celebration. That Tuesday evening, Randy Traywick and Country Lovin' took the stage at Country City USA and sang "God Bless America" and "So Glad to Be Back in the USA." A joyful crowd applauded the band and toasted the release.[16]

A week later marked the closing of the 250-seat Country City USA location. Four years after Hatcher took ownership, she moved to a 400-seat club several blocks down Wilkinson Boulevard. The new location included a thirteen-room motel called the Split Rail Lodge, along with retail space to sell records, western wear, and her ceramics. Hatcher had worked hard to build her club's reputation and develop relationships that could help her find a recording contract for Traywick. Her efforts to book entertainers like Joe Stampley and Gene Watson helped spread the word in Nashville that Country City USA was the place to book solo acts not big enough to fill the Charlotte Coliseum. George Jones, Faron Young, and Moe Bandy played there, as did Gary Stewart, Freddie Hart, John Anderson, and numerous other familiar names. In addition to top-notch country music and the mechanical bull, Hatcher experimented with a variety of cover charges and special events—dance contests, clogging contests, talent nights, bluegrass nights, jam sessions, horseshoe competitions, whatever was popular at the moment.

Mike and Ronnie Traywick drove to Charlotte several times a month to see their cousin. "Country City was the hot spot," says Ronnie. "If you were into country music, that's where you went." Randy stayed busy singing or fulfilling other employee duties. "Lib kept a pretty short leash on him, but at the time, he probably needed it somewhat," Ronnie recalls.[17]

With Country City USA humming along, Hatcher and Traywick started traveling more frequently to Nashville to find a record deal. They'd spend the week pursuing contacts and being turned down before making the eight-hour drive back to Charlotte for the weekend and repeating the process the next week.[18] Dave Barton was a Nashville booking agent for Dick Blake International and its large stable of touring artists. He would call the nightclubs on his list in search of dates to play. Whenever he tried to book an artist into Country City USA, Hatcher would say, "Well, if you get Randy on the Ralph Emery show, I'll take a date." It didn't matter who he was promoting, she asked for a slot on the weekday morning WSM-TV show. Barton eventually arranged the visit, although he didn't think it would help Traywick's career; the show's audience was not in the music business.

But Emery could be a star maker. In addition to the 6:00 a.m. television show, he hosted a late-night, coast-to-coast radio show on WSM-AM and was a Grand Ole Opry announcer. Traywick was in awe of this famous personality. When he walked into the studio around five in the morning, Emery looked at him without saying hello and gruffly asked, "You any good?" Caught off guard, the scared young man managed to say, "Some good." After the show, Emery was friendlier. With a twinkle in his eye, he advised, "Always tell them, 'You're doggone right I'm good.'" Traywick took that as a great compliment.[19]

Traywick was a purist who refused to compromise his choice of traditional country music, and Hatcher supported him. Unfortunately, record labels weren't looking for traditional music. The 1970s had been a period of pop crossover songs, and the urban cowboy momentum continued that trend into the 1980s. Record labels wanted singers who could succeed on both country and pop charts—such as Kenny Rogers, Anne Murray, Olivia Newton-John, Lee Greenwood, and Ronnie Milsap. They certainly didn't want honky tonk music or fiddles and steel guitar.

Still, to have any success, both manager and artist felt they needed to be living in Nashville. Traywick's felony conviction didn't prevent him from leaving North Carolina, so Hatcher purchased an old house at 1610 Sixteenth Avenue South on Music Row in Nashville. On August 27, 1981, she assumed the existing loan balance of $90,081 at a 17 percent interest rate. Her monthly mortgage payment would be $1,431. She hired a manager to run Country City USA. In recent months, the band had been advertised as "Randy Traywick and Country Lovin' and Susan Ledford." After mid-September, the marquee read, "Susan Ledford and Country Lovin.'" Randy Traywick had moved to Nashville to join the never-ending flow of singers searching for recording contracts.[20]

Nashville's title as the "Country Music Capital of the World" can be traced back to October 5, 1925, when WSM Radio first signed on the air. The National Life and Accident Insurance Company owned the radio station, whose call letters referred to National Life's motto, "We Shield Millions." Within a few weeks, WSM debuted what is now the longest-running live radio show in history, the Grand Ole Opry. It was so popular that a venue had to be found to hold the spectators who wanted to watch the performers on the radio show. As crowds grew, the Opry eventually moved to the Ryman Auditorium in downtown Nashville in 1943. Music industry businesses opened offices in the surrounding area, especially after the Castle Recording Studio was established in the Tulane Hotel in 1946. Artists who had been traveling to Dallas to record now had a studio close to home.

The foundation of Music Row was laid in 1955 when brothers Owen and Harold Bradley purchased a house in a once-grand residential neighborhood immediately southwest of downtown Nashville. They turned the house into a recording studio and then expanded the Bradley Film & Recording Studio by building a Quonset hut next door at 804 Sixteenth Avenue South. Its opening coincided with the closing of the downtown Castle Recording Studio. In late 1957, RCA Victor Records built a recording studio on Seventeenth Avenue. The following year, the center of Nashville's music industry migrated from downtown to Sixteenth Avenue South. Marty Robbins, best known for "El Paso" and his *Gunfighter Ballads* album, was one of the first to move his office from its downtown location to an old house on Eighteenth Avenue South. Other publishing companies and entertainers joined him on Music Row, with the recording studios replacing WSM and the Opry area as industry focal points where musicians congregated.[21] Most of these businesses were closer to the north end of the mile-long stretch of Sixteenth and Seventeenth avenues that made up Music Row. The Country Music Hall of Fame and Museum opened in 1967 on Division Street, which crossed the north end of Music Row. At the south end, Belmont University still sits. Founded as a women's college in 1890, it became coed in 1950. Since the early 1970s, taking advantage of its Music Row location, it has developed a strong reputation for music business and performance degrees.

Downtown lost the Opry when it moved in 1974 to the location where it remains today. The current Grand Ole Opry House, the first venue built specifically to house the Opry, was the centerpiece of Opryland USA, a 110-acre entertainment park located thirteen miles northeast of downtown Nashville. The nation's only musical-themed park had opened two years earlier. Featuring unique roller coasters like the Screamin' Delta Demon and water rides like the Grizzly River Rampage, the park also contained a plethora of live outdoor stages that featured new talent. Approximately twenty-five hundred people worked at Opryland every summer, providing employment for local teenagers and opportunities for young singers and musicians who came from around the country to make names for themselves. The music industry in Nashville expanded to support them—instrument shops, management firms, recording studios, and so on. WSM Radio moved from downtown to the new location. To support the thousands of tourists visiting Opryland, the formerly undeveloped area inside Briley Parkway became a sea of hotels, restaurants, and entertainment venues. Nashville native John A. Hobbs teamed with other businessmen to build some of them. They successfully petitioned the Nashville Metro Council to change the name of Elzie Miller Road to Music Valley Drive. At the corner of Music Valley Drive and McGavock Pike, which comes in from Briley Parkway, the group built the Nashville Palace in 1977. Located almost a mile north of the Opry House, the supper club at 2400 Music Valley Drive featured dining, dancing, and live entertainment nightly.

By the time Traywick and Hatcher moved to Nashville, there were two distinct areas supporting the country music industry. Music Row, with its record labels and recording studios, gained its power from record sales and radio play, which leaned toward pop trends. The Opryland/Music Valley scene maintained itself through tourism, with fans who mostly preferred traditional country music. Music Row, in general, did not look to Music Valley in its search for talent. Hatcher and Traywick worked diligently to establish connections in both country music camps. Their two-story, gabled, yellow-brick house sat near the south end of Music Row, about six houses from Belmont University. It was in serious need of repair, as were many in the neighborhood. Traywick used the construction skills learned from his dad to make repairs and remodel the house.

Traywick ran every morning down Sixteenth Avenue to the Country Music Hall of Fame and back up Seventeenth Avenue. "As I made the turn," he remembered years later, "I looked up at the Hall of Fame and wondered what it would be like to have my name and image on a plaque in that building." He worked out to stay in shape, partly because he so enjoyed Hatcher's fabulous cooking. He bought weights and barbells and set up a workout room in the basement. He could do squats with 245 pounds resting on his shoulders. When he could afford to buy exercise machines, he added a few of those.[22] He and Hatcher spent time at the Nashville Palace, which had become the place to hear great entertainment and see familiar faces. Opry stars played there during the week, many of them booked by Opry member Ray Pillow, who would retire in 2017 after fifty years on the Opry stage. A native of Lynchburg, Virginia, Pillow was also a songwriter and publisher and was always willing to help others get ahead.

That included new Nashville residents Hatcher and Traywick, according to Daryl Ray Pillow, who remembers his father inviting the couple to his music room on Highway 96 in Franklin. When they talked about the difficulty of getting people to pronounce and remember the name Traywick, Ray Pillow suggested, "Why don't you go by Randy Ray?" Because Hatcher and Traywick were low on funds, Ray Pillow paid for the early publicity photos of Randy Ray. When a position for restaurant manager opened at the Nashville Palace, Pillow recommended that owner John Hobbs hire Hatcher. Hobbs agreed, making her his employee in September 1982. Hatcher quickly hired Traywick as a dishwasher. She put him onstage with the band for an occasional song. Without this fortuitous opportunity, Traywick might have become one of the many young singers seeking employment on the outdoor stages when Opryland reopened the following summer.

A September ad in the *Tennessean* advertised Daryl Pillow & the Pillow Gang as "live entertainment nightly" at Music Valley's Nashville Palace. "Lib Hatcher, Manager" appeared at the bottom of the ad. Pillow's band played five nights a week when not on tour. Ron Hogan, the band's steel guitarist, remembers, "Randy would be in his kitchen outfit, and he'd get up and sing, and the people would love him." Traywick was introduced as, "He's the dishwasher here at the Nashville Palace and wait till you hear him sing." The people liked him even more, Hogan says, "because he was like the underdog, being the dishwasher." Traywick also did much of the cooking. When an interviewer asked him years later if he was a good cook, he responded, "Well, I cooked. I'm not a great cook. I learned to cook what was on the menu, and I didn't learn much other than that." He added that he occasionally bussed tables but was never a waiter.[23]

Ray Pillow, in an effort to assist Hatcher with apparent problems at Country City USA, told Daryl, "Why don't you go over and work Charlotte for a couple weeks at Lib's place, and let Randy come in here?" Daryl, booked into the Nashville Palace for that two-week period, asked, "Why would I want to work in Charlotte for less money than I'm making at the Palace?" Ray said, "Daryl, we're trying to help them. Just go do that for me." So the Pillow Gang went to Charlotte in mid-October and swapped places with the Country City USA band, which drove to Nashville. "Randy Ray & Country Lovin'" headlined for a week at the Palace.[24]

After years of playing for a dance crowd at Country City USA, Traywick was in for a surprise. "Singing onstage that long for that many people who are the same every night, you run out of things to say," he once explained. "You find yourself thinking, what am I going to say now, after this song? You end up singing a lot and not talking much onstage." He was shocked by the reaction at the Nashville Palace, where the audience sat respectfully and listened to him. "The first night working at the Palace was really a scary night," he recalled. "After that first set, which was about an hour long, I came offstage and I thought, boy, they hated me. Nobody danced. Nobody was loud in the whole show." Ray Pillow settled him down by assuring him the people enjoyed the show, and he would get used to the unfamiliar response. Traywick learned to enjoy working in theater-type situations where people sat and listened. "You feel like they're really paying attention to what you're saying and what you're singing," he said in an interview.[25]

Shortly after the Pillow Gang returned from Charlotte, Hatcher fired Daryl Pillow. He took the matter to court, through the musicians' union, for violating his club contract. Although he won the case, he didn't recoup the money owed to him. "I will say I wasn't a great fan of either one of them for a long time," Pillow says. Still, he admits, "I think Randy is a great traditional country singer." The firing and its aftermath damaged Ray Pillow's relationship with Hobbs, who hadn't objected to Hatcher's actions. Daryl says his father stopped booking talent for the club.[26]

On New Year's Eve, Hatcher presented "A Country New Year's Eve with Tom T. Hall's Band—The Storytellers." She hired most of those musicians to be the club's next band, known as "Nashville." Bass player Leon Watson and keyboardist Drew Sexton both spent time as bandleader. Kenny Soderstrom played fiddle, with Terry Buttram on drums. Sexton invited lead guitarist Rick Money, better known as L D Wayne, to join them, saying, "There's a guy named Randy Ray gets up and sings, from the kitchen." Rick L D Wayne Money joined the band in January 1983. Watson recalls, "Randy would sing with us. Always got a great response. He'd go back and start working in the kitchen again. I'll give him that—he was a worker." Watson found Traywick to be quiet, polite to the audience and the band, and never nervous. "A pleasure to back, onstage," Watson says. "I don't recall him even messing up *once*. You either have that stuff or you don't. It's not something you learn. With him it was natural."

About Hatcher, he says, "Me and Lib never saw eye to eye." Every weekend that a late tour came in, she asked if the band would play overtime, and he asked if she planned to pay extra wages. When she said no, he said, "Well, we won't play over then." Watson thought the relationship between Hatcher and Traywick was "just odd." He remembers Hatcher criticizing twenty-three-year-old Traywick, who responded "like a whipped pup." Watson wanted to tell her to leave Traywick alone. "We'd be on stage rehearsing at the Palace," he recalls, "and she'd come up and *rrr-rrr-rrr* about something. We'd look at each other, and no one would say anything, and Randy would hang his head." Watson calls Hatcher "very strong-willed" and says she treated other Palace employees the same way. "Randy never looked at girls," Watson says. "He was strictly business. When he worked, he worked."[27]

◇ ♦ ◇

The Nashville Network (TNN) started broadcasting from the Opryland USA theme park on March 7, 1983, placing a spotlight on country music and Nashville. The cable and satellite network, owned by WSM and later sold to Gaylord Entertainment Company, brought both popular and new entertainers to national audiences. TNN's flagship show was the ninety-minute primetime *Nashville Now*, hosted for the next ten years by Ralph Emery. Traywick's first visit to *Nashville Now* was as an audience member. Leon Watson, who had left the Palace to tour with singer Shelly West, stopped by one day and overheard Traywick say he hadn't been to the *Nashville Now* show. Watson asked, "What are you doing tomorrow? Meet me here at four o'clock." They went to the TNN studio, where Traywick watched Watson play that evening during West's performance.[28]

Brothers Jimmy and Gary Carter joined the "Nashville" house band, with Gary on steel guitar (replacing Kenny Soderstrom on fiddle) and Jimmy taking Watson's role on bass guitar. Buttram remained on drums, with L D Wayne on electric guitar and serving as bandleader. Traywick would be called out of the kitchen every set. He'd rip off his white apron, put on his suit jacket, rush to the stage to sing four or five songs, and then go back to the kitchen. "He was this incredible singer with a lot of emotion," Gary Carter recalls. "He could deliver a song like the old-timers could." Carter recognized Traywick's talent and songwriting abilities, and he remembers thinking, *Well, man, he's an incredible singer, but there's not a market for him*. Traywick sometimes hung out with the band members during their breaks. "He would come out and play Pac-Man with us," Carter recalls. "He was king of the Pac-Man game."[29]

After the Grand Ole Opry performances on Friday and Saturday nights, the Opry crowd would go to the Palace. The number and diversity of audience members led Traywick to say working in the Palace "was like traveling without going anywhere." There was a different crowd every two or three nights as groups of tourists went home and others arrived for their vacations.[30] Over two million country music fans visited Opryland every summer, with the Opry itself drawing its year-round attendance from across the nation, along with international tourists.

One of the Opry stars who frequented the Nashville Palace was Jeannie Seely, who joined the Opry in 1967 and remains an active performer today. "I knew what a great talent Randy was," she says. "That big voice never seemed like it should be coming out of that guy. Kind of like Brenda Lee—how can that big voice be coming out of that little girl, and that's what I first thought about Randy." She liked his diction. Willie Nelson once told her there was no sense in staying up all night writing song lyrics and then having nobody understand them. A singer must ensure the audience can understand the words being sung. Seely understood everything Traywick sang, which showed a confidence many young artists lack. "It's something they develop," she explains. "It seemed like Randy had that from day one."

Monday nights were "Opry Star Night" at the Palace throughout 1983, with "Randy Ray & 'Nashville'" performing the other six nights. Seely, Little Jimmy Dickens, and numerous other Opry stars took turns performing for the Palace crowd. Seely frequently cleared Hatcher and Traywick to go backstage at the Opry. "It's such a great learning experience for these young people," she says. "It's wonderful to me to see that hunger, knowing they want what I wanted." Traywick later acknowledged such visits by saying, "I got to know a lot of people in town. I could go backstage at the Opry because I knew people who were members, and they'd leave my name at the door. That was nice, to be able to go backstage. I really enjoyed that." Moe Bandy, whose then-recent top ten hits included "Rodeo Romeo" and "She's Not Really Cheatin' (She's Just Gettin' Even)," frequently stopped by the Nashville Palace and watched Traywick perform. "He was working his tail off, y'know," Bandy says of the young singer he'd met several years earlier in Charlotte.[31]

Traywick and Hatcher spent their off-work hours on Music Row, trying to interest record labels in Randy Ray. They met Charlie Monk, who had worked at several Nashville music publishing companies before establishing the Monk Family Music Group, a family-owned and -operated publishing company, in 1983. He had signed Keith Stegall as one of his songwriters. Monk and Stegall both liked Traywick's songwriting and singing. Monk provided a contract to publish Traywick's songs, and he advanced a sum of money. Traywick didn't know the details of the copublishing deal, explaining, "Lib put the last page of the agreement in front of me and said, 'Sign this,' so I did. I was unconcerned about the specifics. I was just glad someone wanted my songs." The agreement gave half the publishing rights to Monk and half to Hatcher. Stegall took Traywick into the studio to record demos on songs each of them had written. But record producers and label executives who heard the songs turned them down.

Hatcher rented a room to Stegall on the ground floor of her house to use as an office. She rented space to the *Radio & Records* trade magazine, which paid Traywick thirty dollars a week to clean the office, an extra income for which he was grateful. Hatcher and Traywick lived on the second floor and had their office there. Dozens of women worked as Hatcher's personal assistants, some for only a few hours, Traywick recalled. "She made her assistants cry, and many of them quit," he said. "A couple went out for lunch and never came back. If I happened to talk to one of the cute girls, I noticed she was soon gone." Hatcher also kept a close eye on Traywick while at the Palace. She showed up whenever he talked to a young female. She said she didn't want him distracted from his pursuit of country music stardom.[32]

Tourists at the Palace asked if Randy Ray and the band had tapes or albums available for purchase. Hatcher approached Hobbs about the possibility of recording a live album. When he agreed to pay for it, Hatcher asked Stegall to produce it. He also agreed. The "Nashville" band still included lead guitarist L D Wayne, Buttram on drums, and brothers Gary Carter on steel and Jimmy Carter on bass. Stegall, though not a member of the band, played piano on the live album because Sexton had recently moved to another nightclub. The band came to the Palace during the afternoons to rehearse already familiar songs, those Randy Ray normally sang during his set. The recording took place after several weeks of marketing the project. The Nashville Palace was packed with more than four hundred people that Friday night in November 1983. Stegall hired Johnny Rosen, who owned a full twenty-four-track recording studio built into a tractor-trailer rig, to do the recording. He set up his audio truck, the band ran a sound check, and the show began. "We played it live, Randy sang it live," Carter says. With the nightclub located on Music Valley Drive, Hatcher used "Music Valley Records" as the label name under which to release the album. Traywick wrote six of the twelve songs and cowrote three. Stegall mixed the album and overdubbed some rhythm guitar and background vocals. He played the songs for numerous record executives on Music Row, but no one was interested. The music was too country.[33]

Traywick made his first appearance on a national television show at the beginning of 1984, as a guest on *Nashville Now* to promote his record album, *Randy Ray Live at the Nashville Palace*. Barbara Mandrell, the Country Music Association's Entertainer of the Year in 1980 and 1981, introduced him as Randy Ray. She said he performed regularly at the Nashville Palace and had recently recorded a live album there. Her introduction was a thrill in itself. He sang "Send My Body (Home on a Freight Train)." When host Emery joked, "Why is that microphone shaking?" Traywick laughed and said, "That's a good question." Emery assured him he was among friends and there was no need to be nervous. Traywick later recalled, "I thought I was gonna shake to death. Singing to a camera is a totally different thing than to stand in front of an audience and sing."[34]

Changes to the band occurred in February when fiddle player Kenny Sears replaced steel player Gary Carter and brought along pianist John Propst. Steve Hill replaced Jimmy Carter on bass. Along with Buttram and Wayne, those five musicians comprised the 1984 band. Today, Sears is retired from the Time Jumpers western swing group and continues to work with Jeannie Seely on the Opry. Sears compares country music to a tree, with the Carter Family and Hank Williams being the trunk, and branches going in all directions. In 1984 there was a huge limb coming out in the pop direction. "Then here came Randy, trying to make it on a tiny twig, so close to the trunk," Sears explains. "With this no-frills, no-nonsense, just sing the song and let it be what it is, with fiddles and steel instead of strings. We all hoped Randy would make it, but we didn't have a lot of faith."

About Hatcher, Sears says, "Libby managed the club well enough. But as an artist's manager, she was feeling her way through. It was obvious to everyone in the band—even back then, we weren't spring chickens, we knew the business pretty well—she was learning on the job." Sears recalls the club being full almost every night. The band would bring up Randy Ray at the end of each set. "We liked Randy a lot, and we wanted to see him succeed, but we couldn't help having a little fun," he says. They would tell him they'd call him up at twenty after, and then they'd introduce him at ten after instead: "For whatever reason, we got a big kick out of seeing him come running around the corner from the kitchen, ripping off his apron." The young singer took the teasing in good humor.

Traywick returned to *Nashville Now* on July 16. Emery introduced the twenty-five-year-old as "the cook who became a singer." His first song was "Ain't No Use," one of his self-penned songs from the album. Since he loved singing Merle Haggard, George Jones, and Lefty Frizzell songs, he initially chose a Haggard classic for his second song. Charlie Monk squelched that idea, telling him *not* to sing the hits of other performers. "Everyone will think you are copying them," Monk advised. "Do your *own* songs." Traywick accepted Monk's wisdom and chose another song from the *Randy Ray Live* album, "I Told You So."[35]

Jeanne Pruett, a singer/songwriter best known for "Satin Sheets," would include "I Told You So" on her October 1985 album, *Jeanne Pruett*. She was the first artist to record one of Traywick's songs.

# 3

# "THERE WAS NO WAY I COULD HAVE NOT SIGNED RANDY."

Martha Sharp moved to Nashville from Virginia in 1963 to be a songwriter. When she signed a contract with Painted Desert Music Corporation, she already had a song playing on pop radio, "The Special Years" by Brook Benton. She wrote Sandy Posey's million-sellers, "Born a Woman" and "Single Girl." Bobby Vee recorded Sharp's "Come Back When You Grow Up."[1]

Sharp was working as assistant to Jimmy Bowen, label head at Warner Bros. Records, in the early 1980s when he moved her into an A&R (artists and repertoire) position before he left the company. She described A&R as "a little bit of everything that's connected with getting the best product into the stores—finding new talent, the songs, getting the best producer for an act, the best studios, the best record mastering facilities, right down to the quality of the vinyl itself." When a Warner Bros. executive asked her what she wanted, she replied, "I'd like to be VP of A&R." She obviously proved her worth, because Warner Bros. named Sharp as vice president of A&R in April 1984, making her the first female vice president at a major record company on Music Row.

Warner Bros. named two female vice presidents that day. Janice Azrak became vice president for press and artist development. Calling herself "a liaison between the artists and their managers and the media," Azrak considered it her responsibility to get the artists as much print, radio, and TV exposure as possible. Although other women on Music Row did similar work, Sharp and

Azrak were the first to be recognized with titles and salaries commensurate with what men received.²

Sharp started looking for a young traditionalist to allow Warner Bros. to compete with MCA's George Strait and CBS's Ricky Skaggs. A CBS Songs employee said she knew the right person. His name was Randy Ray, and Charlie Monk was working with him. Sharp immediately called Monk, who told her she needed to go to the Nashville Palace and hear the young singer. In late November, Monk picked up Keith and Diane Stegall, along with Sharp, and they drove to the Nashville Palace for dinner. "I was blown away," Sharp says as she remembers hearing Randy Ray sing. Traywick (Ray) and Hatcher joined the Monk party at their table, with the shy Traywick soon retreating to the kitchen. Since Sharp said little, he thought she was just another uninterested label representative.³

At that time, Stegall was recording his own album for Epic Records, with Kyle Lehning as producer. Lehning had begun his Nashville career as a recording engineer at the Glaser Brothers studio in the early 1970s, where he had served as engineer and musician on three Waylon Jennings albums. He later produced hit pop records for England Dan (Seals) and John Ford Coley. After that group broke up, Lehning produced successful country records for Seals on Capitol Records. Stegall heard those records and asked Lehning to produce his Epic album.

Lehning was an independent record producer, hired by the artist, with a mutual agreement between the record company and the artist. "I'm assigned to the artist and attached to his contract," he explains. "The artist signs a letter of direction, which allows the record company to pay me. I'm paid from the artist's royalties."

While they were working on that album, Stegall brought in a cassette of a live album he had helped make at the Nashville Palace. He asked Lehning to listen and give an opinion. "I put the cassette on," Lehning recalls, "and I listened to about twenty seconds, and I stopped the cassette and said, 'This is the guy singing live? I think he's incredible.'" Stegall said he'd been unable to get anybody interested in recording Randy Ray. Lehning went to the Nashville Palace to hear for himself and concluded, "He sounded *great*. I thought he had a fabulous voice." Lehning then received a call from Charlie Monk, who was managing Stegall and trying to help Traywick and Hatcher. Monk said Martha Sharp had been to hear Randy Ray and seemed interested. He suggested Lehning give her a call and offer his opinion. "I hear you're interested," Lehning said when he spoke with her. "If you want to do something with him, I'd sure like to put my hat in the ring to work with him." That phone call pushed Sharp into action. She decided to sign Randy Traywick to Warner Bros.

But she wondered, *Oh, my God, how am I going to do this?* She knew record labels wanted pop-sounding acts and that Traywick had been turned down by all the major labels, including hers. Plus, not only was she a new vice president who had never signed an act; she was also a woman and therefore closely scrutinized. She realized the leap she was taking, but she believed Traywick would do well with the proper exposure. She was supposed to get the approval of her boss, the new president of Warner Bros. Records Nashville, Jim Ed Norman, who had initially joined the company as head of A&R in 1983. Instead, she called the corporate business affairs office for help in filling out the paperwork. Then, she says, "I called my boss and said, 'I'm signing this kid.'" She believes the men above her thought, *Oh, we're rid of her now*. They expected her new act to fail and then they'd have an excuse to fire that female VP. They were wrong. "I did what I thought I should do," she says. "There was no way I could have not signed Randy."

Sharp made the standard offer to a new artist: Warner Bros. would pay for recording four sides, including studio time and musician salaries, with the potential for a full album if one of those songs was successful. The press and artist development department was already in action. Azrak and her team went to the Palace to see Traywick perform, and they followed the signing process as it occurred. As soon as he was signed, they added his name to their regular marketing meetings. Nick Hunter, head of promotions, told Sharp, "The name Randy Ray has got to go. It's too hokey." That night she went to bed in her story-and-a-half home. Almost four decades later, she says, "I can see it now. I can see me in that bed, waking up and going 'Travis' and going back to sleep." She slept well that night, with the knowledge she no longer had to worry about a name for her new artist. It was close to the name Traywick, and it was a famous Texas name. "Randy accepted that I was in charge, sort of," she explains. "I think he liked it. I think everybody liked it."[4]

Traywick changed his performing name at the beginning of 1985. The band for the Nashville Palace New Year's Eve party appeared for the last time as "Randy Ray & 'Nashville.'" From then on, the Palace ads said, "Randy Travis & 'Nashville.'" The band also experienced changes. When Kenny Sears returned to the road, Steve Hinson filled the fiddle slot with a steel guitar. David Jones, who today entertains under the name Webb Dalton, joined the band. "I remember people loving Randy's music and his deep voice," he says. "He controlled the room with his voice when he started singing. He didn't need glitz and glamour. People would stop what they were doing and listen."[5]

Lehning and Stegall produced the first four sides recorded by Randy Travis on the Warner Bros. label. The session took place on January 30, 1985, following a song meeting in Martha Sharp's office to decide on the songs. They recorded at Emerald Sound Studio on Music Row. One of the first musicians Lehning called was steel guitarist Doyle Grisham, with whom he had worked since their Glaser Sound Studio days in the early 1970s, when Grisham, from Texas, was becoming well known as a session player. Lehning considers Grisham's sound a big part of Travis's sound from the beginning. "On the Other Hand" was the first song recorded. Pat Higdon from MCA Records had mailed it to Lehning on a cassette marked "Specifically for Randy." Lehning explains, "Pat knew we were looking for traditional country songs. I thought it was a fabulous song, and it seemed to me to fit Randy really well." The second song was "Carrying Fire," which Merle Haggard had recorded for his 1983 album, *That's the Way Love Goes*. The third was "Prairie Rose," at the behest of Jim Ed Norman, to be on the Warner Bros. soundtrack for a western comedy, *Rustlers' Rhapsody*. The final song of the session, "Reasons I Cheat," written by Randy Traywick during his Country City USA days, had appeared on the *Randy Ray Live at the Nashville Palace* album.[6]

"It was magical from the beginning," Sharp says. "Randy was so shy, so cute, so sweet. You could not have asked for a nicer young man to work with." Her initial impression of Hatcher was a "sort of older woman, a little overbearing, who was managing him." The two women developed an amicable relationship. Azrak, a New York native with a rock 'n' roll background, clicked immediately with Travis and Hatcher. "For a quiet, unassuming guy from the South, and this loud, boisterous woman who moved to Nashville with purple hair, we got along great," she says. "I loved him, I loved Lib, I loved working with those guys."[7]

Sharp was so pleased with the four recordings that she issued a contract for a full album, and Lehning immediately began setting up recording sessions. In the contract Randy Travis signed on February 14, 1985, Warner Bros. reserved the option to record a second album if the first one sold well. "I could not have been more elated," Travis remembered years later. "But I still had to go back to work that night cooking catfish at the Nashville Palace." The emcee called him out of the kitchen and announced to the hundred people present that Randy Ray, now Randy Travis, had gotten a record deal. "This is the greatest day of my life," Travis told the crowd.[8]

Things were looking up for the Traywick family in Marshville too. Harold, Bobbie, and their youngest son, Dennis, moved back into the home they'd lost to foreclosure more than two years earlier. Harold had contracted with the Armour Food Company in the 1970s and had overextended himself in the turkey-raising business. He owned a dozen large turkey houses on multiple farms, with thousands of birds and excessive operational expenses. "He made a lot of money for a lot of years, until the market got bad," Dennis says. "He went bankrupt a few times. He could make it; he just sometimes had a hard time keeping it."

At noon on August 16, 1982, the Traywick house had been auctioned on the steps of the Union County Courthouse in Monroe for default in making mortgage payments. North Carolina Federal Savings and Loan purchased it for fifty thousand dollars. A friend remembers Bobbie Rose crying over the phone. Another remembers Harold threatening to shoot everybody involved: "The auctioneer, the judges, anybody who came to the auction. Some people wouldn't come to that auction—scared to come." A friend of Harold's was appointed substitute trustee; he apparently agreed to hold the property until Harold raised the money to buy it back. Harold moved a mobile home onto his mother's property next door, where she continued to live after Bruce Traywick died in 1969. The house remained vacant during the entire foreclosure period. Dennis recalls that as the reason his father placed the mobile home there. With Harold's reputation, nobody wanted to buy the house and live next door to him. In January 1985 the property was released from foreclosure, and sixteen-year-old Dennis and his parents moved back to their home.[9]

In Nashville, Randy had turned twenty-six by the time he made his first appearance as Randy Travis on *Nashville Now*. On May 17 he was introduced by Johnny Russell, a singer/songwriter known for such songs as "Act Naturally" and "Rednecks, White Socks, and Blue Ribbon Beer." Travis sang "Prairie Rose" and then told Ralph Emery he had seen *Rustlers' Rhapsody* a few days earlier.[10] The movie starred Tom Berenger and Andy Griffith; Travis called it "a very funny western." For his second song, he performed Gene Watson's current hit, "Got No Reason Now for Going Home." Emery asked why he was singing a Russell-written song, and Travis answered, "He told me he'd sit on me if I didn't." Russell, who weighed three hundred pounds, usually opened his shows by asking the audience, "Can everybody see me all right?"

Travis didn't sing "On the Other Hand" because he hadn't learned it yet. The single was released exactly two months later, and Travis performed it for the first time before a national audience on August 6, his next *Nashville Now* appearance. Emery always asked questions about his job as dishwasher and cook at the Nashville Palace, so Travis surprised his host by presenting a platter of food—steak, shrimp, and lobster—he'd cooked at the Palace before coming to the studio. "That was one of the few times I saw Ralph close to speechless," Travis recalled.[11]

"On the Other Hand" had been written by Don Schlitz and Paul Overstreet. Schlitz, originally from North Carolina, already had a major hit with the Kenny Rogers recording of "The Gambler." Mississippi native Overstreet was soon to have a number one hit with the Forester Sisters quartet performing "I Fell in Love Again Last Night." The songwriting pair often told the story of how "On the Other Hand" came about. Overstreet suggested a line while they were working on a song, and Schlitz responded, "On the other hand." Overstreet said, "There's a golden band." Schlitz came back with, "To remind me of someone who would not understand." They quickly focused on this new idea and had the song finished in less than thirty minutes. They knew it was good enough to be a hit. When they were told that Randy Travis was going to cut it, Overstreet asked, "Well, who is that?" They had never heard of him. They had hoped someone with name recognition, like George Jones or Merle Haggard, would record it.[12]

The B side of "On the Other Hand" was "Can't Stop Now," a song later recorded by Reba McEntire, New Grass Revival, and Shenandoah. When Lehning used a drum machine on the track, Travis was not happy. "Let's not do that again," he said. They never did.[13]

"On the Other Hand" debuted on *Billboard* on August 31, 1985. Travis sang it on the television show *The New Music City U.S.A.*, which advertised itself as bringing "new faces in country music to America." The single climbed to number sixty-seven and then stalled. To the extreme disappointment of all involved, it dropped off the chart after twelve weeks.

Long before that happened, the Warner Bros. team realized a new song had to be released. Stegall was no longer working with Travis; his time was focused on building his own career. Sharp, Lehning, Travis, and Hatcher began searching through demonstration cassettes and listening to songs submitted by hopeful songwriters. A demo of "1962," sung by T. Graham Brown, caught their attention. Two of Brown's friends from high school in Athens, Georgia, had become Nashville songwriters. Carl "Vip" Vipperman and Buddy Blackmon called Brown and said they had five songs for him to demo. He sang demos on numerous songs that became hits and was about to get his first top ten single in 1985, "Tell It Like It Used to Be." When he sang the straight country number "1962," they asked if he wanted to cut it. "It's too country for me," he told them.[14]

It wasn't too country for Randy Travis. "Kyle and I nearly jumped out of our chairs when we heard it," he recalled. The smooth ballad of a man singing "that same old lost-love story / it's sad but it's true" fit Travis's style perfectly. Lehning suggested changing the title to "1982." Travis had been just three years old in 1962, and the title made him sound old. The songwriters readily agreed to the change. The team went into the studio to record the song they were confident could be a hit. Warner Bros. released "1982" on November 20, with "Reasons I Cheat" from the initial recording session as the B side. Almost six weeks later, "1982" debuted on *Billboard*, and the song kept climbing. It entered the top ten in mid-March of 1986, eventually reaching number six and giving Travis his first hit.

For the past year, in addition to working in the kitchen at the Nashville Palace and performing there, Travis had been opening shows for acts like George Jones and T. G. Sheppard, appearing on television shows, and traveling out of town for concerts from Texas to New York. John Hobbs provided a GMC van with driver Charles Bishop, who was the maintenance supervisor for the Hobbs-owned motels. Hobbs allowed Travis to borrow show clothes from the clothing store he owned. Sharp attended all local performances, recalling, "I was there giving him support, I was." Drew Sexton usually traveled with them to play piano and coordinate with house bands. Travis told an interviewer, "I do three or four things that I've written when I'm on the road. I've been working with house bands, so I don't do anything too complicated. It kind of hurts when they stop playing on you." With his many years of singing in clubs, he knew the songs that house bands played, but they didn't know *his* music—yet.[15]

Azrak was teaching Travis to feel comfortable in front of cameras and working with stylists on his wardrobe for press interviews. He already had a style, thanks to Hatcher, who had jackets with a western flair made for him. "She had a good eye," Azrak explains. "She knew the image they wanted to portray." Throughout his career, Travis's standard concert attire would include black Wrangler jeans, belt with a silver horseshoe buckle, and cowboy boots. He appreciated Azrak's guidance. She showed him videos of himself so that he could see what he was doing. "Randy, you have to start looking up," she told him. He was so shy, he looked at his hands when he talked. "Randy got it," she says. "He was a quick study." Wanting to get to know Travis better, Azrak drove to nearby venues. She arranged interviews and volunteered to help by selling merchandise. "I have memories of me selling merch on the side of the stage," she says. "I remember those days very, very fondly." They carried the merchandise—photos, T-shirts, and the *Randy Ray Live* album—in a medium-size blue plastic suitcase.¹⁶

One of Travis's appearances was as a guest on TNN's special, *Hank Williams Jr. and Friends*, a concert filmed at the Grand Ole Opry House to celebrate the third anniversary of The Nashville Network. Since Travis had no band, he sang "1982" while backed by studio musicians from his recording sessions. Doyle Grisham remembers it as his only live performance with Travis. The "and friends" performers, in addition to Travis, were the Forester Sisters and Pam Tillis—new artists being given a chance for national exposure. Most of the audience consisted of rowdy Hank Jr. fans, who often had to be encouraged to return to their seats. When Travis's turn came to sing, a large group rushed the stage. Startled, he stepped back and looked over his shoulder, as if expecting someone behind him. But, no, the excitement was for him.¹⁷

With his increasing popularity, he and Hatcher had been discussing for months when to leave their Nashville Palace employment. It was a matter of when, not if. Travis played his last evening as an employee on March 1, 1986. The Saturday night show was billed as "Randy Travis returns to the Nashville Palace with his hit single '1982.'" Hobbs willingly let them go, knowing Travis was a once-in-a-lifetime talent and believing the Nashville Palace could take pride in the role it had played in his success. "All we do is give people an opportunity to perform and do what they love," he explained. "We're just a door they happened to walk through." He considered Hatcher a fantastic general manager. Although Hobbs owned the Palace, Hatcher was the boss who handled the staff and ran the operation. She was "all about business," he said, and she treated everyone as if they had a position in a company.¹⁸

When Travis and Hatcher moved to promoting his career full-time, they asked Drew Sexton to put together a band. He'd been playing piano at the Stagecoach Lounge on Murfreesboro Road in South Nashville. Fellow Stagecoach band member Rocky Thacker recalls, "Drew asked me if I wanted to go on the road—if I'd like the job playing bass and singing backup. I had heard '1982.' All it took was one song, and, yeah, I did." Former Nashville Palace steel guitarist Gary Carter, who had played on the *Randy Ray Live* album, joined them in April. Randy Hardison was hired to play drums and Dan Drillen to play lead guitar. They took "Nashville" with them as the name of the band. L D Wayne, who planned to join the group later, stayed at the Palace because of his commitments as bandleader during the tourist season.

While Hatcher and Travis would continue traveling with Charles Bishop in the 1986 GMC van, they needed a vehicle for the band. They purchased a 1977

Chevrolet truck from singer/songwriter Ronnie Reno, who had converted the former Sunbeam bread truck to carry musicians and instruments. It had shag carpet on the walls and floor, along with four bunks for five musicians. Carter says, "The bread truck was hard living." The only air conditioning or heat came from a vent near the driver. "By the time the air got fifteen feet to the back of the bread truck, it wasn't doing any good," Carter adds. They wore shorts and no T-shirts because it was so hot in the summer. It frequently broke down on the side of the road. Carter remembers fumes getting inside at one point, causing several band members to feel lightheaded and dizzy. The bread truck pulled a modified horse trailer filled with band equipment. Sexton drove the bread truck, booked the hotels, handled ground transportation, scheduled backline gear in places where they rented gear—everything a road manager would do. Because Travis's career took off so fast, they stayed on the road and mostly lived in the bread truck.[19]

"On the Other Hand" remained a major disappointment. No one wanted to give up on it. Lehning remembers polling everybody in the inner circle to decide what to do next. They wanted to try again, and some suggested rerecording the song. He says, "I heard it on the radio when it came out the first time, and I didn't know how to make a better record than that." A music critic later wrote, "'On the Other Hand' ought to be required listening for anyone who aspires to produce a record." Lehning credits Nick Hunter with agreeing to rerelease the single. It came out on April 2, 1986.[20]

Two weeks later, Travis and Hatcher flew to Los Angeles. Travis was nominated for New Male Vocalist of the Year by the Academy of Country Music (ACM), an organization founded in 1964 to promote country music in the western states. It had been conducting awards shows since 1968 and had grown into a national organization, with the shows first televised in 1972. This one, held the night before Hatcher's forty-fifth birthday, took place in the Goodtime Theater at Knott's Berry Farm and was broadcast on NBC-TV. The other four nominees were Marty Stuart, who would be inducted into the Country Music Hall of Fame in 2021; Keith Whitley, inducted in 2022 (thirty-three years after he died of alcohol poisoning); Billy Burnette, who joined the band Fleetwood Mac in 1987; and T. Graham Brown, who had sung the demo for "1982" and would later have three number one *Billboard* hits. The five had taped their segments several days earlier, to be inserted into the live broadcast. Travis sang "1982."[21]

Excited about attending his first awards show, let alone being a nominee, Travis wanted to look good. And in a traditional black tuxedo with black bow tie, he did. He didn't expect to win, didn't have a record album out, and was scared to death. "I was shaking," he recalled. Presenter Steve Wariner announced, "The top new male vocalist is . . . ," he paused to open the envelope and then read, "The winner is—Randy Travis!" The dazed Travis "bounded onto the stage as though I'd done it a thousand times—and maybe I had in my mind," he remembered. Backstage he was quoted as saying, "Once I get done shaking, I'll feel better."[22]

George Strait won his second consecutive title as ACM's Male Vocalist of the Year. Two nights earlier, Travis had opened for Strait at the Wiltern Theatre in Los Angeles. A newspaper reviewer commented on how much time Strait must have spent listening to Merle Haggard and George Jones records. He wrote that opening act Randy Travis "is even more strongly in the shadow of Haggard and Jones. There were times during his well-received set that you felt you were at the national finals of the Merle Haggard Sing-Alike Contest."[23]

Then came April 26, the day "On the Other Hand" debuted on *Billboard* at number sixty-four—three positions higher than it had reached in November. The next few months would be life-changing.

Difficult and Defeated are unincorporated towns along Defeated Creek, a Cumberland River tributary flowing through Smith County, Tennessee. Defeated Creek earned its name when early explorers camped along its banks and were driven away by a band of Cherokees in the late 1700s. A century later, officials changed the local post office name from Montrose to Defeated. A government official named the town of Difficult when he couldn't decipher the handwriting of "Williams Crossroad" on a post office application form.[24]

Highway 85 passes between the two towns and runs east into Jackson County toward another small town called Flynns Lick. Azrak, with Hatcher and Travis as passengers in her black Jeep, was driving around the area one day scouting a location to shoot the cover for Travis's debut album. They came to a fork in the road, where a sign pointed in one direction to Difficult and in the other direction to Defeated. They sat in front of the sign and laughed for several minutes. Azrak asked, "Which way do you want to go, Randy? Difficult or Defeated?" They agreed to take Difficult because no one wants to be defeated. Azrak recalls laughing more with Travis and Hatcher during their years together than she did with any other artist. They eventually reached Flynns Lick, where they found the perfect location, an old country store that had been closed for years. On the day of the photo shoot, Sharp rode to Flynns

Lick in the bus with Azrak's team. The film crew dressed up the decrepit old store, hung lights, and added signs borrowed from a Cracker Barrel restaurant. Because Travis already had songs playing on the radio, people knew him. The men who owned the store had called their friends to watch. Azrak remembers people hovering in the background and making comments such as, "Oh, my God, Randy Travis is here!" It was a great day for all concerned.[25]

The album cover for *Storms of Life* shows Travis staring off into the distance as he leans against a 1952 Chevrolet pickup parked in front of the store. Four men in bib overalls sit in rocking chairs on the front porch; one is petting a dog. Feed sacks are piled along the side of the building, next to hay bales provided by Lehning's father-in-law.

Recording the album took almost a year because of the song search. They would find two or three songs they liked, wait for a while, work on those three, and then find a few more. Lehning says, "It might take us six months to find enough songs we liked to be able to get the basic tracks recorded. It could be in three or four clusters of sessions." Travis credits Martha Sharp with finding great songs. "Martha had access to a treasure trove of great traditional country songs that had been pitched to Warner," he once explained. "Oddly, at that time nobody wanted to record them. The whole time Kyle and I were working on the project, she kept searching for the best songs. We'd record something, then Martha would show up with a new song she thought might be even better, so we'd go back into the studio to work on that one." They recorded twenty good songs before selecting the final ten for the album.

Lehning invited Travis to sit with him in his control room at Morningstar Studio in Hendersonville to hear the entire album. When they had listened from top to bottom, Lehning said, "I think that's really pretty good." Travis agreed. Lehning said, "I've done the math. I figure if we sell forty thousand albums, they might let us make another album." Travis responded, "That would be really good." Approval from Warner Bros. to make a second album was Lehning's goal. "It was a joy to be creatively connected with somebody that focused and that clear," he says. Lehning enjoyed working with Travis because he knew who he was as an artist and what he wanted to sing onstage. "He wasn't fixated on becoming a star," Lehning explains. "He was fixated on making the best country music he could make. The thing I loved about Randy from the beginning was how unpretentious he's always been."[26]

Travis thanked Lehning in the album liner notes "for being a great producer." He thanked "Mama and Daddy who always believed and cared"; Janice Azrak, "for 'our' first W. B. album cover"; and Martha Sharp, "for giving me a chance and being my friend." He dedicated the album "With love and appreciation to my manager, Lib Hatcher." He thanked her for "believing when at times it seemed hopeless, for always caring, and for work that should have taken ten people, but was done by one."[27]

Travis and his band were touring steadily throughout the eastern half of the United States. He was being booked by the World Class Talent Agency, whose owners included Barbara Mandrell. Her booking agent, Allen Whitcomb, had heard Travis sing "1982" on the radio in January and immediately called Hatcher to offer the agency's representation, which she accepted. Whitcomb scheduled Travis as the opening act for several different artists, including Mandrell. Travis first opened for her in April, at a show in Milwaukee, Wisconsin. He and his band frequently traveled with Mandrell's group that summer and opened a series of shows for them.[28]

Two of the album's singles were already playing on the radio when *Storms of Life* was released, "1982" and the current, chart-climbing "On the Other Hand." Bobby Tomberlin, who is today a well-known Nashville songwriter, was working as music director at a thousand-watt radio station in Andalusia, Alabama. He listened to "1982" the minute the station received it. He immediately added it to the playlist, along with new songs by Dwight Yoakum and Ricky Skaggs. Because this was the period when country had gone pop, the program director chewed him out and told him to remove those songs from the playlist. Country music was no longer that style and wouldn't be going back, he said. Listeners did not agree. The phone lines lit up with people calling for "1982." Within three weeks, the program director had to rescind his order. "I'm sure a lot of stations never even added it in the beginning," Tomberlin says. "Then it caught on. It brought country back. Constant requests for Randy." After the arrival and smash hit of "On the Other Hand," Tomberlin searched for the previous year's release and couldn't find it. He says, "Warner Bros. may have released it to major markets like Dallas and places like that. Secondary markets may not have even gotten the single."[29] That could be one of the reasons the song failed the first time around.

When Warner Bros. released *Storms of Life* on June 2, 1986, Travis and his band were on tour in Louisiana and Texas. They returned to Nashville in time for Travis to be a presenter at the Sunday evening *Music City News* Awards show that kicked off the annual Fan Fair celebration. A fan-voted event sponsored by trade magazine *Music City News*, the twentieth *Music City News* Awards show was held at the Opry House in Music Valley. Travis joined the Forester Sisters in presenting Single of the Year to the Statler Brothers, a hit-producing quartet for two decades, for "My Only Love." The Forester Sisters, Travis's occasional tour partners, were enjoying their third number one *Billboard* hit in one year.

Several nights later, also during Fan Fair, Travis and his band performed during the Warner Bros. showcase. Fan Fair, sponsored by WSM Radio and the Country Music Association, had been held every year since 1972. Thousands of people planned their summer vacations to attend Fan Fair with its concentration of country music artists. They saw the artists perform and could talk to them at autograph booths. The weeklong event took place at the Tennessee State Fairgrounds in Nashville. Individual record labels organized evening concerts. Travis had performed a year earlier at Fan Fair, without much crowd reaction, when he was an unknown Warner Bros. artist. He already had a fan club, started by Jill Youngblood of Charlotte, North Carolina, when he was still Randy Traywick. She ran the club from her home and traveled to Nashville to operate the booth during Fan Fair. Travis, Hatcher, and Youngblood sat in his autograph booth in 1985 and watched the crowds walk by. A sign advertised, "Randy Travis will be appearing at the Nashville Palace," where he and Hatcher were employees.

What a difference a year made. "When we began the first chords of 'On the Other Hand,'" Travis says about the 1986 show, "the crowd of nearly twenty-five thousand people stood and cheered. It was incredible!" He received a second standing ovation when he left the stage at the end of his set. Watching from backstage, Lehning told Sharp, "Wow, we're in for the ride of our lives."[30]

They didn't know about the other lives being changed by hearing "On the Other Hand." Kevin Jonas, who had competed in the Country City USA talent contest in 1977, was now twenty-one, married, and attending a Bible college. His mother called him and asked if he remembered Randy Traywick. "He's got a song out, and it's blowing up," she said. When Jonas listened to "On the Other Hand," it lit a fire in him to start pursuing music again. "That song changed my life," he says. "I would fly to Nashville and record country songs and then fly home and do worship stuff." In addition to his singing career, he later started managing talent, with his most famous clients being his sons, the Jonas Brothers—Kevin, Joe, and Nick. "Not only was Randy somebody who passed by my life," he says today, "[but] his breakthrough inspired me to open the music business side of my career. So, yeah, there's a definite passion that never left. My kids grew up on country music, and that's why they love Nashville so much. Love working with people from Nashville. That's why they love playing instruments."[31]

David Ball was sitting at a stoplight in Mount Pleasant, South Carolina, when he first heard "On the Other Hand." He'd been planning to move to

Nashville at some point to seek a record deal. When he heard Travis singing on the car radio, he told himself, "That's it. We're going." He moved with his wife and daughter to Nashville, where he would eventually record the platinum-selling "Thinkin' Problem."[32]

The Travis entourage went back on the road immediately after Fan Fair. When Bishop moved from van driver to stage manager, Hatcher asked Gary Carter to drive, which he did for the last two months of the bread truck days. They tried to keep the bread truck and van together on the highway, but Hatcher would say, "We have to pull over in thirty minutes; I've got a radio interview for Randy." Carter would stop at a phone booth, from which Travis would call the radio station. They'd then drive three hours and Hatcher would have another interview set up. "We would do that all day long," Carter says. "We were usually pretty far behind the bread truck."[33]

Most interviewers wanted to know about Travis's wild younger days. "After about the seventh grade, I almost wouldn't go to school," he told one of them. "I went into the ninth grade, and I never did finish that. I got caught driving without a license, drinking, trying to be wild, running with the crowd. I guess I would'a straightened up sooner or later, but I probably would have gone to prison before I did. I may not have lived long enough to straighten out." He talked about Ricky, saying, "My brother did go to prison for a while. He got out and he's got a family now, a couple of kids, and his life has straightened out. He did that on his own."

Looking back, he was embarrassed by his youthful thievery. "I wonder how I could have done a lot of these things," he told one interviewer. "I'd never want to take anything from anybody anymore. I don't want something unless it's mine or unless I work for it. I never want to cheat anybody."

In a reflective mood, he said, "You know, with Mama and Daddy I wish I could go back and re-do so many things. I'm sure what I did broke their hearts. I didn't want to listen to them. For some reason I would listen to Lib. I've learned a lot from her about business and about life in general." He said they could nearly read each other's minds. She stayed with him during interviews to help him remember specifics. With his popularity increasing so fast, he appreciated being able to continue working with the same people and knowing he could trust them. About Hatcher specifically, he said, "She takes care of most of the business end of the music, and I do most of the music. With all the interviews and shows and recording and writing, I do about all I can keep up with, to tell you the truth. We work great together."[34]

In mid-July they headed out for a three-week tour of the West Coast and Texas. Travis talked to interviewers about how his life had changed.

Commenting that he had been home for only four days in April, and it was "a whole change of lifestyle," he said, "I was used to working a sit-down job five or six nights a week and having the day for myself." Now they spent the day driving to the next performance. Interviewers called him "a bachelor who lives in a house on Nashville's Music Row." One wrote that "he has never been married and has no immediate plans in that direction." His relationship with Hatcher would be kept from the public for several more years. Even more than their own desire to keep their private life private, it was a marketing ploy. A handsome bachelor might be expected to sell more records than someone living with a woman eighteen years his senior. One interviewer hesitantly prefaced the question with "If you don't want to answer this, don't." He then said, "There's a little thing in *Time* with Lib. It said you don't foresee marriage. I mean, is your relationship a personal as well as a—" Travis cut him off with, "Huh uh, nah, just work." He added, "I saw that, too. Some people, you wonder where they get their information." Travis was often asked to explain his sudden popularity. "That's a hard question to answer," he usually responded. "I'm part of the traditional country that is making a good comeback. I don't know why it's been a success for me. I love what I'm doing. That's the type of music I love to do and it's all I can do."[35]

Audiences mistakenly thought he was related to Merle Travis, a country entertainer known for his fingerpicking guitar style and coal mining songs like "Sixteen Tons" and "Dark as a Dungeon." That Travis had died three years earlier at age sixty-five, and Randy was initially caught off guard when told, "I was a big fan of your daddy's." He wondered how they knew Harold, so he would ask, "Who are you talking about?" When they said, "Merle Travis," he would explain that he'd never met Merle and they were not kin. He might add, "I was a big fan of his. I wish I could play half the guitar that he could play."[36]

"On the Other Hand" hit number one on *Billboard* on Saturday, July 26. Travis later answered a question about when he knew he'd made it, by saying, "I really began to feel things were looking up when 'On the Other Hand' went to number one." He acknowledged that getting signed to Warner Bros. had been a big vote of confidence, but a record deal didn't necessarily lead to success. With the number one song in the nation, Travis and Hatcher calculated they could afford the sixth musician they'd been waiting to hire. They called fiddle player David Johnson from North Carolina. They'd worked with him earlier, when he had been a member of the Country City USA band. Johnson would be the sole band member to stay with Travis throughout his entire career.

On August 9, *Storms of Life* reached the top of the *Billboard* country albums chart while the Travis caravan was driving to Little Rock, Arkansas. The two number ones, song and album, seemed to bass player Thacker to happen simultaneously. "Everything was starting to pick way up about then," he recalls. "We were finishing dates that had been booked earlier, along with new dates coming in since he was becoming known. I remember being home for hours instead of for days."37

During a rare period of a few days at home, Travis received an urgent early morning phone call on Monday, August 18, from the Country Music Association. Ricky Skaggs, the current CMA Entertainer of the Year, was scheduled to announce the CMA nominations at a press conference, but instead he was in Roanoke, Virginia, at the hospital bedside of his seven-year-old son. Andrew had been riding in a car with his mother on Interstate 81 in western Virginia the previous evening when someone shot into the car and hit him in the face. The boy had undergone surgery and was in stable condition. The CMA representative asked Travis if he could fill in and make the announcements. She told him everything was ready, and he only had to read each category and the nominees.

Travis put on a sports jacket and headed to Music Valley to the Opry House, where he stood onstage in front of a sea of cameras and reporters. Martha Sharp was there to support him. Nervous about reading the cards aloud, he opened the first envelope and read, "And the nominees for the Horizon Award are Dan Seals, Dwight Yoakam, Kathy Mattea, the Forester Sisters, and Randy Travis." Shocked, he looked up and smiled. When he read Single of the Year nominations, and one was "'On the Other Hand,' written by Paul Overstreet and Don Schlitz, recorded by Randy Travis," he grinned and shook his head, saying, "That's me." More was to come. For Male Vocalist of the Year nominees, he read, "George Jones, Gary Morris, George Strait, Hank Williams Jr." Then he paused and choked out, "Randy Travis." Wondering how he could be nominated in the same category as his hero George Jones, he said, "This looks like my day." When he read "*Storms of Life*" as a nominee for Album of the Year, he said, in disbelief, "That's me again."38

The Country Music Association's twentieth annual awards show took place on October 13 at the Opry House. This was the sixth year the Horizon Award had been presented to a rising star. Nominees were required to have demonstrated growth in airplay and record sales, live performance professionalism, and media recognition during the preceding twelve months. Sawyer Brown presented the Horizon Award early in the show. When they called Travis to the stage, he told the audience, "This is quite an honor for me. Mom and Daddy, I love you." He sat quietly and smiled as the three other awards for which he was nominated went to other artists. "I was like a kid gawking at his heroes," he said. Overstreet and Schlitz won Song of the Year for "On the Other Hand."[39]

In the two months between the CMA nomination announcement and the awards show, the bread truck and van were on the road. In September, Travis continued the grueling performance schedule, playing nineteen dates—from Rhode Island to Florida, to Ohio, to New York; then Ohio, Missouri, and Texas; on to Georgia and North Carolina; and back to Texas. Thacker recalls not understanding why the crowds were all of a sudden much bigger. They were playing the small places that had been booked months earlier. "We'd get there and do sound check and there would be lines of people to get tickets to get in," he explains. "We're like, wow, this must be a happening little place. It wasn't. It was all Randy."[40]

As Travis exploded in popularity, he and Hatcher left World Class Talent, taking Allen Whitcomb with them. Hatcher hired Whitcomb on a one-year contract at a straight commission of 5 percent to handle the booking as part of Lib Hatcher Agency Inc., which she founded in October 1986 with Randy Travis as its first client. The incorporation was officially listed as "music industry publishing, recording, managers, and allied activities." Travis's price as a performer kept going up, so they were careful not to book too far in advance.[41]

Hatcher and Travis decided to invest some of their money in real estate. As Travis explained, "Ten or fifteen years down the road, I know I'll be singing, and I want to do it because I want to, not because I have to. I hope to invest the money wisely." In October, "Elizabeth Hatcher & Randy Traywick" signed a $250,000 installment deed to purchase sixty-three acres in Ashland City, Tennessee. The log farmhouse at 117 Smith Street, with a large smokehouse and a summer kitchen, had been built by Braxton Lee in 1811. This began a series of real estate purchases and limited liability companies that would continue over the years. The couple eventually sold this historic property in 2005 for $410,000.[42]

The songs Travis had written were also increasing in value. Hatcher negotiated with Charlie Monk to buy back the songs placed in Monk's company during their earlier copublishing arrangement. The negotiations turned acrimonious when he refused her offer and she threatened a lawsuit. "Although I didn't get too involved in their contentious discussions, I allowed them to happen," Travis said years later, "and for that I felt remorse." He acknowledged that Monk had been instrumental in landing him a recording contract and had believed in him when few others did. Monk eventually spent $35,000 in legal fees, and Travis paid him $250,000 to obtain exclusive publishing rights to his songs. It would be decades before they repaired their relationship.[43]

When the tourist season ended, L D Wayne had fulfilled his commitments at the Nashville Palace. He joined Travis's band in October as lead guitarist and brought drummer Tommy Rivelli with him. Wayne had hired Rivelli to play drums at the Palace when Terry Buttram became too ill to perform. Rivelli had been part of the rhythm section for MTM Records, an independent record label founded in 1984 as a subsidiary of Mary Tyler Moore's production company. Its artists included Judy Rodman, who had won the ACM award for New Female Vocalist of the Year the night Travis won the New Male Vocalist award. Rodman and Travis had then been placed together on a concert tour. Although Travis was using a house band and carrying merchandise in a suitcase, Rivelli remembers thinking, *This dude is on fire*.

The October 1986 band lineup would hold for almost two years: Tommy Rivelli, Rocky Thacker, Drew Sexton, L D Wayne, David Johnson, and Gary Carter. They traveled to the Mississippi State Fair at the end of October in a Crusader tour bus that once belonged to Johnny Lee, the singer of "Lookin' for Love" in the *Urban Cowboy* movie. Rivelli and Wayne were grateful not to have to travel in the bread truck. "They had a driver, and we had our own bunks," Rivelli recalls. A *Newsweek* article reported, "Out of the bus spilled Travis, his mentor-manager Lib Hatcher, a six-man band and carton upon carton of Randy Travis tapes, T shirts, bandanas and bumper stickers. Things were looking up: a month ago the group was caravanning around in a converted bread truck, a van, and a horse trailer." Sherwood Cryer, of Gilley's and mechanical bull fame, owned the 1981 Crusader tour bus. He told Travis and Hatcher to drive it for a while before deciding if they wanted to buy it. They used it for a month, and whenever they asked how much he wanted for it, he would repeat his earlier comment. They bought the bus in November and had it refurbished by Executive Coach in Chicago. The bread truck now carried their concessions.[44]

The third release from the *Storms of Life* album, "Diggin' Up Bones," had been climbing the charts since August. It became Travis's second consecutive chart topper when it hit number one on November 8. Lehning remembers hearing the demo of "Diggin' Up Bones," cowritten by Paul Overstreet, and telling Travis, "I don't know how you can say 'no' to a song that has the word 'exhuming' in it." That word alone was enough to make Lehning want to record it. In the lyrics, the singer recalls how his ex-wife's love is dead and gone:

"I'm diggin' up bones / diggin' up bones / exhuming things that's better left alone."[45]

To add to the high of a second number one record, Travis made a triumphant return to Charlotte to play the Charlotte Coliseum with headliner George Jones. Kathy Mattea was the opening act. This was Travis's first show in Charlotte since leaving the house band at Country City USA five years earlier. Sponsored by WSOC-TV, it was billed as "George Jones and Randy Travis." The Traywicks hung out backstage and met Jones. Many relatives and friends, including Hatcher's father, attended the show. Thacker recalls a carnival atmosphere, with numerous people stopping by the bus to say hello and tell the band members how they knew the singing star. The reception overwhelmed and embarrassed Travis. A reviewer wrote, "When Travis walked onstage, the screams, whistles and popping flash bulbs rivaled the reception given many modern rock stars." Although understandably nervous about performing at home and with his hero Jones, he accepted several plaques and proclamations. The Charlotte mayor proclaimed November 15 as "Randy Travis Day in Charlotte." There was much excitement in the Marshville area about Travis coming to Charlotte to perform. The Marshville town board passed an ordinance to proclaim the date as "Randy Travis Day in Marshville."[46]

Paul Schadt, morning show host for radio station 96.9, The Kat, was leaving the coliseum when he ran into Harold Traywick in the parking lot. Harold opened the trunk of his car, pulled out a gallon of whiskey and two plastic cups, and offered Schadt a drink. He poured himself one when the deejay turned down the offer saying he had to get up early the next day. "He was fun and wide open, and there were no rules to go with Harold," Schadt recalls. "Randy's mom was kind of on the quiet side. Randy didn't come back to town as often as people thought he should. I think it was that turmoil between Lib and his daddy." Harold didn't like Hatcher, Larke Plyler believes, because he thought she was unjustly getting credit for his son's success. Harold had trained his sons in traditional country music, built them a music room, and taught them how to be entertainers. "I think that's where a lot of the tension originally grew," Plyler says, "because he never really got the credit. I can see where he could feel that way."[47]

Travis's hometown had been saluted on October 11 by the television show *Hee Haw*. After the announcement, "*Hee Haw* salutes Randy Travis, hometown Marshville, North Carolina, population, 2,177," the entire cast stood in the *Hee Haw* cornfield and shouted, "Sa-lute!" The program aired on WSOC-TV (Channel 9) in Charlotte. Produced in syndication, it was broadcast on 220 stations and reached eighteen to twenty million households every Saturday night.[48]

*Hee Haw* and *Nashville Now* were the two main television shows on which fans could watch their favorite country singers. Travis made his next *Nashville Now* appearance on December 12. In addition to singing "Diggin' Up Bones," he introduced his newest release, "No Place Like Home," which was written by Paul Overstreet and would peak on *Billboard* at number two. His debut album thus provided two number one and two number two *Billboard* hits, with three of them written or cowritten by Overstreet. Three additional album cuts served as B sides of the singles, two of them written by Travis.

To celebrate *Storms of Life* reaching gold status by selling more than five hundred thousand copies, Warner Bros. hosted a party in November at the Station Inn, a small but well-known Nashville music venue. CEO Jim Ed Norman presented Travis with a large framed gold record. Following the presentation, Travis announced that he had been invited to join the Grand Ole Opry. He shook his head in disbelief, and his voice cracked as he said, "Isn't that something?" He had made his Opry debut earlier that year, on Friday, March 7, with Little Jimmy Dickens introducing him. Singing the Hank Williams classic "I'm So Lonesome I Could Cry," Travis paid tribute to the country legend whose style he was perpetuating.

After a life-changing year of going from restaurant cook/dishwasher playing with house bands to award-winning singer with a number one album and two number one songs, Travis wrapped up 1986 by becoming a member of the Opry on December 20. He was inducted by Ricky Skaggs, who talked about George Jones singing "Who's Gonna Fill Their Shoes" and then said, "I'll tell you one thing, George, one day they're going to be trying to fill *his* shoes." Skaggs introduced Travis by saying, "He's the hottest new star on the horizon today. A nice hand for the great Randy Travis—the sixty-second member of the Grand Ole Opry!" Travis sang "Diggin' Up Bones" and "White Christmas Makes Me Blue." His new Christmas release was the first major-artist single for songwriters Rich Grissom and Neil Patton Rogers.[49] That Travis could now "make" songwriters was another indicator of his changed status.

The *News & Observer* in Raleigh, North Carolina, had this to say about the best of the year's albums: "Country music in 1986 can be summed up in a couple of words. Randy Travis. Travis, the Tar Heel from Marshville, led the so-called new traditionalists to the top of the country charts and won the County Music Association's Horizon Award in the process. If you buy only one country album this year, his *Storms of Life* should be it."[50]

# 4

## "DON'T RECORD 'EM IF YOU DON'T LOVE 'EM."

Harold Lloyd Jenkins took the stage name Conway Twitty at age twenty-four, in 1957, from the towns of Conway, Arkansas, and Twitty, Texas. Beginning with "It's Only Make Believe," he amassed thirty-nine number one hits on *Billboard*, four of them duets with Loretta Lynn. Best known for sensuous love ballads, Conway Twitty directed the messages in his songs to men who had something to say to a woman but didn't know how. He explained in an interview that all a man had to do was "drop a quarter in the jukebox, press the right buttons and squeeze her at the appropriate time and she'll understand."[1]

Travis was scheduled to be the opening act for this country legend during the early months of 1987. Their association came through Jeff Davis of United Talent. Davis had grown up in the booking agency his father, Jimmy Jay (surname Blauw), managed for Twitty. After graduating from high school, Davis spent the next eight years traveling on Twitty's bus and learning from his father to be a promoter. He first saw Travis on *Nashville Now* in August 1985 on the night Travis sang "On the Other Hand" and brought dinner from the Nashville Palace. Davis was so impressed that he told Twitty about the new singer. Twitty listened to Travis's music and decided to place him somewhere as an opening act. Davis called Allen Whitcomb to schedule the event.

That first show, billed as Conway Twitty and opening act "newcomer Randy Travis," took place on May 2, 1986, in Asheville, North Carolina. Davis remembers Travis and Hatcher arriving in a van and the musicians showing up at the Asheville Civic Center in a bread truck. Travis and his "Nashville" band did a sound check while Hatcher hauled in their blue Samsonite suitcase and set up a small merchandise table. Twitty came into the building early to watch Travis's show. He, Davis, and several crew members stood off to the side, in the dark, excited to see this new sensation.[2]

Travis performed during that summer at Twitty City, a major country music tourist attraction in Hendersonville, Tennessee. It contained a small theater where the Twitty organization scheduled performers to play on a regular basis. Travis was being exposed to the large Twitty audience, and his own popularity and huge airplay brought in additional crowds. "Everybody wanted to come see him," Davis recalls. "People who really loved traditional country music were thrilled with Randy Travis. What a breath of fresh air. Established country artists like Conway, like George Jones, like Merle Haggard, were rooting for Randy Travis to make it big. He was turning the tide, so to speak."

The first 1987 show as Twitty's opening act occurred on February 6 in Greenville, South Carolina. On the drive from Nashville, Hatcher called the Warner Bros. office, where she learned *Storms of Life* had gone platinum—Travis's debut album had sold more than one million copies! During the show at the Greenville Memorial Auditorium, they held an impromptu celebration. Having nothing prepared, Davis remembers filling a Hefty trash bag with popcorn to present to Travis onstage. They knew how much he loved popcorn. He once told an interviewer he had a corn popper on his bus and he looked forward to having popcorn every night after a concert.

A conflict arose with the booking two weeks later at shows in Richmond and Fairfax, Virginia. Travis was offered a performance slot as one of three "new traditionalists," along with Steve Earle and Dwight Yoakam, at the Grammy Awards on February 24. With rehearsals and travel time, he couldn't do both. He could either perform with Twitty and miss the Grammys or break his contract. Hatcher and Travis drove to Twitty City in Hendersonville to meet with Twitty and his agents, the father-son team of Jay and Davis. Hatcher asked Twitty to let Travis out of his contract for those two shows. "Conway had the hottest act in the business opening for him," Davis explains, "which meant lots of extra ticket sales. He let Randy out, and we had to scramble to find somebody else to open. Conway understood it and let him go. It was a significant event."[3]

Travis played the Friday date with Twitty in Hershey, Pennsylvania, and then he and Hatcher took an early morning flight to Los Angeles. On the 1987 annual Grammy Awards show, Travis sang "Diggin' Up Bones," which was nominated for Best Country Vocal Performance—Male. In addition to Yoakam and Earle, the other nominees were Hank Williams Jr. and winner Ronnie Milsap, who received the Grammy for "Lost in the Fifties Tonight."[4] Although Travis didn't win, he performed for an audience of more than thirty million people. This vast amount of exposure in households across the nation and around the world gave him recognition far beyond what his touring schedule provided.

During March and April, in addition to the Twitty openers, Travis was one of the performers on the second annual Marlboro Country Music Tour, featuring country quartet Alabama and mother-daughter duo Naomi and Wynonna Judd. Other artists appearing on the seventeen related package tours around the nation were Dolly Parton, Merle Haggard, and George Strait. Advertisements assured fans they would "not only experience some of country music's hottest performers but also help hungry people in their own communities and across America." A portion of ticket sales went to local and national food banks. A local talent contest was held in each city, with the winner opening the package show.[5] Travis joined Alabama and the Judds in Dallas for their second stop on the tour. A reviewer wrote that it must have been hard to designate which was an opening act and which was a headliner, writing, "What with Alabama, Randy Travis and The Judds on the bill, the audience gave up and enjoyed them all equally." That was quite a compliment for Travis, being compared to Alabama, a group described as "the all-time top band in country music, having won every major music award in multiples and sold twenty-five million albums." Travis's thirty-minute set followed the local band that had won five thousand dollars in the Dallas talent roundup. "On the Other Hand" was "probably the best-received song of the night," the reviewer wrote. "Travis was well into the second line before the applause ceased."[6]

After *Storms of Life* was certified platinum and working on its second million in sales, Travis walked into the Warner Bros. office one day and heard some surprising news. As producer Kyle Lehning tells the story, staffers excitedly showed Travis the album's high ranking on the *Billboard* Top Pop Albums chart, which listed the top two hundred albums in all musical genres. "Look at this," someone said. "You're up here with all these pop artists." Travis protested, saying, "Pop! I'm not a pop artist. Get me off there. I'm a country artist." He was upset to be on charts with the biggest-selling acts of the day because they weren't country. The staffers explained that he wasn't on the pop charts; he was selling the kinds of numbers that pop artists sold.[7]

Travis was the first country artist in history to sell a million copies of a debut album in less than a year. *Storms of Life* reached platinum in eight months. Warner Bros. hosted a reception at the Union Station Hotel the first week in March to celebrate the platinum status. Travis assisted CEO Jim Ed Norman in handing out eighty-one framed platinum records to the people who helped make it happen: Lehning, Stegall, Sharp, Hatcher, musicians, songwriters, publishers, and numerous others. Acoustic guitarist Mark Casstevens, who had played on the debut album and would play on every one of Travis's Warner Bros. albums, was happy to attend. Not one to seek the limelight, despite playing on ninety-nine *Billboard* chart toppers in his career, he wanted to join the elite studio players in celebrating Travis's success. Nashville's mayor, Richard Fulton, stopped by during the evening to present Travis with a key to Music City. Travis's second album, *Always & Forever*, was announced as being scheduled for release on May 4. Travis said, "We looked a long time for some great songs for the first album, and I feel like we did that this time, too."[8]

His statement downplayed the effort that had gone into finding time to choose songs and record them, due to his heavy travel schedule. Although producer Lehning could have been heavy-handed in making choices, he preferred consensus. He believed everybody's involvement in a decision was far more creative. Travis, Lehning, Sharp, and Hatcher struggled together to choose which songs to record. All opinions were taken seriously. According to Travis, the goal was to find ten great songs that might make great singles. They refused to settle for a few good songs and then add filler material to complete the album. They didn't look for certain subject matter or specific songwriters, only that it be a great song. Travis told an interviewer, "I have to like the words and the melody. We're real hard on songs. They have to tell a good story, too."

Lehning scheduled their recording sessions around travel dates. When Travis came in off the road too exhausted to sing, Lehning would send him home to rest his voice. They recorded all the songs by the end of January. Lehning then mixed the recordings and made a copy of the complete set for the four decision makers to choose which ten songs to place on the album. Would this sophomore album measure up to the debut album? That was the question on everyone's mind.

Travis and Lehning both referred to the "benefit of the doubt clause" in their recording relationship. They came up with the term simultaneously. If either had strong feelings about a song that the other didn't share, they would at least try it. "We would both know as soon as we started recording the song with the band if it was a good fit or not," Lehning says. He uses the analogy that songs are like clothes, saying, "They might look great on the rack in the store but don't look or feel that good when you try them on." Travis recalls Lehning giving him some of the best musical advice he ever received: "Don't record 'em if you don't love 'em."

During one of the song selection meetings, Martha Sharp excitedly played a demo she had received from Paul Overstreet and Don Schlitz, cowriters of "On the Other Hand." Travis, Lehning, and Hatcher immediately agreed that "Forever and Ever, Amen" could be a hit. They thought almost everyone would be able to relate to a song "celebrating love and commitment and marital fidelity through the years," as Travis described it. He called it "a once-in-a-lifetime song, the kind some singers never find. I felt blessed that Don and Paul had sent it my way."[9]

Overstreet describes the late-night writing session by telling an interviewer, "I knew better than to put it off, because when that opportunity comes, when somebody feels that strong about it, you do it." He had played thirty-six holes of golf at a music business golf tournament that day, followed by the event's dinner. Then Don Schlitz called and said he had an idea for a song they had to write. Overstreet wanted to wait until the next day. He relented when Schlitz said, "No, we've got to do it now." They sat on Overstreet's front porch that night and wrote "Forever and Ever, Amen." Schlitz already had most of the chorus after listening to his wife teaching their young son to recite the Lord's Prayer. The little boy followed the prayer with "Mommy, I love you. Forever and ever, amen."[10]

According to Schlitz, they were so excited with the result that they immediately went into their studio to record the demo. After listening to it, they knew the song was meant for Randy Travis. The first night Travis performed "Forever and Ever, Amen" was at a concert in Kentucky. The audience response of cheering and wanting more told him they had recorded the right song. At a club a few nights later, when he paused before singing the final "A-a-amen," the audience banged on their chairs as though they were at a rock concert. "The response was unlike anything I'd experienced from a country audience listening to a country song," Travis said later. "I sure liked it."

Travis debuted the song to a national television audience at the Academy of Country Music Awards in Los Angeles on April 6. In addition to his performance, he had three award nominations. When Charley Pride announced the Song of the Year winner as "On the Other Hand," Travis joined Paul Overstreet onstage to accept this songwriter award. Overstreet hesitated before saying, "I never think about what I'm going to say when I come up here, cuz I kind of like to wait till the last minute and surprise myself." He thanked Travis for doing an incredible job of singing the song and then concluded by saying, "About two and a half years ago, I was contemplating getting out of the business; I put myself down a hard road, and I gave it to the Lord, and I said, Lord, what do you want me to do, and I guess this is what I'm supposed to do, so thank you." Travis said, "I don't know what to add to that, except I'm glad you didn't get out of the business. And thanks for writing a great song. Thank you, everybody." Travis was named Male Artist of the Year, along with winning Single of the Year for "On the Other Hand" and Album of the Year for *Storms of Life*. He later said he thought he had a shot at winning Album of the Year, and he had tried before the show to think of a few things to say in case he won something. He hadn't thought of enough to cover four awards.[11]

On April 25, "Forever and Ever, Amen" debuted on *Billboard* at number forty-two. It had been released on March 25 as the lead single from the upcoming album *Always & Forever*. The album cover was a simple upper-body shot of Travis leaning against the back of a chair and staring seductively at the camera. "We didn't dress him for that," Janice Azrak says. "That was Randy." He wore his usual gold bracelet and his rings. An early Travis biographer accurately wrote, "The cover depicts a sophisticated, sexy male, while the music inside is full of tradition and roots. It is this combination of the contemporary and the timeless that has become the essence of Randy Travis's image and appeal."[12]

*Always & Forever* was released on May 4, Travis's twenty-eighth birthday. The next night, Travis was a guest on *Nashville Now* along with Conway Twitty and Loretta Lynn. Ralph Emery introduced him by saying, "He went out to California recently to the Academy of Country Music Awards, and he was nominated for four and he won four." To great applause from the audience, Emery listed the four awards and added, "Yesterday was his birthday. And his new album shipped yesterday. And they shipped over a half million copies the first day. He is hot."[13]

It was no coincidence that Travis was on *Nashville Now* with Twitty and Lynn. They discussed their plans for the Country Explosion event that Twitty presented every year the day before Fan Fair began. Twitty told Emery, "This year, Loretta's going to do it with us. And Mr. Randy Travis." Twitty, fifty-three, and Lynn, fifty-two, had recorded and toured together throughout the 1970s. Their suggestive songs led many fans to think they were a couple in real life. They played on that idea and shared a close friendship, although both were married to others. Lynn wrote autobiographical songs like "Don't Come Home

A-Drinkin' (With Lovin' on Your Mind) and "You Ain't Woman Enough (To Take My Man)," as well as her signature song, "Coal Miner's Daughter."

On the *Nashville Now* show, Lynn told Travis she was getting calls about him. "I wanted you to know that, honey," she teased. "A lot of people are coming to see you, not me at all." As she snuggled closer to Travis and put her arm around him, Emery commented to Travis that she seemed to be in love with him. Travis laughed self-consciously. Twitty joked, "I told him, you're sitting there by my girl. It didn't seem to faze him." Twitty switched topics to say how much they admired Travis: "He's a pure country singer, and Loretta and I love him."[14]

The day after the June 7 Country Explosion event at the municipal auditorium, crowds descended on the Nashville Fairgrounds for the opening of Fan Fair. Travis's fan club now boasted three thousand members. Jill Youngblood came from Charlotte to operate his Fan Fair booth. That evening, the crowd moved to the Opry House for the *Music City News* Awards. Travis had been a presenter the previous year. This year he was nominated for four awards. He won Male Artist of the Year and Star of Tomorrow, as well as Album of the Year for *Storms of Life* and Single Record of the Year for "On the Other Hand." He sang the last song of the evening, "Forever and Ever, Amen."[15]

Travis explained his philosophy as a performer by saying, "I enjoy what I do. If you get out there and it looks like you are having a good time, I think people are going to enjoy themselves." A new technology to share that appearance of a good time came through music videos. MTV's music video channel, launched in 1981, quickly became influential in producing pop hitmakers. Country music followed suit when Country Music Television (CMT) premiered its new channel in 1983. The first video aired was a live clip of Faron Young singing "It's Four in the Morning." As CMT grew in popularity, adventurous country performers began making music videos, clamoring for their share of this exciting new outlet.[16]

When Warner Bros. decided to make a video for "Forever and Ever, Amen," many Nashville people considered videos an unnecessary marketing expense. Janice Azrak disagreed. She searched for an appropriate spot for filming and a large enough crowd to be the video audience. Hatcher suggested going to a church and getting a congregation. With the help of the Hillcrest United Methodist Church, they assembled a cast that Travis remembered as "everyday folks from the congregation, including various family members and children, along with several handsome fraternity guys from Vanderbilt University, and a few volunteers from a nearby seniors' center, mixed in with some professional actors." Azrak recalls, "That was an awesome day. The equipment worked, the facility was great; thank God for little favors." She called the finished product classy and "so sweet."[17] The video portrays a wedding reception at the church, with wedding photos taken throughout. After one family photo, the bride asks her brother—played by Travis—to sing. The happy wedding guests lightheartedly pose for photos while he sings. He wraps up the song with "I'm gonna love you forever and ever" as loving couples kiss. The video has become a timeless classic, along with a song that has been played at weddings for more than three decades.

"Forever and Ever, Amen" reached number one on the *Billboard* Hot Country Songs chart on June 13, followed by *Always & Forever* reaching the top of *Billboard*'s Top Country Albums chart a week later. The album would produce four number one songs. It remained at the top of the chart for forty-three weeks, a record not broken until a decade later, when Shania Twain's 1997 album, *Come on Over*, took the top spot. *Always & Forever* would hold on to second place for another twelve years.

After July's full month of touring—from Texas to Wisconsin, Saskatchewan to Wyoming, then to Kansas and back to Wisconsin—the Travis entourage returned to Nashville before taking off again at the end of August. They got as far as Wytheville, Virginia. Travis was "feeling funny" when they left Nashville, and by the time they reached Wytheville, he felt he needed medical help. He spent Thursday night at the Wythe County Community Hospital, with a diagnosis of dehydration from vomiting all night long, caused by food poisoning from a hamburger he had eaten before boarding the bus. "The doctor working with me was the mayor of the town," Travis later said. "I signed an album for him before I left." The Ramada Inn provided rooms for the band at no cost. Flower arrangements and fruit baskets filled his hospital room as townspeople let him know how much they cared. The Thursday and Friday evening shows at the Allen County Fair in Lima, Ohio, had to be canceled, but Travis was determined to make his sold-out Saturday night performance with the Judds at the Indiana State Fair.[18]

And he did. So many fans flooded into the Indianapolis show that more bleachers were added and filled. The promoter then sold standing-room-only tickets until the fire marshal stopped the sales. Those who knew of Travis's illness were gratified to see him looking well. At the end of the evening, his bus headed to Pennsylvania for the next night's concert.[19]

His popularity had increased to the extent that shows that had been booked earlier in the year were drawing crowds exceeding available space at the venues.

On September 18, Travis caused a traffic jam in Knoxville, Tennessee. Before performing at the Tennessee Valley Fair, he had a Friday afternoon autograph session at a store called Records and Things. The crowd started forming at eleven o'clock, and the five hundred extra copies of *Storms of Life* were sold out by three. When Travis and Hatcher arrived in a yellow Cadillac, security guards led them through the screaming crowd into the record store. Travis posed for photos and smiled at each person in line. Amid the chaos in the crowded store, he calmly and politely shook hands with his fans. At a quarter of six, to the disappointment of those still in line, he was rushed outside and through the crowd that pressed against the Cadillac. On the way to the fairgrounds, the radio announcer said the city's traffic jam was caused by crowds on their way to see Travis. The forty-five-hundred-seat Homer Hamilton Theatre couldn't hold the seven thousand people present. Fans were hanging from the gates, standing five-deep by the concrete wall at the rear of the theater, and standing outside the fairgrounds, peeking through the fence from the street.[20]

The next night, after a concert in Cumming, Georgia, Travis and his band headed north on a five-hour drive to Red Boiling Springs, Tennessee. For that Sunday afternoon performance, more than three thousand people sat on the sun-warmed hillside surrounding the outdoor stage at Deerwood Amphitheater. Prior to the concert, Warner Bros. hosted a picnic lunch for special guests in a secluded area under the trees. While everyone was eating, Jim Ed Norman announced he had a special presentation for Travis. He asked, "Do you realize that in the last two years, you have sold over three million records?" The picnickers applauded and cheered as Norman presented Travis with a framed platinum album of *Always & Forever* to commemorate sales of a million albums. *Storms of Life* by then had sold over two million. Taken by surprise, Travis said he didn't realize they'd sold so many.

The surprises weren't over. Norman then said, "Randy, in our tradition of horsing around, we thought it would be appropriate that we hand the reigning king of the new tradition the reins of this horse, named today as New Tradition." Travis, stunned, accepted the reins of the two-year-old quarter horse that had been brought up behind him. Running his hands over the black horse's mane, he said, "Man, is he beautiful. You're giving me this horse?" Norman nodded, telling him he could call it New Tradition or Platinum or whatever he wanted. Travis, who had longed for horses since he'd left North Carolina, led the animal to a nearby clearing to soothe the skittish creature he chose to call Platinum Harry. When Travis took the stage, with the audience standing and cheering, he opened with "What'll You Do about Me." Female fans screamed as he sang "There's No Place Like Home." Throughout the show, women approached the stage to bring him roses and ask for kisses.[21]

◇ ♦ ◇

Hatcher hired Jeff Davis as an in-house promoter in September. She formed Special Moments Promotions, a new company to organize and expand the touring operation, with herself as president and Davis as vice president. Steel player Gary Carter later expressed relief at turning over scheduling duties, saying, "When Jeff came on board, he was a true professional road manager, unlike me and Drew Sexton. He knew what he was doing, where we were musicians just trying to help things roll along." Davis was responsible for touring arrangements and concert promotion, while Allen Whitcomb continued as booking agent and Carol Harper as Hatcher's assistant. The in-house arrangement allowed Davis to both book and promote dates in some of the larger markets. Hatcher wanted to avoid paying a promoter and agent when her company could do the work and take the money, providing it was a venue expected to be profitable. This lessened Whitcomb's ability to book dates because Special Moments handled the lucrative ones. Hatcher took him off commission status and placed him on a lesser salary.

The Hatcher/Travis home on Sixteenth Avenue still served as the office. Davis showed up the first morning and set two file boxes of contracts on the kitchen table. He worked there every day, and when business hours were over, he put everything back in the boxes and cleared the table so the residents could eat supper. When Davis moved from the Conway Twitty/Jimmy Jay organization (United Talent) to the Travis/Hatcher organization (Special Moments Promotions), he moved from riding Twitty's bus to riding Travis's bus. The shows were still promoted by United Talent with Travis as the opening act. Davis prepared for their October tour while Travis concentrated on another upcoming event.[22]

At the previous year's Country Music Association Awards, Travis had won the Horizon Award as country music's rising star. This year he was a finalist in five categories, including the prestigious Entertainer of the Year category. He joined the current winner, Reba McEntire, along with fellow nominees George Strait, the Judds, and Hank Williams Jr., who grumbled, "After thirty years, I ought to be nominated before my hair turns completely gray."[23]

Monday evening, October 12, 1987, country music royalty gathered at the Opry House to celebrate those winners chosen by the seven-thousand-member Country Music Association, composed of professionals from all segments of the country music industry. Host Kenny Rogers announced, "Tonight, for the first time ever, you are going to see performances by all five nominees for Entertainer of the Year. A very big night. Beginning with the young man who started out a year or two ago and zoomed right to the top. Ladies and gentlemen, Randy Travis." The cameras moved to the audience, where Travis rose from his seat, microphone in hand, and started singing "Forever and Ever, Amen." Wearing a glitzy western-cut black suit that sparkled like teeth in a toothpaste commercial, he strolled toward the stage, pausing to shake numerous hands along the way, including those of Ricky Skaggs, George Jones, the Judds, June Carter and Johnny Cash, Rosanne Cash and Rodney Crowell, and Jim Nabors. He paused when he reached Opry matriarch and comedienne Minnie Pearl, sang the chorus, and then kissed her on the cheek before bounding up the steps to finish his song onstage.[24]

Rosanne Cash presented the award for Single of the Year, saying, "When you think about how many singles are produced each year, just being nominated is a miracle." She then called out, "And the winner is 'Forever and Ever, Amen,' Randy Travis." During his acceptance speech, sounding modest and well-spoken, Travis said he'd been watching the awards show for a long time, and it was great to be part of it. He ended with, "I appreciate this very much," and the camera zoomed in on a smiling Lib Hatcher. Album of the Year, presented by the Oak Ridge Boys, went to *Always & Forever*. Travis repeated most of his earlier speech, adding, "Mom and Dad, hello, and thanks to you a lot for a lot of help over the past twenty-eight years." Emmylou Harris announced the nominees for Male Vocalist of the Year as George Jones, Ricky Skaggs, George Strait, Randy Travis, and Hank Williams Jr., concluding, "And the winner is Randy Travis." To great applause, the stunned Travis said, "Thank you again. Ah, a good night for me." Being nominated with people he had admired for years, and then to win the award, brought a sense of disbelief.[25]

Song of the Year went to Paul Overstreet and Don Schlitz for "Forever and Ever, Amen." They had competed against themselves because the previous year's winner, "On the Other Hand," had been nominated a second time. Schlitz commented in his acceptance speech, "I think we're the first people ever to win and lose at the same time." The award made Schlitz the first person to receive three Song of the Year awards, including his 1979 win for "The Gambler." Travis's final two categories, Music Video of the Year (for "Forever and Ever, Amen") and Entertainer of the Year, were both won by Hank Williams Jr.[26]

Then it was time to head to the West Coast for the seven-date Country Explosion Tour, using the title from Twitty's event the night before Fan Fair.

Although Travis had been booked as the opening act, he was by now a bigger draw than either Twitty or Lynn. The ads and newspaper articles put the focus on him. A *Fresno Bee* article said, "Ironically, Travis will be making his Fresno debut as the opening act for Loretta Lynn and Conway Twitty Friday night at Selland Arena. After Monday's awards coup, perhaps they should be opening for him."[27] Next, the buses traveled to Anaheim, twenty-four miles southeast of downtown Los Angeles. A reviewer of that show wrote, "In retrospect, it's not as surprising as it initially seemed that the red-hot Travis, the first country act to have his first two albums go platinum (one million copies), opened the show rather than headlined. Country musicians and fans, more than their rock counterparts, are as *respectful* as they are loyal, and for Travis to leapfrog over two giants from the past would have been downright unneighborly." After saying Travis hadn't "yet developed enough performance confidence to warrant headline status," the reviewer praised his ability to pick great songs, suggesting that if Lynn and Twitty "would hire Travis to find them meatier songs to sink their considerable chops into, maybe they'd get back into the limelight."[28] A reviewer in Vancouver, British Columbia, described Travis by writing, "He has the good looks of a mannish boy, the razor-cut grooming of a white knight, and the graceful style of an old-time movie star." He praised Travis's humility, calling him the headliner, and then quoting him as saying, "This is a nice show to be part of."[29]

After the final three shows in Seattle, Portland, and Salt Lake City, they headed back to Nashville to prepare for the next tour—as co-headliner with the Judds at the Kansas Coliseum in Wichita, Kansas. Patty Loveless was their opening act. Travis and the Judds had become friends while touring around the country on the Marlboro Country Music Tour earlier in the year, followed by the sell-out success at the Indiana State Fair in August. At the recent CMA Awards, the Judds received their third consecutive award as CMA Vocal Group of the Year. "I'm not going to say that music is the most important thing in our lives, but it's right up there with oxygen," Naomi said when accepting the award. Wynonna added, "I want to thank you for allowing a twenty-three-year-old to feel what I feel, and for allowing a mom to enjoy a second childhood."[30]

After returning from Kansas, Travis spent several days in bed with laryngitis, under doctor's orders not to talk or sing. While he cared for his golden voice, plans were finalized for his return to Charlotte as a headliner in front of the hometown crowd. "All of a sudden, overnight it was big business," says Davis. In the two months since he joined the Travis organization, they went from one bus to three buses and four semis, as well as a crew of employees.

Travis's first major headline concerts took place over Thanksgiving weekend. They debuted a new stage set, with monitor covers and backdrop displaying an understated slanted "RT" in maroon and gray. A slide show played his career highlights on a large screen. Travis's opening acts were country legends Gene Watson and Johnny Russell—one more example of how far he had come, from being Watson's opening act and being introduced on *Nashville Now* by Russell.

Friday night they appeared in Louisville, Kentucky. A newspaper critic wrote about headliner Travis: "The man who inspired a sold-out crowd at Louisville Gardens last night to flick their Bics, flash their Instamatics and scream their lungs out on nearly every song seemingly can do no wrong." Exactly a year earlier, Travis and Patty Loveless had opened for George Jones at Louisville Gardens. Loveless remembers Jones wanting an earlier performance slot so that he could get back to his bus and watch television. Travis said no, refusing to outrank him as the closing act. Jones called the two young singers onstage to join him in his show's finale, "Rollin' in My Sweet Baby's Arms."

Saturday night, the entourage was in Charlotte, North Carolina. A matinee had been added to meet demand after the evening show sold out in five hours. The last person to do two shows at the ten-thousand-seat Charlotte Coliseum had been Bruce Springsteen almost three years earlier. Ronnie Traywick remembers visiting briefly with Travis after the Charlotte show. "It seemed like everyone who knew Randy (and a lot that didn't) wanted to get close to the local guy who had done well," he says. Comparing the headlining date to the earlier show with George Jones, Rocky Thacker says it was still carnival-like but more controlled, with more security. Travis was more at ease with the attention. "We met a lot of people from Randy's past," Thacker says. "Everyone you saw seemed to have a story about him. It was very cool to talk to them. We were treated wonderfully." A reviewer described Travis as shyly accepting "the proffered gifts of roses and teddy bears, notes and balloons." He waved at children held high by their moms, and he laughed without missing a lyric when he leaned down to accept one young woman's note. In her excitement, she grabbed the security guard's neck as he escorted her away from the stage. The music, according to the reviewer, was "straight-ahead country, pared to the basics, intelligent lyrics worth singing, sung by a voice that demands listening to."[31]

Travis would soon be reaching a new audience. An entertainer in great demand, he had agreed to headline a USO Christmas tour to Europe.

# 5

# "BY THIS THIRD ALBUM, HE WAS A SUPERSTAR."

In 1941, when President Franklin Delano Roosevelt expressed a desire for a service association that could lift military morale, social reformer Mary Shotwell Ingraham responded. She brought together six civilian organizations to form the United Service Organizations, or USO. The USO is a congressionally chartered but private organization that relies on volunteers and fund-raising. The first and most famous USO entertainer was comedian Bob Hope, who performed his first USO show in 1941 and continued to entertain troops for fifty years, especially during Christmas holidays. He died in 2003, at age one hundred. Many entertainers have followed in his footsteps, with USO tours continuing to this day.[1]

Randy Travis joined those ranks during the 1987 Christmas season. He and Lib Hatcher had been approached while doing a summer concert at Merriweather Post Pavilion, an outdoor venue near Columbia, Maryland. Loretta Lynn's manager, David Skepner, had arranged for the USO's producer of celebrity entertainment to visit them on their bus. Dan Markley, who recruited celebrities and then managed everything associated with the resulting USO tour, told them, "You are going to be challenged in every regard. How you think of presenting your concert, how you travel, what equipment is used, the housing facilities, the local production crew." He said they would be working with "really nice military people who know absolutely nothing about how to put on a show." And they would not be paid.

The couple listened attentively, with Hatcher asking a few questions. Markley said the USO had a contract with The Nashville Network to produce television specials following each tour. After about thirty minutes, Markley finished his pitch. Hatcher looked at Travis and said, "Well, Randy, do you want to do it?" Travis said, "Yeah. I'd like to." Markley says, "Randy's not a natural conversationalist. He's a great one, but he doesn't feel the need to talk all the time." He adds, "It speaks volumes about Randy, and about Lib, too, because they were taking a big gamble. They in no way needed to do this. You couldn't make Randy a bigger star than he was, by going on a USO tour. He thought it was important."

As they were planning their tour, Bob Hope decided in early December to do an around-the-world Christmas tour. Markley was pulled from the Travis tour to put together the Hope production. Hatcher expressed concern about not having Markley with them on their first USO experience. Bob Hope was the only person significant enough to make her accept Markley's colleague as a substitute.[2] Travis's opening act on the tour was a new Warner Bros. act, the McCarter sisters from Sevierville, Tennessee. Jennifer, twenty-three, played acoustic guitar and sang lead, with twins Teresa and Lisa, twenty-one, providing high harmony. They'd grown up singing every evening, summer after summer, outside Silver Dollar City in Pigeon Forge. Jennifer had asked Kyle Lehning for an audition, because he produced her favorite singer, Randy Travis. He referred them to Martha Sharp, who signed them to the label. "We thought Randy Travis was the greatest thing that ever breathed air," Jennifer says.

The USO troupe flew to Fliegerhorst Kaserne, a US Army base in Erlensee, Germany, and crammed as much interaction with the troops as possible into their two days on the base. Following a two-hour show in an aircraft hangar, Travis talked with the soldiers and signed autographs. "I hadn't realized so many of them knew and enjoyed my music," he said later. The troupe also gave performances in Switzerland and Italy. "We had the time of our lives," Jennifer McCarter recalls. "Randy is the nicest human being I've ever met." She doesn't have a high opinion of Hatcher, who had wanted to manage the McCarters until they butted heads over how to dress. Hatcher wanted their style to be gingham shirts and denim skirts. McCarter said no. They had worn gingham dresses for their performances since childhood. Now that they were on a major label and living in Nashville, they wanted sparkly, flashy clothes in the style of Dolly Parton. After their return from Europe, they were never hired again.[3]

During the early part of 1988, Travis swept awards shows and won his first Grammy. At the American Music Awards in Los Angeles on January 25, he won four of the six awards in the country category. He didn't win the other two simply because he wasn't eligible for them. He sang "Forever and Ever, Amen." His guest at that ceremony was Barry Weinberg, athletic trainer for the Oakland Athletics baseball team. They had become friends after being introduced by Nick Hunter of Warner Bros. Travis invited Weinberg to his West Coast shows, and Weinberg invited Travis to Oakland A's games and spring training. "We'd put a uniform on him for batting practice," Weinberg recalls. "Of course, the guys who loved country music were thrilled that Randy was there. He was at the top, the biggest star in that era."[4]

The Grammy Awards presentation was held on March 2 at Radio City Music Hall in New York City. Like the year before, Travis was offered a performance slot for his most recent hit. He sang "Forever and Ever, Amen," which won Paul Overstreet and Don Schlitz a Grammy for writing the Best Country Song. Travis won Best Country Vocal Performance—Male for *Always & Forever*. He later expressed irritation that country music continued to be treated like pop's poor relation, as evidenced by his award not being presented during the televised show. He told an interviewer, "The Judds are selling platinum; George Strait is gold and platinum; Hank Jr. sells millions of records. Country music should be a bigger part of that show."[5]

At the 1988 Academy of Country Music Awards in March, Travis looked like a fashion model in a charcoal gray western-cut suit with silver braid accents. He won Single of the Year and the Schlitz/Overstreet pair won Song of the Year for "Forever and Ever, Amen." During his acceptance speech for Male Vocalist of the Year, Travis thanked Kyle Lehning, "who produces all the things we do. He does a great job." When once asked how he came up with so many different ways of saying thank you for his awards, he responded, "On the way to the stage, I usually try to think of what I'm gonna say and it usually works out pretty good. I'm lucky in that respect—I'm fairly quick thinking of something to say when I'm in a tight spot, I guess."[6] Perhaps that came from his teenage years of explaining his behavior in an attempt to avoid being arrested.

The Nashville Network debuted the TNN Viewers' Choice Awards on April 26, staged in conjunction with TNN's fifth anniversary. Ralph Emery hosted the ninety-minute show in front of an audience of 4,400 at the Opry House, with Willie Nelson and K. T. Oslin as cohosts. It aired live over TNN. About 318,000 TNN viewers had voted via telephone, using a ballot drawn up by a panel of music, TV, and radio industry representatives. Travis won every category in which he was eligible. Near the end of the show, Nelson announced, "Our final award tonight may be the hardest to earn, for the Favorite Entertainer. It takes hours of rehearsal and a deep desire to do whatever it takes to please your audience, and to give them a show." When Travis was announced as the winner, the camera cut to the audience to show Hatcher throwing her arms around Travis's neck. They hugged, grinning, and then he bounded up the steps and onto the stage. He had triumphed over Reba McEntire, Dolly Parton, Ricky Skaggs, George Strait, and Hank Williams Jr., all of whom were producing hit songs before he came along. "I'm very thankful to the people here at The Nashville Network for all they've done for me over the past few years that I've been in Nashville," he said in his acceptance speech, noting that *Nashville Now* was his first television show in Nashville. As usual, he thanked his manager, Lib Hatcher; his "great producer," Kyle Lehning; and Warner Bros. Records, ending with, "This is great!"[7]

The previous weekend, Travis had performed in Ohio as part of the GMC Truck American Music Tour. Tammy Wynette, best known for "Stand By Your Man" and her earlier marriage to George Jones, had been hired by the General Motors Truck Company to host the tour. She opened each show with a thirty-five-minute set before introducing the younger and currently more popular artists on that night's bill. Travis and the Judds appeared with her in Toledo and Richfield. A reviewer in the ten-thousand-person crowd at the Richfield Coliseum noted that Travis, "with his clear, fluid baritone," was so likeable "that even strangers get the feeling they've known him since way back when." The reviewer commented on Travis's "great six-piece Nashville Band," which would surely have pleased Lamont "Monty" Parkey, who was playing his first performance as the band's keyboardist. He had observed Drew Sexton's last night with the group the previous evening in Toledo. After the Richfield performance, tour manager Davis asked Travis, "Well, how did he do?" Travis responded, "I didn't really notice anything. It sounded like it normally does." Overhearing that exchange, Parkey knew he had achieved his goal of playing like Sexton. In the following years, he would surreptitiously make minor changes to ensure the songs sounded exactly like the records themselves.[8]

Travis also participated for a second year in the Marlboro Country Music Tour. Although he didn't smoke, and Hatcher prohibited smoking on his bus, he assured an interviewer that he found no conflict being on a tour that promoted cigarettes. Every show began with a Marlboro welcome video. In one introductory video, Travis says, "Ladies and gentlemen, welcome to an evening of Marlboro Country music." For almost two minutes, the screen shows horses running through a desert landscape as orchestral music plays. Then Travis explains the rules for the local Marlboro Talent Roundup competition and the process of choosing the winner. He ends with, "So congratulations, everybody. I hope you enjoy this evening of Marlboro Country music." At the Mid-South Coliseum in Memphis, in late April he ran into David Jones, whom he had worked with at the Nashville Palace. Jones had won the local Memphis competition, earning him a seventy-five-hundred-dollar prize and the opportunity to open the package show for Kathy Mattea, Travis, and George Strait. "It was special to be able to open for Randy again," Jones recalls. "We both got the key to the city of Memphis, as part of raising money for the Memphis Food Bank." In a photo of the two young men, six-five Jones towers over the five-nine Travis.[9]

On May 9, four days after Travis's twenty-ninth birthday, a sold-out crowd at the civic center in Augusta, Georgia, watched the Marlboro video on the large rear screen before K. T. Oslin took the stage. The surprise was that Merle Haggard—who had to leave early—came out next, granting the headliner spot to Travis, who was excited to be working a show with one of his idols. When Travis came onstage, his screaming female fans tossed roses and cards at him throughout his performance.[10] He made his New York City debut during the Marlboro Country Music Tour's sold-out, four-hour show at Madison Square Garden in Manhattan on May 21. Following the local talent winner, Travis preceded the Judds, George Strait, and Alabama. A reviewer called him "country's hottest vocalist" and said he gave "a beautifully sung performance of his many big hits in his brief two-album career."[11]

Then came Fan Fair and the *Music City News* Awards show in early June. Travis won four awards, as he had in 1987. Three of them were the same categories. But instead of Star of Tomorrow, which went to Ricky Van Shelton (who had followed Travis at the Nashville Palace), he received the top award: Entertainer of the Year.[12]

On June 11, "I Told You So" became the fourth song from *Always & Forever* to hit the top of the *Billboard* chart. "I Won't Need You Anymore" had followed "Forever and Ever, Amen" to number one on November 14. "Too Gone Too Long" arrived on March 12. "I Told You So," Travis's sixth number one and the first that he had written, held the top spot for two weeks. When he had first played it for Lehning, the skeptical producer agreed to record it as one of those "benefit of the doubt" recordings. According to Travis, "When we did it in the studio, it was magic."[13]

Ashland City, the county seat of Cheatham County, lies twenty-five miles northwest of Nashville's Music Row, on Highway 12. In the 1980s, approximately thirty-five hundred residents lived in the town located along the Cumberland River. It is where Travis and Hatcher bought their first joint property and the first property Travis owned, the historic Braxton Lee homestead. About two miles south of the city limits, Little Marrowbone Road lies to the east. Following that curving gravel road up the forested hillside and bearing left on Big Marrowbone Road would bring a traveler to Travis's new home. According to the deed, "Mary Elizabeth Hatcher and Randy Bruce Traywick" purchased fifteen acres of wooded property along Big Marrowbone Road, with a farmhouse along a stream, for $130,000. They moved from Music Row in the spring of 1988 and lived in the Lee homestead while preparing their new home for occupancy.

"I'd like to be able to have horses and a dog again," Travis had said. "I'd like to be able to sleep some place where you don't hear cars going by outside all night long."[14] He liked small towns and loved living on a farm. With a twinge of sadness, he had told an interviewer in 1986, "I live on Music Row. I know it's hard to think of that as 'home.' About all I own is the truck and the van and the trailer. I don't own land or anything like that."[15]

Now he owned land and had a home in the country. He and Hatcher renovated and enlarged the log cabin house, giving it a Southwestern décor and homey atmosphere. Hatcher enjoyed cooking for Travis, choosing his wardrobe, and generally making their house a home. Their socializing, other than music business, was with Hatcher's friends, although they did enjoy attending movies at the Ashland City theater. Travis described himself as a simple person who loved being in the country. "I'm a very laid-back person," he told an interviewer. "Not big on going to the big parties." He relieved the pressure of the music business by riding horses and shooting guns, working out four days a week, and running several days a week.[16]

Hatcher gave him a surprise twenty-ninth birthday party. They celebrated with a Mexican luncheon at the office on Sixteenth Avenue, and he was definitely surprised when his parents and little brother Dennis arrived from Marshville. Harold and Hatcher got along fine that day, and the visit went well. They drove to Ashland City, where Travis showed his family his cabin home on Marrowbone Creek. Another surprise awaited him there. Hatcher presented him with two horses—Red Star Cause, a high sorrel quarter horse, and Smokey's Red Rouge, a tan-and-white Appaloosa. Travis's love of horses had never left him, and these two joined Platinum Harry, his gift from Warner

Bros. the previous September. His parents still owned his first pony, the elderly Buckshot. "I don't like using spurs or a riding crop on a horse," Travis once commented. "I think the best way to train a horse is make friends with it, to win over its trust. If a horse doesn't like or respect you, it won't do anything you want it to do." In addition to riding, he liked guns and loved to get out and shoot targets. Hunting no longer interested him as it had in years past. He owned a shotgun, a 7mm Magnum rifle, a .22 pistol, and an old Winchester pump .22 rifle. "I was content riding horses, practicing my ambidextrous quick-draw techniques with six-shooters, and target shooting on the property," he later said about the Marrowbone home. "I loved to play pool, so we bought a gorgeous pool table that we put in my upstairs studio. Of course, we had a workout area, and I spent several hours a day there."[17]

Travis and Hatcher spent as much time on their newly acquired Silver Eagle bus as they did in their new home. They'd come a long way from that used 1981 Crusader bus they purchased in late 1986 to move up from the bread truck. They traveled in a leased bus for several months while having their purchase refurbished. When the bus was returned with a new interior, it looked so beautiful on the inside that they had the exterior repainted, too, in early 1988. While giving a reporter a tour of his bus, Travis said, "We have, of course, the front lounge, with a couch and a little dinette for a place to eat. We have a microwave and a stove and sink there, too, and a TV, a VCR and a tape player." His bedroom had an almost-full-size bed and a bathroom with a shower. There were also bunks and a lot of closet space. By the end of the year, they had two additional buses, one each for the band and the crew.[18]

Lehning drove to Ashland City for their meetings. "We would sit and listen to songs and decide what we were going to do next," he recalls. "Lib made the most incredible meals. She was a phenomenal cook. And I loved food, particularly the kind she would cook, really great home cooking." They sometimes went to the creek behind the house to shoot pistols, and they occasionally rode horses. "Well, Randy rode the horses," Lehning says. "I sat on the saddle and tried my best not to fall off."[19]

Neighbors remember seeing Travis on his horse. "We would wave at him from the yard," one said. "He'd wave back; he was a very friendly person." Another said, "He rode the backwoods. You couldn't see his place from the road. I tried to let the man have his peace." Fans and tour guides felt differently. It didn't take long before a fence with a locked gate appeared at the end of the Travis driveway. Tour buses tried to navigate the narrow gravel Big Marrowbone Road but eventually stopped coming. Fans came in their cars, especially during Fan Fair week. "People would hang their scarves around the gatepost or open the mailbox and put a package in there," one neighbor says. "Sometimes they'd even walk up our driveway and ask if they could cross the creek and go over there, through the woods."[20]

Alan Ross remembers tour buses stopping near the Travis driveway. The tourists would get off the bus and have their pictures taken, he says, "standing in front of the gates, shut and locked." They'd get back on the bus, which would continue up the road to Ross's driveway to turn around. Ross often saw Travis riding through the woods and on the logging roads. One day the two men were talking about the tour buses, and Travis said he wished he had a way to get around the crowd. Whenever he rode up and pushed the button to open the gate, people chased him down his driveway to get their picture taken with him. Ross suggested, "Why don't you come off the hill in front of your house? It's the old mail route from the early 1800s. My daughter can show you how to get through there." He called his teenage daughter, who swung up bareback on her pony and led Travis through the woods to show him the routes to use. They parted at the gate at the end of his driveway. As Ross tells the story, "Come to find out, Lib was there. And here comes Randy off the side of a hill, riding a horse, and this country girl with long blonde hair was riding there with him, and she took off up the road." He says it was three months before they saw Travis riding again. Other neighbors recall Travis's own bus crawling along the narrow road. One says, "I didn't know that much personal about him; I just knew he was a Grand Ole Opry star and he lived up there."[21]

In June 1988, the Country Music Association sponsored a giant two-week promotion in the United Kingdom, known as "Route '88," to publicize country music and make a bigger splash in London. On June 8 an exhausted but happy Travis left for Europe in the middle of a highly successful Fan Fair. The previous evening, twelve hundred people had attended his fan club dinner at the Nashville Convention Center. Jeff Davis, as vice president of Special Moments Promotions, shared emcee duties with Jill Youngblood, longtime fan club president. Travis's band, Nashville, performed a short acoustic set before he came onstage and debuted some of the songs from his upcoming album, *Old 8x10*. Following his show, Travis signed autographs from nine o'clock until two in the morning.[22]

A concert in Dublin, Ireland, kicked off the twelve-day European tour before they crossed the English Channel to play Paris and Amsterdam. When they returned to Great Britain, Travis performed in several cities at venues ranging from magnificent old theaters to boxing rings. The grand finale of "Route '88" came on June 19, with Travis headlining at the Royal Albert Hall, a five-thousand-seat concert hall dedicated by Queen Victoria in 1871. Its century-plus list of performers has included the Beatles, Janis Joplin, Johnny Cash, Bob Dylan, and Creedence Clearwater Revival. Kathy Mattea opened the show. The steady drumbeat of "Eighteen Wheels and a Dozen Roses" filled the Royal Albert Hall, along with Mattea's voice telling the story of the truck driver who was retiring from the road to be with the woman he loved. Her chart-topping *Billboard* hit from May had been superseded by Travis's "I Told You So," which was number one during the tour. When Travis took the stage and started singing "Storms of Life," he bent to shake a hand reaching up to him and was immediately flooded with waving hands. Several women pulled him forward and kissed his hand. He chuckled when one woman almost pulled him off balance. For his final song, he invited the audience to sing along with the Hank Williams classic "I Saw the Light," saying, "You probably know the words."[23]

Immediately upon Travis's return to Nashville, Warner Bros. threw a party at the West Side Athletic Club to celebrate the fact that his first two albums had sold over five million copies. The record label had mailed invitations to music industry personnel and media representatives. In keeping with Travis's passion for weightlifting and exercise, the theme was "Working Out with Randy Travis." Upon arrival, guests received oversized T-shirts imprinted with "I Worked Out with Randy Travis." Professional trainers entertained the crowd by showing off their physiques while demonstrating lifting exercises. "We were, indeed, expected to exercise at last night's festivities," wrote one reporter the next day. Refreshments included fresh fruit, juices, nonalcoholic beverages, and seafood.[24]

Then came the release of Travis's third album. Originally scheduled for July 12, the release date was moved to June 30 to make *Old 8×10* eligible for the CMA Awards in October. When five hundred thousand copies of *Always & Forever* had been shipped on its release date a year earlier, the demand seemed astronomical. But that didn't compare to the initial order of nine hundred thousand copies placed by stores for *Old 8×10*, giving the album platinum status almost before the first day. It was the largest number of initial units Warner Bros. had ever shipped.[25]

The album cover was a framed square photo (not an 8×10) of the country superstar reclining on a woodpile at his Ashland City home. Life had changed drastically since his previous two album cover photos, but his humble image remained. Wearing a white pullover sweater with blue jeans and boots, his well-exercised physique part of the allure, he looks at the camera with a slight smile, as if patiently waiting for the photo shoot to end. He appears to be enjoying a moment of relaxation from the hectic life of recording, touring, and being interviewed. "By this third album, he was a superstar," Lehning says. "The time we spent together in the studio was carved out of everything that was taking his time. He knew the songs, the lyrics—total pro in the studio. The most difficult thing we ran into, his voice was tired. In the studio, it was always fun." Hatcher, having been heavily involved in song selection, enjoyed the recording process and was usually in the studio.[26] "Lib was in the studio a lot when we were recording," says one sideman. "I think she was in control of most everything Randy did."

Their song search had gotten much easier. "On the first album, we had to have gone through a thousand songs," Travis said. "After the first album, people were more willing to give you their good songs." He said songs were sent to him every day at the office. Lehning and Sharp also received tapes from songwriters themselves or song pluggers who were trying to sell their publishers' songs.[27] The first single, "Honky Tonk Moon," reached the top of *Billboard*'s Hot Country Songs chart on October 8. The title track was never released as a single, although both Lehning and Travis loved the well-written song and thought it could have been a hit. "Old 8×10" was one of five tracks recorded in a session at Ronnie Milsap's studio, Ground Star. Twenty-one musicians gathered in the studio that day, including Travis on rhythm guitar and Lehning on piano. "It was really kind of a musician's tour de force," Lehning recalls. "Randy and I both enjoyed great players, and we were lucky to have them. Their contributions to the records were almost like another set of voices. Even though they were instrumentals, they had unique qualities." That day's session was a throwback to earlier decades when all musicians played together in the studio. "Deeper Than the Holler," an Overstreet/Schlitz song Travis described as "an incredibly well-written song that incorporated images about love, drawn from nature and the beauty around us," was the second single, and it reached number one in January 1989, followed by "Is It Still Over?" in May.[28]

Because this was Travis's third album, both producer and artist had gained enough confidence to take a risk. Lehning wanted to showcase Travis on "Promises," a song he had written years earlier with John Lindley and recorded for the *Randy Ray Live at the Nashville Palace* album. "I felt like putting other musicians on it would be an intrusion," Lehning explains. Travis sang to the accompaniment of his acoustic guitar, with slight background vocals dubbed in later. "He and I were both really proud of that," Lehning says. "He did such a fabulous job of telling that story." Warner Bros. liked it well enough to release "Promises" as a single, but the experiment failed. The song only reached number seventeen, breaking the string of seven consecutive chart-topping songs. Radio stations refused to play the heartbreakingly sad song with the acoustic guitar backing despite its strong, personal vocal performance. "It was the strangest thing," Travis told an interviewer. "So many radio stations wouldn't give it a chance; they wouldn't play it . . . because it was so long and so slow."[29]

It was only a blip. The next single would return Travis to the top.

◇  ♦  ◇

Rumors continued to swirl about the relationship between Travis and Hatcher, especially considering their eighteen-year age difference. When John Hobbs of the Nashville Palace married Libby Murphy and was interviewed in early 1988 for an article where he discussed Travis, readers got the impression that Travis had married Hatcher. Publicist Evelyn Shriver frequently did damage control to squelch rumors. In a newspaper article headlined "Relationship with Blonde Old Enough to Be His Mother," Travis was quoted as saying, "I'm not married to Libby or anyone else." Shriver explained that Hatcher always traveled with Travis as his manager; she decorated his tour bus in his favorite colors, gray and burgundy, and his bedroom had a Jacuzzi. "There are three other bunks, including Libby's," Shriver pointed out. She went so far as to explain that Travis had lived with Hatcher when they first moved to Nashville because they didn't have much money: "Libby was renting rooms in the house to help pay for it, so it was natural that Randy lived there, too." Shriver assured the reporter that Hatcher was sick about the gossip and that Travis didn't have time for a girlfriend.[30]

Travis, in one interview, described a partnership, explaining, "She takes care of the business and I take care of the music." He said he didn't like to push for what he wanted, but Hatcher was willing to do that. He liked to date "the kind of girl with a good sense of humor," one who is "a pretty lady, someone who isn't loud, because I'm not a loud person." He liked women who treated others with respect, something he tried to do.[31] Another newspaper quoted him as saying marriage didn't fit into his career plans. "Someday I would love to get married," he said. "I'll make the time someday. Right now, I don't even have a steady girlfriend."[32] Continuing their subterfuge, Hatcher told a tabloid,

"I'm his manager. I'm not his girlfriend, not his wife, not his mother. I'm his best friend." She added, "He trusts me with his money and his life—to make decisions for him." She said she did the legwork for a project and then they made the final decision together. She was "trying hard to make good investments and take care of his money so he can work when he wants to work, not because he has to."[33]

According to Lehning, "Randy wouldn't say no to anybody. If he ran into somebody at a restaurant, he'd sit and talk to them for thirty minutes." That created a problem for Hatcher, who almost always had a schedule to follow. Travis knew she would pull him away when his time was up. She took the blame for interrupting him, and he didn't have to watch the clock. One irate fan wrote to *Country Music USA* magazine, "I have met Randy in person, and he is kind, sweet, and willing to talk to people, but in the middle of our conversation he was jerked away and pushed on the bus by his manager." Shriver responded by writing that Travis was "lucky if he has two or three days a month when he doesn't have to either do interviews, meet fans, perform a concert, record a song, or in some way be the 'public' Randy Travis. . . . When Lib Hatcher rushes Randy onto the bus it is for his own good and the good of his fans." She reminded readers that a performer's ultimate responsibility was to deliver the product a fan pays for, and that required preserving his voice. Until Hatcher put her foot down, Travis had stayed after every performance to sign autographs for everyone in line. "He would be there sometimes at three in the morning," Hatcher said. "He started getting sick and we had to stop."[34]

Being on the road so much wore everyone out. They toured most of July, August, September, and October, returning to Nashville long enough for the 1988 CMA Awards on October 10. Although "I Told You So" was nominated for both Single of the Year and Song of the Year, it didn't win either award. Travis announced K. T. Oslin as Female Vocalist of the Year. The Male Vocalist of the Year award was presented by Dolly Parton. Wearing a white, low-cut dress, she stepped off the stage and walked to the front row, where she sat in Travis's lap. He laughed nervously as Parton put her hand on his shoulder and told the audience, "Folks, you know that this guy is single." She added, "And I want you to know that if I was twenty years younger and I was single, and you liked little blondes with the big hair and big . . . ideas, then I would be giving you a run for your money!" She returned to the stage and announced the Male Vocalist of the Year as Randy Travis. He began his acceptance speech by saying, "After all that, I find myself trying to remember what I just won!"[35]

◇ ♦ ◇

The Travis operation continued to grow. Hatcher had started the Lib Hatcher Agency in 1986, run by Allen Whitcomb, to handle Travis's bookings. Lib Hatcher Management represented Travis, as well as Gene Watson and other artists. Jeff Davis headed Special Moments Promotions to organize and promote Travis's concerts and tours. Travis Corporation controlled Travis's touring and recording income; it owned the buses and trucks and handled employee payroll. Two publishing companies copyrighted and controlled Travis's works, including the songs reacquired from Charlie Monk in 1986. Hatcher hired Bill Sweeney, experienced in retail management, to run the merchandising department, which included mail orders. As people left other jobs, Sweeney took over those positions. Hatcher and Travis eventually owned eleven businesses at their 1610 Sixteenth Avenue South address on Music Row. Sweeney worked in all of them. He would stay with the company until 2015. He was awed by Hatcher and her "million irons in the fire." He supported her in every business she started, explaining years later, "It's a roller-coaster business, and as things go up and down, some things die off, some things reappear, and you're always trying to keep something going in the company."[36]

Leaving most of the business affairs to Hatcher and Sweeney, Travis fulfilled his publicity role. He was pleased to have a home to show off when CBS's *Entertainment Tonight* sent a television crew to Ashland City to interview him. The profile began with Travis playing with his dog. When asked what his most difficult adjustment had been, he answered without hesitation: "All the days on the road." He explained, "I've never been a person who traveled that much. I'm not one who in younger days looked forward to being able to travel." Along with the success, it was traveling two hundred days a year that "took a lot of adjustment," he said. "Before success, I wasn't scared of anything. I began to get a little scared with the success as it started coming. All the attention. Bigger audiences." He had now become more comfortable working in front of larger audiences. As for future plans, he said, "I'm playing it by ear. I'm not a person who sits and plans what I want to do next year."[37]

Then it was back on tour. By now a seventh member had been added to Travis's band. Tom Rutledge had been in Dolly Parton's band since 1975. When she took a break from touring in 1988 to make a movie, he was at loose ends. His good friend Monty Parkey told him that Travis was talking about hiring a second guitar player, "a swing guy" who could play acoustic guitar, banjo, fiddle, or whatever was needed. Rutledge said he would love to do that. "The crowds were great, the buildings were large, and Randy was riding high," Rutledge recalls about working with Travis. "It was a joyride. I loved the way Randy conducted himself as a man and as an artist. He seemed to try to do the right thing, all the time, and tried to exhibit a good image to the fans and the people he worked with." Steel player Gary Carter served as band leader, and when the musicians had questions he couldn't handle, they took their questions to tour manager Jeff Davis, not Travis or Hatcher. Parkey remembers Travis as "pretty quiet. Generally, he did not run things. If Lib said do this, he did it. And she always had something for him to do."[38]

On November 11, they unveiled image magnification, or I-mag, screens at a concert in Starkville, Mississippi. Jeff Davis remembers the Randy Travis organization as the first regular country music tour to use this new technology. During an earlier conversation about ways to enhance the audience experience, Davis had said, "They want to see and hear Randy Travis. We already have the best sound company and the best sound system available, so they're already hearing him. How can we help them see him?" Having noticed the large video screens at festivals and on the Marlboro Country Music Tour, the Travis/Hatcher/Davis team decided to invest in I-mag screens. By Starkville they were traveling with half a dozen trucks and buses. Counting the opening acts, Davis remembers ordering fifty catered meals. "Today most big tours have way more than that," he says. "In 1988, '89, it was a lot of stuff."[39]

One more band change occurred, after which "Nashville's" seven-member lineup would hold for almost four years. L D Wayne was exhausted from so much touring and decided to take some time off. Fiddle player David Johnson suggested calling Ronald Radford of the Country City USA days in Charlotte. When Travis had opened for Conway Twitty in early 1987 in Greenville, South Carolina, Radford came to say hello. He told Travis, "If your guitar player ever leaves, I'd appreciate an audition." Travis said, "I'll remember that." And he did. Radford was tracked down at a nightclub in Greenville and hired to replace L D Wayne. Radford's first major gig with Travis was a seventeen-day USO tour to Alaska, Japan, and South Korea. "I never had been no farther than Nashville," he says. Since he didn't have a passport, one would have to be acquired in only two weeks. "Randy and Lib were friends with George Bush, Senior," he explains. "Lib called the White House, and Vice President Bush put somebody in charge of it." Hatcher told Radford, "We wanted you to know Vice President Bush put you down as Priority One." The incredulous Radford wondered, *Lord, have mercy, is that dangerous, or what? To be Priority One.*[40]

Travis headlined the 1988 USO Thanksgiving Celebrity Entertainment Tour, with Patty Loveless as opening act. She, along with Ricky Van Shelton, had joined the Grand Ole Opry in June, almost two years after Travis. The USO itinerary included twelve shows for thousands of US military personnel and their families. Travis was reported to have turned down a five-hundred-thousand-dollar Las Vegas engagement for the USO tour.[41] They headed out on November 29, one day after returning from their previous tour. A TNN crew traveled with them to film a special for airing on The Nashville Network. This year, Dan Markley was with them, as was Barry Weinberg, athletic trainer for the Oakland Athletics. Travis had invited Weinberg and then called Markley for permission to include him as well. Markley said no, explaining that there were no straphangers on a USO tour. Everyone had to be essential because taxpayer money funded the transportation. Travis told him the Oakland A's had just played in the World Series, not everybody loved country music, and many soldiers would rather talk baseball and weight training than meet him. Markley advocated for Weinberg and convinced the Pentagon that his inclusion would be a good expenditure of taxpayers' money. "And it turned out to be," he says. "Barry engaged with a lot of people who were not particularly interested in country music but loved to hear what it was like going to the World Series."

The Tennessee Air National Guard in Nashville provided a C-130 aircraft, piloted by Major Bob Doyle (who managed the career of Garth Brooks). Once again, David Skepner served as organizer by talking to the Nashville Air Guard unit, which gained Pentagon approval for a two-week training mission with an airplane and crew to support the tour. Having a dedicated aircraft as a "tour bus" increased efficiency and avoided relying on airline schedules. The four-engine propeller-driven C-130 was slow but reliable. It carried two pallets of production equipment and suitcases and about twenty-two people. There were no actual seats. Passengers sat on a webbed bench along the side. Controlling the temperature and pressure in the loud aircraft was always a problem. Guitar strings would break if not loosened before being loaded. "There are many challenges to touring with USO that would never be faced by people at this level of the entertainment industry," Markley comments. No one complained about discomfort. It was an adventure.[42]

Heading first to Alaska, they arrived at the Anchorage airport and boarded a military plane to Fort Greely, about a hundred miles southeast of Fairbanks. One of the coldest areas in Alaska, it was home to the Cold Regions Test Center

(CRTC). Upon landing, they saw a helicopter lying on its side, still smoldering. Radford wondered, *What in the world have I got into?* The helicopter had been conducting maneuvers when snow in the propellers caused it to crash. Fortunately, no one was injured. "That trip was brutal," Radford recalls. "We flew up and down the Yukon, and at every military post, if there was a tent, it seemed like they'd land the plane and we'd put on a show." They were issued heavy military parkas and boots. Every morning, they would meet in the barracks lobby, get on a bus, and travel to the airfield to board the C-130 for that day's destination. It was so cold that they were told not to touch their hair while outside because it would break off. "I had a bit of a beard, and naturally I had to try it," Radford says. "It broke off in my hand." They experimented by throwing cupfuls of coffee in the air and watching the coffee granulate before it hit the ground.[43] It was quite an experience for a group of Southerners who didn't often see snow, much less frigid temperatures.

Loveless remembers performing in the large hangars. "I was freezing to death trying to get dressed and put my makeup on," she says. "I was given a feel of what it was like to live that life." They were up at four each morning. "Bags at four, bodies at six," she says. "We'd take off to the next place and then play shows that night." They flew to Galena, a forward operating base of Elmendorf Air Force Base, which was inaccessible by road. A local woman offered Loveless a dogsled ride. She wasn't about to miss that opportunity, even when warned she might lose her voice due to the cold. "She wrapped me up real good," Loveless remembers, "and it was just me and her. The only thing you heard was her giving the dogs commands, and the sound of going through the snow. It was beautiful, and quiet. Yes, it was cold, but it was so worth it. And I ended up singing just fine that night." The TNN crew rode on a dogsled ahead of her to film her ride. "They came back maybe half an hour later," Markley recalls, "and poor Patty's eyelids had frozen shut. She had to get medical attention to slowly warm her skin. 'Trouper' does not begin to describe Patty Loveless's participation in that tour."[44]

While in South Korea, Travis accepted an invitation to visit the demilitarized zone (DMZ) that marked the cease-fire line at the end of the Korean War. The areas north and south of the DMZ were still heavily fortified, with both sides maintaining contingents of troops there. This was the site of peace discussions during the Korean War and had been the location of many conferences since then.[45] As they approached the zone in a bus, their liaison provided documents to officials who allowed them to enter the area. "The moment we stepped into the DMZ," Travis remembered, "I noticed immediately that everything looked dark and dreary to the north." They could see armed soldiers in every window of the building. He called the day "a stark reminder of the freedoms we often take for granted in America and the dangerous conditions in which our soldiers serve."[46]

Rutledge recalls visiting the United Nations negotiating building, half in North Korea and half in South Korea. Everywhere they went on their tours, they would receive a briefing on how to dress and behave. For the DMZ visit, they were told no jeans and no ball caps. They had to look somewhat presentable because they would be observed by North Koreans through the windows. When the visitors commented that the American soldiers escorting them looked like offensive linemen in the National Football League, the soldiers explained it was gamesmanship. North Korea sent its tallest soldiers to the DMZ to compete with the Americans in size. "Sure enough," Rutledge says, "there were these giant North Koreans looking in at our giant US troops who were guarding us."[47] There was a line down the middle of the building, with microphone cords lying on the floor and North Korea on the other side of the line. Radford and drummer Rivelli looked at each other, and Rivelli said, "We gotta do it." They stepped over the microphone cords into North Korea and quickly stepped back. Two North Korean guards watched them curiously through the window, and the American soldier inside kept his hand on his weapon. "Please don't do that again," he said.[48]

The soldiers stationed at the DMZ asked Travis and Loveless to sing for them in their underground bunker. Loveless's band members, who had brought along two guitars and a mandolin, accompanied her. When she sang "If My Heart Had Windows," she could see the tears in their eyes—missing home at Christmas. "They were so excited to see me and Randy both," Loveless recalls. "They were just beside themselves over Randy Travis. He was one of them, the way they looked at it." Travis didn't have a guitar; he told Loveless's sidemen, "Well, you know the show." After all, Loveless had spent much of the previous year opening for Travis. They accompanied him on several Christmas songs and hits such as "Diggin' Up Bones" and "Deeper Than the Holler." Lance Dary, who had been a guitarist in Loveless's band since 1986 and would more than a decade later work for Travis, says, "The DMZ in South Korea was the first time I got to play with Randy."

Loveless remembers being told not to point or use gestures. "We had to be really careful about what we did," she says. "And you know, when I think about the DMZ today and what's happening, good-ness. I can't imagine those who are on that line. If anything was to break out, they'd be the first to get it."[49] Markley considers that impromptu show was one of the most memorable ones he ever experienced: "It was almost like you see in the *White Christmas* movie—people in the loneliest, most vulnerable place you can imagine, and then somebody who's as superstar as Randy and as authentic as Randy is in your presence, singing 'I'll Be Home for Christmas.' I think you'd be hard-pressed to say for whom that was more meaningful, for those eighteen-, nineteen-, twenty-year-old soldiers in a conflict setting, or for Randy."[50]

Rivelli calls the annual USO trips his "most cherished and favorite gigs." He remains glad he got to play for the troops. "It was wonderful," he says. "It makes you feel good, y'know. And they enjoyed it so much."[51] Bass player Thacker remembers the soldiers asking all kinds of questions. "They wanted to know what's going on in the NFL, who won the World Series, things like that," he says. "Just hanging with those boys was some of the most memorable things."[52]

When they reached Los Angeles International Airport on the return trip, they had to wait for their luggage to come through Customs before continuing to Nashville. Everybody was exhausted and wanted to get home. The wait at the baggage carousel seemed to take forever. Travis wandered over to a baggage handler who was sitting on his cart, waiting along with everyone else for the luggage to come spitting out. After a few moments, Hatcher sent tour manager David Trask over to get him, but Travis refused to leave. Rutledge recalls the moment as one of the few times he saw Travis defy Hatcher. "He stayed there and talked to him for a long time," Rutledge says, "They had a common interest in horses and some other things, and Randy was telling him about his ranch in Ashland City and whatnot. Lib didn't think that was, I guess, what he should be doing, as a star." Rutledge makes the point that Travis "always had time for the little guy. He remembered when he was a fry cook at the Palace, I'm sure."[53]

Upon their return to Nashville, Travis immediately resumed his grueling schedule. Gary Carter warned Radford, "Ronald, it's gonna blow your mind when the show starts and lights go down. You won't be able to see anything because of the flashes on cameras. Every now and then, you'll feel the stage shake when the women rush the stage." After Radford experienced a few of those shows, he asked Travis, "Randy, what in the world are you doing to cause this?" Travis said, "Ronald, I have no idea."[54]

# 6

## "IT'S A TOUGH JOB."

George Herbert Walker Bush, son of US senator Prescott Bush and Dorothy (Walker) Bush, was a grandson of Wall Street investment banker George Herbert Walker. He enlisted in the US Navy on his eighteenth birthday and became one of the youngest naval aviators in combat during World War II. He and his wife, Barbara (Pierce) Bush, raised a family in West Texas. After serving in several federal government roles, Bush became vice president of the United States in 1980. The Bushes were country music fans, and that included being fans of Randy Travis. They sometimes attended the Houston Livestock Show and Rodeo, where in 1988 Travis set an attendance record for a country music performance, selling 49,702 tickets.

When Bush was elected president of the United States, he invited Travis to perform at one of his inaugural events. The Jefferson Inaugural Freedom Ball was held January 19, 1989, at the J. W. Marriott Hotel at National Place in Washington, DC. That event was their first in-person meeting. Other country artists singing at the gala included Loretta Lynn, Crystal Gayle, the Oak Ridge Boys, and Lee Greenwood. A few weeks later, Travis received a thank-you letter, typed on official White House stationery, beginning, "Dear Randy, Thanks so much for being a part of the Inaugural festivities." Below President Bush's signature was his handwritten note: "Thanks for being with us at the Gala. Great!"[1]

The inaugural gala had occurred during an eventful week for Travis, beginning with a car accident. He was driving his Lincoln Town Car on Marrowbone Road, with Hatcher as a passenger, on their way to a nine o'clock event at a local high school. Travis started to pass a car, and when it turned left, so did he—into the ditch. "Unfortunately, it was a deep ditch," he told a reporter. He and Hatcher climbed through a window to escape. The Tennessee Highway Patrol investigated and pressed no charges. Although they missed the high school event, they spent the remainder of the day working on a video for "Is It Still Over?" at their Music Row house, taking time to visit the West Side Hospital to have Travis's bruises examined. "I'm moving kind of slow; I bruised some ligaments," he told a reporter that day. "I'm playing *Letterman* tomorrow night and then I'm going to do the Inaugural Gala in Washington. Then we're going to come back here, and we'll be looking for songs for the next album." On *Late Night with David Letterman* in New York City, he sang "Is It Still Over?"[2]

He won his second Grammy on February 22: Best Male Country Vocal Performance for *Old 8×10*. While in Los Angeles, Travis accepted an invitation to work out in actor and bodybuilder Arnold Schwarzenegger's private gym. After the workout, Travis and Hatcher had lunch with Schwarzenegger and his wife, Maria Shriver. This began a friendship between the two health-conscious men. Schwarzenegger had recently been named by President Bush as chairman of the President's Council on Physical Fitness and Sports. "I told Arnold I had trouble maintaining my weight," Travis commented years later. "While some people struggled with obesity, I was chronically underweight for my size." Schwarzenegger told him that diet was equally as important as a workout routine.[3]

Travis's February shows included a concert at the War Memorial in Rochester, New York, playing to a screaming audience of ten thousand fans. Conway Twitty opened for him—another example of his changing fortune and acceptance by his predecessors. His I-mag screens were noted by a reporter, who wrote, "And perhaps best of all for the crowd, even viewers from the tip-top of the War Memorial had a terrific view of the singer, since two video cameras projected a sharp, clear image of Travis to a huge screen."[4]

Most of March and April 1989 were devoted to a twenty-three-city tour that paired the reigning CMA Male and Female Vocalists of the Year: Travis as headliner and K. T. Oslin as opener. Tammy Wynette joined them for six shows sponsored by GMC Trucks. The tour opened with two sold-out nights in Greenville, South Carolina, grossing $188,661 and bringing in 11,400 fans. The three-day Travis/Oslin concert series at the Universal Amphitheatre in Los Angeles in mid-August would bring in more than $400,000. When *Amusement Business* tabulated year-end results for the ten top-grossing country concerts of the year, that weekend came in at number eight.[5]

During the short break between the March and April shows, tragedy struck when fan club president Jill Youngblood died of cancer at age fifty-one; her disease had been diagnosed in September. She had moved from Charlotte to Nashville in early 1988, at Hatcher's request, because the fan club had grown too large to manage from a distance. They had agreed it would be more efficient to have the president on site. Youngblood's funeral was held in Charlotte the day before the Travis/Oslin tour resumed.[6]

Three awards shows took place in April 1989. Travis arrived at the ACM event as the reigning Male Vocalist of the Year, with two consecutive wins, along with his second nomination for Entertainer of the Year. Expectations were high. It was a shock when, for the first time since being named ACM's Top New Male Vocalist in 1986, his name wasn't called that evening. George Strait dethroned Hank Williams Jr. as Entertainer of the Year. That didn't mean Travis was no longer at the top. He was named Favorite Male Vocalist at the People's Choice Awards in Los Angeles, and he received his second consecutive Entertainer of the Year award at the TNN Viewers' Choice show in Nashville. When a reporter asked how the TNN award felt after being shut out at the ACMs fifteen days earlier, he replied, "It was a nice feeling. Yeah, it was a pretty nice feeling after losing all of 'em!"

The question then became what would happen at the twenty-third annual *Music City News* Awards show in June. Would Travis maintain his dominance there? When he and Hatcher walked out from backstage at the Opry House to take their seats on June 5, cheers went up from the crowd. Women yelled his name to get his attention. Whenever he looked in their direction, they squealed with delight. The evening's multiple winner was Ricky Van Shelton, who later commented, "When I first moved to Nashville, the first place I sang was at the Nashville Palace. A few months after I showed up, he got his record deal, but he continued to work at the Palace. That's where I got to know Randy."[7] On this night, Shelton won Male Vocalist of the Year, along with three other awards. When accepting his second award, he looked toward his old friend and said, "Randy Travis, tonight I know how you feel!" Later he said, about Travis, "I know why he smiles so much now. It's wonderful." Travis gave the last performance of the evening. Seated on a stool at the edge of the stage, he strummed his acoustic guitar and crooned his current release, "Promises." Then George Jones announced him as Entertainer of the Year. Travis had triumphed over Ricky Van Shelton, Reba McEntire, George Strait, Hank Williams Jr., and the Statler Brothers. Holding his trophy high, he laughed and talked as fans screamed and applauded. Genuinely moved by winning the award for a second year, he said after the show, "I've been lucky to win what I have. I've always said I knew the time will come when I won't win. I've got to be thankful for what I have, and I've had plenty."[8]

The following morning at Fan Fair, on the Tennessee State Fairgrounds, Travis sat in the Warner Bros. booth and signed autographs for a line of fans that had begun forming at five o'clock. When he had to leave, the hundreds in line shrieked with displeasure as the police officers packed themselves tightly around Travis and escorted him from the building. He returned at three o'clock to sign autographs in his fan booth, where the line had begun forming that morning while he was in the Warner Bros. booth. The police tried unsuccessfully to herd the fans into orderly lines as they sought to have their photos taken with the star. Pale and tired from the strain of touring, Travis was recovering from a severe throat infection.[9] But there was no rest. The previous year, he had left in the middle of Fan Fair for a European tour. This year it was to Australia. He and his band arrived in Sydney, New South Wales, and performed their first show at the Sydney Entertainment Centre on June 10, 1989. They had passed through eight time zones and over the International Date Line during their twenty-one-hour flight. The time was now fifteen hours later than in Nashville. Before having an opportunity to rest, they flew to Brisbane, Queensland, for a show the next night and to Adelaide, South Australia, for a show the following evening.

Travis later described the tour as "a smaller audience than we work for here, but basically it was the same. Beautiful people and beautiful country. We went in one day and went to work the next and worked almost every day for two weeks. When we weren't singing, we were sleeping." He said they had fifty pieces of luggage going over and were missing twenty when they arrived. It was mainly equipment, and most of the pieces eventually showed up. That shortage required some adapting when setting up for the shows. Tom Rutledge arrived without his luggage, which came several days later. Fighting jet lag, Travis and his entourage found everyone friendly and welcoming, and they got used to being called "Yanks." In Perth, Western Australia, an outback tour group took the band and crew out in four-wheel-drive Jeeps. Thacker recalls, "Got to see a lot of wildlife we wouldn't have seen otherwise." For the final three nights, they flew to Melbourne in Victoria, to Hobart on the island of Tasmania, and then finished the tour in Auckland, New Zealand. At the Auckland airport, Gary Carter noticed one of their missing pieces of equipment and claimed it. Travis declared Australia to be one of his favorite spots. Overlooking the exhaustion of international travel, he enjoyed the highly enthusiastic audiences and the chance to see the different sights. Thacker says, "It was kind of a whirlwind tour, worth every minute of sleep we lost." With the final show and return trip to Nashville, that long day lasted fifty hours.[10]

Back in Ashland City, Travis and Hatcher welcomed a visitor to their home. Travis had grown up wanting to be Roy Rogers, and now he was hosting his idol. He'd met Rogers the previous year while on tour in California, when he visited the Roy Rogers–Dale Evans Museum in Victorville. Seeing Rogers that day, Travis had reached out to shake his hand and was surprised when the King of the Cowboys grabbed him in a hug and said, "Great to meet you." Travis later told an interviewer, "He's funny, witty, a pleasure to be around. He was just like I thought he would be and that makes you feel good, when it's somebody you admire so much."[11]

Rogers was in Nashville to record for Travis's duet album, scheduled to be released the following year. At the recording session, producer Lehning recalls, "When Roy Rogers walked in, every single guy on the session turned into a six-year-old kid. Everybody started asking questions and talking to him about Trigger and about what he meant to them. He must have heard that all the time." Hatcher and Martha Sharp were also present, as they were at most sessions. After about an hour, Rogers apparently thought the fan questions had gone on long enough. He picked up a guitar and started directing the session. Lehning quickly stepped in, Rogers asked who he was, and Lehning introduced himself as the producer. Rogers said, "It didn't look like there was a producer, so if there isn't anybody to take charge, I'll do it." Lehning explained his ideas, and Rogers agreeably allowed him to do his job on the recording of the signature song "Happy Trails." With all the conversation and all the people coming by that day to have their pictures taken with the King of the Cowboys, there wasn't much time to actually record. "We got Roy's voice down, and the music track, and that was about it," Travis said later. "I'll go back and figure out what parts I need to sing harmony."[12]

Travis brought Rogers with him as a surprise guest when he performed on the Friday night Grand Ole Opry on June 23. They first appeared on Ralph Emery's live television show, *Nashville Now*. When Emery mentioned that Trigger had been stuffed, Rogers told him, "No, say mounted. It sounds better." The audience loved it. And Travis loved having Rogers at his side, walking backstage with him at the Opry and introducing him onstage for a bow. Travis sang several of his *Old 8×10* releases on the two shows. He had a reputation for being friendly and approachable while backstage, remembers Barrett Hobbs, grandson of John A. Hobbs. The little boy who had hung around the Nashville Palace when Travis worked there was now a high school student. If he wanted to impress his girlfriends, he could introduce them to Randy Travis. "Randy would stop and chit-chat and take pictures with us and make sure we felt welcome, in the dressing rooms and hanging out backstage at the Opry," he recalls. It was his first glimpse into Travis's stardom, with everybody wanting photos and autographs. Hobbs says, "He always was a gentleman. Somebody would have a story to tell, and he would listen and respond."

This stardom brought an increased demand for merchandise. By now Bill Sweeney had increased sales to averaging twenty thousand dollars a day, mostly mail order, for everything from T-shirts to the *Randy Travis Coloring Book*. They opened the Randy Travis Souvenir and Gift Shop at 1514 Demonbreun Street, close to the Country Music Hall of Fame, which had been the turnaround point for Travis's daily runs while living on Music Row. The gift shop opened in May, prior to Fan Fair, with the grand opening postponed until August 31, 1989. Although the gift shop contained mementos of Travis's career, the thirty-year-old singer insisted it was not a museum, saying, "A museum seems like something you'd have after you've been in the business for twenty years." The huge back room held the bread truck that had carried the band for sixty thousand miles in 1986. A steady stream of people filed though to view a wall covered with notes and gifts from fans—paintings, embroidery, wooden plaques, decoupage, hand-stitched samplers, even a guitar-shaped mirror. Travis credited Hatcher with most of the ideas, telling a reporter, "She's really good at decorating places and making them look homey."[13]

One of the most popular gift shop items was a cookbook, *Randy Travis' Favorite Recipes*, newly published by the Hatcher Corporation. Filled with traditional Southern recipes and numerous cooking tips, the 118-page cookbook contained five sections, each opening with a full-color photo of Travis working in the kitchen, sometimes wearing a white chef's coat. In the introduction, he said, "I have prepared several of the dishes myself. Most important, these are the things I love to eat." He thanked Hatcher for "some great recipes and many hours of work." Hatcher's recipes included "Lib's Sweet Potato Casserole," "Lib's Gooey Butter Cake," and "Lib's Electric Fry Pan Meat Loaf Dinner," which carried the comment, "This is Randy's favorite meat loaf." Some of the recipes came from his parents, who were both excellent cooks. Travis grew up enjoying Bobbie's pies; the cookbook included her "South Pecan Pie," listed as "Randy's favorite," and "Mama's Apple Pie." Harold had long ago developed a recipe for catfish stew that fed fifty. It was listed in the cookbook as "Randy's Dad's Famous Catfish Stew," along with this explanatory note: "Many gallons of this stew was served on talent night at Country City USA Club in Charlotte, North Carolina, compliments of Harold Traywick."[14]

A reporter who interviewed Travis at his new gift shop wrote that he had to watch his allergies to certain foods, "including dairy products, pork, soybeans, and tomatoes," things he loved. The reporter noted, "It's not unusual for Travis and crew to cook when they're traveling in order to get nutritious meals." There was no mention that Hatcher handled the cooking. Travis told another interviewer, "I don't eat a lot of beef. Unfortunately, I'm allergic to it. But I do love a steak." How many of his dietary restrictions were due to his actual health or Hatcher's direction is debatable. While putting on a cheerful public face, Travis privately chafed under her excessive control over his diet. Years later, he would say, "Lib fretted that I had allergies . . ., but in truth I never had serious problems with allergies." He said some foods adversely affected his voice if he ate them shortly before a show, so he usually waited until after a show to eat, adding, "I didn't regularly use allergy medication, prescription or over the counter. Yet Lib constantly reiterated that I was allergy prone."[15]

Travis enjoyed the many hours he spent on his rigorous bodybuilding regimen. And what he most loved was being with his horses. By mid-1989 he had acquired eighteen horses, including a three-year-old palomino Hatcher had purchased from Roy Rogers: Trigger Jr., a stallion descended from the original Trigger. Travis kept his horses on the two acreages he and Hatcher owned, the Braxton Lee homestead in Ashland City and their home along Marrowbone Creek. Travis took Trigger Jr. to the man who trained the original Trigger and was still training horses in his eighties. "You can make this Trigger kneel," Travis explained in an interview. "And from there, lay down and sit up. Answer you yes and no. I can stand in front of him and make him rear up and stand on his hind legs. If he wants to." Travis told another interviewer, "He's one you won't turn your back on. He'll hurt you if you do, he's bad mean." In the hope of producing a better-tempered Trigger look-alike, Travis planned to breed Trigger Jr. with each of the four mares he owned. He described his ideal horse as "one that's not mean, but kind of playful, one you have to hold back a bit, not one that'll hurt you."[16]

Rocky Thacker remembers how much Travis loved working with horses and how relaxed and welcoming the atmosphere was at the Marrowbone farm. "I felt a little guilty bringing business things out there," he says. "I hated to ripple the calm. Everybody deserves a quiet place to go to." Gibson Guitar had begun endorsing Travis shortly after he became a headliner in late 1987, and Thacker handled the endorsement. He would go to the farm to get Travis's approval on new guitars being sent for his use. Thacker's involvement allowed Travis more time to relax during the short periods they were home. He took care of Travis's guitars, which were normally stored with the band gear unless Thacker took them home for maintenance, such as neck adjustments or string height adjustments. After the release of "Promises," Thacker tuned two guitars and placed them onstage before each show. "That way," he says, "the 'Promises' guitar was always in tune when Randy did that song."[17]

◊ ♦ ◊

The Mastering Lab Hollywood, possibly the first independent mastering facility in the world, was founded in 1967 by audio engineer brothers Doug and Sherwood Sax in California. Doug Sax would become known as the world's greatest mastering engineer. He mastered the Doors' first album in 1967 and Bob Dylan's *Shadows in the Night* in 2015. When Doug Sax died in 2015 at age seventy-eight, his obituary said, "It would not be an exaggeration to say that virtually everyone who has listened to recorded music has heard Sax's work."[18]

Lehning used Sax as the mastering engineer on Travis's albums. "I would always go to Hollywood to master the record with Doug," he explains, "because I loved the way he could make a record sound. He was the best of anybody that did that kind of work. Back then we were doing vinyl. Mastering vinyl is a real art form." The one time Lehning wasn't able to go to California, he sent Sax the mixes of a Christmas album. When Sax called him, Lehning asked how the record was, and Sax said, "Well, that's why I'm calling. I have to tell you, I don't think this is your best work." The minute he said that, Lehning recalls, "My blood sort of chilled." He knew Sax was correct. Warner Bros. had asked Travis in 1987 to record a Christmas album; he and Lehning finished it in 1988, recording mostly familiar songs. They had recorded with the attitude "It's *just* a Christmas album." They would look at each other and say, "That's not really great, but it's probably okay." "That's why I loved Doug," Lehning says. "He was painfully honest. He had great ears, good instincts, and he knew the quality of the work we were doing. He was not just a mastering engineer; he was an artiste."

Lehning told Sax, "You know what, you're right." He immediately called Martha Sharp and repeated what Sax had said. "To her credit, and to Warner Bros. credit," Lehning says, "we stopped the record. And we stopped it because of Doug Sax." Sharp told him to get rid of the songs that were not up to Travis's standards and then wait until the following year to record new songs. *An Old Time Christmas*, on its second attempt, was released on August 14, 1989. It contained classics like "Winter Wonderland" and "Santa Claus Is Coming to Town" as well as Willie Nelson's "Pretty Paper" and an original by Travis and Paul Overstreet that had been released as a single the previous Christmas, "How Do I Wrap My Heart Up for Christmas?" "Silent Night" was replaced by a new Mark Collie/Kathy Louvin song, "Oh, What a Silent Night," which became that year's Christmas single. According to Lehning, they found contemporary songs that felt more like Travis. It became a much better album than it would have been if Sax had not made that phone call. The album was later certified gold for selling more than five hundred thousand units.

While they were redoing the Christmas album, they were working on Travis's regularly scheduled fourth studio album, *No Holdin' Back*, which was released six weeks after *An Old Time Christmas*. Travis and Lehning, working with Sharp and Hatcher, had started with over one hundred songs that they cut to twenty to take into the studio. The first two chosen for the final ten were covers of hits from long ago. "It's Just a Matter of Time" was one of the few Travis recordings not produced by Lehning. Warner Bros. wanted one country artist on a specialty album, *Rock, Rhythm & Blues*, that featured contemporary artists performing classic rock songs by musicians of the 1950s and early 1960s. The album was being produced by Richard Perry, whom Lehning calls "an extraordinarily talented record producer." Perry's credits include Barbra Streisand's album *Stoney End* and "You're So Vain" by Carly Simon. When Travis was chosen for the album, he worried, *Oh Lord, what are they going to come up with for me to sing?* Perry selected "It's Just a Matter of Time," a 1959 pop hit for Brook Benton. Travis willingly recorded the song, but Perry couldn't find a mix that Travis was happy with. Since Lehning mixed as well as produced Travis's music, Perry called to ask if he would mix this one. "Absolutely," Lehning replied. He had no difficulty in mixing it to Travis's liking. Perry had considered having Travis record "Singing the Blues," which spent thirteen weeks as a number one country hit for Marty Robbins in 1956–1957 and was a crossover pop hit. Lehning thought that was a fabulous idea, and Travis loved singing a Marty Robbins song. "It's Just a Matter of Time" and "Singing the Blues" marked the first covers of old hits Travis recorded for an album.

*No Holdin' Back* was released on September 26. Warner Bros. issued three singles from the album. "It's Just a Matter of Time" and "Hard Rock Bottom of Your Heart" topped the charts, while "He Walked on Water" reached number two. Lehning considered "Hard Rock Bottom of Your Heart" more pop than country. "The song was unusual for him," he says. "Once it came to life with his voice, you could say, okay, that's going to work fine." And it did. "Hard Rock Bottom of Your Heart" stayed at number one for four weeks and became the highest-charting single of Travis's career.[19]

Travis and Lehning first heard "He Walked on Water" at a publishing pitch meeting and immediately loved the song, which became Allen Shamblin's first cut in Nashville. Martha Sharp had encouraged him to come to Nashville after listening to a demo tape she had received of his music. Shamblin recalls sitting at the kitchen table when he was four years old and hearing his maternal great-grandfather tell cowboy stories. It was the only time he met the old cowboy, who had lived in Texas in the late 1800s. "When I was a kid, I lived and breathed cowboys," Shamblin says, "so when he told me he had actually been a cowboy, I was fascinated, and I soaked up everything he had to say." The song reminded Travis of his own grandfather, Alexander Bruce Traywick, who lived next door during Travis's childhood. Traywick took the little boy with him whether in a car, on a tractor, or on a horse. "My grandfather is sitting under a mulberry tree, his hat on the ground," Travis reminisced during one of his concerts. "I'm riding around him on a bicycle, he tells me not to run over his hat. A couple more rounds, and I ran over his hat. He lifted me off that bike, the bike stayed upright and kept going. In his generation, he figured if a kid needed a whippin', he should get it then. So he gave me a good one, no doubt about that. When he let go, in my seven-year-old mind, I figured he can't catch me. I ran what I thought was far enough away, and I started throwing rocks at him." His grandfather started throwing rocks back. "There we are," Travis said, concluding his story, "a seventy-year-old man and a seven-year-old kid throwing rocks at each other in the driveway. It's a picture of love."[20]

One of the songs Lehning wanted released as a single was "Somewhere in My Broken Heart." He knew it would be a hit, but Travis struggled with singing the high note in the last line. "I don't know how many takes we did to get that last line," Lehning recalls. "But we finally got it." He was disappointed to hear Travis say, "I'll tell you one thing. I don't want that to be a single." He didn't want to have to sing it every night. "Forty years later," Lehning says, "I'm thinking, why didn't I just tell him to sing it lower? I don't know. Dang it. I did miss a number one there."[21] Billy Dean, who had cowritten the song, recorded it for his 1990 debut album, *Young Man*, and achieved a number three *Billboard* ranking.

A different type of hit—a lawsuit—almost got Travis and his band thrown out of the American Federation of Musicians (AFM). He was scheduled to perform on Labor Day weekend in Las Vegas, Nevada, at Bally's Hotel and Casino, one of four major resort hotels then experiencing a strike by AFM Local 369. The hotels wanted to use taped music in their large-scale production shows and do away with the thirty-six work weeks a year guaranteed to musicians in celebrity rooms. AFM Local 257 in Nashville repeatedly warned Travis and Hatcher not to play the dates. Nashville AFM president Jay Collins told the *Tennessean*, "I was concerned that our members needed to know what was in store for them if they did cross a picket line." He said he tried to warn them what the consequences would be, because Local 369 was serious about filing charges. "Randy supports live music over taped music," publicist Evelyn Shriver told the *Tennessean*. "Originally, he wasn't going to cross the picket line. But we got so many letters and calls from fans—hundreds of letters and phone calls—that he decided to do it." She said he cared more about making his fans happy than making the union happy. Travis later said he decided to play the date after learning how many fans had made plans to attend the shows. He'd also heard the strike didn't have widespread support among Las Vegas union members.

They didn't see what was happening in Las Vegas. As the *Chicago Tribune* reported, "Day after shadeless, desert day, and night after bright, neon night, pianists, trombonists, violists and their colleagues stroll the Strip with signs that urge, 'Honk if you like live music.'" Hatcher and Travis called a band meeting to explain that they were thinking of crossing the strike lines. They said the individual band members had to choose whether to go or stay home, with no repercussions for deciding not to participate. They promised to handle anything that arose because of crossing the line. The band members decided the circumstances of the strike didn't apply to them, and they agreed to go. "I know other country artists that crossed, so it was an easy decision for me," bass player Thacker recalls. "Randy treated us well, and if it was fine with him, it was okay with me. I knew he wouldn't do anything to hurt anyone."

In addition to the Friday, Saturday, and Monday performances at Bally's Hotel and Casino, Travis performed Sunday evening at the Jerry Lewis Theater during the kickoff of the twenty-fourth annual Jerry Lewis Muscular Dystrophy Telethon, which was broadcast for twenty-one hours nationwide with more than fifty celebrity performers. That 1989 Labor Day Telethon brought in a record $42,209,727 in pledges from viewers around the country. Dean Martin, Rodney Dangerfield, Connie Francis, Burt Bacharach, Dionne Warwick, and Bill Medley canceled their shows rather than cross the picket line. "It certainly shouldn't make us proud that all of these major entertainers have honored the picket line, and the first major entertainer not to honor it happens to be one of our local members," Collins of Local 257 fumed.

Local 369 announced it would seek charges against Travis and his musicians that could subject them to fines up to ten thousand dollars each and expulsion from the union. The National Association of Orchestra Leaders then filed a complaint with the National Labor Relations Board, saying the union tried to coerce Travis into bypassing his appearance in an attempt to harm Bally's. All charges were eventually dropped.[22]

The twenty-third Country Music Association Awards show took place at the Opry House on October 9. Travis was the reigning Male Vocalist of the Year and a nominee for Entertainer of the Year. He had been asked to present the award for Female Vocalist of the Year. Anne Murray introduced him by saying he'd been a superstar since appearing out of thin air three or four years ago. She then said, "Let me show you what happened last year to this shy country boy." The screen played the video of Dolly Parton going into the audience and sitting on Travis's lap. After the video, Murray announced Travis, and he walked onstage, not noticing Dolly Parton following him. He began to speak and then stepped back and said, "Oh, no!" as Dolly appeared next to him and said, "Ah, hi, Randy." She told him, "I just wanted to come out and make sure you didn't need me." He said, "Well, I might." He gave her a hug and she walked off. With a big grin, Travis looked at the audience and said, "It's a tough job." He then announced Kathy Mattea as Female Vocalist of the Year.[23] The remainder of the evening did not go so well for Travis. Male Vocalist of the Year went to Ricky Van Shelton, as it had at the *Music City News* Awards. Entertainer of the Year went to George Strait, as it had at the ACM Awards. All three men lost out on Album of the Year, which went to *Will the Circle Be Unbroken Vol. II*, by the Nitty Gritty Dirt Band.

To walk away empty-handed from the biggest awards show of the year was a shock, especially after having won more than forty industry- and fan-voted awards since 1986. Travis acknowledged the inevitability, telling an interviewer, "People in the business are for you when you're beginning, then once you achieve success, they say, 'Well, that's enough—you're over,' or whatever." He said, "It seems like some of those people want to see you not be so successful." As for the fans, he said, "I don't think people *dislike* what you're doing. I think they get used to what you're doing—and they're not going to continue to buy every record you put out or go to every show you do." He was grateful for his success and his support: "I give a lot of thanks to the great songwriters. I have been lucky in having great songs. Of course, I have had great management and publicity, so these things work together."[24]

In the past four years, in addition to the awards, Travis had recorded five albums, sold almost fifteen million albums, had ten number one *Billboard* songs, and toured countless miles around the world. Now it was time for his longest overseas tour ever. He and Hatcher left with their crew on a forty-five-day extended European circuit that would conclude with a third USO tour.

# 7

## "DO YOU THINK HE'S AS CUTE IN PERSON?"

"It was a LONG time to be out of the country," says bass player Rocky Thacker. "We had three weeks of normal touring throughout Europe, then a week off in Amsterdam, then the USO flew us to Egypt, Turkey, Spain, and Italy for three weeks." The tour kicked off in Nottingham, England, on November 1, 1989, and moved across England, Scotland, Ireland, and Wales before crossing the English Channel to France. At a small club in Paris, Travis strode onstage, strapped on his guitar, and greeted the packed house with "*Bon soir*, y'all!" Thacker says, "It brought the house down, and the crowd was in the palm of his hand afterward."[1]

They played their fourteenth and last concert in Utrecht, The Netherlands, and spent Thanksgiving relaxing in Amsterdam. Dan Markley flew from Washington, DC, to meet Travis and Hatcher in Paris and fly with them to Amsterdam. They worked out the details of the USO tour, with schedules changing because of operational or security reasons. A Delaware Air National Guard C-130 picked up the performers in Amsterdam and carried them for the remainder of the tour.[2] Comedy duo Williams and Ree, opening act for the USO show, joined Travis on the Sinai Peninsula. From Idaho and South Dakota, respectively, Bruce Williams and Terry Ree called themselves "The Indian and the White Guy" and had been performing throughout the United States for the past two decades. With their basic show playing on stereotypes held of Native Americans, they drew much of their banter from the locale in which they were performing.

The troupe did two shows on the Sinai Peninsula, one in the northern desert for a US Army component of the international peacekeeping force and one in the south, near a city on the Red Sea. At the northern site, they slept in Quonset huts in the middle of the desert. Markley recalls, "Lib looked at me sideways when we walked into the Quonset hut, as if saying, 'Are you serious?'" He reminded the group, as he often did, "You will get the best of whatever they have. You don't have to ask for it. But they can't give you what they don't have." What they had at the northern location was a Quonset hut. "Randy's generosity of spirit was illuminated by the fact that he wanted to do this, and how he did it," says Markley. "I think it speaks volumes about the person he is. My job was to make sure he enjoyed it and wanted to continue. It was great to collaborate with him."

Everybody wore USO-logo bomber jackets that said "Randy Travis Christmas Tour USO Mediterranean 1989" on the back. Markley compliments the entertainers for their interactions. They weren't just stars on the stage. Through their conversations, they showed the military community, who initially viewed them as exotic, how friendly and personable they were. "That impression was as impactful as the stage performance," Markley says. When offered a helicopter ride, Travis accepted, as did Williams and Ree and several band members. "No seatbelts," Williams recalls. "You were literally hanging out of this helicopter. They're banking and doing all this stuff." Travis sat up front with the pilot and was hanging on for dear life. Williams was thinking, *Okay, we're gonna die here, and the news report will say, "Randy Travis killed with unknown comedy team."* They landed safely, after a spectacularly beautiful tour over the Red Sea with its sparkling clear water.

Their first show in Turkey was at Izmir Air Station, a US Air Force facility on Turkey's western coast; the performers stayed on base in officers' quarters. Then they moved to Incirlik Air Base in the city of Adana, Turkey, where the US Air Force was a tenant of the Turkish Air Force. The base commander took Hatcher, Travis, Williams, Ree, and several of the crew to a restaurant outside the front gate. Williams felt uneasy at seeing guards standing with Uzi submachine guns on the parapets of the restaurant, but the base commander assured them of their safety, and they enjoyed the meal he suggested they order. Prior to the Incirlik performance, the entertainers were instructed not to use political material and not to mention anything about the Turkish government. "That was the first time we came up against something like that," Williams recalls. "We didn't talk about the guys with Uzis at the restaurant. We wanted to. And we thought better of it."[3]

Barry Weinberg came along for the second year, this time enjoying his role as athletic trainer for the current World Series champions, the Oakland Athletics. During the day, he spoke to the troops about conditioning, answered questions about their personal training, and discussed sports in general. The trip gave him a new appreciation of the military. During the evening performances, Weinberg watched the reactions of the crowd: "These are big men, y'know, and it's a Christmas tour, and they're singing songs, and these military guys have tears in their eyes. It meant so much to them for us to come over there. These guys are real people, they're protecting us." Rhythm guitarist Rutledge found the USO shows heartwarming. "The service people were so glad to see us and made us feel so special," he says. "Randy was great with the troops."[4]

After finishing a show in Naples, Italy, the group flew to Rome, but the aircraft carrier where they were scheduled to perform was called into duty. The troupe, which was by now ready to go home, was disappointed not to leave early, but the USO didn't want to pay the cost of changing the tickets. "What at first seemed an encumbrance soon proved to be a blessing," Thacker recalls. "They set up tours of Rome. It was WONDERFUL!" Thacker remembers the USO tours as his personal favorites of all the tours with Travis. "I have all the medals, unit insignia, honor braids, and clothes they wanted us to have or trade Randy's merchandise for," he says. "I bought extra stuff to give away. They are my most treasured souvenirs from my time on the road." He adds, "At the end of seven long weeks, it was time to get home. That was a special time, and at the height of Randy's fame. What a wonderful blessing to have been allowed to be a part of that!"[5]

When they returned from Europe, "It's Just a Matter of Time" was playing on radios everywhere. It was number one on *Billboard*, and *No Holdin' Back* had gone gold by selling half a million albums. Travis, recently chosen as Coke's celebrity spokesperson for 1990, immediately began working on a Coca-Cola Classic commercial. The finished commercial begins with the Travis bus pulling up outside a convenience store. Two teenage clerks inside are watching Travis singing "Can't Beat the Real Thing" on a small television behind the counter. One of them sees Travis walk through the door. Stunned, she smiles and responds, "Hi," when he says hello. The other girl, still staring at the TV screen, muses, "Randy Travis. He's the best. What a voice." She then asks, "Do you think he's as cute in person?" The first one, dreamily watching Travis pull a six-pack of Coke from the cooler, answers, "Uh-huh." As he sets the six-pack on the counter and takes a long drink from one of the cans, the girl watching TV says, "What I wouldn't give to meet a guy like him." The first one says,

"Hey, Julie, wanna ring up this Coca-Cola Classic?" Julie swings around and sees Travis standing there. Her eyes widen in surprise, and she bites her lip as she stares at him. He says thank you as he walks out the door.

Travis explained in a later interview about writing "Can't Beat the Real Thing." He said, "I thought they wanted a commercial, so I wrote a jingle." But they wanted it more like a country song, so he wrote a country song. He was then told, "We like it but it's a little too much like something we've already done. Don't be quite so specific. We love the chorus." He kept the chorus and wrote two more verses. They said they wanted it a little more specific. The night before the recording session, Travis called Don Schlitz and said he needed help. "At one o'clock at night," he recalled, "I was sitting here at the house, and we were singing back and forth to each other on the phone, trying to finish this song." As for filming the commercial, Travis hadn't realized the amount of time and effort required. "It took three days to film a sixty-second commercial," he said. "I don't know how many times we shot these scenes. You shoot walking in the door, you shoot getting off the bus, you shoot picking up the drink, walking to the counter, drinking the drink." He concluded, "I bet I took a drink of Coke forty times to get that one scene. I was very full when I left there that day."[6]

The commercial aired January 22, 1990, during the live broadcast of the American Music Awards, for which nominees were compiled from year-end charts in *Cash Box*, a music industry trade publication. Twenty thousand members of the public selected the winners. Travis was eligible for three of the six country awards that night, and he won them all: Favorite Country Male Artist, Favorite Country Album (*Old 8×10*), and Favorite Country Song ("Deeper Than the Holler"). He tied for the most awards with Milli Vanilli, an international duo that won New Artist awards in both the Pop/Rock and Soul/R&B categories.[7] Travis's time at the top was obviously not over yet.

After a touring breather in January, the Travis troupe hit the road and toured almost nonstop from February through May. They were on the West Coast when "Hard Rock Bottom of Your Heart" hit number one on *Billboard*. They returned to Nashville for the Warner Bros. gala at Union Station Hotel in late March. "In five short years," said CEO Jim Ed Norman while introducing the star, "Randy Travis has sold more than ten million albums and won forty-seven major music awards." Travis held up the Quadruple Platinum trophy for his second album, *Always and Forever*, and said, "I'm learning a lot tonight. I didn't know how many awards I'd won or that I'd sold four million of this one." In his normal self-effacing fashion, he said, "I feel like I've had songs that anybody would have had a hit with." As usual, he thanked Hatcher: "She's always shown support, even when everyone told her she was crazy."

Norman told the audience Travis's career was moving so fast that by the time the celebration was planned and held, he'd sold closer to twelve million than ten million albums.[8]

Their next tour took them for ten days along the East Coast, up to New York and down to Virginia. The first show at George Mason University in Fairfax, Virginia, sold out, so Jeff Davis arranged to add two consecutive nights. The three nights grossed a record $401,165 in sales for the Patriot Center, where the concerts were held, along with a record crowd of 19,611.[9]

One of their hosts scheduled a VIP tour of the White House. On that morning, as Travis recalled later, Hatcher made breakfast on the bus for him and Davis, as she usually did. They were having coffee when the ringing telephone jolted them. Few people knew the number to reach them on the bus. Who could it be? Davis answered and heard an operator say, "Please hold for the president of the United States." Hatcher took the phone. President Bush said, in his neighborly way, "Hey, I hear you're coming over." He then said, "Well, doggone, I'm not going to be here today. Can you come another day?" Hatcher said they could. Next came a call from Tom O'Neill, who had met Travis at the Bush inaugural a year earlier. A member of the Senior Executive Service (civilian equivalent of an admiral), he was a special assistant to the secretary of the Navy and the executive assistant for inaugurals. He was calling to ask how Travis and his entourage planned to get to the White House. He told them their bus was too large to fit through the gates. Hatcher asked if he would pick them up. He arrived the next morning, April 5, in his personal vehicle, a gray 1990 Chrysler.

With Travis, Hatcher, Davis, and Charles Bishop in the car, O'Neill called his Virginia State Police buddies, who pulled alongside and gave them a six-motorcycle police escort on the Virginia roads. Travis remembered, "We *took off*! Those boys were driving like I used to drive when I was a kid, except now we were speeding through busy Washington, DC, traffic. We didn't stop for anything. We roared into town with police lights flashing and sirens blaring." Four U.S. Park Police officers on motorcycles joined them as they crossed the Potomac River. Those four asked if they could get photos with Travis. He readily stepped from the car for a twenty-minute photo session. They then asked if he had seen the monuments. "The officers led us on a high-speed tour of the various national monuments in Washington," Travis recalled. "When we got to the Washington Monument, we roared up the triple-wide sidewalk in front of the monument and circled around the base, lights and sirens still blaring."

When O'Neill pulled up on East Executive Drive at the White House, the Secret Service parked him near a staircase leading to doors guarded by US Marines. Going inside, they were served coffee while they waited for President

Bush's executive secretary to escort them to the Oval Office. "We took Randy in to see President Bush," says O'Neill. "He was overjoyed to see the president, and Bush was a big fan. So was Mrs. Bush. It was one of those nice get-togethers." The president took them into his private dining room and showed them a cupboard containing a row of country music cassette tapes that included Travis's albums. When the president left, O'Neill gave his guests a personalized tour of White House rooms not normally seen by the public.[10]

Travis returned to the White House on May 1, along with a number of sports celebrities, to help President Bush kick off National Physical Fitness and Sports Month. They gathered on the South Lawn at seven o'clock in the morning. "All of us have a stake in making exercise a part of America's fitness and fitness a part of America every day," President Bush said. "And let's pledge to eat a balanced and nutritional diet, avoid excessive alcohol use and, of course, say no to drugs." Speaking to Arnold Schwarzenegger, chairman of the President's Council on Physical Fitness and Sports, Bush said, "Arnold, let's take a look at these workout stations." The participants then took turns hitting golf balls, tossing horseshoes, riding bikes, and other Great American Workout examples.[11]

The White House gathering took place shortly after Travis and Hatcher returned from Hollywood, where they'd attended the Academy of Country Music Awards at the Pantages Theatre on April 25. Hank Williams Jr. led the nominations with six, followed by newcomers Clint Black and Rodney Crowell with five apiece. Travis had three. He lost out to George Strait, who hung onto the Entertainer of the Year title, and to Clint Black, who took the Top Male Artist title. Black was the big winner of the night, with four awards. His debut album, *Killin' Time*, which would produce four number one singles, defeated Travis's *Old 8×10* for Album of the Year.[12]

ACM winners were chosen by the academy's twenty-five hundred members, just as CMA Awards were voted on by that association's six thousand members. Even when those organizations shut Travis out, he could count on fan-voted awards to keep him at the top, as the American Music Awards had done in January. The two fan-voted country music awards shows were combined this year. The *Music City News* Awards had been presented since 1967, with winners decided by the magazine's subscribers. The TNN Viewers' Choice Awards began in 1988, with fans calling The Nashville Network to record their votes. Travis won the top spot of Entertainer of the Year both years and was on his second year as *Music City News* Entertainer of the Year. When it came time for the TNN *Music City News* Awards show in Nashville on June 4, Travis led with five nominations.

Fans could vote through either the magazine or the cable network. And they voted for a new generation of traditional country stars. Ricky Van Shelton won over Travis and George Strait for both Male Artist of the Year and Entertainer of the Year. Shelton said backstage, "I came down the hall and checked to make sure my name was really on it. I feel like I don't deserve it." Clint Black's *Killin' Time* again defeated Travis's album, this time *No Holdin' Back*. Patty Loveless, who had opened for Travis on the 1988 USO tour, received her first award as Female Artist of the Year. The previous year she had been Star of Tomorrow, an award that went this year to Clint Black. During the evening performance, Travis sang his latest release, "He Walked on Water."[13]

It appeared that Travis's reign as consistent award winner might be over. Perhaps it was time to pass the torch. There were plenty of other events to keep him busy. He had celebrated his thirty-first birthday in England after accepting an invitation as the only country artist to participate in the John Lennon Memorial Concert at the Pier Head in Liverpool on May 5. The concert commemorated the ten-year anniversary of Lennon's death, when he had been shot and killed near his New York City home in 1980. Sanctioned by Lennon's widow, Yoko Ono, the show celebrated what would have been Lennon's fiftieth birthday. The performers, who included Cyndi Lauper, B. B. King, Joe Crocker, and Roberta Flack, sang Beatles classics and other songs written by Lennon. By the time actor Christopher Reeve introduced Travis to the crowd of twenty thousand on the banks of the River Mersey, night had fallen and it was cold on the outdoor stage.[14] Travis wore a heavy multicolored jacket and sang "Nowhere Man" while playing his acoustic guitar as the lead instrument. He was backed by a softly playing orchestra that included a steel guitar. The crowd listened quietly and then screamed and cheered at the end of the song.

Dan Markley recruited Travis to headline a government-sponsored show when he produced the entertainment for the G-7 Summit that President Bush held in July in Houston, Texas. "Kind of like with the USO," Markley recalls, "there was no money to do this. Everybody had to be convinced to do it for other reasons." To thank the people of Houston for their volunteerism in making the summit happen, a live television show with Travis as the headliner was organized. Called "Thank You Houston," it took place outdoors on the air-conditioned stage that had been built for the sixteenth G-7 Summit. President and Mrs. Bush attended.[15]

Later that month, Travis took a break from touring for an event that was one of the highlights of his life. TNN had asked him to star in a TV special about an authentic cattle drive on a sixteen-thousand-acre ranch near Red Lodge, Montana. "The cattle drive, that sounded like fun to me," he said. "Riding and working cows and singing around the campfire." Travis didn't consider himself a roper, although he knew how to use a rope from his days of working cattle and horses as a teenager. "I never really got into roping from a horse," he told an interviewer. He preferred riding. Roy Rogers costarred. At age seventy-eight and wearing a pacemaker, Rogers hadn't been on a horse in a long time. During one scene, Travis and Rogers were talking while standing near several horses. When the filming ended, Travis walked away and then heard someone say, "I knew he'd do it." He turned around to see Rogers riding down the hill. "He cantered back to us, and jumped off like he might have been twenty years old," Travis said. "It was so neat for me to be able to see that."

Also in the TV special were actor Denver Pyle and Texas-born singers Michael Martin Murphey and Holly Dunn. Other participants paid to ride along with the stars. The drive lasted five days, with two hundred horses, one hundred head of cattle, ten wagons, fifty cowboys, and seventy-five guests. "People came and experienced it—to work cows, to ride horses, to camp out," Travis said. Every evening featured singing. "We probably had about fifty people around the campfire," Travis related in an interview. "We sat and picked and sang and they sang with us on 'Happy Trails.'"[16] The sixty-minute special, *Randy Travis—Happy Trails*, aired in October.

Jeff Davis, touring director and vice president of Special Moments Promotions, gave an interview to *Amusement Business* in mid-1990, in which he discussed his calculated scheduling approach for Travis's concerts. He alternated summers between fair tours and amphitheater tours to play the same markets in a new way. Travis had played the previous year at Fiddler's Green Amphitheater in Denver, Colorado. Two years earlier, he had been at Frontier Days in Cheyenne, Wyoming. The venues were a hundred miles apart, which made the core audiences different, even though the markets and the media coverage overlapped. This summer he was back at Cheyenne's Frontier Days, where his two appearances drew 22,561 people and broke the two-day attendance record set by the group Alabama the previous year. His second show brought in a crowd of 12,067 and set a one-day attendance record, breaking Clint Black's record from four days earlier. "We try to space Randy's appearances in any market eighteen months apart," Davis explained. "At this point in his career, what affects routing most is to find the freshest markets possible." Because many grandstands at fairs lacked seating capacity, artists with Travis's drawing power and price frequently had to do two shows to make the arrangement financially viable for fair buyers. Two shows in one day could be strenuous, and Davis tried to schedule a day's rest between bookings. Although many artists refused to do two shows, Davis said doing double events was the only way to reach so many fans.

Travis's upcoming September show at the Eastern Idaho State Fair in Blackfoot, a town with a population of two thousand, had sold one hundred thousand dollars in tickets the first day they were on sale. "For Randy Travis to come to Blackfoot, Idaho," one promoter commented, "well, it's really something. It's almost like the President of the United States coming to town." He noted, "Very few acts in this business can sell ten thousand tickets."[17]

Travis's long-awaited *Heroes and Friends* duet album was released on August 31, 1990. It included "Happy Trails," the song Roy Rogers had come to Nashville to record the previous summer. The album was a deeply personal project for Travis. He and Hatcher chose thirteen special people to sing with him, most of whom had helped Travis early in his career. That everyone accepted his invitation showed the stature Travis had attained in a few short years and how admired he was by legendary singers. He had once opened for Conway Twitty, Loretta Lynn, George Jones, Willie Nelson, and Tammy Wynette. Most of the recording was done in Nashville, with three trips to the West Coast. "Duet albums are way more complicated than regular records to make," Lehning explains. They had to juggle many people's schedules and choose songs that satisfied both Travis and his duet partner. Travis and Don Schlitz wrote the title track, which Lehning included as a reprise to bookend the songs on the album. As they began the recording sessions, Lehning had suggested the pair write a song about the record. Travis was already working on the idea. While on tour in Scotland, he had been standing backstage when the thoughts came to him. "I wrote down some lines, then put them aside because I had to go sing," he recalled. After returning to Nashville, he and Schlitz finished the song in one afternoon.

Dolly Parton and Chet Atkins came into the studio to join Travis in recording Parton's song, "Do I Ever Cross Your Mind," Lehning and Travis were awestruck to be in their presence. Atkins played a gut string guitar with his easily recognizable fingerpicking. "The thing I remember most about that day," Lehning says, "is how much fun Dolly and Chet had together. I don't know how long it had been since they worked together in the studio, but they had the best time with each other."[18] Lehning booked a session with Vern Gosdin, known by fellow performers as "The Voice." When he arrived at the studio, he didn't like the song they had chosen. Travis and Lehning loved Vern Gosdin. They looked at each other and told him they would find a song he did like. Gosdin said, "Okay, I appreciate that," and he left. "So we're sitting there with a whole bunch of musicians and no Vern Gosdin," Lehning recalls. They recorded several songs they had been planning for Travis to record later. Lehning booked another session, Gosdin returned, and they recorded "The Human Race."

Lehning describes the George Jones duet, "A Few Ole Country Boys," as "a great song and great performances by two great vocal stylists." The song was written especially for the pair by Troy Seals and Mentor Williams. When Travis first heard it, he thought, *That's amazing—they nailed exactly what I went through listening to George in the early days.* It was released as the lead single from the album. The two singers didn't tour together, so when Travis played the song at his concerts, he sang his part and then flipped his guitar over to show Jones's picture. He would imitate Jones singing and then flip the guitar back to sing his own part. The audience would go wild.

Travis and Tammy Wynette had both come off the road and weren't in the best of voice when they recorded "We're Strangers Again." They redid their vocals and later appeared on Ralph Emery's *Nashville Now* to sing the duet. Emery asked Wynette about making the record. She said, "Randy called and wanted to know if I would be interested in doing a duet with him. I was so excited because I think Randy is responsible for bringing country music back around to traditional country, and he's wonderful to work with." Loretta Lynn wasn't at the tracking session when they recorded "Shopping for Dresses," a song written by Little Jimmy Dickens and Merle Haggard. Dickens had pitched the song for an earlier album, and Travis remembered it when searching for a song for Lynn. She went to Lehning's studio in Hendersonville to add her vocals. "Randy and I loved this song," Lehning says, "because it is so quirky and has such an odd take on romance. But Lib hated the song. I don't know how we ended up getting it through her gauntlet. Randy and I absolutely adored the song and thought it was brilliant, and we managed to get it cut."

Willie Nelson suggested "Birth of the Blues." When Travis listened to the Frank Sinatra recording with orchestra, he said, "No way, we're not doing this song." Lehning asked him to think about it, and Travis began imagining how it would sound as a country song. Because Nelson was working in Las Vegas, Travis flew his crew there, and Lehning booked a studio for Nelson to come in and sing the duet. During one of Travis's California tours, they drove to Merle Haggard's home, where they were scheduled to record in his home studio. Travis thought the Bob Wills western swing classic "All Night Long" would be a perfect fit. Haggard had agreed. They sat on the bus and waited until someone came out and said there would be no recording that day. Lehning later sent the multitrack, and Haggard added his vocals. "Smokin' the Hive" was recorded with Clint Eastwood in Los Angeles. Lehning wanted Eastwood to speak the final line, "You're gonna get stung, boy." Each time he tried, Lehning would say, "No, that's not quite it. Let's do it one more time." As Eastwood became frustrated, Lehning said, "Randy, say it for him the way you said it to me." Eastwood listened and said, "Oh, you want Dirty Harry?" The next take was perfect. Eastwood asked, "Why didn't you say so?" Lehning recalls, "I was too nervous to say, hey, do it like Dirty Harry. I'm lucky he didn't kill me. That was an honor to get to work with him." Lehning calls B. B. King, who sang "Waiting on the Light to Change" with Travis, "the sweetest, kindest person and loved Randy and was well aware of his music and loved country music."[19]

With thirteen wonderful recordings, which ones could be eliminated to fit a ten-song album? Travis and Lehning had been working on *Heroes and Friends* for over a year, and they didn't want to lose any of the songs. Travis had spent much of his own money on the production of this labor of love. To avoid charging fans more for the album, Warner Bros. told Travis he would have to absorb the costs for the three extra songs. The alternative would be to pay a smaller royalty rate. Having heard that reduced royalty deals were a common business practice with longer albums, Travis and Hatcher asked the songwriters and publishers to take a smaller share. Expecting the album to be a million-seller, all agreed. Then the *Tennessean* reported in mid-August that songwriters were complaining about taking a cut to allow Travis to make more money. The article angered Travis because the songwriters went to the newspaper instead of directly to him. "It was kind of an effort to bring the cost of the record down because this is going to wind up to be an expensive record," he told a reporter.[20]

He was touring in the Midwest and had reached Canada by the time the issue was resolved a week later. He and Jim Ed Norman jointly announced they would share the cost of paying full royalty rates to all involved. "My intentions were never to cause financial hardship or to in any way infringe upon the rights of the songwriter," Travis said in a prepared statement. "Hopefully, something good will come out of what has become a personally painful situation." His publicist, Evelyn Shriver, insisted, "He wasn't being greedy. He thought this was the way things were done." She said no one expected such an emotional reaction to the common practice of asking for a lower rate on an album with more than ten cuts.

Although Travis took the heat for the debacle, the actual proposal came from Hatcher and their business manager, Gary Haber. Travis later explained, "As a songwriter myself, I understood that every cut mattered, especially if it was your source of income. But there were a lot of people to satisfy, so Lib and Gary were looking for every way possible to lower expenses. They reasoned that because there were a dozen superstars on the album with me, the sales would be better than most compilation albums and the songwriters would therefore make more than they normally would." He added, "I felt bad about the way that happened. Asking the songwriters to sacrifice was probably a mistake. Besides insulting some of my best friends in the business—the songwriters—when the news went public, it made me appear to be a selfish money grubber."[21]

An incident they mostly kept out of the news occurred at a Nashville restaurant in September, when Hatcher chased away a young waitress who was flirting with Travis. She reportedly stormed from the restaurant after telling him she wasn't going to let some cheap waitress take him away from her. It wasn't the first time such a scene had occurred between the couple, but this time, according to the *National Enquirer*, Travis, thirty-one, stood up to Hatcher, forty-nine, and told her to leave their Ashland City home. Travis was later quoted as saying, "I do owe a lot to Lib—but I don't owe her the rest of my life. She made me, and I made her. But from now on, my relationship with Libby is all business."[22] Hatcher continued as manager and business partner, and they were soon back together. On October 10, 1990, Haber established separate trusts for the couple. He moved their jointly owned homes into the Sandy Creek Trust, with Randy Bruce Traywick as trustee, and the Marrobone Trust, with Mary Elizabeth Hatcher as trustee. Their Music Row office, owned by Hatcher alone, went into the Marrobone Trust. They also signed wills that day, making each other heir and executor. Their real estate investment property belonged to L & R Investments LLC, managed for them by agent Haber.

*Heroes and Friends* was soaring to number one on *Billboard*'s Top Country Albums chart. "A Few Ole Country Boys" peaked at number eight, and the title track reached number three on the *Billboard* Hot Country Singles chart. The album would be certified platinum a year later, Travis's fourth million-selling album.

"A Few Ole Country Boys" was still on its way up the charts when Travis co-hosted the CMA Awards with Reba McEntire at the Grand Ole Opry House on October 8. It was the first time in more than a decade that traditional country artists hosted the show and the first time for either of them. "Everyone says it's an honor to be nominated, and it is," Travis said. "Imagine what it feels like to stand on that stage looking out into the faces of so many of my heroes and introducing *them*, with millions of people watching. Reba was a natural on camera and made my job much easier, and of course the teleprompters displaying our comments and jogging our memories helped a lot."²³ Although both occasionally flubbed their lines, they appeared comfortable and confident. A television reporter at the *Tennessean* reviewed the show as the "best in recent memory," writing, "For Most Congenial Hosts of an Award Show, the award goes to Randy Travis and Reba McEntire, who proved that country music doesn't need crossover acts to host the award show, thank you very much. They handled the hosting chores with perfection."²⁴

In the second half of the show, McEntire announced, "It's now my pleasure to introduce our next Entertainer of the Year nominee, my co-host and good friend, Mr. Randy Travis." When Travis finished the first verse with, "It's good to know there's still a few ol' country boys around," he turned as planned and watched George Jones come onstage, singing, "We heard you were a fast train coming out of Caroline," to a standing ovation. They sang the third verse together, paused while the audience clapped, and then Jones started singing "Heroes and Friends." After two lines, he stopped, allowing Tammy Wynette to come onstage singing the second half of the verse. All three sang the chorus. As Travis started the second verse, "I grew up with cowboys I watched on TV" (a verse he wrote about Roy Rogers), Vern Gosdin and Roy Rogers walked onstage, bringing on another standing ovation, with Gosdin finishing the verse. All five sang the final chorus.

Travis, who had taken home the Horizon Award four years earlier, introduced the previous year's Horizon winner, Clint Black, to announce this year's winner. For the first time ever, all five nominees—Lorrie Morgan, Garth Brooks, Travis Tritt, the Kentucky Headhunters, and Alan Jackson—had already earned gold records for selling five hundred thousand copies of a single. The winner of the 1990 Horizon Award was Garth Brooks. The five nominees for Entertainer of the Year all performed during the show—Travis, Clint Black, Kathy Mattea, Ricky Van Shelton, and George Strait. When Travis introduced Strait's performance, he said he'd been a fan since Strait's first big record in 1981. He announced, "Last year he was named Entertainer of the Year, and he deserved it. This year he is nominated for that same award." He teased, "I wish I could say good luck!" Barbara Mandrell, who had been the first performer to twice be named CMA Entertainer of the Year, came onstage to announce the winner. She proclaimed, "The Entertainer of the Year is—George Strait!"

During a *Nashville Now* segment two nights later, Ralph Emery commended Travis and McEntire for an outstanding job of emceeing. He told them, "If you don't stop emceeing, I'll start singing." When he asked about their upcoming schedules, Travis responded, "Like normal, I know I'm leaving, but I don't know where I'm going." He added, "We leave tomorrow and head somewhere."[25] It was a weekend in Georgia and Alabama where they were headed. On Halloween, Travis appeared again on *Nashville Now*. The evening's show was sponsored by Nestlé, and host Emery played a gangster named Elliot Nestlé. Faron Young called himself Little Flirtie Fanny; he wore a dress and sang "Coal Miner's Daughter." Flirtie Fanny came onstage later in the show with a reddish-brown, floppy-eared dog that was walking upright, taller than Fanny, and wearing coveralls. Emery asked, "Can the dog talk?" The dog answered, "Hi, Ralph." The dog sat down next to Fanny and crossed its legs. A man's hands protruded from the costume's sleeves. At the end of the show, Emery introduced the costumed guests. The dog removed its head to reveal Randy Travis. "That dog suit is very warm," he said. "I can't believe I got talked into this."[26]

In December, Travis returned to Bally's Grand in Las Vegas for five days during National Finals Rodeo week. Guantanamo Bay, Cuba, followed, for the fourth and final USO tour. Williams and Ree once again served as opening act. Naval Station Guantanamo Bay, with five thousand people stationed there, was like a small American town. Markley considered those shows "like doing a mini version of a real Randy Travis concert experience." A Tennessee Air National Guard C-130 flew them from Nashville to Naval Air Station Key West, Florida. There they boarded a US Navy DC-9 jet aircraft for the flight to Guantanamo Bay. Tom Rutledge remembers the show got rained out. "They moved us into a great big hangar," he says, "and mosquitos just about ate us alive."[27]

End-of-year statistics showed Travis as the biggest-grossing country music singer of 1990. His $9.7 million came from seventy-seven concerts attended by 565,627 fans. Second-place Alabama grossed $7.4 million with forty-eight concerts. Third-place George Strait with forty-one shows brought in $6.3 million.[28] As Travis spent weeks on the road, new singers following his example as a country traditionalist continued to nip at his heels. "Today's hot male country music stars sell songs as well as sex appeal," touted a Music City profile. "Read about such singers as Clint Black and Alan Jackson that are following in the steps of Randy Travis to fame and fortune."[29] Jackson's debut album, *Here in the Real World*, was the first album to achieve gold for the new Arista Records label. The *Tennessean* listed nine "hot hunks" of 1990, who were abetted by "hunk vets" like Travis and Strait. A press release in early January announced, "Randy Travis, who was named the top grossing country music concert artist for 1990, has selected hot newcomer Alan Jackson as his support act for the 1991 concert season."[30]

# 8

## "IF YOU SEE WHAT'S WRONG AND YOU TRY TO MAKE IT RIGHT, YOU WILL BE A POINT OF LIGHT."

Both Travis and Jackson appeared to be overnight successes when they had actually worked for years to get their record deals. Both were baritones who started their recording careers with the help of producer Keith Stegall. He would produce Jackson's records for over thirty years, just as Lehning produced Travis's records. Jackson, six months older than Travis, came to Nashville as Travis's first records hit the charts. A fellow pure country traditionalist, Jackson thought Travis's success would help him get a record contract. When that didn't happen, he often commented, as had Travis, that he was "too country" for Nashville. Several months after Travis left the Nashville Palace in 1985 and went into music full-time, the newly arrived Jackson got a job in the mailroom of The Nashville Network. He obtained a contract as a songwriter with Glen Campbell's music publishing company and put together a touring band. Like Travis, he traveled with a van and a trailer, setting up musical equipment in small venues several nights a week. Just as Travis had been nominated for the CMA Horizon Award in 1986, Jackson was nominated in 1990. Travis won in 1986, while the 1990 award went to Garth Brooks. Jackson, a native of Newnan, Georgia, had married his high school sweetheart, Denise Jackson, several years before they moved to Nashville to build a country music career. At six feet, four inches, with longish blond hair and blue eyes, he modeled Travis's unassuming attitude and let it be known he was a married man.[1]

The forty-date Travis/Jackson spring tour began on February 8, 1991, in Huntsville, Alabama, with plans for a summer fair tour and a twenty-date fall tour. Travis and Jackson appeared February 7 on *Nashville Now* to introduce the tour. Tammy Wynette, who would perform with them on several tour dates, joined them. Travis opened the show with "Hard Rock Bottom of Your Heart." Then he walked to the couch next to Ralph Emery's desk. "Let me look at you," Emery said, pulling open Travis's jacket. "You've put on a little weight." Travis revealed he'd been trying to gain weight and had put on twenty-five pounds over a month and a half. He had been 145 pounds (at five feet, nine inches) when he was on the show in October. "I went from medium T-shirts to a large over the holiday," he said. "It was a lot of work." He ate five meals a day, drinking protein shakes with raw eggs between meals. "I'm close to one hundred seventy now," he said. "This is where I want to stay."

The evening spotlighted Travis's new duet album. He sang "Heroes and Friends," Wynette joined him for "We're Strangers Again," and Vern Gosdin arrived to help sing "The Human Race." Jackson performed his current—and first—number one hit, "I'd Love You All Over Again." Travis and Jackson told Emery about two songs they cowrote when Jackson was opening for Travis on the fair circuit the previous August. One afternoon he had gone on Travis's bus for a songwriting session. "Alan was accustomed to trying to write songs while surrounded by the bedlam of a tour bus," Travis recalled. "He and I sat down with two guitars and some notepads. Within an hour we had written two songs. That was a pretty good day of songwriting." B. B. King had asked Travis to write a song for him, and Travis asked Jackson if he had any ideas for a blues song. Jackson said he'd been hanging on to one for a while and hadn't thought of how to write it. The title was "She's Got the Rhythm, I've Got the Blues." They wrote the song in less than forty minutes. Several days later, Jackson said he liked the song and was thinking about recording it himself. Travis told him, "Go ahead, we'll write something else for B. B." King never did get a song written for him. "She's Got the Rhythm (And I've Got the Blues)" became a number one hit for Jackson. The second song they wrote that day was "Better Class of Losers," a number two hit for Travis.[2]

By mid-March, Travis was longing for a break from touring. "It's not hard to get motivated to do a show or to record," he told an interviewer. "I just dread leaving the house after four years on the road. I want to slow down on the touring." When asked if he felt a little bit threatened by up-and-comers like Jackson, he laughed. "Nah, sure don't," he answered. "What I'm really interested in doing is giving the best show we can give 'em."[3]

What he did feel threatened by was a gossip-mongering *National Examiner* article that claimed he wasn't married because he was a closet homosexual. "Randy Travis Angrily Fights Reports He's Gay" screamed the untrue headline of the tabloid that hit the stands just as hundreds of radio station managers and deejays gathered in Nashville for the twenty-second annual Country Radio Seminar. Travis, with Wynette and Gosdin, was scheduled to open the seminar the morning of March 7, in front of a thousand registered attendees at the Opryland Hotel. As Travis waited to go onstage, his thoughts focused on the article with its anonymous quotes and lack of specific incidents. As angry as he'd ever been, he spewed an expletive-laced backstage rant. Bill Mayne, senior vice president of promotions for Warner Bros., tried to calm him. "Just let it alone, and nobody will even bring it up," he suggested. "And if anyone does mention it, say something like, 'As my grandpa used to tell me, consider the source.' They'll get the idea." Travis refused to take that excellent advice.

He went onstage and tried to do his set but found that impossible. "I stopped in the middle and vented to the crowd of listeners," he later said. He denied the gossip and told the audience, "It made me angry. I usually let things slide, but I couldn't this time." The anonymous comment that irritated him most was, "If that guy's not gay, then my grandmother is Willie Nelson." Travis announced, "My advice to you is to buy your grandmother a red bandana and a red wig and teach her to sing through her nose." He later acknowledged he would have been wiser to keep his thoughts to himself. His sense of humor did shine through, though. "I guess it could have been worse," he joked. "I guess they could have said I wasn't country." Mark Casstevens, acoustic guitarist for the performance, remembers being surprised when Travis told the band to stop playing. "That was so strange," he says. "I was wondering who the heck would start that kind of rumor. I admired how firm he was. It obviously bothered him."

The following day, further disregarding Mayne's advice, Travis and Hatcher chose as damage control to release a statement that they had been living together for a number of years; he just hadn't wanted to get married. Although their relationship had long been an open secret, this was the first time they publicly acknowledged it. They consulted an attorney, who reminded them that Travis was a "public person." His only recourse was to sue for malice or defamation of character. Those charges would be difficult or impossible to prove and therefore not worth the effort. The *Tennessean* story "Randy Travis Declares He's Not Homosexual" was spread nationwide over the weekend, with headlines such as "Country Star Travis Denies Story in Tabloid" causing a flood of attention.[4]

By Sunday evening Travis was in Washington, DC, where he debuted his newest song, "Point of Light," for the president of the United States. The occasion was the annual fund-raising gala at Ford's Theatre, site of the assassination of President Abraham Lincoln in 1865. Attendees in addition to President and Barbara Bush included Vice President Dan Quayle, Defense Secretary Dick Cheney, General Colin Powell, and various leaders of Congress, as well as numerous corporate chiefs. The two-and-a-half-hour event raised four hundred thousand dollars for preservation of the active theater with its Lincoln-focused museum. The show turned into a celebration touting the success of the Persian Gulf War. "I was extremely nervous," Travis said the following day. "Because it's not your normal audience. You go out every night and do a show and think nothing of it. You're a little nervous in the beginning, but it passes. Last night, it got worse as I went on."[5] Standing on a stage festooned in red, white, and blue, Travis sang, "If you see what's wrong and you try to make it right / you will be a point of light."

The song was based on the "thousand points of light" mission that Bush had introduced in his acceptance speech for the Republican nomination for US president in 1988. The idea was that money alone could not solve society's ills; it required service by citizens. A year into his presidency, Bush began awarding daily "points of light" honors to groups or individuals who had made significant contributions to solving a specific social ill. Sig Rogich, a White House publicist, contacted the Country Music Association to find a songwriter to put the concept in a country song. Don Schlitz and Thom Schuyler accepted the challenge.

They wrote the song and sent it to Rogich, who returned it with a comment that President Bush liked it but wanted the chorus "a little more sing-songy." They rewrote it to his satisfaction, and then came the search for a singer. Bush, a Travis fan, must have been pleased with the choice. Schlitz played the demo for Travis, who took it to Lehning. They went into the studio and recorded it for immediate release as a single. Lehning told the session musicians that anyone who did not want to participate could sit out. One did, and two others played despite disagreeing with the song's political tone. Travis promised to donate the record's proceeds to the Points of Light Foundation, a private nonpartisan group with Bush as honorary chairman.[6]

Following Travis's debut performance of "Point of Light" and performances by fellow country singers such as Tammy Wynette, Alabama, Alan Jackson, and the Statler Brothers, President Bush came onstage at Ford's Theatre to address the audience. The country music fan said, "The incredible feeling here in this theater tonight shows really what I love best about country music; it hits all the right chords, like caring for your family, having faith in God."[7]

While in the nation's capital, Travis was interviewed by the *Washington Post* about his life with Hatcher. He said they initially denied their relationship because he didn't know how to handle the age difference. Then it became the easiest way to deal with the press. "But it turned around on us," he acknowledged. "When you lie, it usually comes back to you, and I guess that's proof of it."[8]

A few weeks later he was back in Washington, DC, to sing "Point of Light" again. This event was a live CBS television special, *All-Star Salute to Our Troops*, on the evening of Wednesday, April 3. (NBC and ABC networks also presented welcome home salutes in April.) It was held in a huge aircraft hangar at Andrews Air Force Base in Maryland. President and Mrs. Bush were there to welcome home five hundred troops from Operation Desert Storm. The salute featured actors such as Sophia Loren, Charlton Heston, and Alan Alda, as well as singers such as Barbara Mandrell, CeCe Winans, and Gary Morris.[9] Travis later said, "At the close of the show, a huge American flag unfurled as a backdrop behind the band and me. The troops instinctively began cheering. It was truly one of the more emotional patriotic moments of my life."[10]

Not everyone agreed. A Washington-based columnist, Sandy Grady, pointed out that Saddam Hussein was still in charge of Iraq: "Kuwait is burning, refugees clog roads, Kurds are dying. Why are they celebrating?" He wrote, "It was a two-hour commercial for the Gulf War: a videotape montage of the War's Great Moments. Clips of the Commander-in-Chief's Hit Speeches. A swell new song, 'Point of Light.' Flag-waving, foot-stomping cheers."[11]

A New York woman filed a complaint with the Federal Election Commission (FEC) about Travis's performance and the song's radio airplay. The complaint read, "I feel that the current country song 'Point of Light' by Randy Travis is actually a free, frequent, subliminal campaign commercial for George Bush in an attempt to get an early, sneaky start on his 1992 re-election campaign." The woman was a fan who believed Travis and Warner Bros. were "being used as innocent, unsuspecting tools" by the presidential campaign. The FEC responded, "The allegation was that in singing that song, he was making a political statement favoring the president as a candidate. The commission found that was not so. There was no reason to find that there was a violation of the law."[12]

Controversy also arose from the overall concept of President Bush's "thousand points of light" campaign. While some acknowledged that encouraging volunteerism was a good thing, others considered the program to be a cover for shirking governmental responsibility. Organizations that had worked for decades to advocate volunteerism believed there was no teeth in the program and no financial support. It was a feel-good program to make President Bush look like he cared, they said. Travis, of course, was pulled into the controversy. When asked about his position, he stated, "It's not really a political song. When you get involved in politics, you need to know a little bit more about it than I do."[13]

Politics was not his concern; music was. He continued to encourage and support the new singers replacing him on the awards shows. Thomas Goldsmith, who had been writing about Travis for the *Tennessean* since 1986, said, "The Academy of Country Music released its 1991 award nominations. The organization that had given Travis his first major award in 1986 completely shut him out this time. He was last year's top grossing tour artist, had three albums on the charts representing five million in sales, and has put out three Top Five singles—and he didn't rate a single ACM nomination."[14] Although disappointed, Travis understood. "I was real fortunate there for three years," he said. "Things were going great. They still are—the shows are going good and the record is selling good. But the awards don't continue to come. I try to not let it get to me. I know it's time for other people to win. Gosh, I've won over fifty, so I can't really gripe."[15]

Lahaina, on the island of Maui in Hawaii, is the largest city in West Maui of Maui County. It runs along the coast on the northwestern edge of the island, which had doubled in population in the previous two decades—from forty-six thousand in 1970 to one hundred thousand in 1990. Travis and Hatcher enjoyed vacationing there and decided to purchase a vacation home on the island. At the end of April 1990, they bought a two-story, forty-three-hundred-square-foot house on the Kaanapali hillside in Lahaina. Their new home on Lower Honoapiilani Road faced west, across the road and toward the beach along Pailolo Channel, which separated the islands of Maui and Molokai. The sellers were Robert Lyn Nelson and his wife, Uilani. Nelson was a native Californian who had achieved worldwide recognition for his paintings.[16] The Nelsons continued to rent for a year while their new home was being built. During that time, Travis and Hatcher spent their Hawaii visits in a rental house they owned on Lahaina's Front Street.

Travis continued to chafe under Hatcher's control. One night, after one of his "Point of Light" performances in Washington, DC, they were in their hotel suite, along with Jeff Davis, Bill Mayne, Barry Weinberg, and Travis's youngest brother, Dennis Traywick, who was working as a member of Travis's crew. Traywick suggested going to a nearby club where he had heard a great band. "Everyone seemed in favor of the idea except Lib," Travis recalled. "She was wary about me going out with friends, especially to any place where there might be alcohol or attractive women." She told him she planned to buy him a saddle the next morning and they needed to get up early. Travis, feeling crushed, told his friends to go without him. While acknowledging that Hatcher loved him and had poured her life into helping them both succeed, he increasingly questioned whether she was serving his best interests or her own. "It was always there, festering like an infected wound," he said, "even when fantastic things were happening in our lives."[17] They had been a team for a long time, with her the driving force behind most of their decisions. Travis had been described as "polite, quiet and a bit shy," as well as "simple, direct, and honest, with no pretensions or affectations." He loved the singing side of his musical career and was usually content to let her handle the business side. About getting turned down by record labels during his early days in Nashville, he told a reporter, "It's probably for the best that they turned me down when they did, because now I'm more ready for success. I'm singing better now than I was a few years back, and mentally, I'm handling things better."[18]

But how to handle his relationship with Hatcher? He married her.

Hawaii's Bureau of Health Statistics listed the marriage of Randy Bruce Traywick to Mary Elizabeth Hatcher (who became Mary Elizabeth Traywick) on May 8, 1991, at Maui, Hawaii. They held the ceremony on May 25, in front of a waterfall in the courtyard of their Lower Honoapiilani home. Travis, thirty-two, wore a casual shirt with black jeans and boots. Hatcher, fifty, wore a black-and-white checked dress. The only others present were the preacher and two strangers he brought with him to be witnesses. Travis gave his bride a four-carat diamond ring.[19] The wedding was so secret they didn't tell Kyle Lehning, even though he was there until the morning of the wedding. "I'd been there four or five days, and they didn't say a word about it," he says. "They wanted to do that privately, I think." He flew home after completing his recording sessions.[20] The entertainment editor of the *Honolulu Advertiser* reported, not knowing it was a wedding celebration, "Randy Travis, the country music star who's a frequent Maui visitor, found his way with a party of five to the Plantation House Restaurant at Kapalua the other night."[21]

When they returned to Tennessee, their rings gave away their secret. Travis performed his first Nashville concert in three years, headlining at the Starwood

Amphitheatre on Sunday, June 9, the eve of Fan Fair. Alan Jackson and Tammy Wynette appeared with him as part of the GMC Truck American Music Tour. To promote the "Point of Light" theme, barrels and trucks were set up outside the amphitheater to collect cans of food for the Feed the Children organization. The following night, still with no official announcement, Travis appeared on the TNN *Music City News* Awards show at the Opry House. He and George Jones sang "A Few Ole Country Boys" and introduced songs by the Star of Tomorrow nominees. As had occurred the previous year, Travis garnered five nominations and no wins. Finally, on Friday, June 14, Evelyn Shriver sent out a press release announcing that Travis had "married longtime companion and manager Lib Hatcher" at their Maui home on May 25. It said, "Earlier this year, after stories broke that Travis was gay, the couple said they had been living together for twelve years." The newlyweds then returned to Hawaii for a honeymoon. Hatcher was quoted as saying, "We are very happy. We are just trying to get away and have a little rest."[22]

Travis's next album, *High Lonesome*, had been completed and turned over to Warner Bros. to ready it for an August release. It included "Point of Light," which had already reached its height of number three on *Billboard*. The three singles eventually released off the album were cowritten by Travis and Jackson. Travis had said earlier that Jackson recorded one of the first six songs they wrote together, and Travis planned to record three others. "You don't always write six songs and record four of them," he told a reporter. "But we got on a roll and wrote several good tunes all at once. Now we'll probably write six or eight bad ones. That's usually the way it goes."[23] Travis had developed the idea for "Forever Together" during a flight home from England. He needed a paper to write on, so Hatcher gave him the bottom half of a fax memo she was reading. He jotted down his ideas and presented them during the later songwriting session. "He about had it finished," Jackson recalled. "We got together, knocked it out, changed a few lines, and finished a couple he hadn't completed. I thought it was a real pretty song."[24]

So did everyone else. The first release from the album, "Forever Together" became Travis's twelfth number one. "Better Class of Losers" followed and climbed to number two. "I'd Surrender All" reached number twenty. While "Forever and Ever, Amen" was—and still is—an anthem supporting the longevity goal of marriage, "Better Class of Losers" became Travis's signature breakup song.

Travis and his bride returned from Hawaii in late July for another three months of almost constant touring. Following Labor Day, during a few days at home in Tennessee, they attended a Wednesday evening service at the Ashland City Church of Christ. They often went there with friends who were church members. Pastor Dan Harless Jr. sensed the singer had something on his mind. The Travises invited the Harlesses to their home, where the two couples talked for almost two hours. Travis said he would like to be baptized. The couple's baptismal ceremony, with Hatcher being rebaptized, was held during the Sunday evening service at the 250-member church. They had asked to be baptized after the service to avoid causing a disturbance, but Pastor Harless told them the baptism would be an inspiration to the young people in the congregation. Travis later called his baptism "a powerful illustration of the statement that the old Randy was dead, buried in the water and gone, and I was a new person. Thanks to Jesus, I had been raised to a new life here and now and eternal life in heaven to come."[25]

Betty Bitterman, vice president of original programing for the Home Box Office (HBO) network, developed a television series called *Influences*. She got the idea while listening to backstage chatter at an earlier show where performers paid homage to the people who inspired them. The second show in her series aired in October and starred Randy Travis and George Jones. The show begins with Jones and Travis, ages sixty and thirty-two, walking through the packed house at Zanies Comedy Club in South Nashville. It's an intimate setting, with the audience seated close to the low stage. The balcony that surrounds the main floor is full. The crowd cheers in welcome as the two stars reach the stage, pick up their acoustic guitars, and sit on stools. Harmonica player Terry McMillan stands behind them. Travis, who grew up with Jones as a musical hero, is surprised to learn he influenced Jones, whose first number one hit, "White Lightning," came out the year Travis was born. Jones tells Travis, "I was about ready to give up, and then you came out with 'On the Other Hand.'" He says he called radio stations to get the song played, adding, "You gave me a lot of inspiration to want to try harder, and try to make a comeback, y'know."

"I never heard that story before," the astonished Travis says. "I'll tell you what—see if you remember this one." He starts singing "Grand Tour." Jones grins and joins in. They trade off talking about their mutual influences as they sing the classics of Roy Acuff, Hank Williams Sr., Lefty Frizzell, and Merle Haggard. Travis kicks off Haggard's "The Bottle Let Me Down," stops, and says, "Oh, wait a minute. This is embarrassing. I went to the wrong key. The wrong song, too." He points to the set list, which he says has the songs and their keys written down. He throws back his head and laughs when Jones says, "Well, I want you to know I was ready to hit a good lick there, and you messed me up."

"Doggone, I thought I was ready, too," Travis responds. Throughout the show, they obviously enjoy performing together and appreciating each other's abilities. After an intermission, they again walk through the applauding audience to return to the stage. They stand in front of microphones, with a full band behind them, and begin the second segment with "A Few Ole Country Boys." Travis asks Jones to sing "He Stopped Loving Her Today." Jones sings several of his hits while Travis sits on a stool and watches him intently. The crowd responds with wild applause. Travis sings only one of his songs, "On the Other Hand," after which Jones says, "That's my favorite song." He is so impressed, he can only say, "Randy, you just sing—you just sing." Travis appears more interested in listening to Jones and singing the classics of his influences than in showing off his own music. To end the show, Jones starts singing "I Saw the Light" and Travis joins him. The credits roll as they finish the Hank Williams classic, and Travis throws his arm around Jones's shoulders.[26]

Kyle Lehning put together the band of session musicians for the performance. He remembers the evening being a lot of fun, with both Jones and Travis in great voice. Acoustic guitarist Mark Casstevens was excited to be sitting next to Travis. "What a great night that was," he says. "I'd been on so many of Randy's hits that I felt part of a family. Seeing those two, how smoothly they improvised back and forth, here were two titans in country music. I was proud to be a part of that taping."[27]

"A Few Ole Country Boys" was nominated for CMA Vocal Event of the Year but didn't win. The 1991 CMA Awards took place without Travis, who was absent for the first time since winning the Horizon Award five years earlier. He was on the West Coast for his autumn *High Lonesome* tour, which ended in November. Alan Jackson fulfilled his contractual requirement of being the opening act, even though he was more than ready for headliner status, with his third consecutive number one record and six consecutive releases in the top three on *Billboard*. He was billed as "special guest," with newspaper coverage varying from "Travis and Opening Act Draw Crowd, Applause" to saying Jackson "will appear in concert tonight along with Randy Travis."[28]

Travis's first 1992 show was on Valentine's Day in Auburn Hills, Michigan, with Jackson and opening act Trisha Yearwood; she opened many Travis shows that year. To prepare for his tours, Travis spent time working through the song sequence and placement in the show. He balanced new songs with the familiar hits people wanted to hear. Upon finishing his set list, he sent it to Jeff Davis for comment. Although not a musician, Davis as tour manager watched audience responses and had a comprehensive perspective on what worked and what didn't. Travis enjoyed telling jokes, whether poking fun at himself or corny ones that elicited groans as well as laughter. He planned the jokes strategically where they would work best, such as when the band needed extra time to set up for a song.[29]

One of his favorites he positioned as a story told in a country store he visited in his hometown. "Well, maybe you listened to these boys before," he would say. "They weren't always telling the truth, but it was fun to listen to. Now, one day I'm sitting in there, and these boys are talking, and this guy says he's going to tell something that happened this past Sunday at church." Travis's rapid-fire delivery, voice inflection, and obvious joy in telling a story displayed how he had matured as an entertainer. The story begins with the preacher in a creek for a baptism:

> He asks everyone to bow their head, he starts to pray, and I see this guy coming over the hill, he falls down; it's apparent to me he's drunk. I keep watching him. He falls down, gets up, falls down. He ends up in the water with the preacher. And nobody notices this. Preacher says, "Amen." Everyone raises their head; this drunk has ended up right beside him. Preacher turns to him and says, "Are you ready to find Jesus?" The drunk looks sort of strange and he says, "I guess." So he grabbed him and shoved him under the water, pulled him back up and said, "Did you find Jesus?" The drunk's a little out of breath; he says, "No." The preacher looked a little strange at that point, grabbed him again, and shoved him back under the water and held him a bit longer. Pulled him back up and said, "Did you find Jesus?" And the drunk says, "Nooo." Now, the preacher is mad at this point. He grabs this guy, shoves him in the water—I know he held him forty-five seconds; I thought he'd drown him. Pulled him back up, said, "Did you find Jesus?" and the drunk says, "Are you sure this is where he fell in?"[30]

Both his sense of humor and natural politeness showed the night he appeared on *Late Night with David Letterman* in February. He brought guitarist Ronald Radford with him for the performance of "Better Class of Losers." In constant motion while singing, he moves with the music, emphasizing certain notes, always smiling. After finishing the song, he says, "Thank you," lays down the mic, and walks with Letterman to the next sound stage, where they both sit down. Letterman dials a radio station while explaining to Travis, "I want you to get on there and ask them if they can play one of your songs." Letterman says into the receiver, "Hang on a second. I want you to talk to somebody," and hands the phone to Travis, who says, "Hi. Now what I'm calling for is to see, have you already played 'Better Class of Losers' for Dave?"

Letterman pressures him, "Tell her to get it in there." Travis, being a good sport, cheerfully and smoothly says, "If you would, go ahead and play it if you haven't already. If you did, I sure do appreciate it, and I'll turn it back over to Dave now." Taking the phone, Letterman tells the radio deejay, "You play that record, we'll send you a hundred bucks." Travis—understanding the illegality of a "payola" request—falls back in his chair, laughing, stamping his feet and clapping his hands. Letterman hangs up the phone and tells Travis, "Can I do that or not? Can't hurt." Letterman then announces, "The new Randy Travis album, *High Lonesome*, and unless I miscounted, you wrote or cowrote at least five of these songs." Travis acknowledges he wrote three with Alan Jackson and two with Don Schlitz.[31]

While most country bands had a frontman to sing a few songs and warm up the crowd, Travis did not. His "Nashville" band arranged a two- or three-minute music intro to open each concert. "Each year we would change it a bit," recalls steel guitarist Gary Carter. "One year I came up with the idea of doing a montage as an intro. We did ten- to fifteen-second intros of his hits, specially arranged, and then Randy would walk out."[32]

The band members believed Travis would enjoy more opportunities to hang out with them. They acknowledged that Hatcher was "a great businesswoman" but thought she could be less controlling. Monty Parkey's most memorable times with Travis were working out at the gym. "That was the only time he could really get away," Parkey says. Travis would sometimes show up at sound check, saying, "I gotta get away from that woman. She's driving me crazy." His sidemen remember how much he loved to sing. Tom Rutledge recalls, "I'd be sitting there with a guitar, and he'd start singing songs he used to sing in the clubs—he loved to make music." Parkey gave notice that he would be leaving the band when the current tour ended in mid-May. It was the first band change in almost two years. He had been filling in with Alan Jackson's band after that keyboard player's surgery, transferring his equipment between the Travis and Jackson buses. He enjoyed working with Travis and considered him "one of the nicest men I've met in this business." He accepted Jackson's offer of employment because the time seemed right to make the change. Parkey felt Travis would quit touring at some point, based on occasional comments about needing to "quit for a while." During their last show together, Travis expressed regret at losing Parkey, who recalls, "He said a lot of nice things he didn't need to say."[33]

For the first time since Travis's Warner Bros. debut, there was no album of new music in 1992. Instead, the record company released two volumes of hits in September, *Greatest Hits, Volume One* and *Greatest Hits, Volume Two*. Each contained a newly recorded song to entice fans to buy the album. "If I Didn't Have You" and "Look Heart, No Hands" were released as singles, and both rose to number one on *Billboard*. Travis fell in love with "If I Didn't Have You" when he heard the demo. "It was a wonderful, wonderful tune," he recalled. "I thought for sure radio would play that. And I was right, luckily." He had a different reaction to hearing "Look Heart, No Hands." He said, "It was good, but I wasn't real sure of it, and was talked into recording it, by Martha and Kyle. Turns out I'm glad I did, but it was one of those that had to grow on you."[34]

"If I Didn't Have You" hadn't quite topped the chart when Travis made an unannounced appearance at the CMA Awards on September 30. As George Jones finished singing "I Don't Need Your Rockin' Chair," Travis walked up behind him, grabbed him by the arm, and spoke into the standing mic: "There's nobody, sitting at home watching tonight or nobody in this audience that wants to see you retire to your rocking chair, by any means. But—*but*, we do want you to enjoy being the next member of the Country Music Hall of Fame." He held out a plaque, which Jones accepted with a disbelieving shake of the head. Following Jones's thank-you speech, they walked off the stage together.[35] Travis flew to Washington, DC, on December 3 to receive the Bob Hope Entertainment Award at the USO Christmas Celebration. The engraved trophy displayed a glass globe and an eagle to represent his years of performing for American troops around the world. As he recalled later, "I was introduced to General Norman Schwarzkopf and General Colin Powell, the victorious military leaders, as well as Dick Cheney and other political leaders. It was a magical evening, and I was humbled to be the honoree that everyone had gathered to acknowledge."[36]

Then it was off to Las Vegas to the Celebrity Room at Bally's for five 10:30 p.m. shows during National Finals Rodeo week in mid-December. The ten-day competition to determine world rodeo champions brought thirty thousand spectators to town, most of them country music fans. From his Ben-Hur suite at Bally's, Travis could look down on the Las Vegas Strip and see billboards advertising such fellow country stars as Dolly Parton, Reba McEntire, and Ricky Van Shelton. Looking across the living room in his suite, he told a reporter he used to play clubs that could have fit inside the room. His dream back then was to play the Grand Ole Opry. The thought of Las Vegas never occurred to him.[37]

Before the final Saturday show, Travis's six musicians gathered in the living room. This was the traditional annual event where the Travises invited the band to their suite, provided celebratory appetizers, and handed out Christmas bonuses. On the way to the suite, bass player Rocky Thacker and drummer Tommy Rivelli joked about how they hated to have to go there and pick up that check. It was a jovial atmosphere. The mood quickly changed when Travis stood at one end of the room, looked around at each of the faces, and said, "Boys, this is the hardest thing I've ever had to do." Nobody made a sound as he explained he was worn out and needed to take a year or so off. Hatcher jumped in to say that Travis would be working in movies and would return to music after getting some rest. Neither mentioned that they had told Jeff Davis of their plans several months earlier. The three of them had been working to bring the touring machine to a halt. Travis said later, "Several of the guys' heads dropped. Some had tears in their eyes. Most nodded their heads a bit, giving me the impression they understood my decision, but the news was hard on them."

They did understand. "He was burned out," Rivelli recalls. "We'd work six weeks, be off six weeks, but not Randy. Lib had his ass. I applaud him for having that strength, finally, to take hold of the reins." Thacker says, "He was doing interviews and talk shows and stuff. He was busy all year long." Thacker remembers the room got silent, and Hatcher was crying. The news was a punch in the gut to steel guitarist Gary Carter, who had been the bandleader for the past several years, since Drew Sexton's departure. He and Thacker were the only two musicians left from the original band of April 1986. "It hit us as a complete surprise," Carter says. "I'm sure there were people, higher up the chain than the band, that knew about it, but I found out that night." He wondered why Travis hadn't mentioned it to him, considering the amount of time they spent together. Travis usually slept on the bus instead of in a motel room, and Carter picked him up each morning. They would find a gym in every new town. They and Thacker worked out almost every day while on the road. About his boss's decision to take time off, Carter says, "Everybody knew he was getting burned [out]. You could see it. He got to the point where it didn't look like he was enjoying it." The meeting ended with hugs and a few tears. "That night in Vegas we played our last show together," Travis recalled. "It was one of the best, yet most difficult, shows we'd ever done." Thacker concurs: "It was a rough night."[38]

The Travis entourage flew from Las Vegas to Los Angeles to appear Monday night on *The Tonight Show with Jay Leno* at NBC Studios in Burbank. After the show, Rutledge remembers, they stood in the parking lot, where a limo waited to take the Travises to their hotel. The band was headed to the airport for a red-eye flight home. Rutledge thanked Travis for the opportunity to work for him. Travis shook his hand and said, "You're the best acoustic guitar player I've ever worked with. You play what I like to hear, and I want you to know I've really appreciated it." Rutledge has carried those words with him, explaining, "You don't usually get to hear that from the artists you work with."[39]

In the hotel suite meeting, Travis had promised his sidemen four months' severance pay, saying, "If you pick up another job next week, that's great, but you are still going to get paid by me."[40] Lead guitarist Ronald Radford found a job immediately. A friend of his was playing bass with the Marshall Tucker Band in a casino across the street from Bally's. The friend got him a job with that band. "I went from one to the other," Radford says, "and everything worked out great. Of course, I missed working with Randy. That was a great, great job. Playing the big coliseums and the big outdoor stuff. It was nothing but big stuff."[41] Rutledge went to work in January with Brooks and Dunn. Carter joined Faith Hill, whose career was taking off as Travis's had seven years earlier. Carter also ran a successful home recording studio. Thacker and Rivelli were on their way to Hatcher's Sixteenth Avenue office to claim their last severance check when they got a call asking them to join John Anderson's band. They would stay there for twenty-six years.[42] The Travises ended 1992 in Hawaii. "Lib and I retreated to Maui, one of my favorite places on earth," Travis said. "Lib busied herself searching for and acquiring more property, and I enjoyed riding horses in the hills overlooking the turquoise-blue waters of the Pacific."[43]

# 9

## "IT'S SO COMPETITIVE NOW. AND THIS SCARES ME."

Travis had been touring steadily for seven years. By the beginning of 1993, his nine albums had sold more than sixteen million copies. His first five (not counting his Christmas album) went to number one on *Billboard*'s Top Country Albums chart. *Storms of Life*, *Old 8×10*, and *No Holdin' Back* were certified double platinum by the Recording Industry Association of America (RIAA). *Always and Forever* was eventually certified five times platinum (five million albums sold). Travis was in Hawaii when "Look Heart, No Hands" became his fourteenth number one on *Billboard*, where it stayed for two weeks in January. *Greatest Hits, Volume One* and *Volume Two* both went gold by selling five hundred thousand copies apiece.

The Travises usually spent December and January at their Maui vacation home. "I can't think of a better place to go and recuperate after you have been really hitting the road for a year," Travis said. "There's a lot of taking it easy."[1] In Nashville, the radio stations, newspapers, and his office were besieged with calls from fans asking if Randy Travis had retired. Evelyn Shriver issued a press release that said Travis and his wife were relaxing at their home in Hawaii until March. She informed fans that he was writing songs and considering acting roles while taking time off from the road. "This is not to be interpreted as a retirement from the music business," she said. "Randy has toured non-stop for the past seven years to audiences around the world."[2] One unspoken reason for the press release was to squelch a rumor that Travis had AIDS and had gone to Maui to die. "Yeah, I've heard I'm supposed to have AIDS," he told an interviewer.

"That I'm supposed to be gay, all this ridiculous stuff." He said he tried not to let it bother him: "I could live to be eighty years old, and when I die there are still going to be people that say, 'He must've had AIDS. I told you he was gay.'"[3]

The decision to stop touring became irrevocable when Jeff Davis finished selling Travis's buses, trucks, and sound/light equipment, followed by shutting down Special Moments Promotions. With the goal of making his way into the acting world, Travis signed a contract for exclusive representation by Creative Artists Agency (CAA), a Los Angeles–based organization that had recently opened a Nashville office. Hatcher described the new agreement as an opportunity to expand her husband's base to include other career offers. The adjustment to not touring took time. "I felt a little discombobulated, especially at first," Travis said later. He had to get used to not waking every morning in a different town for ten months of the year.[4]

Travis first dabbled in acting when he received an unexpected invitation for a screen test in 1987. "I've never acted before and I don't know whether I could or not," he said at the time, but the screen test "came out decent." The first script was about three cowboys who traveled together on the rodeo circuit. Travis would play a cowboy who, he said, "plays the lottery a lot and wins a million dollars. He goes to LA and gets took for all his money. That's about what I'd do, lose it all." Although that script didn't work out, Travis was chosen for a role in *Young Guns*,[5] a western about the adventures of Billy the Kid during the Lincoln County War in 1878. Travis flew to New Mexico to film his part. His character was listed in the credits as "Gatling Gun Operator." His lines ended up on the cutting room floor. He appeared briefly in the 1988 release, with only his back visible. His parents didn't see him when they watched the movie, leading him to comment, "So you *know* nobody else would recognize me. It was fun but it took three days to get two seconds on film." The experience whetted his appetite for doing more movies.[6]

He frequently read movie scripts but was reticent about taking on a major acting assignment. "We've been offered several scripts over the past few years, with parts ranging from a bum to a policeman," he told a reporter in 1990. "I turned them down because I thought if something was a failure and I was the main character, well, it wouldn't look too good." He made his television acting debut on NBC's comedy *Down Home*,[7] filmed in November 1990 and aired the following March. He played himself in the episode "Strange Bedfellows," where he visited a small Tennessee fishing town to seek solitude while writing new songs. Respecting his desire for anonymity, the regulars at the local café ignored him.[8]

In early 1992, he appeared on Andy Griffith's NBC-TV show, *Matlock*,[9] in an episode called "The Big Payoff." He played Billy Wheeler, a down-on-his-luck musician hired as a house painter. That was a dream come true for someone who watched reruns of *The Andy Griffith Show*. "Andy made me feel welcome and comfortable on the set," Travis said. "He was exactly what and who I had hoped he would be and the kind of person I wanted to emulate." Preparing for a scene in which Travis had to work himself into anger, Griffith came onto his bus to give the novice actor an informal acting lesson. "I was in awe of that," Travis remembered. "I almost laughed a few times when he was talking to me because it sounded so much like Sheriff Andy Taylor talking to Opie." Travis returned as Wheeler in an episode the following year.[10]

In 1993, no longer impeded by a touring schedule, he filmed five movies, four of which were westerns. The non-western was *At Risk*,[11] released in 1994, in which Travis played a homeless man who watched two friends waste away from AIDS. For that role, he grew a full beard. In *Frank and Jesse*,[12] he portrayed outlaw Cole Younger, which also required wearing a beard. Both times, the beard bothered him, and he shaved immediately after finishing the movie. *Frank and Jesse* starred Bill Paxton and Rob Lowe as notorious bank robbers Frank and Jesse James. In addition to his meaty supporting role, Travis enjoyed filming that movie because the director allowed him to do his own stunts. With his background in riding horses, target shooting, and practicing quick draws, Travis was in his element, even giving tips to his costars. "I think I was born too late," he said at the time. "I was probably meant to live back in those days."[13]

He had a cameo but no film credit in the 1994 big-budget film *Maverick*, based on an old James Garner television show.[14] The film credits of 1994's *Dead Man's Revenge* read "and starring Randy Travis,"[15] but as Marshal Harriman he appeared only twice, in the beginning to introduce his deputy marshal and at the end in the climax. The made-for-TV movie aired on the USA cable network the following April. *Outlaws: The Legend of O. B. Taggart* starred Mickey Rooney as a reformed bank robber trying to recover stolen gold while hindered by his three sons, one of whom was Travis.[16] The cast was a collection of Hollywood greats, with the script supposedly written by Rooney. Travis showed up the first day having memorized everybody's lines, as he thought he was expected to do. He spoke his lines, and Rooney responded with dialogue that Travis didn't recognize as being from the script, so he didn't know what to say. Seeing Travis staring at him, Rooney asked, "Do you know when to talk?" "Not really." Rooney said, "When I stop." Telling that story at one of his concerts, Travis concluded, "We pretty much made the whole movie up." After its debut at the National Cowboy Hall of Fame in Oklahoma City on February 14, 1995, Travis commented, "Thankfully, most people were out to dinner for Valentine's Day instead of in the audience."[17]

The movie he wanted everyone to see was his own comedy drama, *Wind in the Wire*, a made-for-TV western filmed in mid-1992.[18] Coproducers were Mark Kalbfeld and Lib Hatcher, who also received credit as executive producer under the name of Elizabeth Travis. Funding came from Warner Bros., the Travises, and a variety of other sources. Jim Shea, with whom Travis had worked on several music videos, wrote and directed the movie. Hatcher made numerous phone calls to convince their actor friends to participate: Burt Reynolds, Chuck Norris, Denver Pyle, Dale Robertson, Lou Diamond Phillips, and Melanie Chartoff. Travis played a singer named Buck who dreamed of being in a Wild West flick. The movie was a behind-the-scenes filming of a western movie, not the western itself. It gave Travis many opportunities for singing, being a cowboy, and getting into fights. His character was hired to find a group of cowboys to go to Hawaii to teach cattle ranching. "It really happened, y'know," Travis explained to Ralph Emery in a May 1993 interview. "They had a lot of cows on the islands, and they didn't know what to do with them." When Emery asked how the cattle got there in the first place, Travis didn't know. He'd read some of the history, about cattle running everywhere and Spanish vaqueros teaching the Hawaiians how to care for them.

To make it appear that Buck was traveling in his search for cowboys to take to Hawaii, parts of the film were shot in New Mexico and Colorado, with other scenes on a buffalo ranch in South Dakota, the Triple Seven Ranch. "We filmed buffalo herds and buffalo stampedes," says Shea's business partner and brother-in-law, Gerry Wenner, who served as director of photography. "We were lucky we didn't get killed." He marvels at Travis's ability to ride and perform stunts. "Randy and Lib treated us really well," Wenner says. "We stayed in nice places and had a great time." He remembers Hatcher as being serious and controlling when it came to ensuring everything went the way she wanted it. Shea, Travis, and Hatcher huddled together to discuss the filming and rewriting throughout the project.[19]

On August 17, 1993, a week before the movie was shown on ABC-TV, Warner Bros. released the ten-song soundtrack to *Wind in the Wire*. In the liner notes, Travis writes, "Thanks to Jim Ed Norman for helping make this possible." While it might be unusual for an artist to thank the label head, this was an unusual album. Travis had made so much money for Warner Bros. Records that Norman was apparently willing to take a risk and provide funds to support Travis's dream of a western album and movie. Warner Bros. had recently created an imprint called Warner Western, following the unexpected success of Michael Martin Murphey's 1990 album, *Cowboy Songs*, the first album of cowboy music to achieve gold status since 1959's *Gunfighter Ballads and Trail Songs* by Marty Robbins. Travis seemed to be a good contender to profit from that new trend.

"It's different than anything I've done before," he told Emery. "I've never recorded western music, although I grew up listening to western music." It was the first album Travis did without Kyle Lehning as producer. Busy with his new job as president of Asylum Records, Lehning recommended their mutual friend Steve Gibson to produce the album. Gibson, who played guitar on all of Travis's albums, had produced Murphey's *Cowboy Songs*. He flew to Maui to set up the recording session and was pointed to the well-equipped studio of jazz guitarist George Benson. "Coming from an environment like Nashville," he explains, "you go into a studio with the knowledge that all musicians are not only the best at their craft, but they understand how the process works." The Hawaiian musicians had never recorded in a studio, and no one explained the process to them. There wasn't time to teach them because Travis was usually on location in the mountains, shooting the movie. Gibson and Travis eventually decided they would have to make the record in Nashville, and Gibson headed home to work on it there.

The new Warner Western imprint was fortuitous for Texas songwriter Roger Brown, who had moved to Nashville a decade earlier. He and Rick Peoples wrote "Memories of Old San Antone" for fun, knowing a western song wasn't commercially viable. Upon hearing the demo, Brown's publisher told him not to write any more of that kind of music. Then Warner Western happened. And Brown's publisher wanted to know if he could write more songs like that. Absolutely! He and Luke Reed, an Oklahoma cowboy, started writing cowboy songs. Brown received a phone call out of the blue from Martha Sharp's assistant, who wanted to know if Brown could change "Memories of Old San Antone" to a song about Santa Fe. He also asked the question songwriters love to hear: "Do you have anything else?" Brown answered yes to both questions. Changing the title to "Memories of Old Santa Fe" required several rhyme changes. He also changed "land of the Navajo" to "land of the Sioux and Crow." When notified that Travis would be recording four of his songs, Brown recalls, "You could have knocked me over with a feather. To get one cut on somebody like that was a great accomplishment. But to get four at once was mind-blowing."

To put that in perspective, a look back at previous albums indicates that Travis, Don Schlitz, and Paul Overstreet never had more than two or three songs apiece. The one exception was *High Lonesome*, with five cuts cowritten by Travis and four by Alan Jackson. For a new writer to have four songs on an album showed the scarcity of original western music in Nashville. When word got around that "Brown got four Randy Travis cuts, pretty quick," it legitimized the unknown songwriter. The experience changed Brown's life, most importantly because he and Travis then wrote songs together and became friends.

Travis and Emery discussed all ten soundtrack songs during their interview. The title track, "Wind in the Wire," was about a cowboy riding the range and hearing the wind in the barbed wire as he bedded down for the night, reminding him of the open range of the old days, when the wire wasn't there and cattle and buffalo roamed free. The Warner Bros. personnel who chose which singles to release were in a quandary over this album despite its high quality. "We didn't have anything that would go to country radio as a product they could sell as a Randy Travis record," Gibson recalls. "Randy picked songs he liked, and I picked a few I thought were good old traditional western pieces. We made the record, and Warner Bros. promotion people said there's nothing here we can use."[20] Travis lacked the audience for a western album. While Michael Martin Murphey was immersed in cowboy culture and had an entire community to buy his cowboy album, Travis's audience was mainstream country music. "Cowboy Boogie" and "Wind in the Wire" were released as singles. Travis later said, "*Wind in the Wire*, my eighth album for Warner Bros., was the absolute worst-selling record I did for them. We didn't even chart a single from it higher than number forty-six on the U.S. music charts." But he had fulfilled his dream of a western movie and western album.[21]

By the time those singles were released, Travis had almost completed his next album, *This Is Me*, which he and Lehning had started recording the previous November. "There are some songs on here a little more rowdy, I guess you'd say, than what we normally do," Travis said. "But we were able to find beautiful ballads, too. An interesting combination of tunes. I'm real happy with it. I hope people like it." With new technology, the format for this and future albums was a CD (compact disc) in addition to, and eventually instead of, a cassette tape.

The first of the album's four singles, "Before You Kill Us All," reached number two on *Billboard*. "It's really different from anything we've done before, instrumentation-wise," Travis said. "It's good to experiment once in a while, totally from left field." They definitely experimented with the video, which placed Travis in a cartoon setting, mourning the rejection of his girlfriend. "I like songs that are humorous but written about a sad subject, kinda like 'Before You Kill Us All,'" he said. The second single, "Whisper My Name," topped the chart. "This Is Me" peaked at number five and "The Box" at number seven. Travis wrote the latter with Buck Moore, about a father who loved his son but couldn't say so. He showed his love by saving family mementos that no one knew about until he died, and they opened the box. "That song tore me up almost every time I sang it," Travis commented. It reminded him of his fractured relationship with his dad.[22]

"I wondered if radio still wanted to play what I was doing," Travis said after *This Is Me* was released on April 26, 1994. "It's so competitive now. And this scares me." He needn't have worried. Reviewers hailed it as his best album since his bombshell debut, *Storms of Life*.[23]

The MGM Grand Las Vegas was the largest hotel complex in the world when it opened on the Las Vegas Strip in December 1993. The building's green "Emerald City" exterior signaled its *Wizard of Oz* theme and the memorabilia to be found inside. The Travises and Jeff Davis had visited the construction site a few years earlier as guests of Richard Sturm, who headed the hotel's entertainment division. Sturm told Travis, "When this gets built, I want you to be the first country artist to perform here." Sturm kept his word. Travis got the call in late 1993 while filming *Frank and Jesse* in Arkansas. He agreed to a four-day weekend in February, even though he had no band, crew, set design, or production manager, and only three months to put a show together. Hatcher called Jeff Davis, knowing he was managing another artist, and said, "It won't be the same going out there without you." Davis replied, "Well, you don't have to." She told him they needed help putting the band back together and building a crew. Davis assured her, "I've always done that for you. I'd be honored to do that again."

Davis and Lehning organized a band that was a mixture of permanent and temporary players. David Johnson immediately returned with his fiddle. Most of the others from the original band were committed to new employers. Acoustic guitarist Mark Casstevens remembers Davis coming into the studio one November day and asking, "How many of you would like to go on the road with Randy?" Everybody initially said yes, but the reality of losing their spots in the highest echelon of session playing, which they'd worked so hard to attain, kept most of them from taking time away from the studio. Casstevens, wanting to back out gracefully, named a price he thought would be too high. Travis accepted, and Casstevens went on the road to cover harmonica, acoustic guitar, and banjo on the upcoming tour. Drummer Paul Leim cherished his lucrative session work but thought touring with Travis for a short time would be exciting. "I'd go out for five days," he says, "get to play with Randy live, and that will be the end of it, right? Of course, it lasted a lot longer than that." Lehning played piano during the opening weekend in Las Vegas, and Tom Rutledge returned temporarily on acoustic guitar. Doing his first major performance in fourteen months, and with a new band, "scared the heck out of me," Travis told an interviewer. "I'm always nervous before I go onstage, and after the first two songs I usually settle down. Well, this took three quarters of the show before I started to feel good."[24]

He was on the road again. The Houston Livestock Show and Rodeo in Texas came next, followed by the Warner Bros. showcase during Nashville's Country Radio Seminar the first week in March. Hundreds of fans poured to the front of the stage to take photos, offer flowers and gifts, and stretch out their hands toward him. Travis was truly being welcomed back. The show was billed "An Evening with Randy Travis and Special Guests." One of those guests was David Ball, who had come a long way since sitting at that stoplight in Mount Pleasant, South Carolina, and hearing "On the Other Hand" on the car radio. He'd moved to Nashville, signed with Warner Bros., and recorded "Thinkin' Problem," a song he wrote with Allen Shamblin, writer of "He Walked on Water."[25]

In April, Travis appeared on the Opry to promote the release of *This Is Me*. He asked former band members Drew Sexton and L D Wayne, who worked on the Opry in Porter Wagoner's band, the Wagonmasters, to back him on "Before You Kill Us All" and "The Box." Wayne then discussed with Wagoner the possibility of him and Sexton touring with Travis. Wagoner magnanimously agreed, offering to use substitutes when scheduling conflicts arose.[26]

Travis told a reporter, "I love the audience, I love the music, I love to sing. I've missed it a lot. But I don't miss the road. We are going to tour some this year, but I'm never going to tour all year long again." When asked if he was shooting his career in the foot, he replied, "Well, it's my foot. I can shoot it if I want to." Having won fifty-eight awards, he acknowledged his role in bringing traditional sounds back to country music. "I was a part of it," he said. "George Strait had a lot to do with it. He was selling half a million records; that was unheard of in those days." He mentioned John Anderson and Reba McEntire singing traditional country music. "Then I came along and was at the right place at the right time," he added with his usual modesty. "I had the right songs come my way, I had great management, the record label was behind me, and I had great press. It just came together."²⁷

He saw two of those three performers the following week at the Los Angeles Universal Amphitheatre, where he presented the Career Achievement Award to John Anderson at the 1994 Academy of Country Music Awards. Travis looked distinctly non-western, except for his boots, which were almost covered by the long trousers of his tan business suit that appeared two sizes too large. His longer hair looked thick and windblown. Travis called Anderson "an early new traditionalist" when summarizing the honoree's life and career. Anderson had first met Travis in the late 1970s when Lib Hatcher and Randy Traywick came to see his show in Georgia. The Florida native couldn't yet afford a band, and his singles didn't reach the top ten. Hatcher booked him into her club, where Traywick led the house band. Within a few years, Anderson had his first number one *Billboard* hits with "Wild and Blue" and "Swingin'."

By the time of the ACM Career Achievement Award, Anderson had had an illustrious career. For the past year, he'd had two of Travis's former sidemen in his band, Rocky Thacker on bass and Tommy Rivelli on drums. "I didn't know what was up," Anderson says about that night. "I knew there must be a reason they had me out there. Because I wasn't presenting or performing." Then Travis came onstage. "That particular award was for inspiring younger people to move into country music," Anderson says. "I find it fitting that Randy was the one who handed it to me. That was a real honor, especially after such a huge star he became. That was a big, big night for me."²⁸

Travis spent the next few months on the road, with "*This Is Me* and I'm Back" the title of his summer tour. By now, the new eight-piece Randy Travis Band, no longer called "Nashville," had come together. Joining L D Wayne, Sexton, Johnson, Casstevens, and Leim were Steve Mandile on acoustic guitar, Steve Hinson on steel, and Paul Fulbright on bass. After three shows at the MGM Grand Las Vegas, a chartered Gulfstream II jet whisked them to Salem, Oregon, for a sold-out Labor Day show at the Oregon State Fair and then to Los Angeles for *The Tonight Show with Jay Leno*. "We did shows in three states in just over twenty-four hours," Travis said. "It was life in the fast lane, and we were riding high again." Casstevens recalls, "Everywhere we went, they loved him. You could see him juiced up and energized. He still had it, and he was accepted." Wayne describes a three-tier operation: "The band is doing their best to play for the wonderful vocalist, and the crew makes our job easy. They set up the stage, tear it down, tune instruments, run monitors, provide sound and lighting, and drive trucks." Years later, Wayne says, "The Randy Travis tour was a well-oiled machine. Randy, band, and crew were a great family and still are to this day." Hinson says, "That was the only band I was ever in that didn't have a bandleader, because we didn't need one. We didn't have to teach anybody anything."

Throughout his career, Travis usually closed his shows with Mickey Newbury's "American Trilogy," a medley made famous by Elvis Presley and consisting of three eighteenth-century songs: "Dixie," "All My Trials," and "The Battle Hymn of the Republic." When Casstevens started touring with Travis, he noticed there was always a huge cheer when the medley began, and he would think, *Randy's really killing it*. After the fourth show, he happened to turn around and see that an American flag had been lowered, covering the entire backdrop. "I had to laugh," he says. "Not only was I unaware we were carrying that huge flag to each show, but I had not understood why there was always a standing ovation at that point."

The band's favorite insider line was, "It is Hoss, ain't it?" They might be backstage, and Travis would look at Wayne and ask, "So who are you?" Then he'd say, "Oh, I know. L D Rick Wayne Hoss Money." He'd pause and add, "It is Hoss, ain't it?" They used the line on each other, and it never failed to crack them up. Casstevens says, "I loved to break up Randy on sessions. I might ask him a question and then say, 'Now is that true, Hoss? It is Hoss, isn't it?' He loved that. He would do it to me, too." All were amazed by Travis's repertoire. "I bet he knew the words and could sing ten thousand songs," Lehning says. "I used to love his sound check. Because he never played his songs. He would play Haggard and Lefty Frizzell and Hank Senior. He had this entire catalog in his soul, in his brain." Band members could call out songs, and he would know them. He was more than just a performer and songwriter. Hinson says, "He loved to sing more than anybody I ever worked for."[29]

Charlie Monk, Lib Hatcher, and Randy Travis at the Nashville Palace, early 1985. (Randy Travis photo collection)

Randy Travis, with manager Lib Hatcher and fan club president, Jill Youngblood, welcoming fans to his first Fan Fair booth, mid-June 1985. The sign announces, "Randy Travis will be appearing at the Nashville Palace," where Travis and Hatcher were both still employed. (Randy Travis photo collection)

Lib Hatcher and Randy Travis, circa summer 1985. (Randy Travis photo collection)

Filming the cover for *Storms of Life* debut album at Flynns Lick, Tennessee, circa late 1985. Randy Travis with store owner and neighbors. (Randy Travis photo collection)

Little Jimmy Dickens introduced Randy Travis for his Grand Ole Opry debut, March 7, 1986. (Randy Travis photo collection)

Three of five nominees for the Academy of Country Music's New Male Vocalist of the Year Award at Knott's Berry Farm, in the Goodtime Theater, April 14, 1986: T. Graham Brown, Randy Travis, and Keith Whitley. (Randy Travis photo collection)

Randy Travis and Roy Rogers prior to their *Nashville Now* appearance, June 23, 1989. (Randy Travis photo collection)

Randy Travis holds his four *Music City News* awards (out of four nominations): Male Artist of the Year, Star of Tomorrow, Album of the Year, and Single Record of the Year, June 8, 1987. (Randy Travis photo collection)

Randy Travis with Johnny Carson on the set of *The Tonight Show Starring Johnny Carson*, August 1989. Judge Honeycutt was watching the show at his home in North Carolina when Travis told Carson the "bring your toothbrush" story. (Randy Travis photo collection)

## A Day Off

Travis riding a camel in Cairo, Egypt, during the 1989 USO tour. (Dan Markley photo collection)

Randy Travis with four US Park Police officers who escorted his vehicle to the Washington Monument and the White House in the District of Columbia, April 5, 1990. (Randy Travis photo collection)

Jeff Davis, Randy Travis, Tom O'Neill, Elizabeth Hatcher, and Charles Bishop at the White House to visit President George H. W. Bush. Washington, DC, April 5, 1990. (Randy Travis photo collection)

Andy Griffith and Randy Travis on the set of NBC-TV show *Matlock* in 1992. (Randy Travis photo collection)

Traywick family. Standing: David, Randy, Ricky, and Dennis. Seated: Sue, Harold, and Rose. Circa 1998. (Rose Arrowwood photo collection)

Randy Travis fishing at Lodge Island Winchester in Wisconsin in 2000, as guest of friend Ray Hillenbrand. They fished for muskie, walleye, and pike. (Randy Travis photo collection)

Route 590 in the Pocono Mountains buckled and collapsed under Travis's 1997 Prevost XL bus while en route to Caesar's Pocono Resort in Lakeview, Pennsylvania. Two tow trucks with cranes worked for more than four hours to get the bus out of the mud-filled ditch, one lifting from each end. March 7, 2004. (Randy Travis photo collection)

Randy Travis (far right) leaving Grayson County jail with unnamed escort and Gary Corley on August 9, 2012. Sherman, Texas. (Photo credit: Chris Jennings/*Herald Democrat*)

Randy Travis's 1998 Pontiac Trans Am at Travis ranch. (Diekman photo collection)

Randy Travis, dressed in a Nashville Palace chef outfit, surprises John Hobbs at his ninetieth birthday party, February 11, 2018. (Barrett Hobbs photo collection)

Marshville, North Carolina, welcome sign, September 2019. (Diekman photo collection)

Randy Travis at Ernest Tubb Record Shop in Nashville to sign copies of *Forever and Ever, Amen: A Memoir of Music, Faith, and Braving the Storms of Life*, November 12, 2019. (Terry Tyson photo collection)

Randy and Mary Travis with Mary's children Cavenaugh Beougher and Raleigh Beougher, attending the CMT Artists of the Year event at the Schermerhorn Symphony Center in Nashville, Tennessee, October 13, 2021. (Debby Wong/ZUMA Press Wire)

Randy Travis with James Dupré, Diane Diekman, Lorraine Paver, and Perry Steilow, backstage at *Music of Randy Travis Show*. Corn Palace in Mitchell, South Dakota, August 28, 2022. (Diekman photo collection)

Randy Travis with little brother Dennis Traywick and cousin Ronnie Traywick, backstage at *A Heroes & Friends Tribute to Randy Travis: 1 Night. 1 Place. 1 Time*. Von Braun Center in Huntsville, Alabama, October 24, 2023. (Diekman photo collection)

Mary and Randy Travis, during testimony at the House Committee on the Judiciary's Subcommittee on Courts, Intellectual Property, and the Internet hearing for "Radio Music and Copyrights: 100 Years of Inequity for Recording Artists." Rayburn House Office Building in Washington, DC, June 26, 2024. (Photo credit: Rod Lamkey/CNP/Sipa USA/Alamy Live News)

# "HE SIGNED AUTOGRAPHS UNTIL THE PLACE WAS EMPTY."

Travis called himself a singer who enjoyed acting and wanted to do more of it. When an interviewer asked in 1995 what stage he was at in his film and television career, Travis smiled and said, "The beginning stage." He added, "I'm at the earn-while-you-learn stage. I don't fool myself into thinking I'm a great actor." He especially liked working in westerns, saying, "I was raised on a horse, and I've been practicing quick draw since I was a kid. That stuff I thought I was wasting my time with finally came in handy." Singing still came first. "There's nothing like performing before a live audience," he often said.[1]

He loved interacting with fans. Kyle Lehning says, "I've been with him hundreds of times, and rarely were we able to go anywhere in public where he wasn't stopped for an autograph or a conversation. I never, ever saw him turn down a request." Lehning especially remembers attending a show in Las Vegas and sitting at a table near the stage in a crowd of fifteen hundred people. Performers Siegfried and Roy ended the show by saying, "And we want to thank our special guest tonight, Mr. Randy Travis." A spotlight shone on Travis, and people immediately began streaming down the aisles, napkins in hand for autographs. After twenty minutes, Lehning suggested it might be time to leave. Travis replied, "Yep, we'll leave in a minute." Twenty minutes later, Lehning suggested again, and Travis said, "Yeah, yeah, we're going to leave in a minute." Lehning looked at Hatcher and raised his eyebrows in question. She shook her head, letting him know this was one area in which she didn't control her husband. "He signed autographs until the place was empty," Lehning recalls. "I have no idea how long we sat there. He would say, 'What's your name and where are you from?' He was genuinely interested in them. When there was nobody left in the club, we went out through the kitchen, and he signed autographs for every busboy and dishwasher and cook in there."[2]

Travis tried his hand at a new project when he coproduced Daryle Singletary's self-titled debut album in 1995. He first heard Singletary on the demo of "Old Pair of Shoes," which Travis recorded for his *Greatest Hits, Volume One* album in 1992. Then several band members saw Singletary performing in a Nashville nightclub. Hatcher signed him to a management contract and worked to get him a record deal. The Georgia native spent the next several years occasionally opening shows and playing with Travis's band. He sang for Travis during rehearsals. Travis's friend James Stroud eventually signed Singletary to his Giant Records label. Their coproduction effort resulted in three hit singles: "I'm Living Up to Her Low Expectations," "I Let Her Lie," and "Too Much Fun." Producing one album was enough for Travis. He said he had a great time doing it but was too busy with his own career.[3]

Travis cowrote three songs for his twelfth Warner Bros. album, *Full Circle*, which he began recording in the spring of 1995. One he didn't write was Roger Miller's "King of the Road," which he had earlier recorded at the request of actor Bill Paxton, who wanted it for the opening credits of his cable TV movie *Traveller*. The two men had been friends since the filming of *Frank and Jesse*. Travis was hesitant to remake such a famous song by the quirky Miller. "You know it's kind of hard to redo a Roger Miller song," he said. "I'm intimidated doing somebody else's material, especially when you are doing material by somebody like Roger Miller. That's in the same league as trying to redo a George Jones song. I thought this was going to be used for the movie and other than that, nobody would hear it." Travis's cover not only made it onto his album but was later released as a single. When he started singing it live, his version was so well received that he included it in his regular show for years.

*Full Circle* was released on August 13, 1996. The origin of the fortuitous title is unknown, as it wasn't a song on the album and wasn't expected to be the end of anything. No one knew it would mark the end of Travis's recording relationship with Warner Bros. Mark Casstevens, who played on all the albums, later remarked, "How lucky I was. I got to be there from *Storms of Life* to *Full Circle*. I went full circle!"[4] Early reviews hailed *Full Circle* as one of the finest releases of 1996, with *Entertainment Weekly* saying, "His million-dollar chops have never sounded better."[5]

By the time Travis went on the road to promote the album, he and Hatcher had closed their Music Row gift shop and moved the bread truck, one of its most popular exhibits, into a storage building at Opryland. The tourist crowd had migrated from Music Row to downtown Nashville. Travis's increased touring pace caused Paul Leim to step down. He recommended his drum tech, Herb Shucher, as a replacement. The two drummers rehearsed the show, with Leim explaining how he played every song and the body cues to watch for. "As a drummer with an artist, you kind of become one with them when you're onstage," Leim says. "Herb did it for the next seventeen years. You don't stay with somebody like Randy Travis unless you're doing a great job."[6]

Warner Bros. released four singles from *Full Circle*, with all four stalling before they reached *Billboard*'s top twenty. "Talk about records that were great but didn't get a shot," Lehning says. He was especially disappointed that "Are We in Trouble Now?" written by Mark Knopfler of Dire Straits, didn't do better. The first and highest-ranking release, it died at number twenty-four.[7] They knew their songs and recordings were high quality, so why the poor sales and lack of radio play? Hatcher blamed Warner Bros. for inadequate promotion. Travis's contract was due for renewal, and Hatcher began talking to other record labels in search of better offers. In an early 1997 meeting with Warner Bros. executives, including label head Jim Ed Norman and country promotions director Bill Mayne, Travis presented the songs he wanted to record next. A label representative disagreed about which ones were best. Hatcher complained that she, Travis, and Lehning were having less say than before about which songs to release. The group got into an argument about how well the company was promoting Travis's music to radio. At one point Hatcher charged, "You don't believe in Randy as a songwriter." Norman and Mayne both denied Hatcher's claims that they had lost confidence in Travis and were no longer promoting him. They pointed out that hurting his career would be hurting themselves. The meeting ended with a lot of hurt feelings. Travis was happy at Warner Bros. and proud of his track record but disappointed with the poor performance of *Full Circle*. He began to wonder if the cause could be lack of promotion. It frustrated him to have concertgoers ask when he was putting out a new album, and he would tell them he had just released one. In the end, as he explained to one reporter, "My contract was up, and we all decided I'd be happier going somewhere else."[8]

Travis and Hatcher were at the ACM Awards in Los Angeles in late April when James Stroud approached them. He and Travis had been friends ever since Stroud played drums on "Forever and Ever, Amen." He had signed Daryle

Singletary to his Giant Records label and coproduced the debut album with Travis. Now he headed the new DreamWorks Records Nashville label, whose owners included famous filmmaker Steven Spielberg and former Warner Bros. label head Mo Ostin. Stroud had pitched Travis as perfect for their new label. After twelve years and twelve albums with Warner Bros., Travis signed with DreamWorks Records Nashville. Although DreamWorks had built its reputation on making blockbuster movies, Travis's recording contract did not mention film. He wanted to keep his singing and acting careers separate, with his DreamWorks contract focused solely on music.[9]

In June he said he was holding four movie scripts and was getting offers after *Frank and Jesse* went on HBO.[10] The 1997 Francis Ford Coppola film, *The Rainmaker*, based on a John Grisham novel, gave Travis a bit part for which he was perfectly cast.[11] He portrayed a juror who flung himself over the top of the jury box to attack a lawyer who'd called him a liar. In the 1997 NASCAR TV movie *Steel Chariots*, he played a former race car driver turned preacher.[12] He had a small part in the Steven Seagal film, *Fire Down Below*,[13] He costarred as Sheriff Sheldon in the movie *T.N.T.*, about a tactical neutralization team of military commandos that comes to his town.[14] That movie gave him a chance to demonstrate his quick-draw skills. He narrated an animated children's home movie, *Annabelle's Wish*, for Christmas release on video.[15]

Travis coproduced his first DreamWorks album, *You and You Alone*, with Stroud and Byron Gallimore. As if indicating a return to his early hard country sound, the cover showed him sitting on a hay bale, his back against a wooden building, and playing his guitar. It was the first album in his career that did not contain a Travis-written song. "That's a little upsetting to me," he said, "but I didn't have time. Things have been so hectic over the last six months I can't think to write." The title track came from the pen of classic country performer Melba Montgomery and her cowriters. She and Vince Gill sang harmony on the recording. "I fell in love with it the first time I heard it," Travis said. "When that chorus came around, it knocked me out." Stroud remembers the initial session, with "The Hole" the first song recorded: "We had these great Nashville players running the song down, getting it right before Randy comes in. We have all done this for quite a while here in Nashville. Randy comes in and sings it for the first time. His voice filled the room. And when we stopped, these great professional musicians gave him a standing ovation. I have never seen that done in this town before. Never."

*You and You Alone* was released on April 21, 1998. Travis and those around him excitedly watched it climb *Billboard*'s country album chart. Within two months it was sitting at number seven. The first single, "Out of My Bones," reached number two on *Billboard* and went to number one on the *Radio & Records* chart. After his earlier feud with Warner Bros. executives, Travis felt vindicated. He had always thought choosing good material was one of his strong points. Signing with DreamWorks and having the first single reach number one proved he was right. Stroud pulled out all the stops to market the new album and its singles. For the Country Radio Seminar in March, the label rented Nashville's downtown Hermitage Hotel and temporarily renamed it the DreamWorks Hotel. Reporters asked about his comeback. Travis corrected them by saying he'd never left. He'd been touring, conducting interviews, and appearing on television talk shows. "I just was gone from radio for a while," he would explain. In that sense, he acknowledged, "It did feel like a comeback when we saw 'Out of My Bones' shoot up the charts as quick as it did."[16]

Two deaths rocked Travis's world in 1998. First came the news that Tammy Wynette had died at age fifty-five. For years she had suffered pain from gastrointestinal problems, but she always pushed through and continued performing. Her memorial service was held on April 9 at the Ryman Auditorium on a cold, windy day with two thousand fans waiting outside for several hours to fill the "Mother Church of Country Music." Travis was one of eight invited performers. He talked about touring with Wynette for the better part of five years, trading a lot of laughs and recipes. "I loved her sarcastic sense of humor," he said. "I'm so glad I could be here today, and I'll attempt to sing this song." Standing in front of an empty bandstand and her portrait, he delivered an a cappella performance of one of her favorite hymns, "Precious Memories." Not a sound was heard in the large auditorium, until the reverential applause as he walked offstage. Naomi Judd came on next. "As the years went by," she said, "we worked together. Randy and Wy and Tammy and I did a GMC tour. We'd park our buses side by side, and we'd eat together." The seventy-minute service concluded with Lorrie Morgan's rendition of "Stand By Your Man."[17]

Although Wynette's death was tremendously sad, it couldn't compare in intensity to the next one. Travis was in California, getting ready to appear at the Amerifest Music Festival in Indio, when his mother died of congestive heart failure on Thursday, May 21. The Travises immediately flew to North Carolina. Tim McGraw agreed to fill in for Travis on the show. Having suffered heart trouble in recent years, Bobbie Tucker Traywick no longer worked in the textile printing plant in Monroe. She celebrated her sixty-first birthday on May 16 with her family at a seafood restaurant in Charlotte. The night before her death, she and husband Harold went to a movie in Monroe. Her funeral was held at the Fountain Hill United Methodist Church in Peachland, and she was buried across the road in the Traywick family cemetery. Travis requested, in lieu of flowers, that donations be sent in her name to the American Tradition, a charity established by the Travises and actor Jon Voight to aid the poverty-stricken. Being with Harold at Bobbie's funeral brought back memories that made a difficult day even more difficult. Travis considered his mother a saint who had always "smoothed some of Daddy's rough spots." She had done her best to instill biblical values in her children, and she modeled grace and mercy. Now she was gone.[18]

Larke Plyler, who had remained a friend of the Traywicks over the years and was still employed by the Union County Sheriff's Office, served as Travis's bodyguard at Bobbie's funeral. "I stayed beside him during the funeral," Larke explains, "and tried to keep the gawkers off of him when they were coming through the visitation." Travis was hesitant to have Plyler move a person along, even those who were clearly there solely to meet a celebrity. Plyler would politely say something like, "The line's long and a lot of people have to get through. There will be other times for a chat." That made Travis apprehensive, despite it being obvious that the person might stand there for thirty minutes if not moved along. "He's such a gentleman," Plyler says, "so 'please and thank you,' 'yes sir,' always so welcoming."[19]

While recording *You and You Alone*, Travis was filming *Black Dog* with Patrick Swayze.[20] "I was in the studio one day, on the set the next, and touring in between," he recalled about that busy five-month period. On the first day of filming in Wilmington, North Carolina, Travis and Stroud walked past Swayze's trailer on their way to a studio on the set. Swayze came outside, and Travis introduced him to Stroud. As they walked off, Swayze said, "If you want me to sing some harmonies or something, let me know." By the time they reached the studio, they had decided to accept his offer. Swayze later came to Nashville to sing harmony on "I Did My Part." In the film, Swayze played a truck driver forced into hauling illegal weapons on a cross-country run. Travis, his sidekick, participated in numerous chase scenes, truck crashes, and attempts to outsmart the villain. Travis credits Swayze with helping him with his lines and with the action in his scenes. Swayze attended the *Black Dog* premiere in Nashville in April 1998, a few days after *You and You Alone* was released.[21] Travis said at the time, "I can't do acting jobs right now. I'm in the process of seeing radio stations, doing interviews, trying to promote *Black Dog* and *You*

*and You Alone* and doing shows. I want to do more acting in the future, but I don't want to do more of that than music. There is no feeling like standing onstage and working for a live audience and feeling that energy."[22]

Shortly after Travis's thirty-ninth birthday, an interviewer asked if success had changed him. "I hope I'm becoming a nicer person," he answered. "I was a mean kid. Even into my early twenties, I was not a nice guy. Extremely bad-tempered. I've been trying to keep that under control. That's something I'll always have to work on." He talked about the many fights, breaking and entering charges, trying to outrun the police, and lots of drugs and alcohol. "I was raised around a lot of fights, a lot of shouting and screaming," he said. "To me that was what life was. Meeting Lib helped me see a different kind of situation. Someone who actually tried to do good things for other people. She and music both made a huge difference in my life." Crediting his wife for management and scheduling skills, he said his job was to show up, answer questions, and remember the words to the songs.[23]

On September 24, 1998, the Travises went before a judge in Davidson County Circuit Court to legally change their names. Travis's petition read, "Petitioner is known to the members of the public by his professional name and desires to change his legal name so that his legal and professional name will be the same." After having signed documents with a variety of name combinations in past years, they acceded to the pressure of their accountant and business manager, Gary Haber, to make the legal change. Randy Bruce Traywick officially became Randy Bruce Travis and Mary Elizabeth Traywick became Elizabeth Travis.[24] Lib started calling herself Elizabeth around this time. Janice Azrak of Warner Bros. remembers struggling with that name change. "I called her Lib for a long time," she says.[25]

Canada passed an immigration law stating that anyone convicted of a crime might be "criminally inadmissible" and not allowed into the country. Pardons would be acceptable for nonviolent felonies. "We knew that was coming," Travis's office manager, Bill Sweeney, recalls. Canada had provided three years' notice before implementing the law. Travis, of course, had a 1977 felony larceny conviction on his record. Sweeney called Larke Plyler, at the time a captain with the Union County Sheriff's Office. Plyler said he thought he could get the governor to give Travis a pardon. Sweeney supplied information from the Travises as Plyler needed it. "Bill was my go-to guy," Plyler says. "I did the paperwork, worked on it so hard, and got the governor to give Randy a pardon for his crimes." Union County Sheriff Frank McGuirt wrote a letter on Travis's behalf. He remembered being in the courtroom more than twenty years earlier when young Traywick requested another chance. He and the other deputies had been skeptical and then surprised when Judge Honeycutt granted probation. During all those years, while legally prohibited from owning weapons, Travis enjoyed target shooting and gun ownership. On March 16, 1999, James B. Hunt Jr., governor of the state of North Carolina, issued a Pardon of Forgiveness for Randy Bruce Traywick AKA: Randy Travis. "It was a long process," Sweeney says, "but they got Randy a complete pardon. So he was allowed to own firearms and get into Canada."[26] A newspaper article announcing the pardon read, "It took a while for Randy Travis to make a name for himself in Nashville. It took a little longer to clear the name he made for himself in Marshville, N.C."[27]

Media coverage about the pardon included reminders of the troublemaker young Randy Traywick had been. In April the Marshville Board of Aldermen announced plans to remove the dilapidated fifteen-year-old signs reading "Home of Randy Travis, Country Music's Finest" that were located inside the town. They planned to build two timeless, classic signs on the edge of town that announced "Welcome to Marshville" and would promote the whole community instead of one person. They suggested they might later "find a better way to bring honor and praise to Mr. Travis."[28] Honor and praise came from Charlotte on May 14 when Travis was inducted as the twentieth member of the North Carolina Music and Entertainment Hall of Fame. State and local officials, radio personalities, friends, and relatives attended the private event in Spirit Square in uptown Charlotte. The event began with the ribbon cutting for the grand opening of the organization's new home. Paul Schadt, morning show host for 96.9 Radio, brought Travis onstage. A bronze bust and large portrait were unveiled, and Randy Travis Day was proclaimed in the state of North Carolina. The mayors of Marshville and Charlotte proclaimed Randy Travis Day in their cities as well. Travis performed a three-song acoustic set, with a standing ovation after each song. During a newspaper interview before the ceremony, a reporter asked why it had taken ten years for him to return to Charlotte for a performance. "I honestly don't know why," Travis answered, adding that he would try to get Charlotte on his tour schedule. A fan responded to the printed *Charlotte Observer* article by writing, "The answer might lie in the news media's continuing to emphasize his 'run-ins' with the law in his teens, rather than his rise to the top of his profession at an early age."[29]

Another article, with the rumor-mongering title of "Travis, Marshville Debunk Rumors of Rift," discussed the rumor that Marshville was miffed at him to the extent of removing the welcome signs that announced his hometown. "I've not done or said anything against Marshville," Travis told that reporter. "Every interview I've done has said I love to go home, and I'd do it more often if I could." Baffled that anyone might think he had a chip on his shoulder, he said, "If anything, I was rough on the folks when I was a kid. I was rougher on them than they were on me." A reader of that article wrote a letter to the editor and asked, "Who do city fathers of Marshville think they are, anyway? They should fly banners, send up balloons and write in the sky that Randy Travis is from their town! I wish Randy were from my hometown—I'd erect a huge sign in my front yard."[30]

Travis had just celebrated his fortieth birthday. Following the Charlotte ceremony, he headed to Raleigh, North Carolina, to kick off a fifty-date tour promoting *You and You Alone*. "The Hole" had reached number nine on *Billboard*, and "Spirit of a Boy, Wisdom of a Man" climbed to number two. Now he was promoting his fourth single, "Stranger in My Mirror," which eventually reached number sixteen.

Schadt remembers Travis always being willing to visit on the radio. "He was a funny guy," Schadt says. "A lot of people I don't think give him credit for his humor." He once brought Travis on the air as a local Randy Travis impersonator. The conversation begins with Schadt complimenting him on his singing and asking when he started doing Randy Travis. "I was doin' him before he was doin' him," Travis as impersonator says. "I should have been the one up there recordin', cuz I've been doing this for so many years. He just literally stole my style."

Schadt says, "You look a lot better than Travis looks, to begin with. So you could have been a bigger star than he is." Travis responds, "I knew that, too. I've been a vegetarian for a lot of years, and so my complexion is really good. And I got more hair and teeth than he does."

When Schadt asks if he has seen Travis act, the response is "Oh, my gosh, I've seen him try. I've seen him try. No doubt, this man is not a trained actor. He's probably just learned to read over the last couple of years or so. He's got problems that we'll never know about."

Finally, Schadt says, "Ladies and gentlemen, of course this *is* Randy Travis," and Travis tells him, "I was wondering how far we were going there!"

"I wanted to see how far you'd beat yourself up."[31]

# "WE ARE PROUD TO CALL SANTA FE OUR NEW HOME."

While on tour in New Mexico in 1990, Travis and Hatcher had fallen in love with Santa Fe. They liked its landscape, adobe architecture, and laid-back cowboy lifestyle. Walking through the town made them feel like they were in a western movie. They started talking about making a western album with an accompanying movie. *Wind in the Wire* was the result. By the end of 1998, the Travises were living in Santa Fe and looking for a permanent home. They found their ideal property along Avenida de Rey, west of Santa Fe. In August 1999 they purchased 209 acres from the King Brothers Ranch, a New Mexico general partnership owned by brothers Bruce, Sam, and Don King, who had built their family homestead into one of the most successful farming and ranching operations in New Mexico. Bruce had recently completed his third term as New Mexico's governor, making him the state's longest-serving governor. The Travises placed their Marrowbone home near Ashland City on the market in 2000 and sold it in 2001. They built an 8,750-square-foot pueblo-style ranch house on the Avenida de Rey property. Completed in 2002, it had ten fireplaces, a large kitchen and living room, a library, and a recreation room. The doors were hand-carved, with the wood beams of the kitchen ceiling covered in stitched leather. Elizabeth decorated the whole house in classic western style. They also built a guest suite and bus garage, along with a swimming pool and a building that looked like a traditional adobe chapel but contained a gymnasium, shooting range, and bowling alley.[1]

Instead of returning to Nashville to record his second DreamWorks album, Travis brought the producers and musicians to Stepbridge Studios in Santa Fe for a four-day session in February 1999. As with the first album, he coproduced *A Man Ain't Made of Stone* with Stroud and Gallimore. It also contained twelve songs, none written by Travis. In the video for the title track, Travis plays a character losing the woman he loves: "But all you ever wanted / was the one thing I never let you see / The tender side of me." The video ends with a surprising and emotional twist. When it appears he is giving his wife a bouquet of roses as a peace offering, he instead kneels at her grave. Travis's "Special Thanks" section in the accompanying booklet acknowledges his father, Harold Traywick, for input on the material in the CD and concludes, "Most of all, thanks to the person most responsible for this career, my wife and manager, Elizabeth Travis."[2]

*A Man Ain't Made of Stone* was released on September 21, 1999. "It shot out of the gates," Travis said, "with some well-written songs and a slightly different sound than people were accustomed to hearing from me. I was excited and felt as though I was starting my career all over again."[3] The *Tennessean*'s reviewer didn't exactly agree, although he thought the songs and voice were good. "Travis retains the rich, smooth voice that's made him one of the most easily identifiable country figures of the last twenty years," he wrote. "But the songs, and Travis, too often struggle against the tide of sound." He concluded, "With a voice as unique as Randy Travis's, it's senseless to camouflage it."[4]

While "camouflage" might be a bit strong for a description of the music, the promotion didn't measure up to that of the first album. "A Man Ain't Made of Stone" was released as the first single. It stalled at number sixteen on *Billboard*, and the following three singles failed to chart higher than number forty-eight. Travis was frustrated by the lack of promotion: "It's such a waste, when you put together an album with this quality of material, and you put out three singles and move on, it's like, man, so much work. Such great songwriting and it got wasted." He told one reporter, "My wife was going into stores in every town we went to, and the records were not there. The country division was new, and they didn't have the distribution in place. If the records weren't out there, you couldn't sell them."[5] DreamWorks Nashville Records was short-lived. The label contracted out distribution, changes occurred, and it was eventually sold. Travis found himself without a recording contract in 2000.

On his forty-first birthday, he was in Reno, Nevada, where he turned on the television and saw the Cerro Grande wildfire burning out of control in Los Alamos, New Mexico. The devastation astounded him. He later said, "Lib wondered from the beginning if there was anything we could do." Upon their return home, they visited the site. Travis recalled, "As we were riding through town, I was trying to think what people might have felt like or how they may have acted when they saw their homes and there was nothing left." Elizabeth said, "It was so sad seeing people out there going through the ashes." They quickly put together a benefit show to help the fire victims. "In two weeks, that's unheard of," Travis said. They held the benefit on Sunday evening, May 28, at the Santa Fe Opera Theater, which waived a ten-thousand-dollar rental fee to make its 2,128 seats available. Tickets to the sold-out show cost fifty dollars, with a limited number of two-hundred-dollar tickets that included a post-concert reception with the Travises.

Actress Ali McGraw introduced Travis. Governor Gary Johnson and his wife, Dee, attended the concert, as did Mayor Larry Delgado. Elizabeth organized a silent auction with three hundred donated items, including artwork from Santa Fe galleries. The following Wednesday, Travis presented the American Red Cross Santa Fe County Chapter with a check for $250,128, raised by the benefit to help fire victims. The Cerro Grande fire had burned forty-eight thousand acres, forced the evacuation of the town of Los Alamos, and destroyed more than four hundred homes.[6] "A lot of country music is about what people live through every day," Travis commented. "Something comes along like this, with so many becoming homeless, you love to help in any way you can." He added, "You're supposed to; it's your duty. If you're not using your success to help raise awareness, something's wrong."

On Friday, a full-page ad appeared in the *Santa Fe New Mexican*, titled "Forever and Ever Amen . . ." and offering "our heart-felt thanks to those of you in the community who without hesitation helped make this event a big success." Following a list of over two hundred names, it concluded with the signatures of Randy Travis and Elizabeth Travis next to the statement, "We are proud to call Santa Fe our new home."[7]

Also on Friday, a television movie that had been advertised around the country, *The Trial of Old Drum*, made its debut, appearing three times that evening on Animal Planet, a spinoff of Discovery Channel.[8] The four-year-old Animal Planet was geared toward a family audience and was the fastest-growing cable network in the United States.[9] Travis narrated *The Trial of Old Drum* as the adult version of eleven-year-old Charlie Jr., whose golden retriever stood trial in 1955 for killing sheep. The story was based on an 1870 court case, *Burden v. Hornsby*, that went all the way to the Missouri Supreme Court. Charles Burden sued for damages after his brother-in-law killed his favorite coon hound,

Old Drum, on suspicion of killing sheep. Lon Hornsby, the defendant, was represented by Tom Crittenden, who later became governor of Missouri and issued the reward that led to the death of Jesse James. The prosecuting attorney, George Graham Vest, had served in the Confederate Senate and would later serve in the US Senate. For his closing argument, he gave a "eulogy to the dog" that won the case and has become known as the source of the saying "A dog is man's best friend." Old Drum, the only dog in US history to stand trial in court, is immortalized in a statue on the courthouse lawn in Warrensburg, Missouri.[10]

In the Animal Planet movie, Old Drum belongs to the fictional Charlie Jr. and is shot but does not die. He is the defendant, on trial for his life. The characters of Burden, Hornsby, Crittenden, and Vest are named for their real-life counterparts. Vest, played by Scott Bakula, delivers the "eulogy to the dog" that was originally given in 1870. The jury finds Old Drum not guilty. Travis appears onscreen as the adult Charlie Jr. at the beginning of the movie and again at the end, where he stands in front of Old Drum's statue and explains how Mr. Vest's speech became famous. About the statue, his character says, "As for me, it's a tribute to the best friend I ever had."[11]

A fifty-city tour to promote *A Man Ain't Made of Stone* in the summer of 2000 included Travis's first-ever concert with a full symphony orchestra. In September the tuxedo-clad singer performed at the Hollywood Bowl with the Los Angeles Philharmonic at an event called "The Bowl Goes Country with Randy Travis." It was the orchestra's first formal collaboration with a country singer. There were a few rough spots in trying to find the right balance between the sixty-seven-piece orchestra and Travis's eight-piece band with its mighty amplifiers. Travis later said, "The sound on the stage was incredible as our band joined with some of LA's finest musicians to recreate a night of music we would always remember."[12]

Travis then began promoting his next album, *Inspirational Journey*. Released on October 31, 2000, it was his first gospel-style album. For four years he had wanted to record a gospel album, but other projects got in the way. The president of Atlantic Christian, Barry Landis, had asked Travis and Kyle Lehning to make an album for his new label, a division of Atlantic Records (owned by Warner Music Group). Travis recorded the album more for personal satisfaction than chart position. "We hoped to record country music with subtle Christian themes," he said about their song search. "We weren't thinking in terms of gospel music, but merely music with a message that would cause people to consider a relationship with God."[13] With titles like "Don't Ever Sell Your Saddle," the inspirational songs straddled the country and gospel genres. Travis cowrote three of the twelve cuts, including the country shuffle "The Carpenter," which Waylon Jennings and Jessi Colter recorded with him.

"The songs get the message across, but they're not hitting you over the head," Travis said during a television interview. "As Christians, we are supposed to live a certain way and I believe that very much and I try, although I fail as a lot of people do. It was important to me that these songs talk about those things without sounding like I am telling you this and you better do it."[14] The only traditional song was "Amazing Grace." It was his mother's favorite hymn, and she didn't live to hear him record it. "That was the only thing she asked me to please record, and although she got to hear some of the songs, I didn't do 'Amazing Grace' 'til close to the end," he told an interviewer. "Boy, I regretted it, too." The famous hymn was written in the 1700s by former slave trader John Newton. "God's power, love, and mercy turned Newton into a different quality of person," Travis said. "Although I couldn't explain it, I knew something like that had happened to me. God had changed my life for the better. Singing the lyrics of that song has become a testimony for me—and an overwhelming emotional experience every time I sing it."

The only song from the album to be released as a single was "Baptism," which Travis expected might be ignored by the same radio programmers who refused to play his traditional music because it was too country. "That is the dumbest remark I have ever heard," he said. "It irritates me to no end." The single entered *Billboard* at number seventy-five and was gone the next week. But it was well received at Travis's live shows. He could relate to the lyrics about a young man being baptized in a muddy river and relinquishing his old ways for a new life. "No matter where I performed it," Travis recalled, "when I reached the part of the lyric that said, 'down with the old man, up with the new,' the audience inevitably broke out in spontaneous applause."

Travis believed both country fans and religious folks would listen to *Inspirational Journey* out of curiosity. "It's a gospel album, but it's not heavily orchestrated or syrupy, and you can't completely take away the country in my voice," he explained. "Some of those who aren't normally that interested in country music—or in me—might be inclined to hear what I have to say about such things as getting baptized or calling on the Lord during hard times. At least, that's what I'm hoping for." He reiterated that he needed to get his temper under control. "I think I inherited that from my daddy," he told an interviewer.

"I'm doing the best I can. I know I'm gonna mess up, but I do repent and seek forgiveness. The Almighty understands that we are works in progress."[15] One of Elizabeth's former employees confirms that terrible temper by saying, "He could get wicked very quickly. He would throw a telephone at you if you looked at him sideways, if he was in a bad mood. But generally, he was very pleasant, very courteous."

When putting his show together for the 2001 touring season, Travis discovered that the first performance to promote *Inspirational Journey* would be at the Miccosukee Casino & Resort in Miami, Florida. "The first night I'm gonna attempt to do gospel songs in this country show is in a casino," he recalled. "I was nervous to the point of shaking, before coming to the first song." He made a comment about singing a gospel song, and someone in the audience called, "Do 'Doctor Jesus.'" That was a song on the album. "I felt a lot more at ease at that point," Travis said. "We've been doing it ever since."[16] To expand his base to religious audiences unfamiliar with him and his music, his management organized an additional tour of acoustic shows in churches and at Christian events, including performances on religious television shows like the *700 Club*. "This has been a new world in one sense," Travis said after his first gospel tour. "For me and a couple of guys playing acoustic guitars in front of a congregation, I even hesitate to say we're doing a show. It's been wonderful. The reception from the congregations we have worked for has been amazing."[17]

His acoustic guitarists were no longer Mark Casstevens and Steve Mandile. Steve Sheehan replaced Casstevens, and Robb Houston replaced Mandile. When Sheehan left in 1998, Lance Dary joined the band. He had first worked with Travis on the USO tour to Asia in 1988. "It was an honor to get asked to be in the band," he says. He appreciated that the Travises allowed the band members to decide on hiring musicians, saying, "I guess they'd come to the conclusion that the guys have got to live with whoever we hire. Of course, Randy and Lib would have the final say, but it was awesome that they relied on the band that way. When I later got to participate in that, I thought it was a really cool thing to be part of." Dary and Houston traveled along on the church circuit. Travis usually kicked off the songs, and Dary played most of the solos. Houston and Dary sang backup vocals. When the full band performed, Houston played acoustic guitar and provided vocals, while Dary was the utility guy. "I'd play mandolin, banjo, gut-string acoustic, twelve-string acoustic, and vocals," he explains.[18]

The entire band was together to record a live performance on December 14 at the Sun Theater in Anaheim, California. The resulting DVD was called

*Randy Travis Live! It Was Just a Matter of Time*.[19] "The title was sort of an inside joke," Travis said. "We'd been talking about doing another live album for years." His one live album had been that long-ago project at the Nashville Palace when he was known as Randy Ray. The title was a takeoff on a previous number one song, "It's Just a Matter of Time," from his *No Holdin' Back* album in 1989. On the DVD, Travis carries a cordless mic as he walks around the stage while opening the show, frequently reaching down to touch hands or accept a bouquet of flowers. Along with a medley of his hits, he sings several songs from *Inspirational Journey*. One of the new songs is "Shallow Water," for which Houston, Dary, and Drew Sexton provide gospel backup harmony. Travis enjoys messing with his band. Singing the last line, "I will not drown," he holds the final note so long that Houston looks at him questioningly. Travis keeps holding the note. Dary drops out. Houston drops out. Sexton points at his throat as he tries to keep up. Finally, he waves his hand in defeat and backs away from the microphone. Travis drops the note and finishes singing "in shallow water," grinning all the while. When introducing the three, he calls Sexton "a great piano player friend for seventeen years or so, and extremely long-winded tonight."

Travis ends the concert with "Diggin' Up Bones." He walks to the front and collects one last bouquet before waving and exiting at the side of the stage. The band finishes the song and leaves the stage. The excited crowd roars when they return for an encore. Travis sings "Runaway Train" while on one knee at the edge of the stage, holding his mic in his left hand and signing his name with his right hand as fans hold out items to be autographed. Image Entertainment Inc. produced the DVD package and released it the following August. In addition to the surround sound video for home theater, it included a twenty-five-song soundtrack on CD and a new audio technology called DVD-Audio. Elizabeth Travis was executive producer.[20]

Although country radio ignored *Inspirational Journey*, Travis did receive recognition from the Christian music industry. The five thousand members of the Gospel Music Association selected him for two Dove Awards in early April. That organization had been honoring outstanding achievements and excellence in Christian/gospel music since 1969. Travis and songwriter Mickey Cates were recognized with Country Recorded Song of the Year for "Baptism," and Travis and producer Kyle Lehning won Bluegrass Album of the Year for *Inspirational Journey*.[21]

On Easter morning in 2001, Travis brought his gospel show to the DeSoto Civic Center on the edge of Memphis, Tennessee. The Colonial Hills Baptist

Church moved its Sunday service to the civic center to accommodate the eight thousand people who came to celebrate with Travis. It was the venue's largest-ever crowd and four times the church's usual attendance. "After all, Randy Travis was there," wrote a reporter, "guitar in hand, his deep, baritone voice reverberating throughout the building as thousands of fans screamed and clapped for the Grammy-winning singer." Travis sang songs from *Inspirational Journey* and talked about how his life had changed since becoming a Christian. At the request of the senior pastor, he included "Forever and Ever, Amen," on his set list.[22]

As much as Travis appreciated his audiences and enjoyed performing for them, he worried about his future recording career. "I don't know where we're going as far as a label," he told a reporter. "I want to continue to record Christian music. But I also want to record country music because of what I am and the way I sing. I couldn't imagine life without country music."[23] The short-lived Atlantic Christian imprint had folded, and Lehning suggested they record an album that the Travises would own. "Then you can pitch it to any label or put it out yourselves," he said. Travis had so enjoyed writing and performing the *Inspirational Journey* songs that he wrote six songs for the new album. During a multiday songwriting session, he and songwriter Mike Curtis wrote seven songs and started four others. One of the songs from that session was "Rise and Shine," which Travis and his two guitarists performed for the first time during the Easter celebration at DeSoto Civic Center: "The Son's gonna rise and shine. / Make the lame walk, the deaf talk, / and give sight back to the blind." The crowd gave them a lengthy standing ovation. "The first four times in a row that we performed the song, we received similar responses," Travis said, still marveling. "The only other song I remember evoking that kind of response, night after night, with people who had never before heard it, was 'Forever and Ever, Amen.' I knew we had struck a chord."

They recorded twelve songs for the album they called *Rise and Shine*. Lehning contacted Peter York, a friend who ran a Christian label, Sparrow, that was distributed by EMI/Capitol. York listened to the record and offered Travis a deal. The contract hadn't yet been signed when Lehning ran into Barry Landis at a NARAS Board of Governors meeting in Nashville. Both men were members of the National Academy of Recording Arts and Sciences, which provided oversight for the Grammy Awards. They hadn't seen each other since the *Inspirational Journey* record almost two years earlier. Lehning described Travis's new album and said they were making a deal with Peter York at Sparrow. Landis responded, "I don't want you to do that. I've taken over Word, and I'd love to have Randy at Word." Word Records was a Christian label under Warner Bros. Records. Lehning told him the contract was already drawn up and Travis would soon sign it. Landis insisted, "I'd really love to have this." Seeing his enthusiasm, Lehning agreed to talk to the Travises.

They liked the idea. Word was a powerful record label in the Christian market, and they already had a good relationship with Landis. Lehning then telephoned York and explained the situation. "In the most absolutely wonderful sort of gentlemanly way you could imagine," Lehning recalls with awe, "he let us out of the obligation to go to Sparrow and let us go to Word." Travis called it "one of the most rare and unselfish acts I've experienced in the music business." Travis signed with Word Records, and Lehning began putting the finishing touches on the album. Lehning was also producing a Sony album for Michael Peterson, who had been named Top New Male Artist at the CMA, ACM, and TNN/*Music City News* awards. Peterson came into the studio one day and said he had found a perfect song for Randy Travis. Lehning listened to "Three Wooden Crosses" and told Peterson, "It's an incredibly good song. I think *you* need a hit." Peterson said, "I don't hear it for me. I hear it for Randy."

Lehning called Peterson's producer, who agreed it was a great song but said the record label wouldn't allow Peterson to record an extra song. "I felt I'd done my due diligence to do right by Michael," Lehning recalls. He then sent the song to Travis, who loved the idea of a farmer, a teacher, a hooker, and a preacher on a midnight bus to Mexico. He thought it was an amazing piece of writing, with its surprise twist and the message that it's not what you take when you leave the world but what you leave behind. He wanted to record it immediately. But record producer Doug Johnson, the song's cowriter, planned for someone else to record it. Disappointed, Lehning told him, "Let me know if you don't do it." The song must have been destined for Travis, because Johnson called Lehning the following day to say, "It's yours."

Travis's schedule didn't permit him to return to Nashville. "It's the only time we've recorded a song that he wasn't there for the tracking session," Lehning recalls. They agreed on what key to use, Lehning booked the session, and Daryle Singletary sang the basic track. Session pianist Gordon Mote, who had never worked with Travis but had worked with Lehning, remembers getting a call from Lehning, who said, "I don't need anything complicated. Just listen to it first. You'll know what to do." Mote had been a Randy Travis fan since *Storms of Life* came out while he was in high school. "I was really excited," he says. "Not only was I getting to work on a Randy Travis album, I was getting to work with Kyle, one of my favorite people. He's a brilliant musician and a brilliant producer." Travis liked the result, and Mote played on all of his future sessions. Travis enjoyed hanging out with the musicians and joking with them. "He didn't put himself above us," Mote explains. "I think that's why everybody loved to work with him. Everybody was really happy to get that call. If Kyle called, you'd do anything you could to move things around and make the schedule work. We all did."[24]

Travis introduced "Three Wooden Crosses" in October when he was invited to be guest soloist at the Billy Graham Crusade in Irving, Texas. Torrential rains poured down on the tarp-covered Texas Stadium as Travis sang four gospel songs with the support of his two acoustic guitarists. Travis was thrilled to meet the famous evangelist and would perform at Graham's later crusades. He came to view his fellow North Carolinian as a father figure.

*Rise and Shine*, now containing thirteen songs, was released on October 15, 2002, by Word Records. "Three Wooden Crosses," issued as a single, debuted on December 7 at number fifty-two on the Hot Country Singles chart. It became Travis's sixteenth number one on May 24, 2003, his first *Billboard* chart topper since "Whisper My Name" in 1994. "It took forever for that record to become a hit," Lehning remembers. "Barry and Word worked that record for months because they believed in it." Mike Curb of Curb Records got involved in the promotion after buying 20 percent of Word Records. Landis became president of Word/Curb Records. (*Inspirational Journey* from Atlantic Christian was eventually absorbed into the Word catalog.) "I think the combination of the folks at Word and Mike Curb's clout got the record the attention it deserved," Lehning says. "If 'Three Wooden Crosses' had been on Warner Bros. at the time, I don't think that record would have been a hit. The guys at Word had nothing to lose, and Randy was the only artist they were promoting to country radio. I give them all the credit in the world for seeing that record through."

One of Word's strategies was to release "Three Wooden Crosses" to smaller radio stations that might be more likely to find room on their playlists. As more and more listeners called stations and asked to hear the song, bigger stations in bigger markets started playing it, even though it was a gospel song from a gospel album. "Three Wooden Crosses" was on the way to the top of the charts when Travis received a GMA Dove Award in April 2003 for *Rise and Shine* as Country Album of the Year. In November the Country Music Association nominated "Three Wooden Crosses" for both Single of the Year (honoring artist and producer) and Song of the Year (honoring songwriters). It won CMA Song of the Year, but no one could compete against a posthumous award for

Johnny Cash, who had died September 12 at age seventy-one. Single of the Year went to his recording of "Hurt."

The following evening, Travis was honored at the Christian Country Music Association Awards. He was named Mainstream Artist of the Year, and "Three Wooden Crosses" won Song of the Year. Travis's recording ended the year at number seventeen on *Billboard*'s year-end chart of Hot Country Songs for 2003. He found himself once again a Grammy winner on February 8, 2004. *Rise and Shine* won Best Southern, Country, or Bluegrass Gospel Album at the Staples Center in Los Angeles. Travis was also nominated for Best Male Country Vocal Performance for "Three Wooden Crosses." He later said, "I didn't win but applauded enthusiastically when Vince Gill received a well-deserved award for his recording of 'Next Big Thing.'"[25]

Travis sang "Three Wooden Crosses" during the Gospel Music Association Awards at Nashville's Municipal Auditorium in April 2004. Wearing a conservative suit with dress shirt and traditional necktie, he looked his Sunday best. His hair, showing a touch of gray at the temples, was cut shorter than in recent years. His full band played softly behind him.[26] "Three Wooden Crosses" won a Dove Award for Country Recorded Song of the Year. The previous year, its album—*Rise and Shine*—had won Country Album of the Year.

Two follow-up singles from *Rise and Shine* were great for Travis's live shows but not successful on mainstream radio. Travis liked to find off-the-wall songs that conveyed their messages with a sense of humor. "I like to laugh," he said, "and I like people who enjoy a good sense of humor." In "Pray for the Fish," the townspeople gather at the river and make bets on whether the man being baptized will get his soul cleansed. The preacher tells them to pray for the fish because "they won't know what's coming when the sins start rolling off the likes of him." Travis thought the lyrics described a man a lot like his former self. "You don't total four cars, two motorbikes and a horse and buggy, get in more than thirty fights and get through all of that without someone taking care of you," he said. "I went through hard drugs and alcohol, so I can talk to people who are going through those situations."[27]

In "Raise Him Up," a young man marries a woman with a fatherless child. The chorus is, "He may not be blood of my blood / but I'm gonna raise him up." The second verse flashes back two thousand years to Joseph, who speaks the same line. In the third verse, when Jesus is in his grave, God says, "He's mine, blood of my blood / and I'm going to raise him up." One night after a show, a man came backstage and said he needed to talk to Travis. Jeff Davis went to the bus to tell his boss someone seemed intent on talking to him.

Travis, as could be expected, said, "I'll be right there." The man explained that his son had married a woman who was pregnant with another man's child. He'd reacted by disowning them. He told Travis, "I heard you sing that song tonight, and it's changed my whole opinion. I'm going home and call my son."

Such stories were becoming more common to Travis as he sang his gospel songs and shared his life story with his audiences. "I had never imagined I might play even a small part of helping somebody find God, that I could influence someone like that in a good way," he later commented. "But similar stories started showing up after our gospel stops across the nation." That created tension in his mind about how to balance religious shows in churches with country shows where drinking and gambling were prevalent. The pastors he consulted assured him his influence might bring people through their doors who would otherwise never come.[28]

One Sunday afternoon, Travis was scheduled to perform at Caesar's Pocono Resort in Lakeview, Pennsylvania. Jeff Davis was driving the Travises from the hotel in their 1997 Prevost XL bus. He had traveled early that morning with the crew buses and trucks to check out the venue. There had been little traffic on the frozen Route 590 in the Pocono Mountains. By the afternoon, however, the snow was melting, and traffic backed up behind the customized tour bus as it slowly rounded the narrow curves. The rear living area was closed off from the front section and had a separate exterior door. A small window between the two sections allowed items such as coffee to be passed through. The Travises were dressing for the show when the bus suddenly pitched sideways into the ditch. The fax machine flew across the bus and landed in a corner. Travis felt as if they were inside a Ripley's Believe It or Not! museum. They crawled along the floor, grabbing anything stable, trying to reach the door. Outside, several men came from a nearby farmhouse and dug a trench by the driver's door to get Davis out. Motorists stopped to assist. They then dug a space to open the back door and help the Travises slide through. Once on the ground, Travis observed that the forty-five-foot bus would have tipped over completely if Davis had tried to steer back onto the road. The asphalt had buckled and the road caved in.

Two monster tow trucks with cranes worked for more than four hours to remove the bus from the mud-filled ditch, one lifting from each end. The engine and undercarriage of the million-dollar vehicle appeared undamaged, and Davis drove the Travises to the resort, where the show went off without a hitch. The regular bus driver, who had been sleeping that afternoon, then drove the Travises home to Santa Fe. Several days later, Travis issued a statement to thank everyone who helped them. He concluded with, "When we planned to release our new single, 'Raise Him Up,' this week, this was not what we had in mind."[29]

In 2004, Fan Fair received a new name: CMA Music Festival (often shortened to CMA Fest). Fan Fair had been created in 1972 by WSM Radio and the Country Music Association to allow fans to mingle with artists who held autograph sessions and performed in concerts. The four-day event was moved in 2001 from the fairgrounds to various venues in downtown Nashville. For one of the 2004 events, Country Music Television decided to promote "CMT's 100 Greatest Love Songs." A team at the network developed the list, hoping to capture the full scope of country music's rich history of love songs. Two of Travis's appeared on the list. "On the Other Hand" was number thirty-nine. The top twelve songs were performed in a two-hour concert at the Gaylord Entertainment Center on June 16. Travis came onstage to sing the fourth greatest love song, "Forever and Ever, Amen." The greatest was "I Will Always Love You," written and sung by Dolly Parton.[30]

Throughout the summer, Travis promoted *Worship & Faith*, his third gospel album, which had been released the previous November. No singles were issued. Because he wanted to record at home in Santa Fe, using Stepbridge Studios, the record company paid to fly Lehning and the musicians to the tracking session. Many of the twenty songs were traditional hymns in the public domain. Word Records wanted a mixture of classics and modern songs known as praise and worship songs. "Most of what I found were more pop sounding, and we're not," Travis told one audience, "so most of you have probably heard these, but probably a little different version."[31] At the Gospel Music Awards in April 2004, Travis had sung "Three Wooden Crosses" and won a Dove Award for Country Recorded Song of the Year. *Worship & Faith* won Country Album of the Year, Travis's third Dove Award for his third gospel album. The following year, in 2005, that album would bring his second Grammy for Best Southern, Country, or Bluegrass Gospel Album. Travis sometimes modified his band to use four musicians for an acoustic-oriented show. "It's a lot of fun," he told an interviewer. "It puts me in mind of when I was a kid, sitting around with friends and family members, playing and singing. You just take away the fighting."[32]

During July 2004, Drew Sexton needed a replacement while recovering from carpal tunnel surgery. Opry keyboardist Joe Van Dyke offered to fill in. He had gotten acquainted with the band members in early 1989 while in

K. T. Oslin's band, when Travis and Oslin toured as reigning CMA Male and Female Vocalists of the Year. Sexton struggled with recurring cancer issues and played the dates he felt well enough to play. "It was still Drew's gig," Van Dyke says. "Whenever he was able to recover, he'd come back." Van Dyke filled in the remaining dates until becoming a permanent band member at the end of the year, when Sexton left for the last time. He died in February 2011, at age fifty-six.[33]

Travis reunited with George Jones in early August for a few dates in Connecticut. They split double bills and performed individual shows. A reviewer wrote, "Both put on shows that were comfortable and appealing despite their simple, unadorned approaches." Jones, seventy-two, and his seven-piece band ran through his hits going back more than four decades. Travis, forty-five, and his eight-piece band focused more on his hits than the recent gospel records. He did, of course, sing "Three Wooden Crosses," and he included "Raise Him Up." Instead of his usual selection of "American Trilogy" for the patriotic ending, he chose his own "America Will Always Stand," a song he had written following the 9/11 attacks. It was the title track of two specialty CDs. Travis had issued the first as a two-song CD in 2001, with all royalties and net proceeds going to the American Red Cross. The second song was "Point of Light" from 1991. Travis wrote on the back cover, "We pray that it will help America and its people, in the worst of times to stay brave and true." The second CD came out in 2004, issued by Time-Life Music as its first-ever album of original music, a collection of Civil War–themed songs performed by country singers.[34]

The last weekend in August 2004, the Travis entourage drove to Ohio for three nights. Patty Loveless, who had traveled with Travis to Asia on the 1988 USO tour, opened for him the first night. Josh Turner, who had recently hit with "Long Black Train" and would become a close friend, opened Sunday night. A Friday night reviewer described Travis as "attired in a natty tan blazer and happy to shake the hand of every single person in the front row." At the Kentucky State Fair on Saturday, Travis asked how many had never been to one of his concerts. When half the crowd gave an enthusiastic shout, he responded, "You didn't have to be exactly proud of it." The reviewer said the show, one hour and forty minutes, "played like a live greatest hits album."[35]

The audience didn't know about the detour taken after the Friday night show. The buses and trucks drove from Kettering, Ohio, to Louisville. While the crew stayed there to set up for the Kentucky State Fair, the others continued driving an additional 165 miles to return to Nashville. Their extra journey was because Lance Dary's twelve-year-old daughter, Felicia, had died several days earlier. She'd been diagnosed the previous November with a rare form of cancer. "It was stage four when we found out," Dary says. "A low number of children get it every year." As her condition worsened, Dary gave up his road work. Robb Houston, who had been replaced by Joe Manuel, happened to be available to step in as second acoustic guitarist. When Dary eventually returned to Travis's band, Manuel left and Houston stayed. During Felicia's illness, Dary recalls, "Everybody, the whole band and crew, they were so awesome. Randy and Elizabeth were really trying to help as much as possible." Band members would call from the road to get updates. "It was a lot of phone calls going back and forth, a lot of praying," Dary says.

The day of Felicia's funeral, Dary and his wife, Terry, were at the church getting ready for the service. They were stunned to see the Travises and the band walk in. The Darys had asked a friend to sing "I'll Fly Away," and a selection of musical instruments was positioned at the front of the church. "Randy and Elizabeth stayed in the pews and sang with everybody, but the guys jumped up and played along with us at the service," Dary reminisces. "They had to go right after. They gave us hugs, and they got to Louisville in time. They changed on the bus and walked onstage and did the show. Such an incredible bunch of guys." Dary sums up the memory by saying, "Randy and Lib and the band came all the way back to Nashville for the funeral. That was really special to us."[36]

# "WE WERE BOTH WRONG."

The original Warner brothers—Sam, Albert, Harry, and Jack—founded Warner Brothers Pictures in 1923 and based their film studio in Burbank, California. Warner Bros. Records was founded in 1958 as the corporation's recorded music division. In 1973 an outpost was established in Nashville, a record label called Warner Bros. Nashville. By 2004, after years of corporate mergers and name changes, Warner Bros. Nashville had become a subsidiary of Warner Music Group, a multinational entertainment conglomerate headquartered in New York City. Warner Bros. owned the masters of the songs Travis had recorded from 1985 through 1996. Although "Three Wooden Crosses" was on Word Records, that label also belonged to the conglomerate. Not wanting to miss out on Travis's latest chart topper, Warner Bros. issued a two-disc anthology, *The Very Best of Randy Travis*, in 2004. "This twenty-song retrospective, which includes sixteen number one country chart-toppers," wrote one reviewer, "reminds us of the greatness of Travis's voice, his generally good taste in production and arrangement, and his ear for strong material."[1]

During the summer and fall of 2004, Travis's tours promoted both that album and the previous *Worship & Faith*. In November, Word Records released his next album, *Passing Through*, a collection of mostly country love songs. Its two singles stayed on the *Billboard* country chart for almost three months apiece but hardly made it into the top fifty. The album earned a Dove Award for Country Album of the Year. Next came *Glory Train: Songs of Faith, Worship, and Praise*, a gospel album released in 2005. Like *Worship & Faith* two years earlier, it was recorded in Santa Fe at Stepbridge Studios, in a bluegrass style with mostly acoustic instruments. The nineteen songs were a mix of new ones and those in the public domain, none written by Travis or released as singles. The album won a Dove Award for Country Album of the Year in 2006 and a Grammy for Best Southern, Country, or Bluegrass Gospel Album in 2007.

In August 2006, Travis appeared on the debut edition of a Country Music Television show called *CMT Cross Country*. The concept was to pair two artists who were similar in musical style yet different. He was matched with Josh Turner, whom he'd met when Turner opened for him two years earlier in Clarkson, Michigan. A friendship had developed when Turner and his wife, Jennifer, visited on Travis's bus after the show. "We talked and laughed and had a great time together," Travis remembered. "Lib took off her manager's hat for that evening and allowed herself to enjoy 'girl stuff.' She showed Jennifer some of the new jewelry I had recently bought her." Turner told the Travises the first song he sang in public, other than in church, was "Diggin' Up Bones." *Storms of Life* was one of the first country albums he owned.[2] Travis was uncomfortable with the praise Turner lavished on him. "When somebody tells you you influenced what they have done, you're the reason they sing the kind of songs they sing, or other decisions they made in life, you don't know how to respond," he once told an interviewer. "Where I came from, y'know, growing up as I did, hearing that I was a good influence to somebody was probably not anything I thought I'd ever hear."[3] By the time they met for *CMT Cross Country*, Travis regarded Turner as a peer, with hits such as "Long Black Train" and "Your Man." Their voices—Turner's bass and Travis's deep baritone—meshed well. They clearly enjoyed performing together, trading off verses and choruses on each other's hits. When Travis came to the "talk about old men" line in "Forever and Ever, Amen," the twenty-eight-year-old Turner playfully pointed at the forty-seven-year-old Travis, who grinned in response.

In 2007 Travis recorded his final Word album, a Christmas record called *Songs of the Season*. He then returned to Warner Bros. as a recording artist. *Around the Bend*, his first straight country CD of the new century, was released on July 15, 2008. He and Lehning had spent a year searching for and recording the "right" songs. "From a purely song performance production standpoint," Lehning says, "this is one of my favorite records," He thought they made "a really solid Randy Travis record," even though "this is when Randy and Lib were starting to become on the outs, and that caused problems." Although Travis rarely covered other people's hits, one of his favorite songs on this album was Bob Dylan's "Don't Think Twice, It's All Right." Travis described "You Didn't Have a Good Time" as being about a person coming to grips with being an alcoholic. The lyrics reflected a man kneeling in a bathroom stall and having a conversation with his conscience. "That's one I could relate to, probably a little more than people should be able to," Travis told an interviewer. "It's one I wish I'd had a hand in writing. I'd love to see it be a single because it would touch people who may be having problems in that area." Several of the songs showed Travis's sense of humor, even in their titles, such as "Everything That I Own (Has Got a Dent)." Its lyrics include, "Why should my heart be any differ-ent? / Everything that I own has got a dent."

The uncluttered album photo emphasizes country-ness with a blue sky and dirt road behind Travis, dressed in a black western shirt with blue jeans. Travis excitedly went on tour, promoting the first single, "Faith in You," which opened with the line, "I don't have faith in technology." The first night he sang it, he told his audience, "The way our record label promotes a single or an album has sure changed in an eight-year period. They're talking to me about stuff like YouTube and downloading and up-linking. As far as I'm concerned, MySpace used to be where you were not." The audience so enjoyed his comment that he repeated it on future shows. The *Around the Bend* tour lasted from July through November and included two rounds in Canada. As much as audiences enjoyed the shows, there was little radio attention. None of the singles even charted on *Billboard*. Lehning thought the long relationship with the record label might have lessened the excitement of promoting Travis again. "*Around the Bend* was a disappointment to both of us because we really liked this record," he says.

Travis signed copies of *Around the Bend* at the Country Music Hall of Fame and Museum on the first Friday in November, following an hourlong interview in the museum's Ford Theater. When interviewer Michael Gray introduced Kyle Lehning and Elizabeth Travis in the audience, Travis said, "Kyle and my wife—these are two of the most important people in my life, as far as this music business and my personal life, too." The Travises were careful to keep the growing cracks in their relationship from public view. Following a discussion of the new CD, Gray asked about using technology, and Travis said he was a cassette person: "I learned how to *use* a CD player. But when I write something, I put it on a cassette." After mentioning he didn't have a cell phone, he told a story about the time office manager Bill Sweeney had sent a broken Motorola analog phone to the house in Santa Fe. Knowing how Travis felt about cell phones, Sweeney included a note that said, "Here's a phone for Randy to shoot." Travis explained to Gray, "I don't practice that much anymore. I still have the speed, but my accuracy's not what it once was. A friend of ours throws this cellphone in the air, I draw a .45 Colt out of my holster, and I hit it dead center of the battery. I actually shot this thing in the air." Elizabeth had then put it in a shadowbox with "Can you hear me now?" inscribed on the front.[4]

On Sunday, Travis and six others received stars on the Music City Walk of Fame across the street from the Country Music Hall of Fame and Museum, which had moved in 2000 from Music Row to downtown Nashville. Josh Turner presented Travis's award in the forty-degree weather. Four years earlier, in California, Travis had accepted a star on the Hollywood Walk of Fame, representing his contributions in the recording category. He was in Washington, DC, when George Jones was feted at the 2008 Kennedy Center Honors in December. Jones sat next to President George W. Bush as Brad Paisley, Travis, Alan Jackson, and Garth Brooks paid tribute with their renditions of his songs. Travis introduced "I'm a One-Woman Man" by saying, "I count myself fortunate to call you a friend, George. Here's one from a few years back."[5]

The 2008 Christmas season saw the release of a DVD that was a joint project of Elizabeth Travis Management and the New Mexico Tourism Department. Elizabeth, as executive producer, provided the idea and the funding. *Randy Travis: Christmas on the Pecos* included the first-ever concert filmed in the depths of the Carlsbad Caverns.[6] The main concert had been filmed at the Walter Gerrells Performing Arts and Exhibition Center in Carlsbad, New Mexico, three years earlier. Travis introduced that show by announcing, "Live in concert from Carlsbad, New Mexico. Welcome to Christmas on the Pecos." He wore a burgundy pullover sweater with his favorite jacket, deerskin leather with fringes, that the famous western designer Manuel had made for him years earlier. To open the show, he sang "Santa Claus Is Coming to Town" and "God Rest Ye Merry Gentlemen."

Because the concert was being filmed, there were pauses and repeated songs due to production issues. Travis wore an earpiece through which the producers talked to him during the show. After finishing one song, he said, "Now the voice in my head tells me they want me to go back and do that song one more time." During breaks when the film crew was trying to iron out problems, Travis told jokes and stories about his days on the road. He acknowledged the presence of recently returned military troops before singing "America Will Always Stand," which he told the audience he had written shortly after the 9/11 terrorist attacks. Most of his selections were traditional Christmas songs along with a few hits his audiences expected to hear. He included one song he reserved for New Mexico audiences, "Sopapilla Song," written by L. D. Burke. About the deep-fried Southwestern bread treat served hot with honey, he said, "All of you probably know what a sopapilla is. That's real important. I like them a lot myself. But I'd never thought of writing a song about them." With lines like "They smell like mama's bread on a warm spring day," "Madre Mia quesadilla red hot chili on a warm tortilla," and "The best to me will always be / honey on a sopapilla," the fun song would never be recorded, but the audience loved it. He'd first performed it during his May 2000 benefit following the Cerro Grande wildfire when he said, "I really like this song. If I'm going to play it anywhere, this is the place to do it."

The underground segments of the concert, which Travis introduced on the DVD by saying, "Now we're going to take you to a very special place—the Carlsbad Caverns," were recorded on May 18, 2006, in the natural wonder buried 830 feet below the Chihuahua Desert floor. To give the appearance of continuity, Travis wore the burgundy pullover sweater he'd worn for the concert five months earlier. Standing next to a huge, ancient rock formation known as the Rock of Ages, he and the forty-member sanctuary choir from the Carlsbad First Baptist Church sang "Rock of Ages." Travis described the room as "a giant underground chamber about a dozen football fields wide, naturally carved out of the rock and magnificently decorated by God with spectacular stalactites and stalagmites." The second song recorded underground and inserted into the DVD was "Silent Night," sung by Travis and the choir.

Recording those two songs was no small undertaking. A twenty-five-person crew hauled a crane, seven cameras, many lights, and much sound equipment across the hot desert floor and into the slow elevators that took them down to the chilly fifty-six-degree caverns. Moisture dripped from the cavern roof, and they tried to minimize the use of lights because of the presence of bats. With the choir members and Travis's band, just getting everyone into the caverns was a long process. "We brought recording equipment and microphones and all kinds of stuff down there," Lehning remembers. "There were lights and power, but we had to have extra lights." Several National Park rangers oversaw the activity. Travis called singing in the spectacular Carlsbad Caverns "one of the most memorable musical experiences of my career."[7]

A next-generation country star also provided Travis with a memorable musical experience when she recorded "I Told You So." Oklahoma native Carrie Underwood had won the fourth season of *American Idol* in 2005, at age twenty-two. Her debut album that year, *Some Hearts*, became the best-selling solo female debut album in country music history, and her "Jesus, Take the Wheel" sat for six weeks at the top of the *Billboard* chart. It won the 2006 Dove Award for Country Recorded Song of the Year, beating Travis's nomination for "Angels." Her second album, *Carnival Ride* in 2007, included a cover of Travis's "I Told You So." She had called to ask if he would mind her recording his song. After saying he certainly wouldn't mind, he joked, "I have several hundred other songs you are welcome to record, too."

When asked his opinion of Underwood's rendition, Travis responded, "I told Kyle Lehning, when we first heard she was doing a version of it, that she will sing it better than I did, because it has those long, high notes. She's made to do that better than I am." Years later, he answered a similar question by reiterating that the song was better suited to her, saying, "Given the fact that I'm obviously a borderline bass and baritone singer, you hear Carrie with the amazing ability on the top end."

Underwood made a guest appearance at the Opry on March 15, 2008. When she finished her song, the crowd rose and applauded. She turned slightly to her right and jumped in surprise to see Travis standing next to her. She put her hands to her face, laughed, hugged Travis, and told the audience, "I thought you guys were standing up for *me*!" Travis then said, "I was asked by the management here at the Grand Ole Opry to come out here and ask you if you would like to be their next member." She accepted, with tears in her eyes, and hugged him again.[8]

Underwood and her record label, Arista, asked Travis if he would agree to a duet of "I Told You So." He went into the studio with Underwood's producer, Mark Bright, to record his vocals. Bright removed the original background vocals and several of Underwood's lines and remixed the recording with Travis's vocals added.[9] Arista Records released the duet as a single, and it reached number two on the *Billboard* country chart in early 2009. Travis and Underwood sang "I Told You So" as guest artists on *American Idol* in March. They would win a Grammy for Best Country Collaboration the following January. With Travis on the radio again, and to claim his Word recordings, Warner Bros. issued two compilations in March 2009. *I Told You So: The Ultimate Hits of Randy Travis* contained thirty-one Warner Bros. recordings on two discs. *Three Wooden Crosses: The Inspirational Hits of Randy Travis* contained twenty Word recordings on one disc.

The year 2009 continued the heavy touring and culminated with Travis receiving two major awards. On September 22, the Academy of Country Music held its second annual ACM Honors at the Schermerhorn Symphony Center in Nashville. Travis had won his first-ever award, Top New Male Vocalist, at the annual ACM Awards in Los Angeles in 1986. This new Nashville event honored legends. The Cliffie Stone Pioneer Award, named for the West Coast musician and producer, went to Travis, Kenny Rogers, Hank Williams Jr., and posthumously to Jerry Reed. Carrie Underwood sang "I Told You So" in honor of Travis. "I feel like I need to be older, or dead," Travis said jokingly about receiving a lifetime achievement award when he was barely fifty years old.[10]

The following month, he was inducted into the North Carolina Music Hall of Fame in Kannapolis. This organization is not to be confused with the North Carolina Music and Entertainment Hall of Fame in Charlotte, where he'd been inducted ten years earlier. The North Carolina Music Hall of Fame was established in 1999, with Charlie Daniels one of its seven initial inductees. The next induction came in 2002 with Ronnie Milsap as the sole new member. The organization then languished until record executives Mike Curb and Eddie Ray revived it and moved it to Kannapolis in 2009. Eighteen new members were added that year but without an induction ceremony. Seventeen were North Carolinians, with the eighteenth being honorary member Mike Curb, born in Georgia. Curb became connected to North Carolina through his involvement with NASCAR when he owned the car driven by Kannapolis native Dale Earnhardt. As founder of Curb Records, he had revitalized Word Records and helped bring "Three Wooden Crosses" to the top of the charts. Now his money and support were bringing the North Carolina Music Hall of Fame back to life. The Travises donated awards and memorabilia to help the fledging operation build a Randy Travis exhibit at the new location. Members continue to be added every year. Travis's 2009 North Carolina Music Hall of Fame bio began: "During the mid-1980s, a group of young performers changed the course of country music by recording songs with a retro sound that harkened back to the traditional sound of country music from the 1940s and 1950s. Randy Travis was a leader in the movement with his baritone twang, his youthful, handsome looks and sex appeal."[11]

With country music as popular as ever in Europe in 2009, one of the biggest broadcasters in the United Kingdom, UTV, hosted its second annual UTV Country Fest in Belfast, Ireland, the first weekend in August. Travis headlined the two-day event. Martina McBride and Connie Smith were other Grand Ole Opry stars on the show. The stage manager was Eamonn McCrystal, twenty-two years old and a recent college graduate. Following the UTV event, the American performers split off on tours throughout Northern Ireland. McCrystal was scheduled to be McBride's stage manager and promoter. But the production company had neglected to arrange proper transportation for Travis, and McCrystal agreed to borrow his father's new Jaguar to drive the Travises around the country for their weeklong tour. At one point, McCrystal was asked if he knew the words to "Danny Boy," and Elizabeth listened to the CD he had recorded. He said he hoped to make music his career. According to Travis, "Lib became enamored with Eamonn, and the two of them talked nonstop any time we were in the car. They continued talking as I got out and went inside the venue for sound check."

At the end of the tour, McCrystal dropped the Travises off at the airport and thought that was the end of it. But a few weeks later, Elizabeth emailed to ask if he would be interested in joining the Travis management team and allowing her to pitch him to the big labels. "I came to America with nothing but a suitcase," McCrystal recalls, "thinking I was gonna visit for a week." His first visit lasted a month, meeting people and making plans. He returned to Ireland, quit his job, and moved to America in early 2010. "It was a whirlwind of a journey, in a couple of months," he says.

Travis stated in his 2019 memoir, *Forever and Ever, Amen: A Memoir of Music, Faith, and Braving the Storms of Life*: "Almost before I knew it, Eamonn was living in our house, eating every meal with us, and traveling on our tour bus to shows." As managers sometimes do, Elizabeth hired McCrystal as an office assistant while waiting for his singing career to support him. He worked for the Elizabeth Travis Management company from 2009 until its closure in 2015. Possessing a flair for organization, McCrystal performed numerous production assistant tasks. He remains awed by the range of his boss's activities, from movie production and music publishing to real estate and interior decorating. In addition to their ranch, the Travises owned at least three rental houses in Santa Fe, four on Maui, and several in Nashville. They bought, renovated, and decorated them all.

Lehning agrees that Elizabeth loved projects and staying busy. He believes Travis was running out of steam in 2009 and needed time to rest. "When Eamonn McCrystal came into the picture, he became a new project for Lib," Lehning surmises. "It was sort of like Randy wanted to take time off, and she didn't." McCrystal became her focus. She tried to promote him in every way possible, including giving him a place on Travis's 2010 tour schedule. Why did Travis consent to that? He later explained, "Things had not been going well between Lib and me for some time. She seemed bored with me and restless, ready for some new venture. To keep her happy, I reluctantly acquiesced to her demands." No recording deal came from Warner Bros., so Elizabeth paid Lehning to produce an album. Lehning initially turned her down, saying he didn't think he was the right person to do it. She asked him again to "please do this," and the ever-loyal Lehning checked with Travis, who told him to go ahead. McCrystal's first US album, *When in Nashville . . .* , was eventually released in 2011.

"I think that shift of focus from Randy to Eamonn was a major factor in their split," Lehning concludes. "I don't have firsthand knowledge of that. But when I was working with Eamonn, Randy would call Lib and ask when she was coming home to Santa Fe."[12] Elizabeth and McCrystal were often on the road, and Travis started drinking wine while home alone. Although he had complained for years about his wife's controlling ways, now he said, "Lib had successfully weaned me away from alcohol more than twenty years earlier, and she had meticulously kept me away from it throughout my career. Now, she didn't seem to care."

After the winter break, Travis appeared on March 6, 2010, at Billy Bob's Texas in Fort Worth. Visiting him on his bus before the show were longtime friends Mary and Ritchie Beougher. The Travises were patients of Dr. Ritchie Beougher. He had been their dentist since they were referred to him by a mutual friend, actor Chuck Norris. When he built a new office, he included a motor home hookup in the back, which allowed them to park their tour bus. The Travises had first met Mary through her brother. Since Travis's early days of stardom, Stubbs Davis in Dallas had been making show shirts for him. During one of their Dallas visits, Stubbs introduced his sister, Mary Davis, who would marry Beougher in 1994. The couple became parents of a daughter and a son. "Lib never let anybody in their life," Beougher recalls. "She was real protective. Well, Lib let Mary in, and they became friends. Lib liked to come to Dallas because Mary would take her shopping. We started having a nice relationship. We went out there with the kids one time to Santa Fe to their ranch."

The Travises asked Mary in early 2009 to assist Elizabeth while she recovered from hip replacement surgery. Mary continued to visit the Travises, to the extent that her husband felt she was neglecting her own family. The Beoughers were already having marital difficulties, and what drove the stake through their marriage was the aftermath of a fire in their house. Early one morning in August 2009, a storm came through Frisco, Texas, and twenty-two lightning bolts hit the ground in a two-mile radius. One bolt struck their chimney and hit a half-inch gas line, starting a fire in the attic. The family escaped outdoors shortly before the ceiling fell in. They moved into a friend's house while their residence was rebuilt. Most of their possessions from more than two decades together were gone.

By that night at Billy Bob's, the Beougher marriage and the Travis marriage were both on the rocks. While the Beoughers visited with Travis on his bus, Mary asked where Lib was. In their twenty years of friendship, they had never seen him without her. He said he thought she and McCrystal were somewhere in Mississippi. Travis returned home that night to an empty house, after an eleven-hour bus ride back to Santa Fe. The next afternoon, Mary called to ask if he was okay. She said she'd never seen him as depressed as he'd appeared the previous evening. After a long conversation, he surprised himself by inviting her to meet him for lunch in Shawnee, Oklahoma, later that week while his bus driver made a rest stop on their way to Nashville. Mary drove three hours north and found the bus in a hotel parking lot. "We were both fragile and vulnerable at that juncture of our lives," Travis writes in his memoir. "Initially we were simply two good friends commiserating in the midst of unraveling marriages. But our relationship soon became much more." He adds, "Before long we were head over heels in love. And unfortunately, we were both still married to other people." Beougher says, "I think Lib got the shaft."

Travis filed for divorce in late April, citing incidents where Elizabeth was spending his money on McCrystal. He moved back to Nashville into the three-bedroom condominium Elizabeth had purchased in his name in upscale Belle Meade. The *National Enquirer* broke the story of the affair and the upcoming divorce, quoting an anonymous source who said, "Lib planted a secret camera on Randy's tour bus and caught him and Mary red-handed." Travis believed that McCrystal, whom he called "a trained gadget guy," had obeyed Elizabeth's orders to install surveillance equipment on his bus. McCrystal finds that accusation ludicrous. "I wouldn't know the first thing about bugging or tapping or any of those things," he says. "Elizabeth would never have known how; her technology goes as far as email. She actually laughed when she read the article, as if she would tap a bus." McCrystal insists Elizabeth found out about the affair through a drastically increased bill for the bus telephone, which was used for faxes and interviews but not personal calls. She requested a copy of the bill from the telephone company and saw the calls made to Mary's number. "That's the way she found out," explains McCrystal. "There was no bugging, there was no tapping, there was no surveillance."

Travis, fifty-one, believed Elizabeth at age sixty-nine was having an affair with twenty-three-year-old McCrystal. "It was clear that Lib was doing everything with the young Irish singer that she had once done with me, back when she had first taken me under her wing as a seventeen-year-old," Travis writes in his memoir. "It all seemed way too familiar." He recites how Elizabeth fired their house manager for discovering an email between Elizabeth and McCrystal that "described the intimate details of their relationship." McCrystal insists that the email the house manager found was one in which he explained he was gay. Elizabeth responded to him with a memory of the problems caused twenty years earlier by rumors that Travis was gay. She warned McCrystal that it wouldn't be good for his career or for the Travises to have that information released. As for the insinuation that Elizabeth was in a romantic relationship with him, McCrystal says, "Aside from the age difference and the other things, you could see this wasn't true, or possible. It was very disappointing that I was a part of their marriage." Lehning believes the two were not involved. "I don't have any knowledge of any relationship between Eamonn and Lib other than a working relationship," he says. "I never saw any physical affection between them. I never saw anything that would even remotely suggest that to me."[13]

Elizabeth continued as Travis's manager, receiving 25 percent of his gross income, considerably higher than the industry norm of 15 percent. "Although we were severing our marriage ties, I wanted to take the high road as much as possible in my dealings with Lib," he said. Years later, when a friend asked why he gave her so much in the divorce settlement, he replied, "I knew I'd make it back. And I wanted to give it to her."

The plan of working together proved awkward. On a June afternoon prior to a show in Arkansas, Jeff Davis helped Elizabeth remove the remainder of her personal possessions from the tour bus. They then traveled to shows in two tour buses—Elizabeth and McCrystal in one, Mary and Travis in the other. McCrystal continued to sing on Travis's shows. A reviewer of a concert in Worcester, Massachusetts, called McCrystal's performance an interruption, saying he "has a fine voice, but in the midst of the unalloyed country that Travis was serving up, McCrystal's *American Idol*–style pop was a little jarring."

The band and crew were courteous to the new partners and tried to ignore the tension between the feuding Travises. "The guys were such professionals that most fans never knew the tension existed," says Travis. "The show went on most nights without a hitch, we played our hits, and the fans went home happy." Lead guitarist L D Wayne agrees, saying, "We stayed out of the divorce stuff. We did sound check, we did the show, and Randy didn't display it on the shows. Our job was to do one thing—play well every night for Randy. And for the people who paid hard-earned money to come see the show."

With no one to hold him accountable, Travis drank more and more frequently. He went from over three decades of Elizabeth's rigid "no drinking at all" standard to complete freedom. Mary partied with him. Although his same age, she hadn't experienced his rebellious years. Lehning suggested to Travis that he hadn't been allowed to grow up the way most people do, having missed some natural development stages of life because Elizabeth took control at such an early stage. "Lib was so concerned that if she let him out from underneath her view, he was going to go completely off the rails," Lehning says. "He trusted her. He gave her all kinds of authority, and she made a lot of really good decisions. As long as the two of them were a couple, it wasn't a problem. When he first started, she might have believed in him more than he did himself."

Those days were long gone. The divorce was finalized on October 28, 2010, after a thirty-four-year relationship and nineteen years of marriage. It was a tough situation for accountant Gary Haber, who had been the financial manager for both Travises for two decades. He selected Travis's divorce attorney, and he provided the attorneys on both sides with a list of Travis assets but without appraisals or evaluations of how to divide the assets. Although the attorneys supposedly split the couple's assets evenly, Travis believed Elizabeth received the profitable ones. Having allowed Haber and Elizabeth to handle the business dealings, he had no real way of knowing. He'd signed whatever documents she told him to sign because he trusted her. He'd been "happy to sing, ride horses, shoot pool, work out, and practice quick draw, leaving everything else to Lib," he admitted. "I abdicated all responsibility, and it wasn't until the divorce that I realized what a vise grip she had on me from the time I moved in with her when I was seventeen till the day I moved out as a fifty-one-year-old man."[14]

Travis, as trustee of the Sandy Creek Trust, transferred the Avenida de Rey home to Elizabeth's Marrobone Trust via a special warranty deed.[15] Elizabeth moved permanently into one of her smaller houses in Santa Fe and placed the ranch property on the market, where it stayed for years. Their Lahaina home in Hawaii was sold in 2012 for over a million dollars. Because of its location on the northern end of Maui, it would survive the devastating Lahaina fire of 2023.

Travis established a new trust and purchased a home near Tioga, Texas, in December. He bought the Chrysalis Ranch, previously a private equestrian center that offered complete training of horses and riders. He and Mary Beougher renovated and enlarged the five-year-old house and decorated it to their western tastes. Travis named Gary Haber as trustee of his ranch trust. The following year, trustee Haber purchased four adjoining portions of land to increase the size of Travis's ranch in Cooke County to over three hundred acres.

Elizabeth and Randy Travis continued as manager and client. "In retrospect it would have been much wiser for Lib and me to simply go our separate ways," Travis stated. "But Lib had been my guardian and manager since long before we married, so we both thought we could separate our emotions from our business relationship. We were both wrong."[16]

## 13

## "I AM WEARING WHAT GOD GAVE ME, AND I AM PROUD OF IT."

At least two years before the twenty-fifth anniversary of Travis's 1986 debut album, *Storms of Life*, discussion began on how to celebrate that life-changing product. The Travises, Lehning, and Warner Bros. eventually decided to record a duet album in the style of *Heroes and Friends* from 1991. While the Travises were going through their breakup and divorce in 2010, they were recording songs for *Randy Travis 25th Anniversary Celebration*. Lehning remembers making the album as "really a fun project" but also "an emotional mess." Travis said, "Lib and I found it incredibly difficult to work together creatively during the time our relationship was disintegrating." But with everyone else, it was "sheer fun."

Half of the songs were new and half were Travis's hits. His current Warner Records A&R representative, Cris Lacy, was heavily involved with the Travises and Lehning in choosing songs and putting the album together. Travis hand-picked every singer on the album, a mix of younger singers and legends he had long known and admired. Elizabeth and assistant McCrystal flew around the country, meeting with potential duet partners and playing examples of the types of songs to record. The young stars included Josh Turner, Carrie Underwood, Brad Paisley, and the Zac Brown Band. Travis and Lehning traveled to Georgia to record "Forever and Ever, Amen" with Brown. "We went to Zac's house near Atlanta," Lehning recalls. "I brought a portable rig, and a couple of guys in his band laid down an acoustic version, and Randy and Zac sang it." Returning to Nashville, Lehning added more musicians to the basic track. "Zac probably changed the sound of 'Forever and Ever, Amen' more than anybody on the other songs," Travis later said. "He had this clear-cut vision of how to redo the arrangement. He wanted to add a back-porch feel to it." Travis enjoyed hearing the new interpretations of songs he had put his stamp on two decades earlier. In many cases, the duet partners selected the songs they wanted to sing. Kenny Chesney chose "He Walked on Water" because he had covered it on shows in his early days.

To sing "A Few Ole Country Boys," Lehning and Travis considered Jamey Johnson a natural choice. He and Travis had developed a friendship through their songwriting sessions after Travis heard him on a demo and invited him to a writing session. Johnson had been a fan since he was a fifth grader in Alabama, when he first heard Travis on the radio. He recalls, "Randy had a serious baritone voice. It was deep and solid, and my voice certainly wasn't deep or solid back then." Johnson's first big show was opening for Travis during Jubilee CityFest in Montgomery, Alabama, in 2002, when he was twenty-six years old. "I saw what he was able to do with a microphone in front of a crowd," Johnson says. "I was blown away." He says the music business doesn't allow friends to see each other "a whole lot 'cuz they're doing exactly what I'm doing—out there touring and traveling. It doesn't make us any less friends." The few hours in the studio were an opportunity to enjoy the company of friends.

John Anderson had performed "Diggin' Up Bones" at an awards show. Travis and Lehning liked his version so well they asked him to sing it on the album. They included an extra verse that hadn't been on the original recording. They sang the extra verse when they appeared together one evening on the Opry in 2011. "We were both smiling pretty big," Anderson recalls. "Sometimes you get the feeling it's sounding pretty good, and the people are liking it, y'know, and I think we both had that feeling. It was a great evening." They ended their performance with a joyful hug. Kris Kristofferson and Willie Nelson came into the studio and sang with Travis on a new gospel song called "Road to Surrender." Alan Jackson joined Travis to sing their cowritten hit songs, "Better Class of Losers" and "She's Got the Rhythm (And I Got the Blues)."

When Travis first heard "More Life," written by Mike Reid and Rory Bourke, he knew he wanted to record it. The song is about a hospitalized man whose nurse gives him pain medication. When she asks if there is anything more he needs, he replies, "More life, more time / More faith and the presence of mind / to breathe deeper, love stronger / stay in the moment one moment longer." Travis called the song "incredibly wonderful writing." Don Henley of the Eagles agreed to sing it, but he said it was a one-person song, not a duet, and he would sing harmony. Lehning calls Henley a major perfectionist with a great ear. At the end of one chorus, where Henley and Travis sang the line "more life" together, Henley didn't like the balance and told Lehning to remove him from that line and let Travis sing it alone. Lehning was amazed by the lack of ego from such a famous singer.

When Travis initially recorded "Promises" in 1988, it had been him and his guitar. Now he sang it with Shelby Lynne and a full band. Lehning asked Mark Casstevens, who had last played acoustic guitar on the *Full Circle* album, to join them for this recording. "This might be the proudest I am of my Randy cuts," he says about the session. "It was sort of a reunion with me and Kyle and me and Randy. They gave me the whole intro." The cut Travis found most meaningful was "Didn't We Shine," a new song he recorded with six longtime friends and people he admired: George Jones, Lorrie Morgan, Ray Price, Connie Smith, Joe Stampley, and Gene Watson. Lehning recorded the session at Sound Emporium and produced it with Don Schlitz, the song's cowriter. Schlitz was in Studio A with the musicians, and Lehning was in Studio B with the seven singers.

Travis described the sessions by saying, "You rehearse a bit, you figure out your keys and modulations, who's singing what part. It fell into place so easily, once we went in the studio and started." He considered all the songs but one "a delight to record." The lyrics of "Someone You Never Knew" described a man in conversation with his lover's husband, telling the husband things about his own wife, "someone you never knew." McCrystal was surprised and honored when Travis asked him to sing the duet, presumably as a thank-you for the work the young singer was doing. Travis took out his guitar, and they agreed on a key and which lines each would sing. "I don't know if Elizabeth put him up to it," McCrystal says. "I don't know the behind-the-scenes story. Randy was always very courteous to me."

There was most definitely a behind-the-scenes story. Elizabeth had been pushing to include her protégé on the album. Travis didn't understand why they would want an unknown Irish singer on an album featuring well-established country artists. "Nevertheless, against my wishes, the song stayed on the album," he said. McCrystal was crushed upon learning that Travis later said, "Fifteen of the sixteen songs on that album were incredible performances." It was a comment unworthy of Travis. Their duet possessed the same high quality as all the others. "It was a bit hurtful," McCrystal acknowledges. He wonders how much Travis objected to the song at the time. "The short time I knew Randy, he could not be bullied," McCrystal says. "He is strong willed and although he was always kind to me, I saw a temper if anyone crossed him."

*Randy Travis 25th Anniversary Celebration* was released on June 7, 2011, within one week of the twenty-fifth anniversary of the release of *Storms of Life*. Although other labels had given their singers permission to record the album, they wouldn't allow singles to be released. As an example, Lehning says, "'Can't Hurt a Man' was a brand-new song with Tim McGraw, and Curb Records wouldn't let us put it out as a single." Still, Travis was happy that McGraw, who had been thinking of recording the song himself, agreed to sing the duet on his album.[1] Twenty years earlier, several duets from *Heroes and Friends* had been released as singles. At that time, Travis was at the top of his fame and able to bring attention to his older duet partners. "A Few Ole Country Boys" had reached *Billboard*'s top ten, and several others charted. Now Travis was the older partner, and perhaps the labels believed their younger artists would be hindered rather than helped by releasing a single.

Travis hit the road to promote his new album. With concerts and promotional events scheduled through Elizabeth's office, he was forced into daily interaction with her. He saw his friends and fellow artists disappearing from his life. "Because Lib's and my divorce was so contentious," he later said, "many of our closest friends found it difficult to be around us, perhaps feeling they had to pick a side. Others apparently thought it was safer to say nothing at all." Travis drank more and more. He generally felt Elizabeth had his best interests at heart, and he hoped they could continue their business relationship. In March he had signed a management agreement prepared by Haber and Elizabeth. Considering his history of signing documents placed in front of him, it's unlikely he read the thirteen-page letter. It acknowledged that they'd operated together for more than twenty years without a written agreement and that they now desired to have a written agreement. Elizabeth's compensation was divided into three categories—before, during, and after their marriage.[2]

The trust between them continued to deteriorate. Elizabeth was present when her ex-husband appeared "out of it" during an early morning television interview in New York City. In front of the production staff, she told Travis, "You look and sound like shit." Her comment so angered him that he slammed his fist into a wall in the Fox News Channel green room. That action made the *New York Post*, with the headline "Country Star Hits the Wall." Travis blamed Elizabeth for purposely overscheduling him on his whirlwind promotional tour. He said he was tired because of a late-night flight from Florida; other sources suggest he was drinking with Mary. He left the studio and later acknowledged that he "spent the next several hours drinking." He returned to the studio for an afternoon interview that he called "a disaster" and said he "hadn't been functioning on all cylinders."[3]

Travis continued to tour all of June and most of July. On Monday, August 8, he fired his ex-wife from being his manager. A three-page letter from attorney Samuel Lipshie to Ms. Travis informed her that she had violated fiduciary duties and obligations, divulged confidential information calculated to damage his reputation and career, and submitted overstated reimbursement requests. The document directed her to no longer discuss Travis's business or personal affairs and to refer all inquiries to Jeff Davis or Gary Haber. Attorney Lipshie gave her three days to turn over "true and accurate copies" of travel expense claims, and he notified her that Jeff Davis would arrive with a moving crew and truck at eleven o'clock the next morning to remove Travis's property. This would include "all personal property not owned by you and other personal items of Mr. Travis (mementoes, awards, Gold Records, plaques and other property purchased by Mr. Travis or gifted to him)." The attorney threatened a court order and a visit from the Davidson County Sheriff's Office if she didn't comply.[4]

Davis brought a four-man moving crew to the Music Row office the next day and spent nine hours loading boxes of career memorabilia, trophies, and framed gold and platinum records, as agreed upon by both parties' attorneys. Travis's framed final thirty-dollar check from cleaning the *Radio & Records* trade magazine office twenty-five years earlier came off the wall. Elizabeth and her staff watched while all of Travis's and Davis's possessions were removed. In a later lawsuit, she described the scene by saying the men came to her office and took "practically all the property and business records located in all three stories therein pertaining to the Defendant's career and the Plaintiff's management thereof." She said the items taken before she could even go through them included "computers with work in progress, files, business records, framed record plaques and photographs hanging on the walls, and many other items which had been accumulated over the course of thirty-four years of personal management service." When Travis's agents were finished, the walls of her office "were left practically bare."

The following day, Travis arrived from Texas and met with his band and crews to reassure them of their employment. Joe Van Dyke remembers Travis giving the band a substantial raise. He says, "It was an indication of what Randy thinks of the people who work for him. It endeared him to us even more."[5]

On the last Sunday in September 2011, Travis headlined the eighteenth annual Crystal Heart Gala at the Worthington Renaissance Hotel in Fort Worth,

Texas. The private fund-raiser, sponsored by the Huguely Memorial Medical Center, attracted five hundred guests to raise money for providing cancer screenings to uninsured and financially challenged patients. Earlier in the day, Travis and Mary ate at a Mexican restaurant. After drinking coffee and taking antihistamines for his cold, he felt weak and wobbly. Jeff Davis asked him before the show if he was okay. Somewhat offended by the question, he said he was fine. Travis was singing his third song, "Three Wooden Crosses," when he collapsed, his guitar flying in one direction as he hit the floor and the microphone stand in another. Crew members helped him off the stage and onto the bus. Several doctors in the audience followed. They examined him and diagnosed dehydration, exacerbated by caffeine and antihistamines. This was reminiscent of his hospitalization in West Virginia in 1988. Then, too, the diagnosis was dehydration, with rest and liquids prescribed. Embarrassed by his collapse and fearful of repercussions to the fund-raising effort, Travis returned his performance fee. He needn't have worried. It was the hospital's most successful Crystal Heart Gala to date. Several months later, he stepped onto the stage with a steady gait and a healthy smile to give a free concert to the same group.[6]

An embarrassment of his own making occurred in February, following the 2012 Super Bowl. He and Mary hosted a party at their Texas ranch that Sunday afternoon. Travis drank more than a few glasses of red wine. After their friends went home, he grabbed a bottle of wine, jumped into his black 1998 Pontiac Trans Am, and headed west. He ended up seventeen miles southwest of his ranch, in the parking lot of the First Baptist Church in Sanger. His wine bottle was half empty when Officer Carl Parker of the Sanger Police Department knocked on the window and asked if he was okay. Asked for identification, Travis stated his name but couldn't find his driver's license. His slurred speech led Parker to ask if he'd been drinking. "Yes, sir, I have," Travis replied. "But I am not driving, as you can see." Parker had difficulty understanding as Travis tried to explain that he'd had a fight with his girlfriend.

Parker returned to his vehicle and radioed the dispatcher, "Subject stating he is *the* Randy Travis and he has a driver's license out of New Mexico." The dispatcher, stunned by the idea this might be the famous singer, answered, "I don't know what to say," before asking if Parker wanted a photo for verification. He didn't need it. Other patrol cars arrived, and Travis was asked to get out. According to the police report and dashcam video footage, he struggled to open the door and then stumbled from the Trans Am. Parker told him he would be going to jail for public intoxication. Travis exclaimed, "Really? Are you kidding me!" Parker said, "Maybe once we get to the jail, we can figure out who . . . get some more information on you, who you are."

When the officers started to handcuff him, Travis said, "You fixing to put handcuffs on me, are you? Is that what you're fixing to do?" One officer replied, "Yes, sir, I need your left hand, please." An officer removed the wine bottle from the front seat and found Travis's New Mexico driver's license. During the twelve-mile ride to the Denton County jail, Travis asked how many hours he had to spend in jail before someone would take him back to his vehicle. Parker told him it would be about four hours and he didn't know if anyone could drive Travis back to his vehicle. "You don't?" Travis asked. "Don't you think you should know that?" He complained about being in handcuffs, saying, "Yeah, I'm about as threatening as a cat." He was charged with a Class C misdemeanor for public intoxication and released on his own recognizance. His car was towed from the church parking lot. Through his publicist, he issued a statement to apologize for his actions, explaining they followed an evening of celebrating the Super Bowl. "I'm committed to being responsible and accountable," he said.[7] In June his attorney entered a no-contest plea in Sanger Municipal Court to a reduced charge of illegal parking. Travis paid a $264 fine and was placed on probation. The violation would be erased from his record on September 23 if those ninety days passed without other offenses in Denton County.

But his troubles weren't over. They were getting worse.

On April 5, 2012, Elizabeth filed a lawsuit against her ex-husband for breaking their management contract. The complaint by Elizabeth Travis Management Inc. (ETMI), recorded in the chancery court for Davidson County, Tennessee, accused Travis of breaching their personal management contract four months into a four-year agreement. It said he failed to provide the required written notice or allow her time to cure the breach. She charged him with violating his duties to act in a professional manner. Referring to his Sanger public intoxication arrest, her complaint stated that his conduct intentionally interfered with her ability to do her job in that it undermined his career. She requested a judgment for damages as well as attorneys' fees and litigation costs.[8] In his counterclaim, Travis insisted ETMI had violated numerous obligations owed to him as his personal manager. He wanted a jury trial. Elizabeth asked the court to either dismiss his counterclaim or rule against him in favor of ETMI.[9]

During these legal machinations, Travis continued touring as he had been doing since early February. He, Mary, and his band spent two weeks in Canada in June. They took a three-day trip to Telemark, Norway, to perform at the Seljord Country Festival on July 26. Travis tried not to think about his ex-wife's lawsuit, but it kept him awake at night. On Tuesday evening, August 7, after returning home to Texas, he and Mary entertained friends for dinner. Their evening included lighthearted conversation, several glasses of wine, and no discussion of legal matters. Exhausted from his travels, Travis took an Ambien sleeping pill and went to bed. In his memoir, he reconstructs what must have happened next. With no memory of that night, he ascribes the blackout and his behavior to mixing Ambien and alcohol.

Ambien, the brand name for the chemical compound Zolpidem, is a sedative-hypnotic drug used to treat insomnia. Its serious potential side effects include memory loss and behavioral changes. One online description includes this note: "Rarely, after taking this drug, people have gotten out of bed and driven vehicles while not fully awake. People have sleepwalked, prepared/eaten food, made phone calls, or had sex while not fully awake. Often, these people do not remember these events."

Travis apparently went downstairs naked and poured himself several drinks. Although not having smoked in years, he felt a sudden craving for nicotine. He jumped into his Trans Am, despite the alcohol, Ambien, and lack of clothes. "Since learning to drive as a teenager," he writes, "I've always enjoyed the thrill of driving fast, so a slow ride to the store was not an option." Once on FM (farm-to-market road) 922, he flew east and turned right on US Highway 377, driving past Tioga and south toward the Tiger Mart convenience store in Pilot Point, about ten miles from the ranch.[10] The store clerk watched a naked man walk through the door and up to the counter, where he ordered a pack of cigarettes. The clerk asked, "What are you doing in this store naked?" "Just give me the cigarettes," the man repeated. The clerk asked how he planned to pay for them. The man glanced at his empty hands, appeared frustrated, and left the store. The clerk immediately called the Pilot Point Police Department but had no idea who the person was, only that he was driving a black sports car.[11] With no cigarettes, Travis headed back up the road, past Tioga, and turned left on FM 922 toward home. He may have fallen asleep while driving.

The Grayson County dispatcher received a 9-1-1 call shortly after eleven o'clock reporting a man lying in the road along FM 922. The nineteen-year-old caller didn't see a vehicle until he drove ahead slightly and saw two lights in the bush. "I don't know if they're headlights," he reported, "but they are bright." The dispatcher asked the young man if he was going to be okay, and he said he was scared. "I want to say it was a white male," he said. "Light brown hair, I'm not sure. I want to say he had no shirt on, but I don't know. I want to stay in the vehicle." Eight minutes into the 9-1-1 conversation, the dispatcher called the Tioga Volunteer Fire Department to report a medical emergency. One minute later, the caller heard sirens and saw lights coming from Tioga. He stayed until the first responders released him.[12]

First on the scene was Elvin Fisk and his engine crew, followed closely by an ambulance that parked next to his fire truck at 11:22 p.m. They could see a dirt-covered person lying facedown in the middle of the highway, with orange cones and construction debris nearby. He was in the eastbound lane of FM 922, right before the bridge that crossed Lake Ray Roberts. Trees and brush covered the surrounding area. Off in the woods were headlights that appeared to be more vertical than horizontal. Several first responders went to see if anybody was in the vehicle. The paramedic who checked the body in the road found "a person laying supine in the middle of the street with multiple abrasions to his arms and left side of his face." The patient response report stated, "Patient responded to stimuli with heavy cursing. Patient jumped to his feet and threatened to choke paramedics and beat us up. He continued to verbally abuse all EMS and fire personnel."

Fisk walked over to introduce himself. The man yelled, "Get the camera out of my face." He apparently mistook emergency flashlights for camera lights and thought people were taking videos of him. Fisk recognized Travis, who was threatening to kill anyone who got close to him. Fisk hollered, "Randy! Randy, come on, man. I'm a fan." Travis headed straight for Fisk, who recalls, "I didn't know what was fixing to happen. He got nose to nose with me. I'm six-two; I didn't realize he was that much shorter than me." Fisk explains his first responder expertise, saying, "I try to calm people by just talking about things." They began a conversation, with Travis telling stories about his life, his parents, growing up, and horses. At no point did he appear physically threatening. "I wasn't ever in fear of him trying to fight anyone," Fisk says.[13]

Deputy Sheriff Bryan Caloway of the Grayson County Sheriff's Office had been dispatched at 11:24 to the call about a male lying unresponsive in the middle of a road. Upon arrival, before he could identify himself, Travis told him, "I am going to kick your ass," followed by, "Do you know who the hell I am?" Caloway wrote in his report, "I informed Mr. Travis I knew who he was and informed him I was there to make sure he was ok." Caloway convinced Travis to sit in the ambulance long enough to have his vital signs checked.

Refusing the offer of a sheet to cover himself, Travis stated, "No, I am wearing what God gave me, and I am proud of it."[14]

Fisk, as assistant chief of the fire department, was initially in charge of the scene. Law enforcement normally waited until patients were medically cleared before assuming control. Once Travis agreed to be checked by the paramedics, he was turned over to the Texas Highway Patrol. Trooper Clifford "Sammy" Bryant had arrived at 11:59 and parked behind a fire truck. He turned on his dash-mounted camera, which would run for the next three hours. Trooper Jim Fortenberry arrived. As the two men walked toward the crashed vehicle to check it out, they discussed the report that came in an hour earlier about a naked man in a convenience store in Pilot Point driving a black sports car. Travis's Trans Am sat in a shallow creek that ran under FM 922. The skin had been ripped off the driver's side when the car slid down the embankment. Fortenberry stuck his head partially inside and recognized distinct odors of alcohol and air bag propellant. They ran the license plate number and notified the communications dispatcher to be discreet with all information, due to Travis's celebrity status. They called for a wrecker to haul the car away.

Bryant approached Travis, who was then seated on the back of a fire truck. "I asked Travis where his clothes were and he angrily responded that that was the stupidest question he had ever heard," Bryant wrote in his report. "I asked Travis how much he had to drink and he again angrily responded that it was a foolish question." When Fortenberry asked what happened, Travis talked about fixing a meal for his girlfriend and her daughter, and how he didn't think they were appreciative. He answered the question about why he was out there by saying, "Just driving, I reckon, just driving." Fortenberry asked if he had a blackout, and he said, "No, I didn't have a blackout, I'm as healthy as a damn horse. I only want somebody to take me home." As he became agitated and angry again, Fortenberry asked for his cooperation. "I will do anything I can to cooperate," Travis said through gritted teeth. "I will cook you goddamn dinner, but just take me home." Fortenberry answered, "I'm not asking for dinner. We'll get this finished as soon as we can."

Bryant gave Travis the choice of going to the hospital or to jail. Travis said if he went in the ambulance he would refuse to get out at the hospital. Bryant then took out a pair of handcuffs and told him he was under arrest. Travis pleaded not to be cuffed, saying sarcastically, "I'm a dangerous son of a bitch." Bryant answered, "You've already threatened to whip me once." To that, Travis replied, "I will before it's over. I will come and find you." Seeing Fortenberry's Taser pointed at him, Travis consented to be handcuffed. Bryant then escorted him to the patrol car and placed him in the passenger seat. The only filming of his nakedness occurred when the dashcam captured him walking past the front of the vehicle. Fortenberry brought a sheet from the ambulance, but Travis refused it, telling Bryant he was fine. Several more hours would go by before Travis returned to his normal self. He never would regain any memory of this night.

During the thirty-four-mile trip to the Grayson County jail in Sherman, the dashcam recorded the conversation between the two men. Bryant asked what happened in the crash, and Travis said, "I don't know. I don't give a rat's ass. My wife-to-be has this argumentative way, so . . .," and he launched into a story about being whipped by his father with a pair of horse reins. "That's what I grew up in," he said. "So you think you got the right to do me this way? Oh, hell, no, you don't. You'll die, mother fucker." Bryant asked what he had done, and Travis replied, "You put these goddamn handcuffs on me." He added, "You goddamn insulted me."

"How did I insult you, Mr. Travis?"

"You insulted me by locking me up in a goddamn cage, basically, with handcuffs behind me, with my dick hanging out. Now—and I'm proud of my dick, it's bigger than most—but, you insulted me. You're a dead man." He continued to make comments such as, "You got sixty rounds fully automatic coming at you" and "I will bury you under a barn." Travis asked why they were going to Sherman instead of Tioga. Bryant explained the crash had occurred in Grayson County. Travis interrupted to say, "There ain't no damn way you could take me to Tioga?" Bryant said Tioga didn't have a jail. Travis didn't care; it had his house.

The dashcam video shows Bryant as consistently polite and courteous in responding to the belligerent complaints. Travis had spent more than thirty years trying to keep his temper and his drinking under control. Now that Elizabeth's restrictions were lifted, replaced by the stress he believed she caused in his life, he reverted to his teenage anger and unresolved issues of growing up with an abusive father. His inhibitions were completely gone, and his long-held anger spilled out, overriding any concern for consequences or responsibility. Still, at no point did he become physically abusive.

They drove through the secure entrance gates of the Grayson County jail shortly after one o'clock. Travis wanted the handcuffs removed, but Bryant said he first needed to read him the statutory warning. As Bryant read, Travis continued to ask questions and berate him. He told the trooper to "goddamn finish and please get the handcuffs off." Bryant said he was trying to finish but Travis kept interrupting him. At the end of reading the warning, Bryant asked if Travis would consent to a breath test. Travis said no. Bryant explained he would then have to get a search warrant for a blood specimen. Leaving Travis handcuffed, Bryant drove to the Texas Department of Public Safety in Sherman. He opened the passenger door and placed the sheet around Travis before escorting him into the office and seating him in a chair. The dashcam inside the patrol car continued to record the sound through the open doorway.

As Bryant prepared the search warrant paperwork, Trooper Fortenberry arrived to assist. "I did nothing. I killed nobody," Travis complained to him. "I'm sitting here goddamn naked, thanks to you people." Fortenberry told him, "We didn't take your clothes off, sir." When the signed search warrant arrived, Bryant told Travis they were going to the hospital. Travis asked, as he had previously, to call his girlfriend. Once again told no, he repeated that both Bryant and Fortenberry were dead men.

Arriving at the Wilson N. Jones Hospital, Bryant removed Travis from the patrol car, telling him to calm down. Travis said he was "as calm as a center seed in a cucumber." Wrapped in the sheet, he was taken inside the emergency room entrance and into an examination room. Other than telling Bryant it was illegal to draw his blood, he caused no problems with the hospital staff. A doctor examined him and discharged him as fit for confinement. Travis didn't complain of injuries, despite his swollen eye and cuts on his face. The staff gave him blue disposable pants and shirt, which he put on before being handcuffed again and returned to Bryant's patrol car. They reached the jail shortly after 2:30 a.m. Bryant completed the booking paperwork and released Travis to the jailers to place him in a holding cell. He was charged with a misdemeanor DWI first offense and a felony charge of retaliation for threats against law enforcement officials. His blood alcohol content registered .210 per 100 milliliters of blood. The legal limit in Texas was .008.[15]

Travis continued asking for permission to call his girlfriend. Finally, after the booking process was completed, the call was made. The ringing phone woke Mary at about four in the morning. Hearing that Travis was in jail, she reacted by reaching for the other side of the bed. He wasn't there. She had no idea what to do. She called a longtime friend, Al Weir, and said, "Al, I don't know what's going on." Weir called a deputy sheriff friend in Denton County, who tracked down Travis's location in Grayson County and called Weir with the story of what had happened that night. Weir called Mary to say he was on his way to Sherman, a forty-five-minute drive from his house.

By that time, word had spread and news reporters were gathering in front of the jail. Gary Corley, whose Sherman law firm handled commercial litigation, received a call from an attorney friend who joked that Corley was no longer the most infamous person in Grayson County, as Randy Travis was in their jail. Corley responded, "We can't have Randy Travis in the Grayson County jail. Bye." A Travis fan, Corley threw on shorts and flip-flops, a T-shirt and ball cap, and headed to his office. He looked up the charges against Travis and prepared two bonds. He then went to the jail, where he pressed the button on the wall and announced himself. Just then he heard the clanging doors, watched them swing open, and saw Travis step into the vestibule. Those doors banged shut and another set opened to release him. "He comes out," Corley remembers, "he's in a hospital gown, and he's got a horrible black eye." Two women were sitting in the lobby waiting for their relatives to be released. They asked, "Oh, Mr. Travis, can we have a picture with you?" Corley assumed his protective lawyer demeanor and told them, "Ladies, look, he's not interested in taking pictures with y'all at this time." But the drugs and alcohol had worn off, and Travis was once again the humble celebrity who appreciated his fans. Contradicting the attorney, he said, "No, that's okay." The women handed Corley a phone. He took two photos of them with Travis and handed the phone back. Years later, Travis would chuckle at the memory of that photo.

Corley took off his orange University of Texas ball cap and put it on Travis's head, saying, "You need this worse than I do." Travis didn't object. It was one of Corley's favorite caps, he says, "so I hated to part with it, but for Randy Travis I would." Corley told Travis the television news cameras were set up outside, and if Travis would keep the cap down and follow him to his truck, Corley would take him wherever he wanted to go. At that moment, Al Weir entered the room and Travis greeted him happily. After being told from which exit Travis would be released, Weir backed his truck to that door and waited for Travis to come out. The media and several onlookers were there as Weir helped his friend into the truck. He asked, "Randy, what happened?" "I don't know" was the hesitant reply. Weir drove westbound on old Highway 82, trying to lose the people following them. He asked, "What made you leave the house? You were naked!" Travis said, "No." Weir told him, "What the hell? Why do you think you're wearing those paper clothes?" Travis looked down at his clothing and said, "Damn." Weir asked, "You don't remember that?" Travis answered, "No, I don't remember anything." After a pause, he said, "That doesn't look good, does it?" His sense of humor somewhat restored, he joked, "Well, I guess any press is good press." Weir recalls the moment, saying, "Even though he was disoriented, he had a good attitude about it."

Speeding down the road, Weir succeeded in losing their pursuers. Travis said he was thirsty and Weir gave him a bottle of water. Then he said, "I gotta get something to eat. I'm starved." Weir said okay and Travis added, "And you're buying." That cracked Weir up: "Yeah, with all the money you have on you?" At the Sonic Drive-In in Whitesboro, Weir purchased an egg sandwich for his passenger. He had already called Mary, who met them there in her Range Rover. They then headed to the ranch, where they had to drive past news trucks to get to the locked gate at the end of the driveway. Helicopters flew overhead. Once inside the house, Travis still seemed disoriented. Weir suggested Mary take him to the hospital and get him checked out because he didn't seem right. Plus, he had glass in his scalp and dried blood on his face. Mary cleaned him up the best she could, not understanding why he hadn't received medical treatment at the hospital in Sherman. She waited until dark so that they wouldn't be seen and then took him to the Baylor Emergency Medical Center in Aubrey to get his wounds cleaned and the glass removed. He was diagnosed with a concussion.[16]

The mug shot showing his black eye and scratched face traveled around the world, along with headlines such as "Randy Travis Wandered Naked into Convenience Store" and "Randy Travis Arrested Naked, Charged with DWI." The Republican National Convention canceled his appearance the following week. Eleven other concert promoters canceled his shows during the initial flurry of negative publicity. The Trans Am was towed to the Travis ranch, where it remains today. It had to be moved into a grove of trees to hide it from helicopters flying overhead. Singer Jamey Johnson calls it "the Trans Ambien."

Travis had a week to recuperate before heading to Franklin, Ohio, for his next concert. Acoustic guitarist Lance Dary remembers standing on the stage, wondering how the fans would react and what Travis would say. The band brought the boss onstage to the tune of the humorous Ray Stevens song "The Streak," which includes the lyrics, "Here he comes / There he goes / And he ain't wearin' no clothes." Travis came onstage and paused for a moment. Dary popped his earbud out to hear what the crowd was yelling: "Just sing, just sing! We love you." And Travis sang. Dary says, "They'd already forgiven him. Which is a pretty amazing connection to have with your fans."[17]

# 14

## "IN FACT, I WAS FEELIN' MIGHTY FINE."

Travis's legal troubles continued. Fortunately, he was not charged for the convenience store incident in Pilot Point, and his record in Denton County was cleared as scheduled in September. His court case in Grayson County was expected to be heard in January. Concerning Elizabeth's ETMI lawsuit in Nashville, a jury trial was scheduled for October 1 but then canceled. A judge issued a case management order, and the Travises' attorneys spent the remainder of the year with motions and telephone conferences. Both parties were given until February to file additional motions.[1]

Several newspaper columnists focused on Thanksgiving by choosing their top turkeys of the year. One placed Travis on a list of "the top flops and fools of 2012." Another, with a headline of "These Celebrities Deserve a Dressing Down for Their Bad Behavior This Year," said, "Let us pray that Randy Travis, who was found drunk outside a church after a Super Bowl party, then was found naked in the road after crashing his Pontiac Trans Am in August, gets help. Forever and ever, amen."[2]

Travis, by then, was back in the studio to record his next album. Instead of new songs, he wanted to pay tribute to the singers who had influenced him and whose songs shaped his life. He and Lehning were discussing their next Nashville sessions when Travis received an offer from a new friend. Pierre de Wet contacted Travis with an invitation to visit his winery and recording studio in Bullard, Texas, south of Tyler. He had been raised in South Africa on a farm named Kiepersol. He came to the United States with two baby daughters and two suitcases after his wife died of cancer. He eventually developed Kiepersol Enterprises, planting vineyards in 1998 and then opening a winery and steak house. For whatever reason, de Wet wanted a recording studio, so he purchased equipment secondhand from Willie Nelson's studio near Austin and built Studio 333. He told Travis in a phone call, "I cook you the best steak you've ever had. And we play music." Travis and Mary accepted his invitation to visit Kiepersol. After a great meal, the guests played music in de Wet's living room until four in the morning. De Wet offered Travis the use of the studio for his next recording session.

Lehning was less than thrilled when Travis said he wanted to record the upcoming album at a studio built by a winery owner near Tyler, Texas. Lehning wondered what kind of studio it could possibly be. He agreed to go to Texas and check it out. When he arrived at Travis's ranch, the news got worse. Travis said a friend, Al Weir, would take them there—in his helicopter. "I'd never flown in a helicopter," Lehning explains. "I figured, well, if I'm gonna die, it might as well be with Randy." Weir arrived in his Bell 206 Long Ranger and landed on Travis's property. Travis sat up front, while Lehning and Mary strapped themselves into the rear seats of the four-seat helicopter. Lehning's apprehension quickly went away. "It was awesome," he says. "Al was a great pilot, and it was a beautiful day." They landed on the Kiepersol property, which was surrounded by tilled fields and nearby mansions interspersed through the tree-covered landscape. Lehning inspected the studio, fully expecting to tell Travis it wasn't up to standards. He was wrong. Only two additional pieces of equipment were needed, and de Wet purchased them according to Lehning's specifications.

In mid-November, Lehning and his adult son, Jason, flew in from Nashville and met Travis and the band at the studio. It was the first time Travis had recorded an album using his own band. The songs were those he normally played at sound check. "I'd go to his sound checks from time to time," Lehning recalls, "and they would have so much fun playing these old songs he grew up singing. When it came time to make this record, these guys knew these songs backwards and forwards. They played like they wrote them." Lehning wanted to call the album "Sound Check Volumes I and II." They recorded thirty-two songs over a four-day period, taking time out for two concerts. Saturday evening Travis played in Vinton, Louisiana, about four hours from Tyler. The buses then traveled five hours to San Antonio, Texas, for a Sunday evening show at the Majestic Theatre, returning to Tyler to resume recording on Monday and Tuesday. The two Lehnings remained at the studio to edit the songs already recorded. Throughout the sessions, de Wet sat in the control room with Lehning, enjoying his role as honorary producer. His family and staff treated the visitors like royalty, turning their food requests into delicious meals.

"It was so much work in so little time," L D Wayne remembers. "It was almost overwhelming, but we got it done, and Randy was in great vocal form." The musicians knew from experience how their boss wanted the music to feel. Lance Dary says, "I was one of the new guys, and I was in my sixteenth year." Joe Van Dyke considers the experience "a real highlight of my career." He enjoyed the creative process, with everybody suggesting parts as they put together a recording rather than playing live and trying to copy a recording already made. Van Dyke says Travis had fun working with the band and paying tribute to artists who had influenced him. They covered songs ranging from Ernest Tubb to Kris Kristofferson, Marty Robbins to Waylon Jennings, with the largest number coming from Merle Haggard. Some were Haggard's hits, and some were his western swing versions of older classics, such as Louis Armstrong's "Big Butter and Egg Man" and "Pennies from Heaven."

They rerecorded "More Life," which they had been performing on their shows since the *25th Anniversary Celebration* album came out. Robb Houston sang Don Henley's part. The song had become one of their favorites. "Even the first night we did it live," Dary recalls, "it took on such a meaning. Everybody in the band, I know, was thinking of a specific person. By the fifth time we did it, the song was dripping with emotion. Everybody brought their own thing to it while staying true to the record." That camaraderie permeated their long weekend of recording at Studio 333. After returning to Nashville, Lehning added background vocals and additional instruments. Warner Bros. planned to release two volumes of *Influence: The Man I Am*, the first in October 2013 and the second the following year. The leftover songs went into the vault, along with Travis's other unreleased recordings from earlier years.[3]

Travis finished the touring season with his usual December week in Las Vegas during the National Finals Rodeo, this year at the Golden Nugget. He returned to Texas to face the DWI case in Grayson County. Judge James Corley Henderson of the Grayson County Court scheduled the arraignment and plea conference for January 31, 2013, at four o'clock. Larry Friedman from Dallas and local Sherman attorney John Nix represented Travis. When Nix had been recommended to join the defense team, he went to Tioga to meet fifty-three-year-old Travis, and they became friends. "Highly intelligent, a musical genius," Nix says. "He thought some people were trying to take advantage of him, but other than that, he had a childlike sweetness to him. His whole thing was about making whoever he was with happy. I couldn't have asked for a sweeter client." Nix ordered an independent test of Travis's bloodwork, which came back with an unidentified chemical, in addition to alcohol. "My argument was always that it was Ambien," Nix says.

Judge Henderson issued a pretrial order concerning media access. While courtroom proceedings would be open to the public and transcripts could be obtained from the court reporter, photographs and recordings inside the Grayson County Courthouse were prohibited. To provide background and context shots of the location, media representatives were allowed to take photographs inside the courthouse and its west courtroom from one o'clock until half past two. No interviews were allowed inside the building that day. "It was a jam-packed courtroom," Nix remembers. "I had prosecutors with the DA's office asking me if they could come back and meet him. It was a real circus. The *New York Post*, the *Washington Post*, it was traveling around the wire. Even around the courthouse square, people were sitting out there, trying to get a look at him." Nix credits Travis's long experience in front of crowds with helping him get through the day. "He was cavalier about it," Nix says. "That case was the biggest we've ever had around here, not because of the content but because of who it was."

Travis was charged with "Driving While Intoxicated, with a blood alcohol content greater than 0.15." The Class A misdemeanor carried a maximum penalty of a year in the county jail and a four-thousand-dollar fine. The sticking point in the plea agreement discussions prior to the trial date had been what to do about the felony charge of retaliation. District Attorney (DA) Joe Brown was a Randy Travis fan who believed Travis hadn't been himself that night. But he *had* threatened the troopers. Such behavior couldn't be tolerated. The Texas Department of Public Safety (DPS) wanted Travis held accountable. The resulting compromise dropped the felony charge but required Travis to spend thirty days in an inpatient treatment facility. In the plea agreement, he consented to his punishment: 180 days of confinement probated for twenty months (meaning he would be supervised by the court but would avoid jail time), a fine of two thousand dollars plus court costs, one hundred hours of community service, thirty days of inpatient alcohol/substance abuse treatment at Enterhealth Treatment Center, an ignition interlock device on his vehicles, and routine drug tests. In return, the state agreed to "file no charges other than Driving While Intoxicated."[4]

The Grayson County Criminal DA's Office issued a press release that announced Travis's plea agreement and gave a summary of his behavior the night of his arrest. DA Brown explained that Travis's belligerent behavior was the reason his punishment was greater than for most first-time DWI offenders. In addition to inpatient treatment, Brown said, "His fine and community service requirements are more than double what is usually received, and his probation term is the maximum available, and longer than the usual eighteen months. All of that is appropriate in light of his behavior with the officers. I spoke at length with the officers involved, and they were in agreement with the outcome."[5]

At the January 31 arraignment, Judge Henderson approved the plea agreement and then ruled on another motion, one that would take years to settle. Travis's attorneys asked the court to order the "videos and their transcripts" from the night of the arrest be destroyed or at least prohibited from public release. DA Brown objected, reminding the court that the plea agreement removed the felony charge of retaliation but did not include destroying dashcam videos. Arguing that the public had a right to know what was happening on the roadways and how law enforcement was responding, his statement said, "The State contends that the public's confidence in the fairness of the criminal justice system is of a legitimate concern to the public, and the facts contained on the videos at issue are highly relevant to this concern."

Judge Henderson determined the video was confidential and therefore exempt from the Texas Open Records Act. He ordered "all copies of the DPS dashboard video, and any transcripts of said video" destroyed, with the exception of one copy held by the Grayson County District Attorney's Office. He gave the DA sole discretion to hold the copy until it was no longer needed for detecting or prosecuting crime. It would then be destroyed. It was not to be viewed outside the office. He agreed with the district attorney's desire to publicly confirm his correct charging decision and to recognize the highly professional conduct of the arresting officer. "However," he wrote, "this legitimate concern of the public and elected public officials does not demand the disclosure of every intimate and private detail."

Travis immediately went to work to fulfill the requirements of his sentence so that what he called "the horrendously embarrassing police video of me naked" would be destroyed. "I paid the fine," he said later, "went to rehabilitation, and did more than one hundred eighty hours of community service, working with various charities, singing for kids at McDonald's restaurants, and that sort of thing."[6]

◊ ♦ ◊

Kim Hughes, a Texas filmmaker from Odessa living in Dallas, wanted to build her professional reputation. Her brother advised her to make a short film that starred a celebrity and then show it at film festivals to gain recognition and obtain funding for larger projects. She considered short films amateurish, but she prayed that night about finding a suitable project. Because she didn't want to make a short film, she added a list of requirements to her prayer, including, "Lord, if I'm going to write a short film, it has to have Randy Travis." When the Lord answered every one of her requests, she knew the project was meant to be. She began by writing a twenty-minute film, *The Virtuoso*, about an aspiring musician who discovers he is the biological son of his idol, a country music legend. Roy Taggert rejects young Jonah Anderson but changes his mind on his deathbed and wants to reconcile. Kim's husband, Dr. Kent Hughes, offered to find Travis, and Mary answered the phone when Hughes called the ranch. He said his wife had written a movie, "and she feels strongly that Randy is meant to play the leading role." Mary invited them to the ranch. The two couples became instant friends. Dr. Hughes, a renowned plastic surgeon, would soon play a significant role in Travis's life. Travis liked the script, especially the overarching theme of redemption. Even though it was only a short DVD production, it looked like a cool project.

With the Taggert character cast, Hughes needed a young singer to portray Jonah. She remembered someone her brother had earlier called to her attention on YouTube, saying, "If I had a voice like that, I wouldn't do anything but sing." She did some research on James Dupré, who had recently moved from Louisiana to Nashville to pursue music full-time, and then emailed him to explain she had written a script for a short film with Randy Travis in the lead role. Would Dupré be interested in playing his character's son? "I had started thinking maybe one day I'll try my hand at acting," Dupré says about receiving her email. "I didn't know whether I'd be good or not. I told Kim I'm not an actor, but I would love to try." She said she'd seen his YouTube videos, and he looked comfortable in front of a camera. It was such a small role he didn't need to worry about it.

*The Virtuoso* was filmed in Dallas in February 2013. Dupré remembers being super nervous about meeting Travis. "The first day on the set, Randy walked in with his guitar, and he immediately came to me," Dupré says, "and he said, 'Hey, let me show you this song I just finished writing with my buddy.' He started singing this brand-new Randy Travis song. I was like, man, is this really happening? It was surreal." Dupré adds, "He showed me the ropes and gave me tips about different scenes we were doing. Meeting him and getting to work with him was a great experience."

While Kim Hughes worked on finishing her short film, which would eventually become much more, Travis and Dupré returned to music. Travis had received a personal note from George Jones about his final show, which he planned to give in Nashville in November. "I sure would like it if you would come to be with me that night," Jones wrote. "Heck, maybe do a song or two with me. Please let me know if you can celebrate my career with me. I might be eighty-one years old, but I'm not in the grave yet." Travis happily accepted.

Unfortunately, Jones died on April 26, 2013, after being hospitalized for a respiratory infection. Travis and Mary were among Jones's friends who attended a private visitation on May 1. The following morning, crowds began gathering outside the Opry House before sunrise to honor Jones on the day of his funeral. Numerous country music stars spoke and sang during the three-hour memorial service. Political figures such as Tennessee governor Bill Haslam and former first lady Laura Bush spoke.[7] Travis wore a black tuxedo and black cowboy boots. Sitting on a stool on the Opry stage in front of funeral bouquets and a portrait of Jones, he sang "Amazing Grace" while softly strumming his guitar. The traditional hymn was a Jones standard and had become one for Travis as well. His performance was reminiscent of fifteen years earlier, when he'd stood on the Ryman stage in front of Tammy Wynette's portrait and sung a hymn in her memory. Both times, his voice was the only sound in the packed auditorium.

He had already recorded a George Jones tribute song that was being readied for release. Cris Lacy of Warner Bros. contacted Travis several days after Jones's death to say she had a song she'd like him to record. Popular songwriter Keith Gattis had written "Tonight I'm Playin' Possum," which begins by announcing Jones's death with the line, "In case you haven't heard / he stopped loving her today." Referring to Jones by his nickname of "Possum," the singer plans to spend a long night listening to "every last song he ever sung." Gattis was in the studio the day Lehning and Travis recorded his song. Joe Nichols was there to sing with Travis. With number one hits that included "Brokenheartsville" and "Tequila Makes Her Clothes Fall Off," thirty-six-year-old Nichols had grown up on Travis's music. *Storms of Life* was one of his favorite albums as a child. "He sounded like the old guys but he's a new guy," Nichols remembers. "I've always wanted to mimic the guys I thought had the good country, manly qualities I wanted. Randy Travis was among the best. Range-wise, some of his songs were so low, and he was capable of singing so high, it's really impressive." When Lehning invited Nichols to record with Travis, Nichols responded that it would be an honor to do a duet with Randy Travis: "I don't care what the song is. He's one of my heroes."[8]

It was Travis's last recording session.

While in Nashville, Travis settled the year-old lawsuit with ex-wife/manager Elizabeth. On May 7 mediator Tracy Shaw reported to the district court judge for the Middle District of Tennessee, "The parties appeared and participated in mediation. All matters in controversy were resolved." Terms of the agreement were not released.[9]

Then, when Travis thought his troubles were behind him, with the Tennessee case settled and his Texas plea agreement fulfilled, he was hit with news of a partial release of the dashcam video. Greg Abbott, attorney general of Texas, and the Texas DPS had filed objections that asserted Judge Henderson lacked jurisdiction to order DPS to destroy the video. Judge Henderson twice denied their requests to set aside the protective order. DPS and the attorney general disregarded his ruling and granted release of a portion of the dashcam video, redacted to not show Travis below the waist. They said Texas law on public information requests required them to release the video.

Travis was outraged. Having completed the requirements of his plea agreement, he felt betrayed by the state of Texas for releasing a video that he believed had been destroyed. He called the release a violation of his privacy and insisted the state hadn't held up its end of the deal. However, Travis had just begun his two-year probation, and Judge Henderson had ordered the video to remain as evidence until the case was closed. Its existence shouldn't have been a surprise. But the state's willingness to release it to media outlets came as a shock. Travis sued the DPS and Attorney General Abbott, arguing that his actions at the time were not voluntary because he was exhausted, intoxicated, sleep-deprived, medicated, and suffering from a post-collision concussion.[10]

After filing his lawsuit against the Texas authorities, Travis went to Louisiana to film a movie. *Christmas on the Bayou* was a romantic drama about an overworked divorced executive, played by Hilarie Burton, who returns to her hometown to spend Christmas with her family.[11] Travis's character, the owner of a small general store, plays a pivotal role in the outcome of the story. His scenes were filmed inside an old feed and hardware store that had been closed for half a century. Dust particles floated in the air throughout the filming. The movie would be released for that year's holiday season.

Travis was back in Nashville on June 7 for CMA Fest, where he was one of a group of artists and songwriters taking part in an afternoon "Remembering

George Jones" panel discussion. As part of his presentation, Travis debuted his latest recording, "Tonight I'm Playin' Possum." The hundreds of fans and industry professionals present gave him a rousing standing ovation. That evening, he sang it for the CMA Fest crowd of thousands at the NFL stadium LP Field (renamed Nissan Stadium in 2016). The crowd cheered all through the song. The following week, Warner Bros. released the duet version of "Tonight I'm Playin' Possum" as the first single from the upcoming album, *Influence Vol. 1: The Man I Am*.

Travis played several show dates in late June, ending with an appearance with Loretta Lynn at RiverEdge Park in Aurora, Illinois, on June 29. While on the road, he and acoustic guitarist Robb Houston enjoyed working out together. "The workouts helped relieve stress, as well," he recalled about that summer. "In fact, I was feelin' mighty fine." Wherever they were, if the hotel didn't have a decent exercise room, Jeff Davis would find them a local fitness center. Lance Dary says, "I'd be crawling off the bus at eight in the morning, when Robb and Randy were already running around the parking lot, headed to the gym. They definitely had their workout routine." It gave Travis an additional opportunity to interact with the public. "I guess they were surprised to see us," he said about running into fans at the gym, "but I enjoyed meeting folks and tried to spend time talking with them."

Travis's band members continued to enjoy working with him, and he frequently let them know how much he appreciated their musicianship. "That's the main thing I remember about working with Randy," steel guitarist Steve Hinson says. "Every time he turned around and looked at me during the show, he'd make me feel like I was worth a million dollars, and he was so glad I was there. Every night." Dary recalls, "One of my favorite things in the Randy Travis Band was going down the road at two o'clock in the morning, we'd have what I call Country Music 101. Steve Hinson would be in the jump, David Johnson would be on the stairs, me and L D, and Bill Cook, we'd be huddled around, listening to music." They listened to the stories on the radio that went along with the songs being played and to each other's road stories. "It was a country music history lesson," Dary says. Joe Van Dyke called it the Golden Hour. There was excitement in the air and the adrenaline rush still going from the evening's show experience. He especially enjoyed listening to Hinson, who considered it his duty to entertain the band on the bus. "He has an encyclopedic knowledge of the history of Nashville," Van Dyke says. "He knows who worked with who when."[12]

As farewells were said after the Aurora concert, and the buses and trucks headed to their destinations in Texas and Tennessee, everyone looked forward to returning to their travels and performances after the Independence Day holiday break. An upcoming tour in Canada was scheduled to kick off on July 10 with an appearance at the Deadwood Mountain Grand Event Center in Deadwood, South Dakota. A newspaper announcement said Travis's show promised to "pull favorite after favorite from a treasure trove featuring more than twenty-five years of his distinct, award-winning country sound." The club manager was quoted as saying, "His demeanor is equally as down-home as his music, and we are looking forward to hearing his voice ring through our event center."[13]

It was not to be.

# "LORD, PLEASE GIVE HIM BACK TO ME."

During an early 2012 interview, Travis repeated what he had said many times in interviews. He loved writing songs, loved recording in the studio, loved playing even though he didn't consider himself a good player. "But, ultimately," he said, "to walk on a platform in front of a live audience and sing these songs, and joke with an audience and hear that laughter and hear them sing along, there's nothing like that. It's the greatest thing I have ever experienced." Referring to his *25th Anniversary Celebration* album, he said, "If I am fortunate enough to live twenty-five more years, I hope I remain healthy, vocally healthy, strong enough to continue writing and recording. Because of the way I feel about what I do onstage, I hope I can still do that in twenty-five years." He wanted to go through the rest of life just being happy. "I am fortunate enough to be with someone now, a lady named Mary who is a beautiful woman," he said. "I enjoy her more than anybody I've ever met in my life."[1]

Following an Independence Day pool party at his ranch on Thursday, July 4, 2013, he was looking forward to the three-week tour of Western Canada. On Friday, he omitted his normal four-hour workout because they spent the morning packing the tour bus. It took extra planning to prepare for unpacking everything for inspection if required by Canadian Customs and Immigration. At some point during the morning, Travis started having trouble breathing. He told bus driver George Hampton he was going to take a break. Sitting in the cool house and drinking water didn't make him feel better. After lunch, he and Mary held an eight-hour meeting with business advisors from Nashville and

Dallas. Travis attributed his sluggish feeling to missing his morning workout. Perhaps he was getting a cold. He went to bed early but was unable to sleep. By Saturday morning, he was so congested that he allowed Mary to take him to the emergency room in Aubrey, twenty-eight miles away. The doctor at Baylor Emergency diagnosed him with walking pneumonia and gave him a prescription for antibiotics and an inhaler. That evening, he struggled to breathe. He again went to bed early but didn't sleep.

By Sunday morning, he and Mary were seriously concerned. They planned to leave Tuesday afternoon to meet the band in Deadwood. Would he be able to sing by Wednesday evening? Worried, Mary took him back to Baylor Emergency in Aubrey. Their friend Al Weir met them there around noon, and the three of them walked together into the emergency center. Mary filled out the paperwork at the front desk; she and Randy had exchanged durable powers of attorney a year earlier. "I can't breathe," Travis kept saying. "I can't get my breath." Breathing brought pain. The nurse who led them back to the examination room told Travis she had always enjoyed his music. She acknowledged he wasn't feeling well but asked if she could have his autograph. "Sure," he answered, smiling at her as he signed the clipboard with his last-ever right-handed signature.

The emergency room doctor said Travis now had full-blown pneumonia and needed to go to Baylor Medical Center at McKinney. Both of his lungs were filled with fluid. Paramedics placed him on a gurney and wheeled him to the ambulance, which took him nineteen miles to McKinney. Mary and Weir followed in their vehicles. While Weir parked in the visitors' section, Mary stopped in front of the emergency entrance and jumped out to follow her fiancé inside. Travis was rushed to the intensive care unit (ICU) and hooked to an IV. As the doctors tried to force air into his lungs, he kept telling them he couldn't breathe. Mary asked, "How can he get air if both lungs are full?" The effort was putting a strain on his heart. The doctors asked everyone to leave the room while they inserted an Impella 2.5, a tiny pump the diameter of a coffee stirrer. The process consisted of placing a catheter in an artery in Travis's left groin and sending the "left ventricle assist device" all the way to his heart. Able to only whisper, Travis told Mary, "Don't worry. I'll be fine."

While Mary went to park her car in the visitors' lot, Weir returned to Travis's room, where a nurse was attending to the patient. Suddenly, the heart monitor started screaming, and the line on the screen stopped moving. Travis's heart had stopped. A medical team rushed into the room. A doctor slapped defibrillator paddles on Travis. Nothing happened. He tried again. The heart monitor started blipping. Travis was alive! Weir looked on in shock. The thought raced through his mind: *We were just talking to Randy. An hour ago, he signed an autograph, with a smile on his face. How could we be there, and he just flatlined?* Weir met Mary in the hallway to tell her, "Randy died, and they brought him back."

Throughout the day and into the evening, Travis was kept sedated to ease the burden on his heart. Mary and Weir stayed by his side. Weir called Jeff Davis, Dennis Traywick, and several others to update them. As midnight approached, Mary told him to go home and get some sleep. Travis's condition worsened during the night. Mary insisted he be taken to the Heart Hospital in Plano. The McKinney doctors were in contact with Dr. William Gray, director of cardiovascular services at Baylor Medical Center in Plano. He conferred with Dr. Michael Mack, medical director of cardiovascular disease. They agreed "a higher level of specialized care" was needed. The unconscious Travis was transported twenty-two miles to the Heart Hospital at Baylor Plano. Dr. Mack met him and Mary there at 5:30 on Monday morning. Weir joined them a short time later.

After a series of tests, Dr. Mack diagnosed Travis with viral cardiomyopathy, a virus that attacks the heart. The virus had weakened his heart and caused his lungs to fill with fluid. "Viral cardiomyopathy can sit dormant for four to six weeks before attacking," Dr. Mack explained. "Then it does its damage to the heart in twenty-four to forty-eight hours, stretching the lungs and masking as pneumonia." That was why Travis had been misdiagnosed and why the virus attacked so quickly. Dr. Mack asked where they had been four to six weeks prior, and Mary told him they were in Lafayette making a movie, five weeks to the day. She described filming scenes in an old feed store that had been closed for fifty years. Dr. Mack surmised that might be where Travis contracted the virus.

When other doctors suggested replacing the Impella 2.5 with an Impella 5.0, Dr. Mack determined there wasn't time to wait for it to work. He made a long incision in Travis's right groin area and connected him through a series of tubes to a form of life support called extra-corporeal membrane oxygenation. The machines took over all heart and lung functions.[2] A statement released by Travis's publicist on Monday notified the world that Randy Travis, fifty-four, had been admitted to an unidentified Texas hospital on Sunday, suffering from viral cardiomyopathy. News media reports filled in the blanks by summarizing Travis's recent alcohol incidents and quoting "talking head" retired cardiologists who made pronouncements such as "The singer's hard-drinking lifestyle is a possible factor in his illness." The news reports mentioned, accurately, that heart problems ran in the family and discussed his mother's death and a heart attack experienced by brother Ricky Traywick the previous year.[3]

Travis's mother had died in 1998 at age sixty-one, after years of dealing with heart problems and fluid buildup. Bobbie Tucker Traywick's death certificate listed the cause of her death as "congestive heart failure with ischemic cardiomyopathy, weakened heart muscles due to coronary heart disease."[4] Ischemic cardiomyopathy describes a heart muscle that can't pump well because of damage from ischemia (lack of blood supply to the muscle). In a later press conference, Dr. Mack explained that Travis suffered "an acute viral illness" that "seems to have tipped over a more chronic condition. He has what's called idiopathic cardiomyopathy, which means he has scarring of his heart muscle." A biopsy of his heart muscle confirmed old scar tissue. "This is not the appearance of either drugs or alcohol causing the heart condition," Dr. Mack said. "Mr. Travis does have a family history of cardiomyopathy. It is more likely related to that."[5]

On Tuesday, Jeff Davis, Kyle Lehning, and Dennis Traywick arrived from Nashville. Davis had been home Saturday afternoon, working on tour details, when bus driver Hampton called and said, "Randy's really sick." The next day, Mary called to say, "Hey, Jeff, Randy's in an ambulance going to the hospital, and I'm following him." Then came Weir's call in the evening. Davis remembers, "When you hear that kind of news on the phone when you're seven hundred miles away in Nashville, you just gotta go there." He spent Monday tracking down trucks and buses that were on their way to South Dakota, notifying band members that the Canadian tour was on hold, and contacting promoters to cancel the early dates.

Tuesday evening, a group of doctors met with Travis's team of family and friends in the hospital conference room. One doctor suggested holding a press conference because the hospital was inundated with calls. Media trucks and reporters lined the streets. On Wednesday morning, Dr. Gray issued a short video statement summarizing the events. Dr. Mack explained his diagnosis of viral cardiomyopathy, saying, "Since his transfer, his condition has stabilized, and he is showing signs of improvement." Not mentioning that Travis was in an induced coma, he concluded with thanks: "On behalf of Mr. Travis's family, friends and associates, we would like to express our extreme gratitude for the overwhelming affection and support Mr. Travis has received."

Late Wednesday morning, the doctors began slowly bringing Travis out of the induced coma. Around two o'clock, Dr. Mack asked Mary, Dennis, and Jeff Davis to join him in his office. His request sounded ominous. They didn't realize how bad it would be. He told them, "Randy has suffered a massive stroke."

Dr. Mack theorized that a blood clot had reached Travis's brain during the time he was being revived after his heart stopped beating at McKinney on Sunday. After seventy-two hours in a coma, it was too late for medication to reverse the effects. In addition, his brain was swelling. "We've got to do surgery to relieve the pressure on his brain by six o'clock tonight or we'll lose him," Dr. Mack told Mary. He explained that the swelling had already caused the midline of two cranial sections to shift a distance of eight centimeters. At twelve centimeters, Travis would die. There was a three-to-four-hour window. "You have to decide what you want to do," Dr. Mack said. Travis's family and close friends gathered in the conference room, where the doctors showed them X-rays of his brain and explained possible approaches. Jeff Davis remembers, "They said we had three choices. And all three choices ended with 'or he'll die.'" Lehning says, "We were sitting there talking to the doctors, trying to decide what ought to happen. It was hard to know what the right thing to do was."

Dr. Mack outlined seven critical aspects that had to go right in order for Travis to survive the surgery. First, he had to breathe on his own when they took him off life support. The other six medical issues included having no blood clots. It reminded Mary of a hurdle race, where he had those hurdles to get over to make it to the finish line of the surgery. "We couldn't believe what we were hearing," Davis says. "The responsibility of trying to hopefully make the right decision for him; we all loved him so much, it was devastating. I just doubled over. Put my hands on my knees and couldn't stand up for a minute."

Dr. Mack then told them, "Even with the surgery, we have only a one to two percent chance that Randy will survive." Weir recalls thinking it just kept getting worse. Mary remembers, "It didn't take any time to do the math on that. One to two percent is one hundred percent over zero."[6] During the evening's emergency surgery to prevent the swollen brain from choking off its own blood supply, the doctors removed a bone flap from Travis's left hemi-cranium, the frontal temporal parietal and occipital lobe. The piece of bone was approximately three by four inches. Once it was removed, only the relatively thin layer of the scalp protected the dura, the covering of the brain. To preserve the bone, the doctors made an incision on the left side of Travis's abdomen, above the pelvic bone and over from the belly button. They inserted the bone flap in a subcutaneous pocket of fat below the skin surface. It was a sterile environment where the skull bone would live for the next three months, having access to nutrition supplied by Travis's body.[7]

The hospital sent out a publicity notice at 8:10 p.m. that read, "As a complication of his congestive heart failure, Mr. Randy Travis has suffered a stroke and is currently undergoing surgery to relieve pressure on his brain." About the four-and-a-half-hour surgery, Mary says, "It seemed like about four-and-a-half years." Then Dr. Mack came into the waiting room with the good news: Travis had survived. The next forty-eight hours were touch and go. Doctors warned Mary, "If he does survive, he will probably never be able to speak or walk again." Mary prayed, "Lord, please give him back to me." As the swelling in his brain subsided, he began to improve, although remaining in critical condition. Ricky Traywick and Rose Arrowwood arrived from North Carolina on Thursday to be with their brother.[8]

Friday night, after midnight, singer John Anderson, along with bass player Rocky Thacker and drummer Tommy Rivelli, showed up in the hospital room. They had played a concert in Arlington and were on their way back to Nashville. Jeff Davis had called Rivelli to notify him of Travis's stroke. Since they were already in Texas, Rivelli and Thacker asked Anderson if they could stop by to see their former boss. "I don't know if we really should have been there or not, but it seemed good to go say hello," Anderson recalls. "Tommy and Rocky went out of their love and respect of having worked with Randy so long, and I went along with them out of love and respect, also." Thacker says, "Randy was unconscious. I do remember Tommy making jokes to Randy in his ear. And Randy kinda squeezed both of our hands." They all prayed together by his bedside. "It was a touching night," Anderson remembers.[9]

Monday afternoon, Mary joined Dr. Mack and Dr. Gary Erwin at a press conference. After Dr. Mack summarized the situation, Dr. Erwin, a pulmonary and critical care specialist, explained that Travis remained on intravenous medication to help support his heart while they were decreasing the doses and starting him on oral medications. He was still on a ventilator to help him breathe. Dr. Erwin said, "He is awake, alert, interacting with his family and friends, and beginning to start some early physical therapy." Mary said, "He is responding well to voices, and he sees and understands, and he's miles beyond where any of us thought he would be a few days ago." She added, "This could have occurred anywhere at any time, and we were in the finest place we could be to have the best outcome we could ever have."

Josh Turner brought his family for a visit. His wife, Jennifer, and her mother took Mary out to eat, to give her a break from the hospital. Turner, noticing Travis's Gibson Dove guitar that Mary had brought to the hospital, began a private concert that lasted over an hour. He sang his songs, Travis's songs, classic country hits, and gospel songs. Travis's head was completely bandaged, he had a tube in his throat, and he couldn't see or talk. But he could hear and feel.

Travis was thrilled when his band members arrived from Nashville. They came into his room two at a time, sounding heartbroken, and he was unable to reassure them or let them know how much he appreciated their presence. Guitarist L D Wayne had talked to the band's bus driver, John Hill, who drove for Nitetrain Coach, the company that leased band buses to Travis's organization. Nitetrain offered the band a company bus at no charge, and Hill volunteered his time. He announced, "Okay, band and crew, we're going to see Randy." The band members pitched in to pay for fuel on the roundtrip to Plano, Texas. Numerous other friends stopped in for visits. Al Weir and Bill Blythe visited daily. Blythe, who lived in Plano and considered Weir his best friend, had developed a close friendship with Travis and Mary after Weir introduced them several years earlier.

In the July 15 press conference, Dr. Erwin had said Travis would be at the Heart Hospital for another two to three weeks to stabilize his heart and begin aggressive physical therapy. When discharged, he would be transferred to an inpatient facility to continue therapy. "We anticipate it will take months to recover from the stroke," Dr. Erwin said. For that inpatient facility, Mary chose the Stallworth Rehabilitation Hospital, part of the Vanderbilt University Medical Center system, in Nashville. She thought being back in the music community with his band members and so many friends close by would be helpful. By now the Canadian tour had been canceled and the band members released to find other employment until touring could resume. On July 31, Travis was discharged from the Heart Hospital Baylor Plano.[10]

The eighty-bed Vanderbilt Stallworth Rehabilitation Hospital opened in 1993 as a collaboration between Vanderbilt University Medical Center and Encompass Health. In twenty years it had become a leading provider of inpatient rehabilitation for stroke and brain injury, offering speech, occupational, and physical therapy, along with full-time nursing care.[11] Travis arrived from Texas on a miserable two-hour flight in an air ambulance that lacked air conditioning. Strapped to a stretcher, he was soaked with sweat as the pilot fought the turbulent weather buffeting the small plane. Mary and an air medic were the only others on board.

Once settled at Stallworth and in an established routine, Travis enjoyed receiving visitors. He sat up in bed and acknowledged the many friends who stopped by. One nurse brought in a guitar at the end of his work shifts to play and sing for Travis. These daily visits somewhat assuaged Mary's extreme disappointment that Stallworth had no music therapy program. She had taken it for granted that a premier rehab center in Music City, eight blocks from Travis's former Music Row home, would have such a program. There wasn't even a piano in the building.

Travis's blurred vision added an extra layer of difficulty to his rehab. His eyesight slowly started to improve as he began seeing outlines of shapes and people. It would take nine months for his vision to return to normal, where he could go back to using reading glasses.

Rehabilitation took a backseat when Travis contracted a hospital-borne staph infection. His breathing problems resurfaced. He appeared to have pneumonia, and his lungs collapsed. Twelve days after arriving at Stallworth, he was transferred to the ICU at Vanderbilt Medical Center, suffering from life-threatening sepsis (blood poisoning). The infection had spread throughout his body. Once again hooked to machines, he was barely conscious as his weight dropped to almost one hundred pounds and his body systems deteriorated. A tracheotomy tube protruded from his throat, and he wore a helmet to cover the missing portion of his skull. He looked so bad that his friends who came to visit thought it was the last time they would see him alive. Travis's lungs collapsed for the third time. The infections couldn't be controlled. Medical professionals warned Mary to prepare for the worst. In a semi-coma, Travis felt Mary grab his hand and heard her ask if he wanted to keep fighting. He squeezed her hand as a tear trickled from his eye. That told everyone he wanted to live.

"Strength, hope, love, faith, and prayers," Mary later said was what got them through this period. "The prayer warriors who were out there," she explained, "the fan mail streaming in, the phone calls and texts and things like that. They helped give us strength." She relied on Travis's record label and publicist to keep the world informed of his condition. "I didn't have the wherewithal to be involved with that," she said. "What was important to me was thinking about a way to get him back to us. To educate myself, I read a lot and learned a lot. It was a fast course in nursing. When no one else was there, I was suctioning and adjusting, I was watching monitors."

"More Life," one of the songs Travis had recorded in Tyler, Texas, became Mary's theme song. She played it repeatedly in the hospital. They were living the lyrics, where nurses ask if there's anything more you need, and the answer is "More life, more time." Once again, Mary prayed, "God, please give him back to me. I don't care how you give him back, just please let me have more time." During the third week at Vanderbilt, Mary consented to a risky adjustment to the antibiotics. The new medication was so strong it could only be administered for a short time before it started doing more harm than good. Fortunately, it succeeded in bringing down the staph infection. Travis slowly improved.

After those rough weeks, Mary longed to be home in Texas. She called Al Weir to say she wanted to bring Travis back to Baylor. Weir asked Ray Davis, owner of the Texas Rangers Major League Baseball team, if he would fly to Nashville and pick up Travis. He agreed, inviting Weir and Bill Blythe to travel with him. They were shocked at the sight of their friend when his gurney was loaded onto the private jet on September 6. "Randy looked terrible," Weir recalls. "It was sad." Tubes protruded from the thin, pale body still racked with blood poisoning. Dennis Traywick, who lived near Nashville, gave his big brother an emotional farewell. Two nurses boarded the plane with Travis and Mary. They landed at Addison Airport, nine miles north of downtown Dallas. A Baylor ambulance met them and carried Travis back to the Heart Hospital in Plano, where he was once again under the care of Dr. Mack. Several days later, Dr. Mack removed the tubes from his lungs, which then reinflated and allowed him to start breathing normally. After ten days at the Heart Hospital, when Travis was no longer toxic with the staph infection, he was transferred to the Baylor Institute of Rehabilitation in downtown Dallas. Weir and Blythe visited every day, bringing delicious food to supplement the hospital meals Travis and Mary had grown weary of eating. Knowing Travis loved milkshakes, they brought those daily to fatten him up. They competed to see who could bring better "outside" food. Many friends visited, always a thrill for Travis, even though he couldn't speak his appreciation.

As Travis stabilized, the doctors discussed when it would be safe to replace the bone flap. Dr. David Barnett, chief of neurosurgery at Baylor University Medical Center in Dallas, examined Travis at the rehabilitation hospital and then transferred him to Baylor University Medical Center for surgery on October 14, 2013. Although Dr. Barnett would normally perform the surgery by himself, Mary requested that renowned plastic surgeon Kent Hughes assist with the closure of the scalp. "Obviously, this is Randy Travis," Dr. Barnett says. Dr. Hughes and his wife, Kim, had been close friends since Travis starred in *The Virtuoso*. The couple stayed with Mary at the hospital during those dark hours when Travis's survival was in question. Kim was still working on her movie.

Dr. Barnett removed the section of bone from its pocket in Travis's abdomen and replaced it on his skull. "Neurosurgeons are known to be excellent brain surgeons, working around the skull," he comments, "but maybe what we're not known to be is excellent at making things look pretty and perfect on the outside." After the initial closure, he turned the surgery over to Dr. Hughes, who accomplished a perfect skin closure, with a barely noticeable incision and minimal external scar tissue. The operation went perfectly, according to Dr. Barnett. Travis handled the anesthesia well, and there were no problems whatsoever. Two days later, Travis was returned to the rehab hospital. "It was an absolutely miraculously beautiful job on Randy's skull," Kim Hughes says. "His head had been sunk in where they took the skull out. It would be like a hardboiled egg, where you have one place that's dented real deep. Now Randy has his confidence back."[12]

Out in the music world, two events that had been planned more than a year earlier went on as scheduled but in much different forms. On October 1, Warner Bros. released *Influence Vol. 1: The Man I Am*. Although there could be no promotional tour, the album did get reviewed. One reviewer gave it an A+ rating, along with the comment, "It will probably be my pick as the top country album of the year." The review stated, "There's no doubt that this collection of covers comes from a serious lifelong fan of hardcore country music, and not someone who pays empty lip service to the music of the American common people."[13] The album included the duet with Joe Nichols "Tonight I'm Playin' Possum." On November 22, the date George Jones had planned to play his final concert in Nashville, with Travis as one of his guests, it was instead a tribute to Jones's memory. Titled "Playin' Possum: The Final No Show," the event at Bridgestone Arena drew a sold-out crowd of sixteen thousand. Halfway through the evening, actor Jon Voight took the stage to raise the spirits of Randy Travis, over six hundred miles away in rehab. "Let's form a human chain of love for Randy," Voight announced. He then led the crowd in a cheer of "We love you, Randy!"[14]

A few days later, Travis was discharged from Baylor Institute of Rehabilitation. After almost five months in hospitals, he and Mary left early in the morning, unnoticed. Travis could barely see and was in a wheelchair. As Mary pushed him through the hospital doors, he raised his left arm above his head and said, "Bye!" He and Mary were home on the ranch by Thanksgiving. Travis had spent six weeks in a coma, undergone two brain surgeries and five tracheostomies, and lost more than a third of his body weight. He had suffered through serious infections and been poked with innumerable needles and tubes. He could not talk or walk. He had to relearn simple functions such as flushing a toilet and operating a television remote.[15]

But he was home. Now would begin the grueling outpatient rehab.

# 16

# "I THINK YOU WOULD BE THE PERFECT PERSON TO MANAGE RANDY TRAVIS."

Travis began outpatient therapy at Select Rehabilitation Hospital of Denton, Texas, in November 2013. Physical therapist Tim Massengill remembers "pretty big" deficits and significant injury. He says Travis worked "really, really hard" at the vigorous regimen prescribed for him. They first worked on trying to stand. Many people with strokes have trouble bending their affected leg. "In RT's case," Massengill explains, "his knee would buckle, so getting him to stand on that side was difficult. It wasn't weak, just how he responded to pressure. Trying to take a step, advance his good left leg, he couldn't do that when I first saw him. I haven't seen many patients who tend to have that pattern due to the damage to their brain. It made transfers, like getting him from his wheelchair to the table, very challenging." Massengill and the other therapists assigned challenging exercises to lessen the boredom of doing things over and over. "You're crazy," Travis would say about some of what they expected him to do.

"Randy had expressive aphasia," Massengill says, "where he knew what you were saying, but the damaged part of the brain affected his word formation, the ability to process and think of words. He could pull out one or two words, but he might struggle to put three or four together. He knew the word he wanted to use. He couldn't get it from his brain to his talk." Travis could get his messages across, though. He would laugh as he mocked the therapists. "No" was a favorite word. He might throw his hands up like "What? What?" But he continued to drive himself, determined to improve.[1]

Aphasia is a neurological disorder that occurs with a third of the 795,000 strokes each year in the United States. It has a greater negative impact on a person's quality of life than cancer or Alzheimer's disease because the person is unable to communicate and interact with others. Although over two million Americans have aphasia, 85 percent of the general population have never heard of it. Aphasia is more common than Parkinson's disease, muscular dystrophy, or cerebral palsy. Travis's stroke wiped out portions of his brain that deal with speaking, as well as diminishing his ability to read and write. It did not affect his intelligence.

For almost two and a half years, Mary drove him the thirty-mile distance five days a week. "By the time we had our coffee and got dressed, it was time to go back to rehab," she later said about their daily routine. Friends and family sometimes provided their transportation. "You find days that you have your little victories, and they keep you going," Mary told an interviewer. "Then there's days you feel totally defeated. You have to sift through your soul and figure out if you want to keep going forward." What made it possible for her to keep going was seeing the fight in her sweetheart and his strong determination. "Just the look in his eyes and to see that smile the world knows, the Randy Travis smile," she said.[2]

"The challenge of rehab is taking what we do in the clinic and turning it into a daily, functional thing at home," Massengill says. "One of the hardest things someone in Randy's situation has to do is adapt to the new reality of 'this is what I was, this is where I am now.'" He would sometimes go to the ranch on his days off to practice maneuvering in Travis's home environment—walking on the stone porch, around the pool, through the house on the rugs, up and down the staircases. Massengill helped Travis design tasks to perform at home to continue the carryover from the clinic. He set up Travis's Chuck Norris Total Gym to allow his patient to perform a one-leg squat. Travis would ask how many he had to do, grumbling that it was too hard and that his leg hurt. Mary was always there to encourage her fiancé, never allowing him to give up when the frustration overwhelmed him. In addition to rehab, Travis had a business to manage. After the daily therapy sessions, the couple would often go off to handle other commitments. Massengill praises Mary by saying, "The role of being significant other, caregiver, and brand manager, those three roles are incredibly hard. I wouldn't want to do even two of those."[3]

After the first few weeks at home, Mary knew she had to get Travis away from the house and back with friends instead of spending so much time alone. The couple first went to a Tanya Tucker concert in Fort Worth. Mary stayed on the lookout for friends' concerts in the local area. Travis credits that effort as one of the best things she did to help with his rehabilitation. Shortly before Christmas, they were watching *Forrest Gump* when fire trucks drove up the hill to the ranch house, sirens blaring and lights flashing. Mary rolled Travis to the front porch, where a group of neighbors and firefighter friends serenaded him with Christmas carols. He bobbed his head in enjoyment as twenty people sang off-key versions of "We Wish You a Merry Christmas" and "Jingle Bells." He gave them all hugs and stood up in his wheelchair to wave good-bye. Mary continued to surround him with music, as she had done during their months in the hospital. He mouthed the words to familiar songs. The lyrics were firmly held in his right-brain memory, even if he couldn't speak them. When she first played his own songs upon their return home, he cried. It took a year before he was willing to listen to his former self. As he adjusted to hearing his recordings, he mouthed the words to those songs.

Music also played a role in therapy. It multitasks the brain to work on two things at once, such as walking while singing. "Sometimes if we add a mental load, it changes how people walk and move," Massengill says. "That's a good challenge." One of their favorite songs was the Lionel Richie and Kenny Rogers recording of "Lady." The therapists would sing a refrain, and Travis could eventually belt out a rough version of "La-dy-y." He would laugh at Massengill's terrible singing, and there would be smiles and humor all around. The person who contributed the most to getting Travis to sing again was Tracy Miller, who worked in the clinic's marketing office. She began by bringing her keyboard to play for Travis during her lunch hour and then started joining in the therapy sessions for the multitasking efforts. When she asked for a song Travis loved and might be able to sing, Mary suggested "Amazing Grace." Travis perked up when he heard that melody but could not put words and music together. The two women worked with him every day for months, one syllable at a time, until he could sing a full verse.[4]

When Mary heard that Neal McCoy was headlining a Smiles for Life charity benefit in Dallas on February 7, 2014, she loaded Travis and the wheelchair into their SUV. At the venue, McCoy invited them to join him for his meet and greet. Fans saw for the first time how seriously the stroke had debilitated Travis. They looked shocked and offered prayers and get-well wishes. Travis felt energized to be greeted by his fans. In April the couple drove to Mesquite, where Josh Turner was performing at the rodeo. Turner was astonished to see Travis, having last seen his friend seemingly on his deathbed. When Turner introduced Travis during the show and Mary rolled the wheelchair a few feet onto the stage, the crowd erupted in a prolonged standing ovation. At the end of May, a few weeks after Travis's fifty-fifth birthday, they traveled on his tour bus to Thackerville, Oklahoma, to a Dolly Parton concert. During her show, she announced, "There are some people you love and admire for their talents. Tonight, one of those people is here. Randy Travis, wherever you are, I hope you are enjoying the show." Two of Travis's former sidemen reunited with him. Tom Rutledge had played acoustic guitar in Parton's band for years, and keyboardist Monty Parkey drove one of the buses. They went on his bus, and he was as thrilled to see them as they were to see him.[5]

On August 19, Warner Bros. released, with little fanfare, the second volume of the songs recorded in Tyler, Texas. One newspaper reported, "Despite some health setbacks, Randy Travis has a new album out today. *Influence Vol. 2: The Man I Am* is a collection of the crooner's covers of classic country songs." Whereas the first volume closed with Travis and Joe Nichols singing "Tonight I'm Playin' Possum," the second volume closed with Travis's solo version.[6]

In September, Mary drove Travis to Denison, Texas, to attend the Four Rivers Outreach fund-raiser banquet. Leaning on a walking stick, he concentrated on every labored step as he walked slowly into the hangar at the North Texas Regional Airport. He reached his table, victorious. Sixteen months earlier, as part of his required community service, he had performed a forty-minute set at the Four Rivers fund-raiser. Playing his guitar, he sang songs and told stories about his songs and movies. Concluding the show by inviting keynote speaker Larry Gatlin to join him in singing "Amazing Grace," he said, "I did this the other day for George Jones's memorial." Now, in 2014, he was still on probation in Grayson County, but his court supervision had stopped a year earlier, and his case would close as scheduled in January.

By November he was learning to write left-handed and trying to play his guitar. He could form chords with his left hand, but his paralyzed right hand could not strum the strings. They had been home from the hospital and in rehab for over a year when Mary suggested driving to Nashville. She wanted to test his long-term memory, of which doctors had repeatedly warned not to expect much. The first breakthrough came while they were driving east on I-40. Travis pointed to an overhead sign and read the word "Na-ash-ville." It was a turning point for them, giving hope that his brain was recovering. During their Nashville stay, Mary drove to locations familiar to Travis where she had never been. One was Flynns Lick, several hours east, where the cover for his debut album, *Storms of Life*, had been photographed just under thirty years earlier. As she rounded a bend on a narrow road, Travis reacted with excitement. He recognized the store, even though it was mostly a pile of rubble now. A day later, while driving through the Ashland City area, he remembered the roads and directed Mary where to turn. He took them to the house he had lived in twenty-five years earlier. They were overwhelmed to realize the stroke had not destroyed his long-term memory. Filled with joy, they spent several days driving around, with Travis excitedly pointing out familiar sights. They returned home feeling rejuvenated and optimistic.

In February they were back in Nashville, this time to discuss financial matters with Warner Music executives, including CEO John Esposito. The meeting was chaired by A&R vice president Cris Lacy, who would soon be named one of *Billboard*'s 2016 Women in Music for her executive role. She had been Travis's A&R representative since his return to the label in 2008. Prior to accepting that A&R position in 2005, she had spent ten years as a song plugger for various publishing companies. This was Travis's first visit to his record label since his stroke. After updating everyone on health issues, Mary asked why he wasn't receiving royalty payments. The executives said he had not recouped his advances, as there had been many draws against royalties over the years. How could that be, with the millions of records he had sold? The executives appeared uncomfortable talking about issues usually discussed with managers, not artists alone. But Travis had no management and no one looking out for him. He couldn't speak for himself, and Mary was struggling to learn the music business. No one knew what to do. Then Lacy had an idea.[7]

That was the day they met the man who would change their future.

Tony Conway spent thirty-three years as a talent agent with Buddy Lee Attractions, which for many years was the biggest talent agency in Nashville. He represented Willie Nelson, Kris Kristofferson, George Jones, and many others. He first met Travis when Lib Hatcher asked for his representation in 1984; he declined because he had too many clients at the time. Several years later, as Travis approached stardom, Conway represented new acts, including Ricky Van Shelton, Lorrie Morgan, and Patty Loveless. Travis needed co-headline talent to increase the size of his crowds. Conway booked acts into those slots and traveled along on the tours. Plus, as Tammy Wynette's agent, he participated in the GMC Truck American Music Tour in 1988. He enjoyed hanging out with Travis and Hatcher on the road, and Travis was intrigued by the legendary artists Conway represented. Conway became president of Buddy Lee Attractions in 1987 and co-owner in 1998, shortly before Buddy Lee died from cancer. Lee asked Conway to stay at the agency for the next ten years. Owning half the company and with no intention of going anywhere, Conway agreed. Ten years to the day, he resigned and sold his half to the Lee family. He was ready to start his own company, which he did in 2010 by establishing a management company and boutique talent agency called Conway Entertainment Group.

He was working in his office the day Cris Lacy called and asked him to come to her office. She said, "I've got Randy Travis and Mary here, and I told them I think maybe you could help them." He walked the four blocks to Warner Music, where he and Travis held an impromptu happy reunion. After being introduced to Mary, he listened as the group discussed what could be done to help Travis. "I think you would be the perfect person to manage Randy Travis," Lacy told him. With Travis in a wheelchair and unable to verbally communicate, Conway didn't know what he could do to help, although he wanted to assist in whatever way he could. Feeling somewhat overwhelmed, he said, "Let me think about this and see if I can come up with some ideas." Travis's contract with Warner Music was expiring, and everyone agreed there was no reason to renew it.

Several days later, Conway told Travis it would be an honor to represent him. They signed a management agreement on March 2, 2015. Conway wanted to find a way that Travis could make a living, and he assured the couple that everything would be done first class. He and his staff began brainstorming. Travis had almost no income, and half of his royalties were owed to his ex-wife. His huge medical bills were only partially covered by insurance; policies had lapsed due to unexplained nonpayment. Following the death of accountant Gary Haber in 2014, Travis had no access to his financial records. While Elizabeth had been Travis's manager, she negotiated a contract that gave Warner Music's merchandise company total rights to sell Travis's merchandise. The large advance she received had not been earned back before his stroke. With no touring or merchandise sales, Warner Music couldn't recoup its investment. Conway asked label head Esposito if Warner Music would consider wiping the recoupment off Travis's account. Fortunately, Esposito agreed. That allowed Travis to start receiving his quarterly royalty checks.

Conway's major goal was to get Travis into the Country Music Hall of Fame. As a member of the CMA Board of Directors for more than twenty years, he knew how the process worked. "There's no way anybody can make somebody a member of the Country Music Hall of Fame," he explains. "There's no real way you can lobby or convince anybody. It's a technical and surgical process." The board appoints a twelve-person nominating committee, which comes up annually with five nominees in each of three categories. The ballots are sent to a group of six hundred people to select the winners. These voters, chosen in secret by the CMA Board of Directors, must have been making their incomes in the country music industry for at least ten years. They are appointed for life, unless they miss a year of voting, in which case they are removed. With all six hundred people being in country music businesses—artists, entertainers, entertainment lawyers, CEOs of record labels, talent agencies, management companies—and a large majority of them living in Nashville, Conway believed he knew most of them. He simply didn't know who they were. He began a quest of talking to everybody he knew, reminding them of "this iconic, one-of-a-kind, changer of country music" who was so deserving of being in the Country Music Hall of Fame.

For Travis's first national public appearance after his stroke, Conway worked out a deal with the Academy of Country Music during its fiftieth anniversary awards show, to be held at the home of the Dallas Cowboys, AT&T Stadium in Arlington, Texas. The April 19 event broke the Guinness world record for "Highest Attendance at an Awards Show Broadcast" with a crowd of 70,252. When Lee Brice was introduced as "last year's ACM Song of the Year winner," he sang the chorus of "Forever and Ever, Amen" and then explained it had won Song of the Year in 1987. He said, "The man who sang it has had an amazing comeback to be with us tonight. Ladies and gentlemen, the great Randy Travis." The camera switched to Travis in the audience. The crowd immediately jumped up in a standing ovation. Travis shakily stood, waved, and nodded as the applause continued. His bride smiled adoringly up at him.[8]

Randy Travis and Mary Davis Beougher, both fifty-five, had been married at the nondenominational Denton Bible Church on March 21, 2015. The Beougher divorce had been finalized a year earlier, and Travis's rehab was far enough along that they decided it was time. Travis had re-proposed to Mary on Christmas Day, after learning enough words to present her with a ring and ask her again to marry him. They purchased their marriage license in early March and scheduled a date with Pastor Tommy Nelson. When the day arrived, they called Bill Blythe and asked him to meet them at the church. They said they wanted him to help them sell some Longhorn cattle. He thought it was strange to be selling cattle at a church, but he put on khaki slacks and a white golf shirt and drove to Denton, where he was surprised to be asked to participate in the wedding. The groom wore a black jacket, shirt, and jeans. The bride wore an ivory dress with sleeveless bodice and floor-length frilly skirt. Pastor Nelson conducted a traditional wedding ceremony, with Blythe and Penny Wootten, the pastor's assistant, as witnesses. The newlyweds went out to eat and then home. That was their honeymoon.[9]

In November, Kim Hughes released her movie, which she had turned into a full-length feature film with a new title, *The Price*.[10] Travis's stroke occurred six months after filming the short film *The Virtuoso*. Hughes's original intent had been a film she could show at festivals to gain exposure. Not knowing if Travis would ever act again, she realized her film had become more important than just a short film. "People don't watch short films," she says. "He acted so beautifully and did such a great job, I needed to make it into a feature film. Because I was so proud of his work." The original twenty-minute film focused on Travis's character, Roy Taggert, a famous country singer who refused to acknowledge as his son the aspiring country singer Jonah Anderson, played by James Dupré. On his deathbed, he calls Jonah and asks for forgiveness. Hughes gave Mary the role of Taggert's former lover and Jonah's mother. With screenplays running about a minute per page, Hughes needed to write seventy pages to add more than an hour. "It took a bit of stretching my skill to create a story to wrap around what had already been recorded as a short and be able to film it without the lead actor and fill sixty more minutes," she explains. She placed Dupré in the leading role and changed the plot to a television show where Jonah Anderson wins a record deal. They filmed the new scenes in early 2014. Hughes spent the next year finalizing her movie and blending in Travis's scenes. "Everything turned out fabulously beautiful, and I'm proud of it," Hughes says. "And Randy was proud of it." It was later released on DVD and Netflix.

*The Price* enjoyed a small theatrical release in a handful of cities, including with the Travises in attendance in Nashville and Dallas. Hughes was disappointed in Warner Music's refusal to support the Nashville screening. "Warner squashed it," she says. "They wouldn't put out news press or articles or let anyone know about it. As an independent filmmaker, it was hard for me without anyone to promote it. His band came, his producers came, friends came to the premier. Randy was really happy. But it made me sad that none of the fans knew it was playing there."[11]

By this time Travis had signed a new recording contract with Warner Music. Tony Conway calls it "historic and unprecedented" for a label to contract with an artist who can't go into the studio and record. However, the unreleased songs Travis and Lehning had recorded over the years could be promoted as "new" material. Lehning searched through his own catalog and the Warner Bros. vault and found fourteen fully produced singles, which he remixed with modern technology. But the new album couldn't be released without verifying ownership of the songs, and no paperwork was found to document the sale of the Giant Records recordings to Universal.[12]

Shocking news came to the Travises at the end of January when Pierre de Wet died of a heart attack at age sixty-one. His preplanned funeral called for a celebration of life, and he had often said he wanted Travis to sing at his funeral.

More than a thousand people attended the celebration on February 3, 2016. Mary wheeled her husband onstage and helped him stand at the microphone. In his first time singing before an audience since his stroke, he began the first verse of "Amazing Grace." The crowd immediately joined in and sang along with him. Feeling victorious, Travis knew he would sing again.[13]

The Travises were in Nashville when Tony Conway asked them to meet him at the Country Music Association office for a special interview with CEO Sarah Trahern. He said it would be about upcoming events, with a video filmed for a CMA special on country music. They went into the atrium of the CMA office, where two chairs were set up with microphones, lights, and video cameras. Staff members seated the couple and put the mics on them. Trahern walked in, greeted them, and asked if they were ready to start the interview. As the cameras rolled, she said, "Well, we are not going to interview you today. We wanted you to be in Nashville so we could tell you some news about you and the Country Music Hall of Fame." They looked at each other in confusion. Trahern said, "Randy, it is my honor to inform you that you have been elected to go into the Country Music Hall of Fame." Their confusion turned to shock. Mary hugged her husband and started crying. She asked, "Are you telling us the truth? Is this really happening?" Trahern assured them, "Yes, you are going into the Country Music Hall of Fame." Travis cried with joy. Conway hugged them both and congratulated them. He remembers, "All three of us are crying and need a Kleenex." Trahern made them promise not to tell anyone, even family members, until the CMA made its announcement. The Travises promised, "Yes, yes," as they hugged and cried, repeating, "I can't believe this is really happening."

They were back in Nashville on March 29 for the CMA's press conference in the rotunda of the Country Music Hall of Fame and Museum. Press and industry leaders, members of the CMA Board of Directors, and members of the Hall of Fame filled the room. Brenda Lee, of "Rockin' around the Christmas Tree" fame, introduced Fred Foster as the first of three 2016 inductees. Foster, eighty-four, had founded Monument Records and helped build the careers of many country music stars. The Non-Performer inductee said, "I've always been a big dreamer, but this is too big. I'm truly honored to be coming into the Hall with two of the greats, Charlie Daniels and Randy Travis." When Lee came back onstage, she joked, "Well, since Fred has let the cat out of the bag, you can all go home." She then announced Charlie Daniels as Veterans Era Artist. Daniels, seventy-nine, fiddle-playing leader of the Charlie Daniels Band, was best known for "The Devil Went Down to Georgia."

Lee began her introduction of the Modern Era Artist by saying that very few figures in country music stand out as signposts along the way. After calling the inductee one of the trendsetters "who fearlessly predict and influence the future of the genre," she said, "Born on May 4, 1959, in Marshville, North Carolina—we're well-represented by North Carolina today, aren't we—he grew up on a rural farm and began performing as a child with his brother. A reckless boy, he clashed with his father and dropped out of school, getting into scrapes with the law that continued until he won a country music singing contest at a club in Charlotte." During her introduction, she said, "As I told him backstage, in my opinion, he is the one who started the movement of what we know as country music today." She choked up as she described how the artist spent six months in the hospital following a stroke. "He fought back harder and with courage, and he is now able to walk. Please welcome our Modern inductee, Randy Travis, with his adoring wife, Mary Davis Travis."

When they reached the speaker stand, Travis said, "Uh, uh, thank you." He struggled to get more words out, but they wouldn't come. With a grin, he settled for "Okay. Thanks" as he motioned for Kyle Lehning to join them. Mary then said, "I've been asked to take on this daunting task of being the voice for this man who so eloquently put words to melodies to make beautiful music for the world to enjoy." She expressed his gratitude, gave anecdotes of his early career, and praised him effusively. "There's too many people to thank," she said, "who have been a part of his life—his band; his crew; Kyle Lehning; Martha Sharp; Elizabeth Hatcher; Jeff Davis, who was on the road with him for so long; Warner, for believing in him from the start and being with him still today; for all the fellow artists and writers he had the opportunity to work with. Thank you for the people who have been our friends and have stood beside us through the last three years after spending the months in the hospital when they said there was no hope for him." Travis smiled and nodded in agreement as she talked.[14]

During the summer of 2016, as the Travises looked forward to returning to Nashville in October for the official induction ceremony, they stayed busy attending numerous events. "We love going to hear other people play music," Mary told an interviewer. "Music is his soul. That's what he gave to the world, and now the world likes to give it back to him." She added, "The best therapy is living. I think environment and stimulation, as far as how you live your life, that's when things start coming back to you and words start showing up." She explained that they'd been told many times during their months in the hospital that whatever speech came back would happen in six months and there was no hope after that. "It was frustrating to know they put a deadline on it,"

Mary stated. "There's every day a new word or two words put together. Those are the exciting things. The brain doesn't have a deadline."[15]

They were back in Nashville in June for the annual Country Radio Seminar gala, during which Travis was honored with the Artist Career Achievement Award, acknowledging his contributions to the promotion of country music and country radio. Josh Turner sang three of Travis's songs during the celebration. Earlier that month, the Travises made a surprise appearance at Nissan Stadium during the annual four-day CMA Music Festival. Charlie Daniels was so thrilled to see Travis standing in front of him that he reached out and squeezed his fellow Hall of Fame inductee's cheeks. Daniels brought Travis onstage to wave to the crowd, resulting in what a reporter called "one of the most emotional moments of the festival."[16]

In August a three-judge panel of the Texas Court of Appeals, Third District, ruled on Travis's lawsuit from three years earlier. The judges said the dashcam video from the night of Travis's arrest did not fall within the state law's medical exemptions and that Travis had "put himself in public by driving unclothed while intoxicated." His lawyers immediately appealed the decision. (A year later, the Texas Supreme Court would let the ruling stand, and the three-hour video was released to the public.)[17]

The Travises forced their frustrations aside as they planned for the 2016 Country Music Hall of Fame Medallion Ceremony. The March press conference had been livestreamed to allow the public to watch, but the actual induction is an invitation-only concert and ceremony. Much to the disappointment of the large country music community, it is not filmed for public broadcast. Mary provided the CMA with an invitation list, planned the couple's attire, and discussed with her husband what to say and whom to thank.

They were getting ready to leave for Nashville when Dennis Traywick called on October 8 to say their father had died. The news hit Travis doubly hard; Harold had been planning to attend the medallion ceremony. Although the pair seldom got along, Travis knew his father was proud of him. Matt Arrowood, who lived with his grandfather, recalls that Harold had chest pains all through the night but refused to go to the hospital. Matt fed the horses in the morning and returned to the house to find his grandfather lying between the couch and the coffee table. It appeared he fell when he was walking into the living room to sit down. Harold Bruce Traywick's death certificate showed "acute myocardial infarction" as the immediate cause of death, with contributing conditions of coronary artery disease and type II diabetes mellitus. He was eighty-three years old and had never remarried in the eighteen years since Bobbie Rose died. Survived by his six children and their families, Harold was buried next to his wife in the Traywick family cemetery in Peachland, under the impressive headstone he had designed after her death. The Travises went to North Carolina for the October 12 funeral and then drove to Nashville.[18]

The official induction of the new Hall of Fame members took place on Sunday evening, October 16. Demonbreun Street was blocked off in front of the Country Music Hall of Fame and Museum, with fans lining the ropes to watch the celebrities walk the red carpet into the building. Travis, in his wheelchair, was escorted by Mary and her two children, Cavanaugh and Raleigh, along with manager Tony Conway. They waved at the crowd and stopped frequently to have photos taken. Roger Brown, whose songs had appeared on Travis's *Wind in the Wire* album, attended the ceremony with Fred Foster. While waiting backstage, Brown wanted to say hello to the busy Travis but didn't want to bother him. Foster told him he would regret it if he didn't go say hello. "Randy lit up when he saw me," Brown says. "I knelt by his chair and told him how incredibly proud of him I was. He kept patting my arm and saying, 'Yeah, okay.'" When Brown moved to leave, Travis grabbed his arm and hung on while speaking the word "friend." Brown recalls, "I was a wreck—had to go back to Fred's room and compose myself."[19]

The 776-seat CMA Theater was filled to capacity when the museum's CEO, Kyle Young, came onstage to welcome the crowd. One of the guests in the audience was physical therapist Tim Massengill. He felt fortunate to be invited, and he wasn't going to miss it. He'd said hello to the Travises but stayed out of the way. "I remember it being Randy's night," he says. Massengill was the only person in the theater who knew the surprise the Travises were planning. He wondered if they'd be able to pull it off.[20]

After the inductions of Foster and Daniels, CEO Young summarized Travis's career and then quoted Merle Haggard: "Down the road, somebody is going to idolize Randy Travis." Young concluded, "We're a long way down that road now, and time has proven Merle Haggard right." Alan Jackson kicked off the third musical tribute, singing "On the Other Hand" after telling Travis, "You opened the door to a lot of guys and girls who wanted to sing real country music." Brad Paisley called Travis "a beacon of light on the radio," adding, "You are one of the greatest singers we've ever had." He sang "Forever and Ever, Amen." Garth Brooks sang "Three Wooden Crosses" before saying, "Name me any artist from any genre in the history of all music that took a format, turned it a hundred eighty degrees back to where it came from, and made it bigger than it has ever been before." Brooks pointed at Travis and invited him to the stage. Paisley and Mary assisted the honoree in climbing the stairs to the stage, where Brooks placed the medallion around his neck.

Mary took the microphone to speak her husband's thanks. She choked up as she said, "Today God's proof of a miracle stands before you." She then announced, "Ladies and gentlemen, heroes and friends, tonight I want to give back to you the voice of Randy Travis." Holding a cordless mic in his left hand, Travis gave his famous grin after Mary told him, "Okay." He responded, "Okay," and started singing. The stunned audience softly joined in when he carefully growled the words, "Amazing grace, how sweet the sound." He looked down instead of at the audience as he sang, as if concentrating on the effort. Mary rubbed his back and sang the four verses along with him. Brooks stood next to him, obviously overwhelmed, with his head thrown back and his eyes closed, as he mouthed the words. Finishing the song, Travis unceremoniously handed the microphone to Mary. The room erupted with a thunderous standing ovation.

In 2001 Travis had said singing "Amazing Grace" was "an overwhelming emotional experience every time I sing it." He had no idea how overwhelming an emotional experience it would be for everyone who heard him sing those lyrics fifteen years later. "I as his manager was in complete shock," Conway says. "I was with Randy and Mary that night, in the dressing room and everywhere, but they never told me what they had planned. They had been practicing and rehearsing for weeks, maybe even months."

The ceremony concluded with the traditional performance of "Will the Circle Be Unbroken?" led by the Oak Ridge Boys and including their fellow Hall of Fame members. Travis sat onstage in his wheelchair and sang along as best he could. During the reception in the sixth-floor event hall with its forty-foot glass windows overlooking the downtown skyline, there were congratulations and hugs from all the living members of the Hall of Fame as well as from family and friends and industry leaders. "It will be a day that goes down in the history of Country music as so special that it will never be repeated," says Conway.[21]

At age fifty-seven, Randy Travis achieved the goal he'd held since he began performing as a child.[22] Although the stroke had damaged his body, and he could no longer give the performances he once gave, he was forever enshrined with his heroes and friends in the Country Music Hall of Fame.

# EPILOGUE

Becoming a member of the Country Music Hall of Fame hasn't changed Travis's unpretentious attitude. He and Mary live in a beautiful ranch house on several hundred acres near Tioga, Texas. He intends to spend his life on the ranch, with its population of horses, cattle, buffalo, and donkeys. His heart muscles have healed, he is strong and healthy, takes very little medication, and his vocal cords are in excellent condition. He is in a wheelchair because of his paralyzed right side. He propels himself with his feet and holds them in the air when someone pushes him, which gives him control. When he wants to stop, he plants his feet on the floor.[1]

Shortly after his Hall of Fame induction, the CMA hosted its fiftieth annual awards ceremony. An eleven-minute opening medley at Nashville's Bridgestone Arena honored past winners and included Travis and Charlie Daniels as new Hall of Fame members. The medley ended with hosts Brad Paisley and Carrie Underwood leading the ensemble in singing the 1987 CMA Single of the Year, "Forever and Ever, Amen." They held Travis's arms as he stood smiling and looking around throughout the song. He put a microphone to his mouth to sing the final "A-a-a-me-en."[2]

Seventeen-year-old Randy Traywick had said, "If I ever get to the stage of the Grand Ole Opry, I guess I'll know I made it." As Randy Travis, he has been a member since 1986. When the Opry celebrates its Centennial in October 2025, he can be expected to participate. In September 2015, he returned to the Opry for the first time since his stroke. The evening celebrated Jeannie Seely's forty-eighth anniversary as an Opry member. Tanya Tucker escorted Travis onto the Opry stage as he leaned on a five-foot walking stick. He celebrated his sixtieth birthday at the Saturday night Opry on May 4, 2019, standing proudly among a dozen of his former band members who gathered for the occasion. He and Mary occasionally appear backstage at the Opry. Travis doesn't want to be announced; he enjoys being with the artists and watching the show. While the Grand Ole Opry is almost one hundred years old, and the Opry House celebrated its fiftieth anniversary in 2024, Opryland itself is long gone. In one of the poorest decisions in the history of business decisions, Gaylord Entertainment demolished the park and replaced it with a shopping mall. After twenty-five years as Nashville's largest tourist attraction and a driving force behind the vibrant music industry, it abruptly closed at the end of 1997. By then, Travis was house hunting in Santa Fe.[3]

Today the Travises regularly appear at music events, which are therapeutic for Travis as he interacts with friends and is revered by fans. Showing up unexpectedly at performances is something he can still do. Younger singers feel encouraged and supported by his presence. North Carolina native Scotty McCreery, the 2011 winner of *American Idol*, grew up a Travis fan, with "Forever and Ever, Amen" one of the first songs he learned to play on guitar. Fifteen minutes before his 2017 show at Billy Bob's Texas in Fort Worth, McCreery saw Travis sitting outside his bus. "I had like a freak-out oh-my-god moment," he remembers. "This is the guy whose songs influenced me my whole life, and he's at our show. It made me super nervous." Mo Pitney—who cowrote his traditional hit "Country" with Bill Anderson and Bobby Tomberlin—grew up in Illinois with Travis as an inspiration. "Randy had the best God-given instrument for country music I think I've ever heard," he says. Tracy Lawrence, who graduated from high school just before Travis's career exploded, says, "I want everybody to remember the impact he had on our industry and how much he changed the face of country music at a time when things were getting really pop." The 1990s hitmaker, whose number one songs include "Sticks and Stones" and "Time Marches On," adds, "He was a huge, huge influence on me, and I credit him for keeping what I consider real country music alive."[4]

Tony Conway worked for months to organize a Travis tribute at the Bridgestone Arena. He hoped to sell out the venue and raise funds to help the Travises pay their medical bills and support the newly established Randy Travis Foundation, a 501(c)3 nonprofit charity dedicated to stroke rehabilitation, finding a cure for viral cardiomyopathy, and providing opportunities for at-risk children to participate in arts and music programs in schools. Conway wanted eighteen artists to sing Travis's eighteen top hits. "Everybody we called said they would be there," Conway remembers. "We had so many artists that we had to ask some of them to do duets on Randy's songs." Jeff Davis rounded up former members of Travis's stage crew to recreate a set from years past. Kyle Lehning and Steve Gibson brought their expertise from producing Travis's albums. The sold-out event, *A Heroes & Friends Tribute to Randy Travis: 1 Night. 1 Place. 1 Time*, was a tremendous success. Nashville's mayor kicked off the evening by declaring February 8, 2017, "Randy Travis Day." Travis's band played for over three hours nonstop to back more than thirty artists who performed the all-star salute. The Travises, wearing western-cut, yellow leather jackets, sat at the edge of the stage to watch the performances and greet the entertainers. Closing the show, Garth Brooks said, "There isn't anybody that's in country music today or in the last twenty years that doesn't owe their career to Randy Travis. I know that for sure. I'm one of those guys." He sang "'Forever and Ever, Amen" and held the microphone for Travis to sing the final "Amen." Travis led the night's all-star cast in singing "Amazing Grace."[5]

Marshville, North Carolina, honored its hometown boy in September 2017 during its annual two-day Boll Weevil Jamboree. In a Saturday afternoon ceremony on Main Street, city leaders unveiled new signs that read "Town of Marshville . . . Home of Randy Travis." The signs would be placed next to the "Welcome to Marshville" signs along U.S. Highway 74, at either end of the town. The Travises spent hours posing for photos and listening to stories from fans and friends.[6] The following February, Travis surprised longtime friend John Hobbs, benefactor of Randy Traywick and Lib Hatcher in the early 1980s, by appearing at his ninetieth birthday party, wearing a Nashville Palace chef's outfit and carrying a tray. "He was walking a little bit at that point," recalls Barrett Hobbs, "and he went to take orders at my grandfather's table. That meant so much, for Randy to take the time, struggling, to come in and make my grandad laugh at his last birthday party." The Travises often visited over the next sixteen months, until Hobbs died.[7]

During the June 2018 CMA Fest in Nashville, Travis received the inaugural Cracker Barrel Country Legend award. It honored country musicians with over three decades in the music business, past partnerships with Cracker Barrel's music program, and a strong influence on present-day artists. Travis proudly wore cowboy boots for the first time since his stroke. It was also the first time in five years he stood without leg braces. The Lucchese Boot Company had made him a pair of double-zipped boots that supported his legs and ankles without metal braces. The following evening, the Travises attended CMA Fest at Nissan Stadium. Luke Bryan, a top-selling country artist and the newest *American Idol* judge, took the stage just before midnight to close the festival.

After performing several of his hits, he noticed Travis in the audience and immediately sang "On the Other Hand." He then announced, "I've been wanting to sing to you for a long time, buddy. That was unrehearsed." He followed with "Diggin' Up Bones" before returning to his set list.[8]

The Travises attended a wedding reception in Lafayette, Louisiana, in November, where only the groom, James Dupré of *The Price*, and his bride, Kelsie Menard, knew they were coming. "Randy and Mary were so gracious with my family and really made our guests feel privileged to be there," Dupré says. "People around here are still talking about it almost five years later." At the ASCAP Country Music awards on November 11, Garth Brooks and Carrie Underwood presented Travis with the 2019 ASCAP Founder's Award. He and Mary radiated joy as they stood onstage to accept the prestigious award, first given to Stevie Wonder in 1984, followed by Paul McCartney and Bob Dylan.[9]

The Ernest Tubb Record Shop on Lower Broadway in Nashville held a book signing the next night for Travis's memoir, *Forever and Ever, Amen: A Memoir of Music, Faith, and Braving the Storms of Life*. Ken Abraham, an author well known for collaborations with celebrities, had done a masterful job of interviewing people, researching Travis's life, and producing a story that sounded like Travis was doing the talking. An author's note said, "Because of certain circumstances I have experienced, I have relied on a number of individuals to help describe and fill in some details of this story." Record shop manager Terry Tyson worked with Zach Farnum, whose 117 Entertainment Group handles Travis's marketing and publicity, to arrange the event. When Travis came through the door and was wheeled past the life-size bronze statue of Ernest Tubb, he smiled up at the Texas Troubadour and tipped his ball cap. Tyson recalls, "Everybody was so overjoyed to get a picture with him, sit beside him, tell him how much they loved him, what his music meant to them, and how his songs touched their lives."[10]

Travis still plays a role in the music industry. In 2023, Cris Lacy, co-president of Warner Music Nashville, wanted to do something to counteract the preponderance of artificial intelligence (AI) technology making fake recordings of famous voices. Wondering how Warner Music could use AI for constructive ends, she remembers, "The first thing that came to mind was we would give Randy Travis's voice back." With that idea, she called Travis's longtime record producer, Kyle Lehning, and asked for his thoughts.

He was skeptical but intrigued. He contacted the Travises, who felt they had nothing to lose by trying. Warner Music connected Lehning with a company called My Vox, whose technicians asked for a selection of Travis's vocals with no instrumentation. Lehning pulled out forty-two lead vocal tracks from songs recorded between 1985 and 2010. Using those samples, with music and harmony voices stripped away, John Clancy and Arianna Broderick of My Vox built an AI model of Travis's voice. They sent Lehning a link and password so that he could access the model. He would have to insert a vocal track from another singer, a "donor vocal," wait for the model to change the donor's voice into Travis's voice, and then insert the artificially generated voice into the original recording.

"They sent it to me in early November, and I just didn't know what to do with it," he says. "The idea sounded creepy." He sat on it for several weeks before remembering an unreleased James Dupré record he had coproduced for Warner Music in 2011. He liked "Where That Came From," and he thought Dupré's excellent vocal performance sounded similar to how Travis sang. Lehning pulled up the recording, exported Dupré's vocals into the model, and watched for about five minutes as the conversion was processed. He exported the converted vocal back into the original session and physically lined up the waveforms with Dupré's vocals. "Then I, with some fear and loathing," he recalls, "hit play, and I'll be damned if Randy's voice didn't come out of the speakers. It freaked me out!" Travis, rather than Dupré, was now singing "Where That Came From."

Lehning and his right-hand recording engineer, Casey Wood, worked for several weeks to tweak the vocal. Although there were no pitch issues, certain words seemed a little out of tune with the character of Travis's voice. They made minor adjustments to the phrasing, such as moving a word or a line. "It's really not so much how it sounds; it's how it feels," Lehning explains. The person providing the donor vocal must pronounce words in a similar fashion. For example, if the donor doesn't tail off the end of a line the way the singer would, it sends a negative message. "The public wouldn't know why it didn't feel authentic," Lehning says, "but they'd sense that something's off."

In mid-December, he sent the recording to Lacy for her reaction. "She called me back, blubbering," he says. They were now ready to let the Travises hear it. "Mary was a basket case, listening to his voice again," Lehning remembers. She filmed her husband listening to the recording on headphones. "He was just really happy with it," Lehning says about watching that video. "When I saw his reaction, to me that was worth everything, to see him be so excited about hearing that."

Travis then joined Lehning in the studio, reminiscent of those joyful days of yesteryear, as they prepared the record for release. Lacy arranged to release the song the weekend of Travis's sixty-fifth birthday and to make the announcement on a *CBS Sunday Morning* segment that aired on May 4, 2024. "Where That Came From" debuted at number forty-five on the *Billboard* Country Airplay chart, Travis's first solo chart record since 2005. It was also one of the very first AI songs to be recorded and released with full artist consent and involvement. The team is now working on recording future songs and showing how to use AI for positive purposes.[11]

Partly as a result of this publicity, the Travises were invited to appear at a hearing held by the House Judiciary Subcommittee on Courts, Intellectual Property, and the Internet. During the June hearing on Capitol Hill, Mary spoke for her husband in supporting the American Music Fairness Act (AMFA), a bill that would create performance royalties for sound recordings broadcast over radio airwaves. "Of all the things we do differently than we did one hundred years ago, one thing remains the same—the voice is still the mandatory bridge between the writer and the listener," she stated. "How did someone determine that writers and publishers would get paid for terrestrial radio play, but artists, musicians, and producers shouldn't?"[12]

While the US Congress continues its debate on radio play equity, Tony Conway works on ideas to keep Travis in the public eye, to help his recovery and bring in an income. With Zach Farnum publicizing the events and Jeff Davis producing them, he developed a live concert to take on the road. The *More Life* tour appears several times a year around the nation. James Dupré sings Travis's hits, backed by Travis's band. Via a video from an earlier concert, Travis introduces the band members. As each is mentioned on screen, a somewhat older person waves from the stage. The Travises sit at the edge of the stage, under a spotlight. For the finale, Travis stands by Dupré as they close with "Amazing Grace."[13]

In addition to attending awards shows and their friends' concerts, the Travises stay busy with philanthropic activities and events sponsored by the Randy Travis Foundation. In all of his interactions, Travis encourages people to be stroke *survivors* rather than stroke *victims*. When people marvel at his cheerful demeanor, knowing his life has changed so drastically, Mary points out her husband's tremendous improvement since coming home from the hospital. They were at such a low point, and they have come so far.

As they work through the adjustment to their new lifestyle, Randy Travis continues to influence the entire music industry, and his songs continue to inspire and delight.

# APPENDIX A
## *Album Discography*

### *Storms of Life* (June 2, 1986)

Warner Bros. (LP 9 25435–1) (Cassette 9–25435–4) (CD 9 25435–2)
    On the Other Hand (Paul Overstreet/Don Schlitz)
    The Storms of Life (Troy Seals/Max D. Barnes)
    My Heart Cracked (But It Did Not Break) (Ronny Scaife/Don Singleton/Phil Thomas)
    Diggin' Up Bones (Al Gore/Paul Overstreet/Nat Stuckey)
    No Place Like Home (Paul Overstreet)
    1982 (Buddy Blackmon/Vip Vipperman)
    Send My Body (Randy Travis)
    Messin' with My Mind (Joseph Allen/Charlie Williams)
    Reasons I Cheat (Randy Travis)
    There'll Always Be a Honky Tonk Somewhere (Steve Clark/Johnny MacRae)

### *Always & Forever* (May 4, 1987)

Warner Bros. (LP 9 25568–1) (Cassette 9 25568–4) (CD 9 25568–1)
    My House (Paul Overstreet/Al Gore)
    Good Intentions (Randy Travis/Marvin Coe)
    What'll You Do about Me? (Dennis Linde)
    I Won't Need You Anymore (Troy Seals/Max D. Barnes)
    Forever and Ever, Amen (Paul Overstreet/Don Schlitz)
    I Told You So (Randy Travis)
    Anything (Ronnie Scaife/Phil Thomas)
    The Truth Is Lyin' Next to You (Kent Robbins/Susan Longacre)
    Tonight We're Gonna Tear Down the Walls (Randy Travis/Jim Sales)

## *Old 8×10* (June 30, 1988)

Warner Bros. (LP 9 25738–1) (Cassette 9 25738–4) (CD 9 25738–2)
    Honky Tonk Moon (Dennis O'Rourke)
    Deeper Than the Holler (Paul Overstreet/Don Schlitz)
    It's Out of My Hands (Randy Travis/John Lindley)
    Is It Still Over? (Ken Bell/Larry Henley)
    Old 8×10 (Joe Chambers/Larry Jenkins)
    Written in Stone (Mac McAnally/Don Schlitz)
    The Blues in Black and White (Wayland Holyfield/Verlon Thompson)
    Here Is My Heart (David Lynn Jones)
    We Ain't Out of Love Yet (Gene Pistilli/Larry Henley)
    Promises (Randy Travis/John Lindley)

## *An Old Time Christmas* (August 14, 1989)

Warner Bros. (LP 9 25972–1) (Cassette 9 25972–4) (CD 9 25972–2)
    Old Time Christmas (Stewart Harris)
    Winter Wonderland (Felix Bernard/Richard Smith)
    Meet Me Under the Mistletoe (Mark Irwin/Joe Collins/Betsy Jackson)
    White Christmas Makes Me Blue (Rich Grissom/Neil Patton Rogers)
    Santa Claus Is Coming to Town (Fred Coots/Haven Gillespie)
    God Rest Ye Merry Gentlemen (Public domain)
    Pretty Paper (Willie Nelson)
    Oh, What a Silent Night (Mark Collie/Kathy Louvin)
    How Do I Wrap My Heart Up for Christmas? (Randy Travis/Paul Overstreet)
    The Christmas Song (Mel Torme/Robert Wells)

## *No Holdin' Back* (September 26, 1989)

Warner Bros. (Cassette 9 25988–4) (CD 9 25988–2)
    Mining for Coal (Ronnie Samoset/Matraca Berg)
    Singing the Blues (Melvin Endsley)
    When Your World Was Turning for Me (Dallas Frazier/A. L. "Doodle" Owens)
    He Walked on Water (Allen Shamblin)
    No Stoppin' Us Now (Randy Travis)
    It's Just a Matter of Time (Brook Benton/Belford Hendricks/Clyde Otis)
    Card Carryin' Fool (Byron Hill/Tim Boys)
    Somewhere in My Broken Heart (Billy Dean/Richard Leigh)
    Hard Rock Bottom of Your Heart (Hugh Prestwood)
    Have a Nice Rest of Your Life (Verlon Thompson/Mark D. Sanders)

## *Heroes and Friends* (August 31, 1990)

Warner Bros. (Cassette 9 26310–4) (CD 9 26310–2)
    Heroes and Friends (Randy Travis/Don Schlitz)
    Do I Ever Cross Your Mind? (Dolly Parton) w/Dolly Parton and Chet Atkins

Birth of the Blues (Lew Brown/B. G. DeSylva/Ray Henderson) w/Willie Nelson
All Night Long (Johnny Gimble/Bob Wills) w/Merle Haggard
The Human Race (Tim Mensy/Jimmy Phillips/Gene Dobbins) w/Vern Gosdin
Shopping for Dresses (Merle Haggard/Jimmy Dickens) w/Loretta Lynn
Waiting on the Light to Change (Gary Nicholson/Richard Leigh) w/B. B. King
A Few Ole Country Boys (Troy Seals/Mentor Williams) w/George Jones
Walk Our Own Road (Bernie Nelson/Lisa Palas) w/Kris Kristofferson
We're Strangers Again (Merle Haggard/Leona Williams) w/Tammy Wynette
Smokin' the Hive (Byron Hill/Remington Wilde) w/Clint Eastwood
Come See about Me (Conway Twitty) w/Conway Twitty
Happy Trails (Dale Evans) w/Roy Rogers
Heroes and Friends (Reprise)

## *High Lonesome* (August 27, 1991)

Warner Bros. (Cassette 9 26661–4) (CD 9 26661–2)
    Let Me Try (Allen Shamblin/Chuck Cannon)
    Oh, What a Time to Be Me (Randy Travis/Don Schlitz)
    Heart of Hearts (Kevin Welch/Michael Henderson)
    Point of Light (Don Schlitz/Thom Schuyler)
    Forever Together (Randy Travis/Alan Jackson)
    Better Class of Losers (Randy Travis/Alan Jackson)
    I'd Surrender All (Randy Travis/Alan Jackson)
    High Lonesome (Gretchen Peters)
    Allergic to the Blues (Alan Jackson/Jim McBride)
    I'm Gonna Have a Little Talk (Randy Travis/Don Schlitz)

## *Greatest Hits, Volume One* (September 15, 1992)

Warner Bros. (Cassette 9 45044–4) (CD 9 45044–2)
    If I Didn't Have You (Max D. Barnes/Skip Ewing)
    1982
    Hard Rock Bottom of Your Heart
    On the Other Hand
    Honky Tonk Moon
    An Old Pair of Shoes (Jerry Foster/Art Masters/Johnny Morris)
    I Told You So
    Too Gone Too Long
    Heroes and Friends
    Deeper Than the Holler
    Reasons I Cheat

## *Greatest Hits, Volume Two* (September 15, 1992)

Warner Bros. (Cassette 9–45045–4) (CD 9 45045–2)
    Look Heart, No Hands (Trey Bruce/Russell Smith)
    Forever and Ever, Amen

No Place Like Home
Is It Still Over?
He Walked on Water
Take Another Swing at Me (Paul Craft)
Promises
Diggin' Up Bones
I Won't Need You Anymore
It's Just a Matter of Time
I'd Do It All Again with You (Randy Travis)

## *Wind in the Wire* soundtrack (August 17, 1993)

Warner Bros. (Cassette 9 45319-4) (CD 9 45319-2)
Down at the Old Corral (Roger Brown/Luke Reed)
Cowboy Boogie (Robert Blythe)
Blue Mesa (Roger Brown/Luke Reed)
Memories of Old Santa Fe (Roger Brown/Rick Peoples)
Roamin' Wyoming (Roger Brown/Luke Reed)
Wind in the Wire (Stewart MacDougal/David Wilkie)
The Old Chisholm Trail (public domain)
Paniolo Country (Marcus Shutte Jr.)
Hula Hands (Jean Harris/William D. Beasley/J. T. Adams)
Beyond the Reef (Jack Pittman)

## *This Is Me* (April 26, 1994)

Warner Bros. (Cassette 9 45501-4) (CD 9 45501-2)
Honky Tonk Side of Town (Troy Seals/Eddie Setser/Jerry Phillips)
Before You Kill Us All (Keith Follese/Max D. Barnes)
That's Where I Draw the Line (Roger Brown/Trey Bruce)
Whisper My Name (Trey Bruce)
Small Y'all (Bobby Braddock)
Runaway Train (Larry Gatlin/Jerry Steve Smith)
This Is Me (Tom Shapiro/Thom McHugh)
The Box (Randy Travis/Buck Moore)
Gonna Walk That Line (Jamie O'Hara/Kieran Kane)
Oscar the Angel (Don Schlitz)

## *Full Circle* (August 13, 1996)

Warner Bros. (Cassette 9 46328-4) (CD 9 46328-2)
Highway Junkie (Chris Knight/Sam Tate/Annie Tate)
Price to Pay (Craig Wiseman/Trey Bruce)
Long on Lonely (Short on Pride) (Bob McDill/Dickie Lee/Bucky Jones)
Would I? (Mark Winchester)
Future Mister Me (Randy Travis/John Lindley)

Don't Take Your Love Away from Me (Everlon Thompson/Mark D. Sanders)
   Are We in Trouble Now? (Mark Knopfler)
   If It Ain't One Thing, It's Another (Bobby Carmichael/Tony Stampley/Joe Stampley)
   I Wish It Would Rain (Randy Travis/Ron Avis)
   King of the Road (Roger Miller)
   I Can Almost Hear Her Wings (Randy Travis/Buck Moore/Eddie Lee)
   Ants on a Log (Skip Ewing/Johnny Rees)

## *You and You Alone* (April 21, 1998)

DreamWorks (DRMD-50034)
   The Hole (Skip Ewing/James Dean Hicks)
   Out of My Bones (Gary Burr/Sharon Vaughn/Robin Lerner)
   Spirit of a Boy, Wisdom of a Man (Trey Bruce/Glenn Burtnik)
   Only Worse (Kent Robbins/John Jarrard)
   One Word Song (Max D. Barnes/John Jarrard)
   I Did My Part (Billy Livsey/Don Schlitz)
   Horse Called Music (Wayne Carson)
   I'm Still Here, You're Still Gone (Kevin Brandt/Ralph Murphy)
   Easy to Love You (Deanna Bryant/Danny Orton)
   Stranger in My Mirror (Skip Ewing/Kim Williams)
   You and You Alone (Melba Montgomery/Leslie Satcher/Tim Ryan Rouillier)
   Satisfied Mind (Tony Arata)

## *A Man Ain't Made of Stone* (September 21, 1999)

DreamWorks (004 450 119–2)
   A Little Bitty Crack in Her Heart (Shawn Camp/Jim Rushing)
   A Little Left of Center (Steven Dale Jones/Billy Henderson)
   A Man Ain't Made of Stone (Gary Burr/Robin Lerner/Franna Golde)
   The Family Bible and the Farmer's Almanac (Lee Thomas Miller/Bob Regan)
   A Heartache in the Works (Chet Biggers/Melba Montgomery)
   No Reason to Change (Troy Seals/Mentor Williams)
   Where Can I Surrender? (Rock Killough)
   I'll Be Right Here Loving You (Jeffrey Steele/T. W. Hale)
   Once You've Heard the Truth (Chuck Jones/Leslie Satcher)
   In a Heart Like Mine (Skip Ewing/Donny Kees)
   Day One (Max D. Barnes/Jimmy Yeary)
   Thirteen Mile Goodbye (Gary Burr/Gerry House)

## *Inspirational Journey* (October 31, 2000)

Word Records (9 47893–2)
   Shallow Water (Tom Kimmel)
   Baptism (Mickey Cates)

Which Way Will You Choose? (Ron Block)
Doctor Jesus (Tony Stampley/Justin Bolen)
Drive Another Nail (Marty Raybon/Michael A. Curtis)
See Myself in You (Tom Kimmel/Tom Prasada-Rao)
Feet on the Rock (Troy Seals/Buck Moore)
Don't Ever Sell Your Saddle (Kim Tribble/Bobby Whiteside)
The Carpenter (Randy Travis/Ron Avis/Chip Taylor) w/Waylon Jennings and Jessi Colter
Walk with Me (Randy Travis/Les Bohan)
I Am Going (Randy Travis/Buck Moore)
Amazing Grace (John Newton)

## *Randy Travis—America Will Always Stand* / 2-song benefit CD (2001)

Madacy (M2N2 5137)
America Will Always Stand (Randy Travis/Becki Bluefield/Michael Curtis/Yvonne Sanson/Doc Walley)
Point of Light

## *Rise and Shine* (October 15, 2002)

Word Records (WD2–886236)
Raise Him Up (Robb Royer/Rivers Rutherford)
Rise and Shine (Randy Travis/Michael Curtis)
When Mama Prayed (Paul Overstreet/Rory Lee Feek)
I'm Ready (Randy Travis/Ron Avis)
Three Wooden Crosses (Kim Williams/Doug Johnson)
That's Jesus (Randy Travis/Michael Curtis)
Pray for the Fish (Phillip Moore/Dan Murph/Ray Scott)
Jerusalem's Cry (Randy Travis/Lance Dary/Pastor Matthew Hagee)
Keep Your Lure in the Water (Randy Travis/Michael Curtis/Pastor Jeff Perry)
If You Only Knew" (Rob Mathes/Phil Naish)
Everywhere We Go (Randy Travis/Michael Curtis)
The Gift (Ray Scott/Phillip Moore)
Valley of Pain (Rob Mathes/Allen Shamblin)

## *Worship & Faith* (November 11, 2003)

Word Records (WD2–886273)
He's My Rock, My Sword, My Shield (public domain)
Farther Along (J. R. Baxter/W. B. Stevens)
How Great Thou Art (Stuart K. Hine)
Just a Closer Walk with Thee (public domain) [duet with John Anderson]
Shall We Gather at the River (Robert Lowry)
You Are Worthy of My Praise (David Ruis)

Love Lifted Me (James Rowe/Howard Smith)
Softly and Tenderly (Will L. Thompson)
Sweet By and By (Sanford Filmore Bennett/Joseph Philbrick Webster)
Blessed Assurance (Fanny J. Crosby/Phoebe Knapp)
I'll Fly Away (Albert E. Brumley)
Turn Your Radio On (Albert E. Brumley)
Open the Eyes of My Heart (Paul Baloche)
In the Garden (C. Austin Miles)
Above All (Paul Baloche/Lenny LeBlanc)
Will the Circle Be Unbroken (Charles Gabriel/Ada R. Habershon)
We Fall Down (Chris Tomlin)
Peace in the Valley (Rev. Thomas A. Dorsey)
The Unclouded Day (Josiah K. Alwood)
Room at the Cross for You (Ira Stanphill)

## *The Very Best of Randy Travis* (August 3, 2004)

Warner Bros. (8122–78996–2)
Diggin' Up Bones
On the Other Hand
Forever and Ever, Amen
Too Gone Too Long
I Told You So
I Won't Need You Anymore
Honky Tonk Moon
Deeper Than the Holler
Is It Still Over?
It's Just a Matter of Time
Hard Rock Bottom of Your Heart
He Walked on Water
Heroes and Friends
Forever Together
Better Class of Losers
I'm Gonna Have a Little Talk
If I Didn't Have You
Look Heart, No Hands
Whisper My Name
Three Wooden Crosses

## *Passing Through* (November 9, 2004)

Word Records (WD2–886348)
Pick Up the Oars and Row (Jamie O'Hara)
Four Walls (Don Rollins/Harry Stinson/D. Vincent Williams)
That Was Us (Craig Wiseman/Tony Lane)

Angels (Harvey McNalley/Buck Moore/Troy Seals)
Running Blind (Roger D. Ferris)
My Daddy Never Was (Tony Lane)
A Place to Hang My Hat (Shawn Camp/Byron Hill/Brice Long)
Right on Time (Al Anderson/Sharon Vaughn)
My Poor Old Heart (Shawn Camp/Gary Harrison)
I'm Your Man (Randy Travis)
Train Long Gone (Dennis Linde)
I Can See It in Your Eyes (Randy Travis/Pastor Matthew Hagee)

## *Glory Train: Songs of Faith, Worship, and Praise* (October 25, 2005)

Word Records (WD2–886402)
This Train (Sister Rosetta Tharpe)
Swing Down Chariot (public domain)
Precious Memories (Sister Rosetta Tharpe)
Shout to the Lord (Darlene Zschech)
Down by the Riverside (Sister Rosetta Tharpe)
Nothing but the Blood (Robert Lowry)
Were You There? (public domain)
Up Above My Head (I Hear Music in the Air) (Sister Rosetta Tharpe)
He's Got the Whole World in His Hands (public domain)
Heart of Worship (Matt Redman)
Jesus on the Main Line (public domain)
Through the Fire (Gerald Crabb)
Here I Am to Worship (Tim Hughes)
Oh Death (Gerald Crabb)
Nobody Knows, Nobody Cares (Sister Rosetta Tharpe)
Since Jesus Came into My Heart (Charles H. Gabriel/Rufus H. Gabriel)
Oh How I Love Jesus (Frederick Whitfield)
Are You Washed in the Blood? (public domain)
Precious Lord, Take My Hand (Thomas A. Dorsey)

## *Songs of the Season* (September 25, 2007)

Word Records (WD2–887146)
(There's No Place Like) Home for the Holidays (Robert Allen/Al Stillman)
Have Yourself a Merry Little Christmas (Ralph Blane/Hugh Martin)
O Holy Night (Adolphe Adam/John Sullivan Dwight)
Go Tell It on the Mountain (public domain)
Labor of Love (Andrew Peterson)
Angels We Have Heard on High (public domain)
Let It Snow! Let It Snow! Let It Snow! (Sammy Cahn/Jule Styne)
Away in a Manger (William J. Kirkpatrick)

O Little Town of Bethlehem (public domain)
Nothin's Gonna Bring Me Down (At Christmas Time) (Pat Alger)
The First Noel (William J. Kirkpatrick)
Joy to the World (George Frideric Handel/Isaac Watts)
Our King (Randy Travis)

## *Around the Bend* (July 15, 2008)

Warner Bros. (43254–2)
Around the Bend (Tania Hancheroff/Marcus Hummon/Tia Sillers)
You Didn't Have a Good Time (Kris Bergsnes/Jason Matthews/Jim McCormick)
Every Head Bowed (Brent Baxter/Brandon Kinney)
Love Is a Gamble (Hugh Prestwood)
Faith in You (Tom Douglas/Joe Henry/Matt Rollings)
Don't Think Twice, It's All Right (Bob Dylan)
Dig Two Graves (Ashley Gorley/Bob Regan)
Turn It Around (Noah Gordon/Matt Kennon)
From Your Knees (Leslie Satcher)
Everything That I Own (Has Got a Dent) (Tony Martin/Mark Nesler)
'Til I'm Dead and Gone (Shawn Camp/John Scott Sherrill/Sarah Siskind)

## *I Told You So: The Ultimate Hits of Randy Travis* (March 17, 2009)

Warner Bros. (518189–2)
*Disc One:*
Diggin' Up Bones
Forever and Ever, Amen
I Told You So
He Walked on Water
Promises
Three Wooden Crosses
Deeper Than the Holler
On the Other Hand
Too Gone Too Long
We're Strangers Again
Look Heart, No Hands
1982
Better Class of Losers
I Won't Need You Anymore
Faith in You
Love's Alive and Well (Steve Jones/John Scott Sherrill)
*Disc Two:*
Honky Tonk Moon

Would I
It's Just a Matter of Time
Forever Together
No Place Like Home
A Few Ole Country Boys
Is It Still Over?
Whisper My Name
Before You Kill Us All
Heroes and Friends
This Is Me
King of the Road
The Box
Are We in Trouble Now?
Turn It Around
You Ain't Right (Kelley Lovelace/Phil O'Donnell/Tim Owens)

## *Three Wooden Crosses: The Inspirational Hits of Randy Travis* (March 2009)

Warner Bros. (WD2–887820)
   Three Wooden Crosses
   Four Walls
   Angels
   Just a Closer Walk with Thee
   In the Garden
   Faith in You
   Love Lifted Me
   Blessed Assurance
   Softly and Tenderly
   Raise Him Up
   He's My Rock, My Sword, My Shield
   Sweet By and By
   Everywhere We Go
   Rise and Shine
   Were You There?
   He's Got the Whole World in His Hands
   Shall We Gather at the River?
   Pray for the Fish
   Swing Down Sweet Chariot (public domain)
   Will the Circle Be Unbroken?

## *Randy Travis 25th Anniversary Celebration* (June 7, 2011)

Warner Bros. (524503–2)
   Everything and All (Troy Jones) w/Brad Paisley

A Few Ole Country Boys (Troy Seals/Mentor Williams) w/Jamey Johnson
Forever and Ever, Amen (Paul Overstreet/Don Schlitz) w/Zac Brown Band
He Walked on Water (Allen Shamblin) w/Kenny Chesney
T.I.M.E. (Roger Springer/Tim Menzies) w/Josh Turner
Love Looks Good on You (Gordie Sampson/Hillary Lindsey) w/Kristin Chenoweth
Better Class of Losers/She's Got the Rhythm (And I Got the Blues) (Randy Travis/Alan Jackson) medley w/Alan Jackson
More Life (Mike Reid/Rory Bourke) w/Don Henley
Can't Hurt a Man (Brad Warren/Brett Warren/Lance Miller) w/Tim McGraw
Promises (Randy Travis/John Lindley) w/Shelby Lynne
Is It Still Over? (Ken Bell/Larry Henley) w/Carrie Underwood
Road to Surrender (Angela Russell/Buffy Lawson/Gary Duffey) w/Kris Kristofferson/Willie Nelson
Diggin' Up Bones (Al Gore/Paul Overstreet/Nat Stuckey) w/John Anderson
Someone You Never Knew (Fred Wilhelm/Kyle Jacobs) w/Eamonn McCrystal
Too Much (Donny Lowery/Gary Nichols) w/James Otto
Didn't We Shine? (Don Schlitz/Jesse Winchester) w/George Jones/Lorrie Morgan/Ray Price/ Connie Smith/Joe Stampley/Gene Watson
Everything and All (Troy Jones)

## *Influence Vol. 1: The Man I Am* (October 1, 2013)

Warner Bros. (535880–2)
    Someday We'll Look Back (Merle Haggard)
    Big Butter and Egg Man (Percy Venable)
    What Have You Got Planned Tonight Diana? (Dave Kirby)
    Ever Changing Woman (Dave Kirby/Curly Putman)
    Pennies from Heaven (Johnny Burke/Arthur Johnston)
    Thanks a Lot (Eddie Miller/Don Sessions)
    Trouble in Mind (Richard M. Jones)
    My Mary (Jimmie Davis/Stuart Hamblen)
    Saginaw, Michigan (Bill Anderson/Don Wayne)
    I'm Always on a Mountain (When I Fall) (Chuck Howard)
    You Asked Me To (Waylon Jennings/Billy Joe Shaver)
    Why Baby Why (Darrell Edwards/George Jones)
    Tonight I'm Playin' Possum (Keith Gattis) w/Joe Nichols

## *Influence Vol. 2: The Man I Am* (August 19, 2014)

Warner Bros. (544762–2)
    I'm Movin' On (Hank Snow)
    Set 'em Up Joe (Vern Gosdin/Buddy Cannon/Hank Cochran/Dean Dillon)
    Are the Good Times Really Over? (Merle Haggard)
    You Nearly Lose Your Mind (Ernest Tubb)

There! I've Said It Again (Redd Evans/David Mann)
That's the Way Love Goes (Lefty Frizzell/Sanger D. Shafer)
Sunday Morning Coming Down (Kris Kristofferson)
Don't Worry 'bout Me (Rube Bloom/Ted Koehler)
Only Daddy That'll Walk the Line (Jimmy Bryant)
For the Good Times (Kris Kristofferson)
California Blues (Jimmie Rodgers)
Tonight I'm Playin' Possum (Keith Gattis)

## Single Releases as Randy Traywick (1979)

Paula Records (PAULA 431 and PAULA 429)
    She's My Woman / All the Praises
    Dreamin' / I'll Take Any Willing Woman

## *Randy Ray Live at the Nashville Palace* (November 1983)

Music Valley Records (LP) (RR 1215)
    Ain't No Use (Randy Bruce Traywick)
    If It Was Love That Kept You Here (Randy Bruce Traywick)
    Free Rider (unknown)
    You Ain't Seen Nothing Yet (unknown)
    One Last Time (unknown)
    Reasons I Cheat (Randy Bruce Traywick)
    Call Somebody Who Gives a Damn (Randy Bruce Traywick)
    I Told You So (Randy Bruce Traywick)
    Promises (Randy Bruce Traywick/John Lindley)
    Send My Body (Home on a Freight Train) (Randy Bruce Traywick)
    Future Mister Me (Randy Bruce Traywick/John Lindley)
    Good Intentions (Merle Haggard/Melvin Coe/Randy Travis)

# APPENDIX B
## *List of Awards*

| | | |
|---|---|---|
| 1986 | Academy of Country Music (ACM) | Top New Male Vocalist |
| 1986 | Country Music Association (CMA) | Horizon Award |
| 1987 | Academy of Country Music (ACM) | Male Vocalist of the Year |
| | | Single of the Year—"On the Other Hand" |
| | | Album of the Year—*Storms of Life* |
| 1987 | *Music City News* Awards | Male Artist of the Year |
| | | Star of Tomorrow |
| | | Album of the Year—*Storms of Life* |
| | | Single Record of the Year—"On the Other Hand" |
| 1987 | Country Music Association (CMA) | Male Vocalist of the Year |
| | | Single of the Year—"Forever and Ever, Amen" |
| | | Album of the Year—*Always & Forever* |
| 1988 | American Music Awards | Favorite Country Album—*Always & Forever* |
| | | Favorite Country Song—"Forever and Ever, Amen" |
| | | Favorite Country Video—"Forever and Ever, Amen" |
| 1988 | Grammy | Best Country Vocal Performance, Male—*Always & Forever* |
| 1988 | Academy of Country Music (ACM) | Male Vocalist of the Year |

|      |      |      |
|------|------|------|
|      |      | Single of the Year—"Forever and Ever, Amen" |
| 1988 | TNN Viewers' Choice | Favorite Entertainer |
|      |      | Favorite Male Performer |
|      |      | Album of the Year—*Always & Forever* |
|      |      | Favorite Video—"Forever and Ever, Amen" |
| 1988 | *Music City News* Awards | Entertainer of the Year |
|      |      | Male Artist of the Year |
|      |      | Single of the Year—"Forever and Ever, Amen" |
|      |      | Album of the Year—*Always & Forever* |
| 1988 | Country Music Association (CMA) | Male Vocalist of the Year |
| 1989 | American Music Awards | Favorite Country Male Artist |
|      |      | Favorite Country Album—*Always & Forever* |
|      |      | Favorite Country Song—"I Told You So" |
| 1989 | Grammy | Best Country Vocal Performance, Male—*Old 8×10* |
| 1989 | People's Choice Awards | Favorite Male Vocalist |
| 1989 | TNN Viewers' Choice | Entertainer of the Year |
|      |      | Album of the Year |
| 1989 | *Music City News* Awards | Entertainer of the Year |
| 1990 | American Music Awards | Favorite Country Male Artist |
|      |      | Favorite Country Song—"Deeper Than the Holler" |
|      |      | Favorite Country Album—*Old 8×10* |
| 1992 | United Services Organizations (USO) | Bob Hope Entertainment Award |
| 1999 | Charlotte NC | North Carolina Music and Entertainment Hall of Fame |
| 2001 | Dove Award (Gospel Music Assn) | Country Recorded Song of the Year—"Baptism" |
|      |      | Bluegrass Album of the Year—*Inspirational Journey* |
| 2003 | Dove Award (Gospel Music Assn) | Country Album of the Year—*Rise and Shine* |
| 2003 | Christian Country Music Assn | Mainstream Artist of the Year |
|      |      | Song of the Year—"Three Wooden Crosses" |

| | | |
|---|---|---|
| 2004 | Grammy | Best Southern, Country, or Bluegrass Gospel Album—*Rise and Shine* |
| 2004 | Dove Award (Gospel Music Assn) | Country Recorded Song of the Year—"Three Wooden Crosses" Country Album of the Year—*Worship & Faith* |
| 2005 | Grammy | Best Southern, Country, or Bluegrass Gospel Album—*Worship & Faith* |
| 2005 | Dove Award (Gospel Music Assn) | Country Album of the Year—*Passing Through* |
| 2006 | Dove Award (Gospel Music Assn) | Country Album of the Year—*Glory Train* |
| 2007 | Grammy | Best Southern, Country, or Bluegrass Gospel Album—*Glory Train* |
| 2009 | Dove Award (Gospel Music Assn) | Country Album of the Year—*Around the Bend* |
| 2009 | ACM Honors | Cliffie Stone Pioneer Award |
| 2009 | Kannapolis NC | North Carolina Music Hall of Fame |
| 2010 | Grammy (with Carrie Underwood) | Best Country Collaboration—"I Told You So" |
| 2016 | Country Radio Seminar (CRS) | Career Achievement Award |
| 2016 | Nashville TN | Country Music Hall of Fame |
| 2018 | CMA Music Fest | Cracker Barrel Country Legend Award (inaugural) |
| 2019 | ASCAP | Founder's Award |

# APPENDIX C
## *Members of the Randy Travis Band*

**Piano/keyboard**
Drew Sexton (April 1986–1988)
Monty Parkey (April 1988–May 1992)
Drew Sexton (Feb. 1994–July 2004)
Joe Van Dyke (July 2004–July 2013)

**Lead guitar**
Dan Drillen (April 1986–Oct. 1986)
Rick L D Wayne Money (Oct. 1986–1988)
Ronald Radford (Nov. 1988–Dec. 1992)
Mike Blasucci (Feb. 1994–fall 1994)
Rick L D Wayne Money (fall 1994–July 2013)

**Steel guitar**
Gary Carter (April 1986–Dec. 1992)
Tommy Hannum (Feb. 1994–July 1994)
Steve Hinson (Aug. 1994–July 2013)

**Bass guitar**
Rocky Thacker (April 1986–Dec. 1992)
Larry Marrs (Feb. 1994–Aug. 1994)
Paul Fulbright (Sept. 1994–2003)
Bill Cook (2003–July 2013)

**Drums**
Randy Hardison (April 1986–Oct. 1986)
Tommy Rivelli (Oct. 1986–Dec. 1992)
Paul Leim (Feb. 1994–Mar. 1996)
Herb Shucher (1996–July 2013)

**Acoustic guitar**
Tom Rutledge (Sept. 1988–Dec. 1992), (1994)
Mark Casstevens (Feb. 1994–1995)
Steve Mandile (Sept. 1994–1996)
Steve Sheehan (1996–1997)
Robb Houston (1997–1999)
Joe Manuel (2000–2004)
Lance Dary (1998–July 2013)
Robb Houston (2004–July 2013)

**Fiddle**
David Johnson (summer 1986–Dec. 1992) (Feb. 1994–July 2013)

# ACKNOWLEDGMENTS

It was the summer of 1986 when I first heard Randy Travis. I lived in Virginia Beach, Virginia, and was on my way to Susie's Nashville East, a little nightclub where I enjoyed listening and dancing to a live country band. "On the Other Hand" came on my car radio, tuned as always to WCMS-FM. I've been a Randy Travis fan ever since. I purchased *Storms of Life* and his next six album cassettes as soon as they came out. I followed Randy's life and career throughout the decades as I completed my US Navy career and then wrote biographies of Faron Young and Marty Robbins. I am happy to once again be working with the University of Illinois Press, director Laurie Matheson, project manager Tad Ringo, and publicist Michael Roux.

Lorraine "Kayo" Diekman Paver and Perry Steilow served as my traveling companions and research assistants and offered their support throughout the years of this project. Kayo completed the index. In addition to being grateful to them, I'm grateful to God for my health and ability to be a runner. I developed many ideas and solved many problems in my head during my daily runs.

One of the first people who agreed to talk to me was Rick L D Wayne Money, longtime lead guitarist in the Randy Travis Band. He gave me names and dates to help me develop a list of band members. Leon Watson helped organize the band reunion; he found a venue and notified the musicians of the event. Thanks to both L D and Leon for their early assistance and their interviews, and thanks to the other band members who shared their memories. I am indebted to record producer Kyle Lehning, who provided hours of information about finding and recording songs along with stories of his long friendship with Randy. I could not have written so thorough a book without Kyle's help. He invited Kayo, Perry, and me to his home, and we enjoyed our visit in his beautiful studio with its spiral staircase.

Thanks to Randy's family members, friends, fellow entertainers, and other associates who willingly shared their memories. Matt Arrowood gave Kayo and me a tour of the Traywick homeplace where his uncle had grown up. Rose Arrowood and Dennis Traywick welcomed us into their homes to talk about their brother. Elizabeth Travis has lived in Santa Fe since she and Randy divorced. She closed her management company in 2015 and sold her Music Row office. She turned down my requests for interviews.

Kathleen Campbell, senior archivist at the Country Music Hall of Fame and Museum in Nashville, Tennessee, was most generous in opening the archives whenever we visited Nashville. Thanks to Patrick Smith, register of deeds of Cheatham County, who provided documents and told us about the historic house Randy once owned. Kayo, Perry, and I drove around Ashland City until we found the Braxton Lee homestead.

Those at various courthouses who provided information include Belinda Collins in the Circuit Court Clerk's Office, Nashville; Joyce Brooks and Aubrey Frantz in the US District Court, Middle District of Tennessee, Nashville; Craig Price, assistant criminal district attorney for Grayson County, Texas; Deana Patterson, Grayson County clerk; and the young women at the Union County Courthouse in Monroe, North Carolina. Katie Davis of the Union County Public Schools in Monroe found yearbook photos for me.

My online writers critique group, the Internet Writing Workshop, was an invaluable resource in helping me improve the chapters as I wrote them. Janaki Lenin, Cathy Moser, Ellen Dreyer, and Sheri McGregor stuck with me to the end. Special thanks to Cathy Moser, who edited my final manuscript and helped me condense it. Members of the Biographers International Organization provided encouragement, especially my fellow participants in the Pop Culture Roundtable.

Thanks to publicist Zach Farnum for introducing me to Randy and Mary, and to Jeff Davis and Tony Conway for their interviews and assistance. A final thanks and all my gratitude to Mary and Randy Travis for their gracious hospitality, numerous invitations, and for answering my questions. I've truly enjoyed getting acquainted with them.

No book of this magnitude gets written without assistance from a lot of people. My apologies to anyone I missed. You were all a great help to me.

# NOTES

**Chapter 1. "Bring your toothbrush."**

1. Randy Travis with Ken Abraham, *Forever and Ever, Amen: A Memoir of Music, Faith, and Braving the Storms of Life* (Nashville: Nelson Books, 2019), 10–11; Randy Travis, telephone interview with Bob Allen, January 23, 1987.

2. Kenneth Honeycutt, telephone interview with author, December 5, 2019; Union County NC District Court # 76CR 004824.

3. Don Cusic, *Randy Travis: The King of the New Country Traditionalists* (New York: St. Martin's Press, 1990), 22; Union County NC District Court # 77CR 000460.

4. Travis and Abraham, *Forever and Ever*, 14–15.

5. Honeycutt interview.

6. Travis and Abraham, *Forever and Ever*, 15; Cusic, *Randy Travis*, 23.

7. Robarde Traweek (1668–1730), FamilySearch (accessed August 16, 2024); https://www.findagrave.com/memorial/35969473/berryman-traywick (accessed August 16, 2024).

8. Bland Simpson, "Moonshine," *Encyclopedia of North Carolina* (Chapel Hill: University of North Carolina Press, 2006), https://ncpedia.org/moonshine (accessed August 16, 2024); Jerry Helms, telephone interview with author, November 9, 2021; Matt Arrowood, telephone interview with author, October 29, 2021.

9. Helms interview; Dennis Traywick, interview with author, July 19, 2021.

10. Dennis Traywick interview; Ronnie Traywick, telephone interview with author, November 29, 2021; Travis and Abraham, *Forever and Ever*, 9; Timothy Griffin, interview with author, July 22, 2021.

11. Dennis Traywick interview; Travis and Abraham, *Forever and Ever*, 5, 9.

12. Helms interview; Travis and Abraham, *Forever and Ever*, 3; Cusic, *Randy Travis*, 4; Dennis Traywick email to author, November 28, 2021.

13. Rose Traywick Arrowood, interview with author, July 22, 2021; Dennis Traywick interview; Steve Dougherty, "Winners: Home at the Range No More, Randy Travis Flexes His Nashville Muscle," *People Weekly,* November 10, 1986.

14. Travis interview with Allen.

15. Travis and Abraham, *Forever and Ever,* 9; Randy Travis, "Five Things You Didn't Know," *Great American Country*, 2011, https://youtu.be/-yukBe4jZCw (accessed August 16, 2024).

16. Dennis Traywick interview.

17. Dougherty, "Winners: Home at the Range No More."

18. Randy Travis, interview with Ralph Emery, early April 1987; Cusic, *Randy Travis,* 11–14; Travis and Abraham, *Forever and Ever,* 5–7.

19. Travis and Abraham, *Forever and Ever,* 7; Dennis Traywick interview; Helms interview.

20. Ronnie Traywick interview; Helms interview.

21. Cusic, *Randy Travis,* 18; Travis and Abraham, *Forever and Ever,* 9–11; Union County NC District Court # 76CR 000536; Dennis Traywick interview.

22. "Helping Children of Adults with Alcohol Use Disorder," Leah Miller, mental health counselor, updated January 6, 2023, https://alcohol.org/helping-an-alcoholic/children-of-alcoholics/?msclkid=a6f20852b6c811ecb66edad8919e6873 (accessed December 19, 2024).

23. *Country Aircheck Weekly*, "WSOC Turns 50" (Issue 766, July 26, 2021), 1; Cusic, *Randy Travis,* 21.

24. Helms interview; Travis and Abraham, *Forever and Ever,* 13–14.

25. Kevin Jonas Sr., telephone interview with author, November 9, 2020.

26. Travis and Abraham, *Forever and Ever,* 14; Jonas interview; Cusic, *Randy Travis,* 21; Gay Ryon, "Randy Traywick Wins Talent Contest," *Union News and Home* (Marshville, NC), May 5, 1977.

## Chapter 2. "It's too country."

1. Don Cusic, *Randy Travis: The King of the New Country Traditionalists* (New York: St. Martin's Press, 1990), 24–26; Kathy Haight, "Managing Randy," *Charlotte Observer*, October 16, 1988.

2. Cusic, *Randy Travis,* 25–26; Larke Plyler, telephone conversation with author, January 3, 2020; Ron Alridge, "Fan Club Petitions WSOC In Praise of John Harper," TV/Radio, *Charlotte Observer,* July 26, 1976.

3. Gene Watson, telephone interview with author, January 25, 2022; Cusic, *Randy Travis,* 26; Jack Hurst, "Randy Travis' Hard Road," *Chicago Tribune*, 1987.

4. Plyler conversation; Country/Bluegrass announcements, *Charlotte Observer,* May 13, 1977, June 24, 1977, July 7, 1978; Randy Travis, telephone interview with Bob Allen, January 23, 1987.

5. Randy Travis with Ken Abraham, *Forever and Ever, Amen: A Memoir of Music, Faith, and Braving the Storms of Life* (Nashville: Nelson Books, 2019), 17; Gene Watson, telephone interview with author, January 25, 2022.

6. Joe Stampley, telephone interview with author, November 5, 2019; Travis and Abraham, *Forever and Ever*, 19–20; Joel Whitburn, *Top Country Singles: 1944–2001*, 5th edition (Menomonee Falls, WI: Record Research Inc., 2002), 357; Robert K. Oermann, "He'll sing country forever and ever—Amen!" *The Tennessean*, June 27, 1987.

7. Gene Watson interview.

8. Randy Travis, with host George Jones, *The George Jones Show*, TNN series late 1990s; Randy Travis, interview with Ralph Emery, early April 1987.

9. Moe Bandy, telephone interview with author, December 16, 2019; Cusic, *Randy Travis*, 31.

10. Travis and Abraham, *Forever and Ever*, 16; Travis interview with Allen.

11. Travis and Abraham, *Forever and Ever*, 17–18; Cusic, *Randy Travis*, 27–28; Larke Plyler email to author, March 23, 2020.

12. Larke Plyler conversation.

13. Jeff Bridges, dir., *Urban Cowboy*, Paramount Pictures, 1980; Fun Crew USA, "The History around Mechanical Bulls," August 29, 2017, https://www.funcrewusa.com/resources/history-around-mechanical-bulls (accessed August 16, 2024).

14. Mary Beth Markley, "Ride 'em Cowboy, Only $2 a Buck," *Charlotte Observer*, August 13, 1980; Plyler conversation; Kathy Haight, "Young Star to Play 2 Shows at Coliseum for Hometown Crowd," *Charlotte Observer*, November 27, 1987.

15. Ronald Radford, telephone interview with author, October 12, 2021.

16. John Wildman, "Flags Fly as Spirit Soars Here," *Charlotte News*, January 21, 1981.

17. Country/Bluegrass announcements, *Charlotte Observer*, February 6, 1981; Cusic, *Randy Travis*, 29; Ronnie Traywick, telephone interview with author, February 14, 2022.

18. Travis interview with Allen.

19. Dave Barton, telephone interview with author, November 27, 2019; Travis and Abraham, *Forever and Ever*, 21; Randy Travis on *Nashville Now*, May 5, 1987.

20. Warranty Deed from Samuel T. Scott and wife, Janis T. Scott, to Mary E. Hatcher, Book 5790, Page 302, Davidson County, TN, recorded September 1, 1981; Country/Bluegrass announcements, *Charlotte Observer*, September 18, 1981.

21. Diane Diekman, *Twentieth Century Drifter: The Life of Marty Robbins* (Urbana: University of Illinois Press, 2012), 63–64.

22. Travis and Abraham, *Forever and Ever*, 22, 28.

23. Daryl Pillow, telephone interview with author, February 15, 2022; Cusic, *Randy Travis*, 45–46; Nashville Palace advertisement, *The Tennessean*, September 26, 1982; Ronald Hogan, telephone interview with author, March 5, 2021; Randy Travis, with hosts Ted and Tom LeGarde, *Down Home Down Under* TV show, 1990.

24. Pillow interview; Nashville Palace ad, *The Tennessean*, October 12, 1982.

25. Travis interview with Allen; Travis interview with Emery.

26. Pillow interview.

27. Nashville Palace advertisement, *The Tennessean*, December 26, 1982; Rick L D Wayne Money, telephone interview with author, September 30, 2019; Leon Watson, telephone interview with author, July 5, 2021.

28. Watson interview.

29. Gary Carter, telephone interview with author, November 1, 2019.

30. Travis interview with Allen.

31. Bandy interview; Jeannie Seely, telephone interview with author, March 5, 2020; Nashville Palace ad, *The Tennessean*, August 14, 1983; Travis interview with Allen.

32. Jim Bessman, "Monk family puts focus on nurturing environment (Songwriters & Publishers), *Billboard* (115, no. 8), February 22, 2003; Cusic, *Randy Travis*, 41–43, 47; Travis and Abraham, *Forever and Ever,* 27, 30.

33. G. Carter interview; Travis interview with Allen; Travis and Abraham, *Forever and Ever*, 30–31.

34. Travis and Abraham, *Forever and Ever*, 33–34; Robert K. Oermann, "Country with Capital C Suits Hit Maker Randy Travis to a T," *Tennessean Showcase*, August 10, 1986.

35. Kenny Sears, telephone interview with author, September 28, 2019; Travis and Abraham, *Forever and Ever*, 34; Cusic, *Randy Travis*, 64.

## Chapter 3. "There was no way I could have not signed Randy."

1. Phil Sullivan, "Martha Sharp Inks Pact," *The Tennessean*, April 11, 1965.

2. Robert Oermann, "Warner Bros. Names Two Female V.P.s," *The Tennessean*, April 11, 1984; Martha Sharp, telephone interview with author, October 24, 2020.

3. Randy Travis, telephone interview with Bob Allen, January 23, 1987; Sharp interview; Don Cusic, *Randy Travis: The King of the New Country Traditionalists* (New York: St. Martin's Press, 1990), 71–72.

4. Kyle Lehning, telephone interview with author, October 19, 2020; Sharp interview; Cusic, *Randy Travis*, 72–73; Janice Azrak, telephone interview with author, April 27, 2022.

5. Nashville Palace advertisements, *The Tennessean*, December 16, 1984, and January 6, 1985; Rick L D Wayne Money, telephone interview with author, September 30, 2019; Webb Dalton (David Jones), telephone interview with author, April 8, 2021.

6. Doyle Grisham, telephone interview with author, June 13, 2022; Lehning interview; Kyle Lehning, email to author, February 27, 2022.

7. Sharp interview; Azrak interview.

8. Randy Travis with Ken Abraham, *Forever and Ever, Amen: A Memoir of Music, Faith, and Braving the Storms of Life* (Nashville: Nelson Books, 2019), 38.

9. Dennis Traywick, interview with author, July 19, 2021; Deed of Book 359, page 687, Union County, North Carolina, dated September 13, 1982; Cusic, *Randy Travis*, 2–3.

10. Hugh Wilson, dir., *Rustlers' Rhapsody*, Paramount Pictures, 1985.

11. Cusic, *Randy Travis*, 77–78; Travis and Abraham, *Forever and Ever*, 34.

12. "Travis 'Handed' Hit Second Time Around," Nashville Beat, *The Tennessean*, August 10, 1986; Randy Travis, telephone interview with Bob Allen, January 23, 1987; Travis and Abraham, *Forever and Ever*, 37–38.

13. Lehning email.

14. "Gary Morris to Host 'Music City,'" *The Tennessean*, September 22, 1985; T. Graham Brown, interview with Biff Collie, May 1, 1989; Travis and Abraham, *Forever and Ever, Amen*, 40.

15. Thomas Goldsmith, "Country's Paying Off for Randy Travis," *The Tennessean*, February 8, 1986; Travis and Abraham, *Forever and Ever,* 29, 41; Sharp interview; Lehning interview; Barrett Hobbs, telephone interview with author, May 11, 2022.

16. Azrak interview.

17. Grisham interview; "Hank Jr. and Friends to Party," *The Tennessean*, February 16, 1986; Alan Mayor, *The Nashville Family Album: A Country Music Scrapbook* (New York: St. Martin's Press, 1999), 164–65.

18. Nashville Palace advertisement, *The Tennessean*, February 23, 1986; Hobbs interview.

19. Rocky Thacker, telephone interview with author, September 28, 2019; Rick L D Wayne Money, telephone interview with author, September 30, 2019; Gary Carter, telephone interview with author, November 1, 2019.

20. Lehning interview; Michael Bane, "Record Reviews," *Country Music*, September/October 1986.

21. Academy of Country Music website, https://www.acmcountry.com/about-us (accessed August 16, 2024); Cusic, *Randy Travis*, 87.

22. Mark Price, "Nashville Discovering Singer from Marshville," *Fayetteville (NC) Times*, April 30, 1986; Travis and Abraham, *Forever and Ever*, 43–44; Jeff Wilson, "It's 'Hats' Off for Country Musicians Strait, Alabama," *San Pedro (CA) News-Pilot*, April 15, 1986.

23. Robert Hilburn, "Taking the Strait and Narrow Way," *Los Angeles Times*, April 14, 1986.

24. Mark Kennedy, "Speck-on-the-Map Towns in Tennessee," *Herald-Journal* (Winchester, TN), February 19, 1989; Edward Albright, *Early History of Middle Tennessee* (Nashville: Brandon Printing Company, 1909), 120.

25. Azrak interview; Sharp interview; Randy Travis with host Ralph Emery, *Nashville Now*, summer 1986.

26. Lehning interview; Travis and Abraham, *Forever and Ever*, 46.

27. Randy Travis, *Storms of Life* record album liner notes (Warner Bros. Records, 1986).

28. Price, "Nashville Discovering Singer"; Scott Faragher, *Music City Babylon: Inside the World of Country Music* (Birch Lane Press, 1992), 140.

29. Bobby Tomberlin, telephone conversation with author, December 27, 2021.

30. Travis and Abraham, *Forever and Ever*, 47–48.

31. Kevin Jonas Sr., telephone interview with author, November 9, 2020.

32. David Ball, telephone interview with author, September 28, 2019.

33. Carter interview.

34. Robert K. Oermann, "Country with Capital C Suits Hit Maker Randy Travis to a T," *The Tennessean*, August 10, 1986; Robert K. Oermann, "He'll Sing Country Forever and Ever—Amen!" *The Tennessean*, June 27, 1987; Wayne Bledso, "Travis Sings Pure Country," *Knoxville (TN) News-Sentinel*, November 21, 1986; Randy Travis, interview with Ralph Emery, early April 1987.

35. Jim Lewis, "Overnight Success Has Paid His Dues," *Fresno (CA) Bee*, July 25, 1986; Joe Edwards, "Country Music Star Began Twinkling in Kitchen," *Tulare (CA) Advance-Register*, July 14, 1986; Randy Travis, telephone interview with Bob Al-

len, January 23, 1987; "Randy Travis Is Hot Country Property," *Daily News-Journal* (Murfreesboro, TN), July 13, 1986.

36. Travis interview with Emery.

37. Randy Travis, *Entertainment Tonight*, November 9, 1988; Rocky Thacker, email to author, March 27, 2022.

38. Travis and Abraham, *Forever and Ever*, 49–50; Robert K. Oermann, "Music Row" column, *The Tennessean*, August 20, 1986; Robert K. Oermann, "'New Breed' Stars Top CMA Award Nominations," *The Tennessean*, August 19, 1986.

39. "CMA's Horizon: Award for Rising Artists," *Billboard*, August 29, 1981, 58; Travis and Abraham, *Forever and Ever*, 50.

40. Thacker interview.

41. Travis and Abraham, *Forever and Ever*, 51; "Incorporations," *The Tennessean*, November 30, 1986; Faragher, *Music City Babylon*, 141.

42. Bruce Honick, "Rally 'round the Flag," *Nashville Scene*, June 1987; Installment Deed signed by Elizabeth Hatcher and Randy Traywick and recorded in Book 248, page 848, Register's Office for Cheatham County, Tennessee, October 31, 1986; Warranty Deed recorded in Book 147, page 33, Register's Office for Cheatham County, Tennessee, April 25, 2005.

43. Travis and Abraham, *Forever and Ever*, 48–59.

44. Tommy Rivelli, telephone interview with author, July 5, 2021; David Gates, "A New Honky Tonk Hero," *Newsweek*, October 27, 1986; Travis interview with Emery; Power of Attorney, State of Tennessee, County of Davidson, signed by Randy Bruce Traywick Travis, November 14, 1986.

45. Lehning interview.

46. Kathy Height, "George Jones, Randy Travis Sing," *Charlotte Observer*, November 16, 1986; Thacker email; Dennis Traywick, email to author, May 26, 2022.

47. Paul Schadt, telephone interview with author, February 6, 2020; Larke Plyler, telephone interview with author, January 3, 2020.

48. "*Hee Haw* Will Salute Marshville," *Union News & Home* (Marshville, NC), October 1986; Joe Edwards, Associated Press, printed as "Buck Out," *Arizona Republic*, December 28, 1986.

49. Travis and Abraham, *Forever and Ever*, 43, 60, 63; "Travis Christmas Tune Erases Songwriters' Blues," *Tennessean Showcase*, December 21, 1986.

50. Bill Morrison, "Wrapping the Best of This Year's Albums, Country," *News & Observer* (Raleigh, NC), December 12, 1986.

## Chapter 4. "Don't record 'em if you don't love 'em."

1. "Twitty to Sing Ditties at Hershey," *Pottsville (PA) Republican*, February 5, 1987.

2. Jeff Davis, telephone interview with author, March 18, 2022; Randy Travis with Ken Abraham, *Forever and Ever, Amen: A Memoir of Music, Faith, and Braving the Storms of Life* (Nashville: Nelson Books, 2019), 52.

3. Davis interview; Johna Blinn, "His Passion Is Popcorn," *Courier-Post* (Camden, NJ), April 24, 1986.

4. Travis and Abraham, *Forever and Ever*, 64.

5. "Country Music Tour Opens Sunday," *Asbury Park (NJ) Press*, March 5, 1987.

6. Shirley Jinkins, "Marlboro Performers Smoke 'em," *Fort Worth (TX) Star-Telegram*, March 14, 1987; "Critic's Choice/Marlboro Country Tour," *Fort Worth (TX) Star-Telegram*, March 6, 1987.

7. Kyle Lehning, telephone interview with author, October 19, 2020.

8. Thomas Goldsmith, "Opry Spotlight: Randy Travis Celebrates Platinum Mark," *The Tennessean*, March 6, 1987; Mark Casstevens, email to author, January 16, 2023.

9. Kyle Lehning, interviewed by Paul Kingsbury, Country Music Foundation Oral History Project, November 3, 1987; Randy Travis, telephone interview with Bob Allen, January 23, 1987; Kyle Lehning, email to author, March 24, 2022; Travis and Abraham, *Forever and Ever*, 45, 65–66.

10. Bill Conger, "Paul Overstreet, Hall of Fame Country Songwriter & Artist, Talks about His Classic Hits Including 'Forever and Ever, Amen' and 'Love Can Build a Bridge,' and His Own Albums," *Songwriter Universe*, June 30, 2022.

11. Travis and Abraham, *Forever and Ever*, 66–68, 70.

12. Janice Azrak, telephone interview with author, May 24, 2022; Don Cusic, *Randy Travis: The King of the New Country Traditionalists* (New York: St. Martin's Press, 1990), 123–24.

13. "Randy Travis on *Nashville Now*," May 5, 1987.

14. "Cruisin' with Conway Twitty & Randy Travis Promo Spot," *Nashville Now*, May 5, 1987.

15. Cusic, *Randy Travis*, 162; Bruce Honick, "Rally 'round the Flag," *Nashville Scene*, n.d.

16. Shawn Williams, "Randy Travis: Dishrags to Riches," *Music City News*, June 1987; Andrew Leahey, "Flashback: CMT Airs First Country Music Video," *Rolling Stone*, March 6, 2015, https://www.rollingstone.com/music/music-country/flashback-cmt-airs-first-country-music-video-37213/ (accessed August 16, 2024).

17. Janice Azrak, telephone interview with author, April 27, 2022; Travis and Abraham, *Forever and Ever*, 67.

18. Don Rhodes, "Album Autograph Was Part of Doctor's Bill," *Augusta (GA) Chronicle-Herald*, May 1, 1988; Robert Oermann, "Hospital Gives Randy Travis the Royal Treatment—Literally," *The Tennessean*, August 29, 1987; "Travis Concert Delayed," *Lima (OH) News*, August 28, 1987.

19. Diane Samms Rush, "Travis and the Judds," *Wichita (TX) Eagle-Beacon*, November 12, 1987.

20. Wayne Bledsoe, "Thousands Flock to See, Hear Randy Travis," *Knoxville (TN) News-Sentinel*, September 19, 1987.

21. Thomas Goldsmith, "Randy Travis Gets 'Platinum' Horse, Wows Record Concert Crowd of 6,000," *The Tennessean*, September 21, 1987; Travis and Abraham, *Forever and Ever*, 79–80.

22. Davis interview; Travis and Abraham, *Forever and Ever*, 53; Scott Faragher, *Music City Babylon: Inside the World of Country Music* (Birch Lane Press, 1992), 141–44; Gary Carter, telephone interview with author, November 1, 2019.

23. Jim Lewis, "CMA Nominees Announced," United Press International, August 18, 1987.

24. Thomas Goldsmith and Robert K. Oermann, "Hank Jr., Randy Travis Take Top CMA Awards," *The Tennessean*, October 13, 1987.

25. Country Music Association Awards 1987.

26. Goldsmith and Oermann, "Hank Jr., Randy Travis Take Top CMA Awards."

27. Ken Robison, "Randy Travis Takes the Traditional Route to Success," *Fresno (CA) Bee*, October 18, 1987.

28. Randy Lewis, "Travis, Lynn and Twitty in Anaheim," *Los Angeles Times*, October 26, 1987.

29. Tom Harrison, "New Blood in Country," *The Province* (Vancouver, BC, Canada), October 28, 1987.

30. Goldsmith and Oermann, "Hank Jr., Randy Travis Take Top CMA Awards."

31. Davis interview; Kathy Haight, "Young Star to Play 2 Shows at Coliseum for Hometown Crowd," *Charlotte Observer*, November 27, 1987; Kathryn Duncan, "Thousands See Travis in Program of Hits," *Charlotte Observer*, November 29, 1987; Cary B. Willis, "Randy Travis in Concert, Last Night," *Courier-Journal* (Louisville, KY), November 28, 1987; Patty Loveless, telephone interview with author, July 26, 2023; Ronnie Traywick, email to author, May 26, 2022; Rocky Thacker, email to author, May 5, 2022.

## Chapter 5. "By this third album, he was a superstar."

1. United Service Organizations, https://www.uso.org/about (accessed August 16, 2024).

2. Dan Markley, telephone interview with author, November 10, 2022.

3. Jennifer McCarter, telephone interview with author, June 9, 2022; Randy Travis with Ken Abraham, *Forever and Ever, Amen: A Memoir of Music, Faith, and Braving the Storms of Life* (Nashville: Nelson Books, 2019), 81.

4. Don Cusic, *Randy Travis: The King of the New Country Traditionalists* (New York: St. Martin's Press, 1990), 148; "BMI Won't Penalize Defecting Songwriters," *The Tennessean*, December 2, 1987; Barry Weinberg, telephone interview with author, October 3, 2022.

5. Larry Nager, "Travel Style Shows Singer's Success," *Indianapolis Star*, April 26, 1988.

6. "Randy Travis Wins Top Male Vocalist," Academy of Country Music Awards, April 1988; Stacy Harris, "Randy Travis at 30," *Country Song Roundup*, October 1989, 10.

7. "Travis Sweeps TNN Awards," *Music City News*, May 1988, 20; Steve Green, "Randy Travis Dominated the Nashville Network's First-Ever Viewers' Choice," United Press International, April 26, 1988.

8. Tyler Mahan Coe, "Another Lonely Song: The Tammy Wynette & George Richey Story," CR030/PH16, January 18, 2022, https://cocaineandrhinestones.com/tammy-wynette-george-richey (accessed August 16, 2024); Mark Faris, "Travis Is Down-Home at Coliseum," *Akron (OH) Beacon Journal*, April 18, 1988; Lamont "Monty" Parkey, telephone interview with author, September 20, 2021.

9. Don Rhodes, "Album Autograph Was Part of Doctor's Bill," *Augusta (GA) Chronicle-Herald*, May 1, 1988; "Randy Travis in Marlboro Country Music Message—1988,"

CMHOF digital collection, FV.2012.2707, digitized October 7, 2016; Webb Dalton (David Jones), telephone interview with author, April 8, 2021.

10. Donna NeSmith, "Is The Hag Playing Second Fiddle to Randy Travis?" Magazine unknown, May 1988.

11. Jim Bessman, "City Country: Alive and Kicking," *New York Post*, May 24, 1988.

12. "Travis Wins 4 Music City News Awards," *Clarion-Ledger* (Jackson, MS), June 7, 1988.

13. Travis and Abraham, *Forever and Ever*, 45; Kyle Lehning, email to author, March 24, 2022.

14. Warranty Deed signed by Mary Elizabeth Hatcher and Randy Bruce Traywick and recorded in Book 184, page 280, Register's Office for Cheatham County, Tennessee, September 8, 1987; Thomas Goldsmith, "Country's Paying Off for Randy Travis," *The Tennessean*, February 8, 1986.

15. Randy Travis, telephone interview with Bob Allen, January 23, 1987; Robert K. Oermann, "Country with Capital C Suits Hit Maker Randy Travis to a T," *The Tennessean*, August 10, 1986.

16. Randy Travis, *Entertainment Tonight*, November 9, 1988.

17. Dennis Traywick, email to author, August 2, 2022; Travis interview with Allen; Travis and Abraham, *Forever and Ever*, 57–58; Michael Leccese, "Country Star Saddles Up," *Clarion-Ledger* (Jackson, MS), May 15, 1988; Cusic, *Randy Travis*, 160; Bruce Honick, "Rally 'round the Flag," *Nashville Scene*, n.d.

18. Travis interview with Allen; Larry Nager, "Travel Style Shows Singer's Success," *Indianapolis Star*, April 26, 1988.

19. Kyle Lehning, telephone interview with author, October 23, 2019; Kyle Lehning, email to author, April 24, 2022.

20. Nancy Vaden, telephone interview with author, December 17, 2019; William Dill, telephone interview with author, December 28, 2019.

21. Alan Ross, telephone interview with author, December 17, 2019; JoAnn Jones, telephone interview with author, December 28, 2019.

22. Cusic, *Randy Travis*, 152, 160–61.

23. Jeff Davis, telephone interview with author, March 18, 2022.

24. Robert K. Oermann, "Randy Travis to Preview His New LP," *The Tennessean*, June 24, 1988.

25. "Truckloads of Travis," *Music City News*, September 1988.

26. Kyle Lehning, telephone interview with author, June 16, 2022.

27. Travis, Entertainment Tonight.

28. Travis and Abraham, *Forever and Ever*, 86; Lehning interview.

29. Lehning interview; Thomas Goldsmith, "Laid-Back Randy Travis Learns to Live with Peaks and Valleys of His Career," *Tennessean Showcase*, October 22, 1989.

30. "Forever and Ever Not Quite Yet, Amen," *Nashville Banner*, May 2, 1988; Norma Langley, "Relationship with Blonde Old Enough to Be His Mother," *San Antonio (TX) Express News*, July 31, 1988.

31. Helen and Tom Dorsey, "Travis Overcame Outlaw Ways of Youth," *Des Moines (IA) Register*, August 14, 1988.

32. Jerry Sharpe, "Riding to Fame on Country Road," *St. Louis (MO) Post-Dispatch*, May 18, 1988.

33. Kathy Haight, "Managing Randy," *Charlotte Observer*, October 16, 1988.

34. Lehning interview; Cusic, *Randy Travis*, 173–74; Wayne Bledsoe, "Thousands Flock to See, Hear Randy Travis," *Knoxville (TN) News-Sentinel*, September 19, 1987.

35. Travis and Abraham, *Forever and Ever*, 89–90.

36. Cusic, *Randy Travis*, 187–88; Kim Heron, "Making Country Music Hot Again," *New York Times Magazine*, June 25, 1989; Bill Sweeney, telephone interview with author, May 20, 2020.

37. Randy Travis, *Entertainment Tonight*, November 9, 1988.

38. Tom Rutledge, telephone interview with author, September 17, 2021; Lamont "Monty" Parkey, telephone interview with author, September 20, 2021.

39. Jeff Davis, telephone interview with author, March 18, 2022.

40. Rick L D Wayne Money, telephone interview with author, September 30, 2019; Ronald Radford, telephone interview with author, October 12, 2021.

41. "Travis & Loveless on Tour for USO," *Music City News*, January 1989.

42. Markley interview.

43. Radford interview.

44. Patty Loveless, telephone interview with author, July 26, 2023; Markley interview.

45. "Demilitarized Zone, Korean Peninsula," *Encyclopaedia Britannica*, https://www.britannica.com/place/demilitarized-zone-Korean-peninsula (accessed August 17, 2024).

46. Travis and Abraham, *Forever and Ever*, 93.

47. Rutledge interview.

48. Radford interview.

49. Lance Dary, telephone interview with author, November 2, 2021; Loveless interview.

50. Markley interview.

51. Tommy Rivelli, telephone interview with author, July 5, 2021.

52. Rocky Thacker, telephone interview with author, September 28, 2019.

53. Tom Rutledge, at Randy Travis band reunion, Nashville, Tennessee, July 18, 2021.

54. Radford, interview with author.

## Chapter 6. "It's a tough job."

1. Randy Travis with Ken Abraham, *Forever and Ever, Amen: A Memoir of Music, Faith, and Braving the Storms of Life* (Nashville: Nelson Books, 2019), 85–86, 105; President George H. W. Bush, letter to Randy Travis, January 31, 1989.

2. Thomas Goldsmith, "A Car Wreck Doesn't Hinder Randy Travis," *The Tennessean*, January 18, 1989.

3. Travis and Abraham, *Forever and Ever*, 94; Pat Harris, "Stargazing," *Music City News*, April 1989.

4. Barbara Isaacs, "10,000 Cheer Randy Travis' Country Tunes," *Democrat and Chronicle* (Rochester, NY), February 20, 1989.

5. "Sellouts Posted for First Dates of Travis–Oslin Tour," *Amusement Business*, March 18, 1989; Robert Oermann, "Music Row: Trade Mags Judge Top Country Hits," *The Tennessean*, January 3, 1990.

6. Don Cusic, *Randy Travis: The King of the New Country Traditionalists* (New York: St. Martin's Press, 1990), 162; "Longtime Randy Travis Fan Club President Dies," *The Tennessean*, March 29, 1989.

7. Stacy Harris, "Randy Travis at 30," *Country Song Roundup*, October 1989, 10.

8. Joe Edwards, "Van Shelton Wins Four Music City News Awards," Associated Press, June 8, 1989; "Country Music Honors Its Own," *Journal News* (White Plains, NY), June 6, 1989.

9. Cusic, *Randy Travis*, 177–78.

10. Susan Jarvis, "From a Stormy Beginning, Success Overtakes Randy," *Sun-Herald* (Sydney, Australia), May 28, 1989; Randy Travis, interview with the LeGarde twins on their show *Down Home Down Under* # 5, 1990 (available at https://www.youtube.com/watch?v=nCmsfGyXNfU); Rocky Thacker, email to author, August 29, 2022; Tom Rutledge, email to author, August 20, 2022; Lydia Dixon Harden, "Randy Travis: On Top of the World," *Music City News*, September 1989.

11. Vincent Creel, "Randy Travis and Roy Rogers Ride Happy Trails Tonight," *Seattle Times*, October 17, 1990.

12. Kyle Lehning, telephone interview with author, September 30, 2022; Travis interview with LeGarde twins.

13. Kim Heron, "Making Country Music Hot Again," *New York Times Magazine*, June 25, 1989; Barrett Hobbs, telephone interview with author, May 11, 2022; Thomas Goldsmith, "Travis Opens Gift Shop," *The Tennessean*, August 31, 1989.

14. Hatcher Corporation, *Randy Travis' Favorite Recipes* (Olathe, KS: Cookbook Publishers, 1989).

15. Beverly Garrison, "Diggin' Up (Soup) Bones," *The Tennessean*, September 13, 1989; Travis and Abraham, *Forever and Ever*, 57–58.

16. Thomas Goldsmith, "Laid-Back Randy Travis Learns to Live with Peaks and Valleys of His Career," *Tennessean Showcase*, October 22, 1989; Travis interview with LeGarde twins.

17. Thacker email.

18. Robert Harley, "Mastering Engineer Doug Sax: 1936–2015," April 9, 2015, https://www.theabsolutesound.com/articles/mastering-engineer-doug-sax-19362015-1/ (accessed August 17, 2024).

19. Lehning interview; Thomas Goldsmith, "Laid-Back Randy Travis."

20. Thomas Goldsmith, "Opry Spotlight: Writer Uses Nostalgia for Travis Hit," *The Tennessean*, June 15, 1990; Randy Travis, Four Rivers Outreach Banquet, Sherman, Texas, May 10, 2013.

21. Lehning, telephone interview.

22. Mary T. Schmich, "Taped Tunes Put Musicians on Picket Lines in Vegas, *Chicago Tribune*, August 21, 1989; Thomas Goldsmith, "Travis' Gigs in Vegas Rile Union," *The Tennessean*, September 7, 1989; "Music Group Challenges Union's Action to Halt Travis Concert," *The Tennessean*, September 7, 1989; Goldsmith, "Laid-Back Randy

Travis"; Pat Harris, "Star Gazing: Travis Walks the Line," *Music City News*, October 1989; Thacker email; Rutledge email.

23. Travis and Abraham, *Forever and Ever*, 91–92.

24. Goldsmith, "Laid-Back Randy Travis"; Harden, "Randy Travis: On Top of the World."

## Chapter 7. "Do you think he's as cute in person?"

1. Rocky Thacker, email to author, September 29, 2022.

2. Dan Markley, telephone interview with author, November 10, 2022; Tom Rutledge, telephone interview with author, September 17, 2021.

3. Markley interview; Bruce Williams, telephone interview with author, September 28, 2022.

4. Tom Rutledge, email to author, October 3, 2022; Barry Weinberg, telephone interview with author, October 3, 2022.

5. Thacker email.

6. Undated video, Coca-Cola Classic commercial featuring Randy Travis, 1989.

7. John Antczak, "Milli Vanilli, Travis Top Music Awards Winners," *The Tennessean*, January 23, 1990.

8. Robert Oermann, "Opry Spotlight: Randy Travis Praised for Hard Work," *The Tennessean*, March 30, 1990.

9. Lisa Zhito, "Touring Strategies Help Travis Capture the Fair Market, Tap Others," *Amusement Business* 102, no. 33 (August 20, 1990).

10. Randy Travis with Ken Abraham, *Forever and Ever, Amen: A Memoir of Music, Faith, and Braving the Storms of Life* (Nashville: Nelson Books, 2019), 105–108; Tom O'Neill, telephone interview with author, November 4, 2022.

11. George H. W. Bush, "Remarks on Signing the National Physical Fitness and Sports Month Proclamation, 1990–05–01," George H. W. Bush Presidential Library and Museum, https://bush41library.tamu.edu/archives/public-papers/1831 (accessed August 18, 2024); Pat Harris, "Stargazing," *Music City News*, June 1990, 92.

12. Jeff Wilson, "Hank Williams Jr. among Top ACM Nominees," *The Tennessean*, February 28, 1990.

13. Robert K. Oermann, "Randy Travis Leads the Pack in Music Award Nominations," *The Tennessean*, February 1, 1990; Thomas Goldsmith and Robert K. Oermann, "Ricky Van Shelton Leads as Fans Voice Choices," *The Tennessean*, June 5, 1990.

14. Robert K. Oermann, "Opry Spotlight: Randy Travis Praised for Hard Work," *The Tennessean*, March 30, 1990; Lee Grimsditch, "John Lennon Memorial Concert That Saw Crowds Flock to the Pier Head in 1990," *Liverpool Echo*, March 7, 2002.

15. Markley interview.

16. Thomas Goldsmith, "'Singing Cowboy' Randy Travis Hits the Trail," *Tennessean Showcase*, October 14, 1990; Vincent Creel, "Randy Travis and Roy Rogers Ride Happy Trails Tonight," *Seattle Times*, October 17, 1990; Randy Travis, interviewed by Ralph Emery, May 21, 1993.

17. Zhito, "Touring Strategies Help Travis."

18. Kyle Lehning, telephone interview with author, September 30, 2022; Jim Abbott, "Singing with the George Bush Jitters," *Daily Press* (Newport News, VA), March 22, 1991.

19. Lehning interview; Media Information, "Randy Travis—Duets," Warner Bros. Records, undated; Randy Travis, *Nashville Now*, February 7, 1991.

20. Robert K. Oermann, "Music Row: Travis Duets at Root of Controversy," *The Tennessean*, August 22, 1990; Goldsmith, "'Singing Cowboy' Randy Travis Hits the Trail."

21. Robert K. Oermann, "Music Row: Randy Gives Songwriters Their Due," *The Tennessean*, August 29, 1990; Travis and Abraham, *Forever and Ever*, 99.

22. Jim Nelson, "I'm a Free Man!" *National Enquirer*, October 30, 1990.

23. Travis and Abraham, *Forever and Ever*, 100.

24. Sandy Smith, "Television: CMA Show Deserves an Award, Too," *The Tennessean*, October 10, 1990.

25. Ralph Emery, *Nashville Now*, October 10, 1990.

26. *Nashville Now*, October 31, 1990.

27. Markley interview; Rutledge interview.

28. The Arts in Brief: Travis Top Money-Maker," *Globe & Mail* (Toronto), January 7, 1991.

29. Music City Profile, *The Tennessean*, September 23, 1990.

30. "1990 Hits a High Note for Music City Music," *The Tennessean*, December 29, 1990; "Randy Travis and Alan Jackson to Tour in 1991," Evelyn Shriver Public Relations, January 9, 1991.

## Chapter 8. "If you see what's wrong and you try to make it right, you will be a point of light."

1. Laurie Werner, "Fast Track Jackson," *The Tennessean*, October 7, 1990.

2. Randy Travis with Ken Abraham, *Forever and Ever, Amen: A Memoir of Music, Faith, and Braving the Storms of Life* (Nashville: Nelson Books, 2019), 104; Randy Travis, interviewed by Michael Gray at the Country Music Hall of Fame, November 7, 2008; "Randy Travis and Alan Jackson to Tour in 1991," Evelyn Shriver Public Relations, January 9, 1991.

3. Shirley Jinkins, "Road-Weary Randy Travis Yearns to Slow Touring Pace," *Florida Today* (Cocoa, FL), March 15, 1991.

4. Robert K. Oermann and Thomas Goldsmith, "Country Radio: The New Wave," *The Tennessean*, March 11, 1991; Thomas Goldsmith, "Randy Travis Declares He's Not Homosexual," *The Tennessean*, March 9, 1991; Travis and Abraham, *Forever and Ever*, 113–14; Mark Casstevens, telephone interview with author, January 11, 2023.

5. Jim Abbott, "Singing with the George Bush Jitters," *Daily Press* (Newport News, VA), March 22, 1991.

6. Teresa Simmons, "From Its Humble Beginnings as a Catch Phrase . . .," United Press International, May 13, 1991; "Randy Travis Hits No. 17 with 'Point of Light' Song," *Honolulu Star-Bulletin*, May 29, 1991; Travis and Abraham, *Forever and Ever*, 115; Mark Casstevens, email to author, January 14, 2023.

7. "Gala Becomes Victory Celebration," *Park City Daily News* (Bowling Green, KY), March 11, 1991.

8. Thomas Goldsmith, "Are We Taking Randy Travis for Granted?" *Journal of Country Music* 14, no. 1, date unknown.

9. "Troops Honored Tonight," *Honolulu-Star Bulletin*, April 3, 1991.

10. Travis and Abraham, *Forever and Ever*, 116.

11. Sandy Grady, "America Revels as Kurds Die," *Honolulu Advertiser*, April 5, 1991.

12. Beth Fortune, "Travis Song Plugs Bush, Says Complaint," *Nashville Banner*, September 14, 1991.

13. Jason DeParle, "'Thousand Points' Illuminate Good, Bad of Bush Agenda," *New York Times*, May 29, 1991.

14. Goldsmith, "Are We Taking Randy Travis for Granted?"

15. Robert K. Oermann, "Travis 'Points' to Future," *The Tennessean*, June 8, 1991.

16. Don Chapman's column, *Honolulu Advertiser*, April 17, 1991.

17. Travis and Abraham, *Forever and Ever*, 116–17.

18. Don Cusic, "The Real Randy," *Daily Press* (Newport News, VA), March 22, 1991.

19. Travis and Abraham, *Forever and Ever*, 120–21.

20. Kyle Lehning, telephone interview with author, December 7, 2022.

21. Wayne Harada, "Show Biz," *Honolulu Advertiser*, June 4, 1991.

22. Oermann, "Travis 'Points' to Future"; Pat Harris, "The Secret's Out," *Music City News*, July 1991; Thomas Goldsmith and Robert K. Oermann, "Fans Pick Ricky Van Shelton," *The Tennessean*, June 11, 1991; "Forever and Ever," *Honolulu Star-Bulletin*, June 16, 1991.

23. Jim Abbott, "Singing with the George Bush Jitters," *Daily Press* (Newport News, VA), March 22, 1991.

24. "Forever Together: Writers, Randy Travis & Alan Jackson," *Music City News*, March 1993.

25. Travis and Abraham, *Forever and Ever*, 120; Frances Meeker, "Baptism Makes Travis a 'Brother in Christ,'" *Nashville Banner*, November 8, 1991.

26. Marc Ball and John Lloyd Miller, dirs., *Influences: George Jones and Randy Travis*, Country Music Association (production), HBO (distributor) special, October 1991.

27. Casstevens interview; Kyle Lehning, telephone interview with author, January 16, 2023.

28. John Burnes, "Travis and Opening Act Draw Crowd, Applause," *St. Louis Post-Dispatch*, November 23, 1991; "Alan Jackson Featured in Concert," *Town Talk* (Alexandria, LA), November 16, 1991.

29. Travis and Abraham, *Forever and Ever*, 84, 125–26.

30. Randy Travis, "It Was Just a Matter of Time," live performance, Sun Theatre, Anaheim, California, December 2000.

31. Randy Travis and David Letterman, *Late Night with David Letterman*, February 1992, https://www.youtube.com/watch?v=QMNLK1FYFy0 (accessed August 6, 2024).

32. Gary Carter, telephone interview with author, November 1, 2019.

33. Tom Rutledge and Lamont "Monty" Parkey, at Randy Travis Band reunion, Nashville, Tennessee, July 18, 2021; Lamont "Monty" Parkey, telephone interview with author, September 20, 2021.

34. Randy Travis, interviewed for *This Is Me* video, filmed on the set of *Frank & Jesse* in Fort Smith, Arkansas, December 1993.
35. 26th Country Music Association Awards, September 30, 1992.
36. Travis and Abraham, *Forever and Ever*, 116.
37. Robert Hilburn, "Country Cashes In," *Los Angeles Times*, December 27, 1992.
38. Tommy Rivelli, telephone interview with author, July 5, 2021; Rocky Thacker, telephone interview with author, September 28, 2019; Gary Carter telephone interview with author, November 1, 2019.
39. Rutledge, Randy Travis Band reunion.
40. Travis and Abraham, *Forever and Ever*, 126–27.
41. Ronald Radford, telephone interview with author, October 12, 2021.
42. Rivelli interview; Tom Rutledge, telephone interview with author, September 17, 2021.
43. Travis and Abraham, *Forever and Ever*, 127.

## Chapter 9. "It's so competitive now. And this scares me."

1. Richard McVey II, "Randy Travis: The Leading Man," *Music City News*, July 1997.
2. Robert K. Oermann, "Despite Rumors, Travis Plans to Keep on Singing," *The Tennessean*, January 6, 1993.
3. Michael Corcoran, "Travis Tries to Shrug Off Cruel Rumors," *Greensboro (NC) News & Record*, August 24, 1993.
4. Randy Travis with Ken Abraham, *Forever and Ever, Amen: A Memoir of Music, Faith, and Braving the Storms of Life* (Nashville: Nelson Books, 2019), 71, 127; "Creative Artists Agency Signs Randy Travis," *The Tennessean*, February 26, 1993.
5. Christopher Cain, dir., *Young Guns*, Morgan Creek Entertainment (production), Twentieth Century Fox (distribution), 1988).
6. "C/W Singer Considers Acting," *Times-Gazette* (Ashland, OH), May 1987; Lydia Dixon Harden, "Randy Travis: On Top of the World," *Music City News*, September 1989.
7. Barton Dean, creator, *Down Home*, Savage Cake Productions, Paramount Television, NBC-TV, 1991.
8. "Travis Tries 'Down Home' TV," *The Tennessean*, December 4, 1990.
9. Dean Hargrove, creator, *Matlock*, Dean Hargrove Productions, Viacom Productions, NBC-TV, 1992.
10. Travis and Abraham, *Forever and Ever*, 123–24; Randy Travis, telephone call to Fox Nashville, July 3, 2012.
11. Elana Krausz, dir., *At Risk*, 1994.
12. Robert Boris, *Frank and Jesse*, Trimark Pictures, 1994.
13. Nancy Sweid, "Randy Travis," *Country Weekly*, April 12, 1994; Randy Travis, interviewed for *This Is Me* video, filmed on the set of *Frank and Jesse* in Fort Smith, Arkansas, December 1993.
14. Richard Donner, dir., *Maverick*, Warner Bros., 1994.
15. Alan J. Levi, dir., *Dead Man's Revenge*, Finnegan/Pinchuk Productions, 1994.
16. Rupert Hitzig, dir., *Outlaws: The Legend of O. B. Taggart*, Entertech Releasing, Hanover House, 1995.

17. Travis and Abraham, *Forever and Ever*, 128–29; Randy Travis, Four Rivers Outreach Banquet, Sherman, Texas, May 10, 2013.

18. Jim Shea, dir., *Wind in the Wire*, Planet Video Inc., 1993.

19. Travis and Abraham, *Forever and Ever*, 129–30; Randy Travis, interviewed by Ralph Emery, May 21, 1993; Gerry Wenner, telephone interview with author, January 26, 2023.

20. Roger Brown, telephone interview with author, December 27, 2022; Steve Gibson, telephone interview with author, December 19, 2022.

21. Travis and Abraham, *Forever and Ever*, 130.

22. Kyle Lehning, telephone interview with author, January 16, 2023; Travis interview for *This Is Me* video; Travis and Abraham, *Forever and Ever*, 133.

23. Shirley Jinkins, "Revitalized: Travis Turns Time Off into Triumph," *Fort Worth (TX) Star-Telegram*, September 28, 1994.

24. Travis and Abraham, *Forever and Ever*, 131–32; Lehning interview; Jeff Davis, telephone conversation with author, October 5, 2023; Tom Rutledge, telephone interview with author, September 17, 2021; Mark Casstevens, telephone interview with author, January 11, 2023; Paul Leim, telephone interview with author, January 4, 2023; Jinkins, "Revitalized: Travis Turns Time Off into Triumph."

25. Travis and Abraham, *Forever and Ever*, 132; Jim Bessman, "Country Music Hunks Lookout!" *Billboard* (reprinted in *Cincinnati Post*, March 24, 1994); Tom Roland, "Randy Travis Dismounts to Plug 'Normal' Album," *The Tennessean*, February 27, 1994; David Ball, telephone interview with author, September 28, 2019; "Ball Has No Problem 'Thinkin'," *The Tennessean*, July 31, 1994; Jack Hurst, "Travis Tunes Up for New Tour," *Abilene (TX) Reporter-News*, March 18, 1994.

26. Rick L D Wayne Money, telephone interview with author, September 30, 2019.

27. Lydia Dixon Harden, "There's No Place Like Home," *Music City News*, April 1994.

28. John Anderson, telephone interview with author, January 31, 2023.

29. Travis and Abraham, *Forever and Ever*, 133; Casstevens interview; Lehning interview; Steve Hinson and Tom Rutledge at Randy Travis Band Reunion, July 18, 2021; Money interview; Leim interview.

## Chapter 10. "He signed autographs until the place was empty."

1. Diane Samms Rush, "Randy Travis Talks about His Drinking and Drugging Days," *Wichita (TX) Eagle*, June 27, 1996; "Where He Belongs," *American Cowboy*, May/June 1995.

2. Kyle Lehning, telephone interview with author, October 19, 2020.

3. Randy Travis, interviewed for *This Is Me* video, filmed on the set of *Frank and Jesse* in Fort Smith, Arkansas, December 1993; Randy Travis with Ken Abraham, *Forever and Ever, Amen: A Memoir of Music, Faith, and Braving the Storms of Life* (Nashville: Nelson Books, 2019), 135–36; Paul Leim, telephone interview with author, January 4, 2023; Jay Orr, "Randy Gets His Act Together," *The Tennessean*, June 15, 1998.

4. Travis and Abraham, *Forever and Ever*, 122; Lehning interview; Brian McCollum, "A Comfortable Randy Travis Comes 'Full Circle' with New Album," Knight Ridder/Tribune News Service, August 5, 1996; Randy Travis, Four Rivers Outreach Banquet,

Sherman, Texas, May 10, 2013; Mark Casstevens, telephone interview with author, January 11, 2023.

5. Robert K. Oermann, "He's Back!" *The Tennessean*, September 7, 1996.

6. McCollum, "A Comfortable Randy Travis Comes 'Full Circle'"; Leim interview.

7. Lehning interview.

8. Mario Tarradell, "Welcome Back? Randy Travis Never Left," *News & Record* (Greensboro, NC), May 1, 1998; Travis and Abraham, *Forever and Ever*, 141–42.

9. Chet Flippo, "Travis Makes DreamWorks Debut," *Billboard*, March 14, 1998; Orr, "Randy Gets His Act Together"; Travis and Abraham, *Forever and Ever*, 141–42.

10. Oermann, "He's Back!"

11. Francis Ford Coppola, dir., *The Rainmaker*, Paramount Pictures, 1997.

12. Tommy Lee Wallace, *Steel Chariots*, Buena Vista/Walt Disney Television, 1997.

13. Felix Enriquez Alcalá, dir. *Fire Down Below*, Warner Bros., 1997.

14. Robert Radler, dir., *T.N.T.*, Interlight Venture Corporation/New Cinema Corporation, IVC/NCC Entertainment, 1997.

15. Roy Wilson, dir., *Annabelle's Wish*, Ralph Edwards Productions, 1997; Richard McVey II, "Randy Travis: The Leading Man," *Music City News*, July 1997.

16. Steve Morse, "Digging Out Randy Travis Is No Longer 'Alone' in the Music Business," *Fresno (CA) Bee*, July 5, 1998.

17. Tammy Wynette's Memorial Service, April 9, 1998, https://youtube/pz8PN17-QDs (accessed August 20, 2024).

18. "Travis' Mom Taught Son to Love Music," *News & Record* (Greensboro, NC), May 22, 1998; *Music City News* article, August 1998; Travis and Abraham, *Forever and Ever*, 8; Dennis Traywick, interview with author, July 19, 2021.

19. Larke Plyler, telephone conversation with author, April 21, 2020.

20. Kevin Hooks, dir., *Black Dog*, Universal Pictures, 1998.

21. Orr, "Randy Gets His Act Together"; Richard McVey II, "20 Questions with Randy Travis," *Music City News*, June 1998; Travis and Abraham, *Forever and Ever*, 144.

22. Tarradell, "Welcome Back? Randy Travis Never Left."

23. Orr, "Randy Gets His Act Together"; McVey, "20 Questions with Randy Travis."

24. Bill Sweeney, telephone interview with author, May 20, 2020; Randy Bruce Traywick Petition for Name Change in the Circuit Court for Davidson County, Tennessee, No. 98C2625, September 24, 1998; Mary Elizabeth Traywick Petition for Name Change in the Circuit Court for Davidson County, Tennessee, No. 98C2626, September 24, 1998.

25. Janice Azrak, telephone interview with author, April 27, 2022.

26. Sweeney interview; Larke Plyler, telephone conversation with author, January 3, 2020; Wendy Goodman, "Pardon Me, Singer Says, for Youthful Indiscretions," *Charlotte Observer*, March 26, 1999.

27. "All's Forgiven," *Courier-Journal* (Louisville, KY), March 29, 1999.

28. Wendy Goodman, "Generic Signs May Replace Marshville's Travis Tribute," *Charlotte Observer*, April 20, 1999.

29. Kenneth Johnson, "Country Roads Take Him Home," *Charlotte Observer*, May 15, 1999; Roger Hart, "Lay Off Randy Travis, and Maybe He'll Visit," *Charlotte Ob-*

*server*, May 18, 1999; Randy Travis Will Be Inducted into North Carolina Hall of Fame and Will Be on Hand for Grand Opening of the New Charlotte-Based Hall of Fame Building," PR Newswire, May 12, 1999.

30. Mark Price, "Travis, Marshville Debunk Rumors of Rift," *Charlotte Observer*, May 16, 1999; Barbara Garrison, "Why Doesn't Marshville Show Pride in Travis?" *Charlotte Observer*, May 23, 1999.

31. Paul Schadt, telephone interview with author, February 6, 2020.

## Chapter 11. "We are proud to call Santa Fe our new home."

1. Emily Heffter, "12 Avenida De Rey," *Today*, April 30, 2014.

2. Randy Travis, *A Man Ain't Made of Stone*, DreamWorks (004 450 119–2), 1999.

3. Randy Travis with Ken Abraham, Forever and Ever, Amen: A Memoir of Music, Faith, and Braving the Storms of Life (Nashville: Nelson Books, 2019), 143.

4. Tom Roland, "Album Reviews: Randy Travis," *The Tennessean*, September 20, 1999.

5. Randy Travis telephone interview with Chet Flippo, August 18, 1999; Thomas Kintner, "Randy Travis Has His Own Crosses to Bear," *Hartford (CT) Courant*, August 6, 2004.

6. Ellen Berkovitch, "Randy Travis Gives Benefit Concert Sunday," *Santa Fe (NM) New Mexican*, May 26, 2000; Dale Lezon, "Entertainers Pitch In Some Serious Relief," *Albuquerque (NM) Journal*, June 6, 2000; Andres Ybarra, "Travis Raises Funds for NM Fire Relief," *Carlsbad (NM) Current-Argus*, June 8, 2000; Mike Dano, "Red Cross Receives More Than $1 Million to Help Forest-Fire Victims in New Mexico," *Albuquerque (NM) Tribune*, June 9, 2000; Shonda Novak and Mark Hummels, "El Mitote: Fried Music," *Santa Fe (NM) New Mexican*, June 4, 2000.

7. "Forever and Ever Amen . . .," full-page ad signed by Randy and Elizabeth Travis, *Santa Fe (NM) New Mexican*, June 9, 2000.

8. Sean McNamara, dir., *The Trial of Old Drum*, Lions Gate Films Home Entertainment, 2000.

9. Mary McNamara, "Animal Planet: Where the Wild Things Are," *Los Angeles Times*, April 26, 2000.

10. "Old Drum Story," Johnson County (MO) Historical Society (jocomohistory.org) (accessed August 21, 2024).

11. *The Trial of Old Drum* (2000), https://youtube/xiOZ8Msaofw (accessed August 25, 2024).

12. Randy Lewis, "Travis & the Philharmonic Share a Country String Thing," *Los Angeles Times*, September 11, 2000.

13. Kyle Lehning, telephone interview with author, March 6, 2023; Travis and Abraham, *Forever and Ever*, 149–51.

14. Mario Tarradell, "His Career at a Crossroads, Randy Travis Looks for Inspiration," *Dallas Morning News*, December 8, 2000.

15. John Roos, "For Randy Travis, It's God and Country," *Los Angeles Times*, December 14, 2000; Nick Krewen, "Inspired Journey," *Country Music*, February/March 2001.

16. Randy Travis interviewed by Michael Gray, Country Music Hall of Fame, Nashville, Tennessee, November 7, 2008.

17. Nick Krewen, "Inspired Journey."

18. Lance Dary, telephone interview with author, November 2, 2021.

19. Steve Binder, dir., *Randy Travis Live! It Was Just a Matter of Time*, Image Entertainment Inc., 2000.

20. Travis and Abraham, *Forever and Ever*, 146–47; *Live: It Was Just a Matter of Time*, Sunset Theater, Anaheim, California, December 14, 2000, DVD by Image Production Services; "Image Entertainment Announces August 28 All-Format Release of 'Randy Travis Live: It Was Just a Matter of Time'," *Business Wire*, June 20, 2001.

21. Jim Patterson, "Rock Band Third Day Triumphs at Christian Music Awards," *Johnson City (TN) Press*, April 27, 2001.

22. Sheila Edmondson, "Thousands Sing Easter Praise with Randy Travis," *Commercial Appeal* (Memphis, TN), April 16, 2001.

23. Tarradell, "His Career at a Crossroads"; Gordon Mote, telephone interview with author, March 24, 2023.

24. Mote interview with author; Lehning interview; Travis and Abraham, *Forever and Ever*, 149–52.

25. Shirley Jinkins, "Country Tradition Follows Travis in New Gospel Role," *Fort Worth (TX) Star-Telegram*, October 19, 2002; Lisa Zhito, "Second Coming," *Country Music*, August/September 2003; Peter Cooper, "Travis, Worley Selected for CCMA Awards, *The Tennessean*, November 7, 2003; Lehning interview; Travis and Abraham, *Forever and Ever*, 155.

26. Randy Travis, GMA Dove Awards at Municipal Auditorium, Nashville, Tennessee, April 28, 2004.

27. Travis and Abraham, *Forever and Ever*, 154; Thomas Kintner, "Randy Travis Has His Own Cross to Bear," *Hartford (CT) Courant*, August 6, 2004.

28. Lehning interview; Travis and Abraham, *Forever and Ever*, 154.

29. Randy Travis in Tour Bus Accident," United Press International, March 8, 2004; Travis and Abraham, *Forever and Ever*, 154–57; "Randy Travis' Bus Runs into a Ditch," *Odessa (TX) American*, March 9, 2004; Jeff Davis, conversation with author, June 24, 2023.

30. John Gerome, "The Best Country Love Songs," *Livingston County Daily Press* (Howell, MI), June 17, 2004.

31. Lehning interview; Randy Travis performance at Calvary Assembly of God, Orlando, Florida, late 2003.

32. Travis interview, Country Music Hall of Fame.

33. Joe Van Dyke, telephone interview with author, June 22, 2023.

34. Thomas Kintner, "Travis and Jones Connect Country Generations," *Hartford (CT) Courant*, August 7, 2004; "Civil War–Themed Album Completed," *Abilene (TX) Reporter-News*, March 4, 2004.

35. Ron Rollins, "Randy Travis Is a Friday Night Steady," *Dayton (OH) Daily News*, August 28, 2004; Laura Younkin, *Courier-Journal* (Louisville, KY), August 30, 2004.

36. Dary interview.

## Chapter 12. "We were both wrong."

1. Mike Regenstreif, "Randy Travis: *The Very Best of Randy Travis*," *Harbour City Star* (Nanaimo, BC), August 21, 2004.

2. Randy Travis with Ken Abraham, *Forever and Ever, Amen: A Memoir of Music, Faith, and Braving the Storms of Life* (Nashville: Nelson Books, 2019), 159–65; Kyle Lehning, telephone interviews with author, October 23, 2020, March 6, 2023, and March 30, 2023.

3. Randy Travis, interview with Mike Dupree about *More Life* documentary, January 11, 2012.

4. Randy Travis interviewed by Michael Gray, Country Music Hall of Fame, Nashville, Tennessee, November 7, 2008.

5. George Jones Tribute at Kennedy Center Honors, December 7, 2008.

6. Charlie O'Dowd, dir., *Randy Travis: Christmas on the Pecos*, Elizabeth Travis, executive producer, filmed May 2006, FilmNewMexico, TV special released 2008.

7. Lehning interviews; O'Dowd, *Randy Travis: Christmas on the Pecos*; Shonda Novak and Mark Hummels, "El Mitote: Fried Music," *Santa Fe New Mexican*, June 4, 2000; Travis and Abraham, *Forever and Ever*, 108, 160–61; Karen Polly, "Director Says Filming of Christmas Special a Success," *Carlsbad (NM) Current-Argu*, December 15, 2005; Mary and Randy Travis, conversation with author, Pilot Point, Texas, August 16, 2023.

8. Randy Travis, interviewed by Jim and Barb from KCQ, 98 FM, broadcasting live at the CMA Awards, November 7, 2007; Randy Travis, on "The Hot Seat" at Kissin' 102.1.com, Wichita, Kansas, May 14, 2012; Travis and Abraham, *Forever and Ever*, 163–64.

9. Mark Bright, telephone interview with author, May 15, 2023.

10. Peter Cooper, "Legends, Leaders Get ACM Honors," *The Tennessean*, September 23, 2009.

11. North Carolina Music Hall of Fame website: https://northcarolinamusichalloffame.org/ (accessed March 3, 2024); David Menconi, "All about Carolina Music," *News & Observer* (Raleigh, NC), December 20, 2009.

12. Lehning interviews; Travis and Abraham, *Forever and Ever*, 167–70; Eamonn McCrystal, telephone interview with author, May 2, 2020.

13. Lehning interviews; Travis and Abraham, *Forever and Ever*, 108–109, 167–70, 176–77; Eamonn McCrystal, telephone interview with author, May 2, 2020; "Randy Travis Cheatin' Heart," *National Enquirer*, July 22, 2010; Mark David, "Randy Travis Says 'Amen' to Condo in Nashville," *Variety*, July 18, 2019; Dr. Ritchie Beougher, telephone interview with author, February 24, 2024.

14. Rick L D Wayne Money, telephone interview with author, September 30, 2019; Bill Blythe, telephone interview with author, November 4, 2022; Travis and Abraham, *Forever and Ever*, 178, 183; Stuart Munro, "Randy Travis Recovers from Rocky Start at Indian Ranch," *Telegram & Gazette* (Worcester, MA), September 13, 2010; Lehning interview.

15. Randy Travis, Special Warranty Deed, Napa County, California, October 24, 2010.

16. LinkedIn post for Chrysalis Ranch, https://www.linkedin.com/company/chrysalis-ranch (accessed August 23, 2024); Travis and Abraham, *Forever and Ever*, 177–80.

## Chapter 13. "I am wearing what God gave me, and I am proud of it."

1. Eamonn McCrystal, telephone interview with author, May 2, 2020; Eamonn McCrystal, email to author, April 17, 2023; Kyle Lehning, telephone interview with author, March 30, 2023; Randy Travis with Ken Abraham, *Forever and Ever, Amen: A Memoir of Music, Faith, and Braving the Storms of Life* (Nashville: Nelson Books, 2019), 181–83; Jamey Johnson, telephone interview with author, September 1, 2021; Randy Travis, interview with editorial director Bill Werde, "Randy Travis Q&A @ Billboard about 25th Anniversary Album," *Billboard*, March 28, 2012; John Anderson, telephone interview with author, January 31, 2023; Cindy Watts, "25 Years after Landmark Album, Travis Celebrates 'Storms,'" *The Tennessean*, June 14, 2011; Mark Casstevens, telephone interview with author, January 11, 2023; Randy Travis, interview with Mike Dupree about *More Life* documentary, January 11, 2012.

2. Randy Travis letter to Elizabeth Travis Management, management agreement, March 29, 2011.

3. "Country Star Hits the Wall," *New York Post*, June 8, 2011; Dr. Ritchie Beougher, telephone interview with author, February 24, 2024; Zach Farnum, email to author, April 28, 2024; Travis and Abraham, *Forever and Ever*, 184–85.

4. Samuel D. Lipshie letter to Elizabeth Travis, "Termination of Elizabeth Travis and Elizabeth Travis Management Agreement," August 8, 2011.

5. *Elizabeth Travis Management Inc., Plaintiff, v. Randy Travis, Defendant*, Chancery Court for Davidson County, Tennessee, Case 12–0526-IV Complaint, April 5, 2012; Joe Van Dyke, telephone interview with author, June 22, 2023.

6. "Huguley Memorial Medical Center's Crystal Heart Gala," *Fort Worth (TX) Star-Telegram*, October 5, 2011; Travis and Abraham, *Forever and Ever*, 187–89.

7. Omar Villafranca, "Sanger Release Dashcam Video of Randy Travis Arrest," NBC 5 Dallas–Fort Worth, February 14, 2012; Travis and Abraham, *Forever and Ever*, 190–91; "Randy Travis Gets Drunk after Fight with Girlfriend," *TMZ*, February 6, 2012.

8. Elizabeth Travis Management Inc., Plaintiff, Case 12–0526-IV.

9. *Randy Travis, Defendant and Counter-Plaintiff*, "Answer to Complaint and Counterclaim for Declaratory Judgment," US District Court for the Middle District of Tennessee, Case 3:12-cv-00497, May 24, 2012; *Elizabeth Travis Management Inc., Plaintiff, v. Randy Travis, Defendant*, "Answer to Counterclaim for Declaratory Judgment," US District Court for the Middle District of Tennessee, Case 3:12-cv-00497, June 20, 2012.

10. Travis and Abraham, *Forever and Ever*, 194–95; "Ambien," https://www.msn.com/en-us/health/drugs/ambien/hp-ambien (accessed March 3, 2024).

11. "Randy Travis Wandered Naked into Convenience Store," World Entertainment News Network, August 13, 2012.

12. Grayson County, Texas, 911 call, August 7, 2012; James Fortenberry, Texas Highway Patrol Offense Report concerning Randy Bruce Travis, August 10, 2012.

13. Jonathan Perales, patient response report for Randy Travis, August 7, 2012; Elvin Fisk, telephone interview with author, May 10, 2023.

14. Bryan Caloway, Grayson County Sheriff's Office Incident Report, case number 13–08–2438, August 10, 2012.

15. Trooper Clifford S. Bryant, Texas Highway Patrol Division Offense Report on Randy Travis, August 8, 2012; Fortenberry, Offense Report; Trooper Bryant dashcam video, August 8, 2012; Fisk interview.

16. Al Weir, telephone interview with author, November 4, 2022; Gary Corley, interview with author at Gary Corley Law Office, Sherman, Texas, October 20, 2022.

17. Lance Dary, telephone interview with author, November 2, 2021; Travis and Abraham, *Forever and Ever*, 199–200; Johnson interview; Mary Travis, conversation with author, Travis ranch, August 18, 2023.

## Chapter 14. "In fact, I was feelin' mighty fine."

1. "Civil Docket for Case # 3:12-cv-00497," US District Court, Middle District of Tennessee.

2. Wade Tatangelo, "My Picks for Top Turkeys of 2012," *Bradenton (FL) Herald*, November 18, 2012; Lisa Gutierrez, "2012 Turkeys," *Kansas City (MO) Star*, November 22, 2012.

3. Randy Travis with Ken Abraham, *Forever and Ever, Amen: A Memoir of Music, Faith, and Braving the Storms of Life* (Nashville: Nelson Books, 2019), 205–207; Al Weir, telephone interview with author, April 20, 2023; "The Kiepersol Name," https://www.kiepersol.com/origin-story-kiepersol-tree (accessed August 23, 2024); Lance Dary, telephone interview with author, November 2, 2021; Kyle Lehning, telephone interview with author, March 30, 2023; Rick L D Wayne Money, telephone interview with author, September 30, 2019; Joe Van Dyke, telephone interview with author, June 22, 2023.

4. John Nix, telephone interview with author, November 4, 2022; Judge Henderson, *State of Texas v. Randy Bruce Travis*, No. 2013–1–007, "Plea Conference and Pretrial Management Docketing Order," January 21, 2013; Judge Corley Henderson, *State of Texas v. Randy Bruce Travis*, No. 2013–1–007, "Pretrial Order Concerning Media Access and Courtroom Decorum," January 29, 2013; Joseph Brown and Randy Travis, *State of Texas v. Randy Bruce Travis*, No. 2013–1–007, "Plea Agreement and Sentence Recommendation," January 31, 2013; Travis and Abraham, *Forever and Ever*, 211–12.

5. Joseph D. Brown, Grayson County Criminal District Attorney press release, January 31, 2013.

6. Lawrence Friedman, *State of Texas v. Randy Bruce Travis*, No. 2013–1–007, "Evidentiary Motion for Destruction of Evidence," January 13, 2013; Joseph Brown, *State of Texas v. Randy Bruce Travis*, No. 2013–1–007, "State's Response to Defendant's Motion for Destruction of Evidence," January 29, 2013; Judge Corley Henderson,

*State of Texas v. Randy Bruce Travis*, No. 2013–1–007, "Protective Order Regarding Certain Evidence and Findings of Fact," January 31, 2013.

7. Kim Hughes, telephone interview with author, January 14, 2021; Audris Ponce, "Permian Grad Directs 'The Virtuoso,'" *Odessa (TX) American*, June 5, 2014; James Dupré, telephone interview with author, October 24, 2020; Chris Talbott, "Music City Mourns Country Legend George Jones," *Brownsville (TX) Herald*, May 3, 2013; Travis and Abraham, *Forever and Ever*, 207, 214, 217–18.

8. Kyle Lehning, telephone interview with author, March 30, 2023; Joe Nichols telephone interview with author, October 23, 2021; Travis and Abraham, *Forever and Ever*, 221.

9. Tracy Shaw, *Elizabeth Travis Management, Inc., Plaintiff and Counter-Defendant v. Randy Travis, Defendant and Counter-Plaintiff*, "Report of Rule 31 Proceeding," US District Court for the Middle District of Tennessee, Case 3:12-cv-00497, May 7, 2013.

10. Greg Abbott, *State of Texas v. Randy Bruce Travis*, No. 2013–1–007, "Texas Department of Public Safety's Objection to and Motion to Set Aside Protective Order," March 11, 2013; Judge Corley Henderson, *State of Texas v. Randy Bruce Travis*, No. 2013–1–007, "Findings of Fact and Conclusion of Law Relative to Texas DPS's Objection to and Motion to Set Aside Protective Order," May 14, 2013.

11. Leslie Hope, dir., *Christmas on the Bayou*, Active Entertainment/Lifetime Television, 2013.

12. Dary interview; Steve Hinson at Randy Travis Band Reunion, July 18, 2021; Travis and Abraham, *Forever and Ever*, 221–23; Van Dyke interview.

13. "Randy Travis Returns to Deadwood," *Black Hills Pioneer* (Spearfish, SD), April 11, 2013.

## Chapter 15. "Lord, please give him back to me."

1. Randy Travis, interview with Mike Dupree about *More Life* documentary, January 11, 2012.

2. Mary Travis interview with Mike Dupree, September 11, 2020; Randy Travis with Ken Abraham, *Forever and Ever, Amen: A Memoir of Music, Faith, and Braving the Storms of Life* (Nashville: Nelson Books, 2019), 225–31; Al Weir, telephone interview with author, November 4, 2022; Mary Travis, telephone conversation with author, June 30, 2023.

3. Charlotte Libov, "Singer Randy Travis Battles Heart Virus," *Newsmax*, July 9, 2013.

4. Medical Examiner's Certificate of Death for Bobbie Tucker Traywick, North Carolina Form DEHNR 2164 (Revised 9/91) Vital Records, filed May 28, 1998.

5. "Randy Travis's Physicians Speak," Baylor Scott & White Health Media Newsroom, press conference, July 15, 2013, https://news.bswhealth.com/en-US/releases/randy-travis-physicians-speak (accessed August 24, 2024).

6. Mary Travis interview with Dupree; Jeff Davis and Kyle Lehning, interviewed for *Randy Travis: More Life* documentary, released in 2021; Travis and Abraham, *Forever and Ever*, 231–34; "Randy Travis's Physicians Speak," Baylor Scott & White Health Media Newsroom, video statement, July 10, 2013; Weir interview.

7. David W. Barnett, MD, telephone interview with author, July 20, 2023.

8. Travis and Abraham, *Forever and Ever*, 233; Kim Hughes, telephone interview with author, January 14, 2021; Mary Travis interview with Dupree.

9. Rocky Thacker, telephone interview with author, September 28, 2019; John Anderson, telephone interview with author, January 31, 2023.

10. "Randy Travis's Physicians Speak" press conference; Travis and Abraham, *Forever and Ever*, 234–35, 239; Rick L D Wayne Money, telephone interview with author, September 30, 2019; Bill Blythe, telephone interview with author, November 4, 2022; Mary Travis, conversation with author, August 18, 2023.

11. Stroke Rehabilitation Hospital Nashville | Vanderbilt Stallworth Rehabilitation Hospital (encompasshealth.com) (accessed March 3, 2024).

12. Weir interview; Travis and Abraham, *Forever and Ever*, 239–45; Mary Travis interview with Dupree; Hughes interview; Barnett interview.

13. Don Chance, "Travis' 'Influence' One of Year's Best," *Times Record News* (Wichita Falls, TX), October 11, 2013.

14. Chris Talbott, "Stars Honor George Jones," *Paducah (KY) Sun*, November 23, 2013.

15. Travis and Abraham, *Forever and Ever*, 247–48.

## Chapter 16. "I think you would be the perfect person to manage Randy Travis."

1. Tim Massengill, telephone interview with author, March 5, 2023; Randy Travis with Ken Abraham, *Forever and Ever, Amen: A Memoir of Music, Faith, and Braving the Storms of Life* (Nashville: Nelson Books, 2019), 249–51.

2. Mary Travis, interview with Mike Dupree, September 11, 2020; Mary Travis, Houston Aphasia Recovery Center's "Let's Talk" Virtual Luncheon, March 31, 2021.

3. Massengill interview.

4. Massengill interview; Travis and Abraham, *Forever and Ever*, 249–51; Alicia Dennis, "What Happened to Randy Travis?" *People*, March 17, 2014.

5. Tom Rutledge at Randy Travis Band Reunion, July 18, 2021; Travis and Abraham, *Forever and Ever*, 251–52; "Randy Travis Makes Rare Appearance at Dolly Parton Gig," World Entertainment News Network, June 4, 2014.

6. "Tuesday—Listen," *News-Press* (Fort Myers, FL), August 17, 2014.

7. Travis and Abraham, *Forever and Ever*, 253–58; "Randy Travis Makes a Stop in Denison on His Road to Recovery," KTEN Channel 10 (Sherman-Denison, TX), September 18, 2014; Four Rivers Outreach Banquet, Sherman, Texas, May 10, 2013; John Nix, text message to author, December 4, 2023.

8. Tony Conway, telephone interview with author, July 13, 2023.

9. Bill Blythe, telephone interview with author, November 4, 2022; Travis and Abraham, *Forever and Ever*, 260; Zach Farnum, email to author, April 28, 2024; Dr. Ritchie Beougher, telephone interview with author, February 24, 2024.

10. Kim Hughes, dir., *The Price*, Trumpett Productions, 2015.

11. James Dupré, telephone interview with author, October 24, 2020; Kim Hughes, telephone interview with author, January 14, 2021.

12. Conway interview.

13. Travis and Abraham, *Forever and Ever*, 262.

14. Tony Conway, email to author, July 21, 2023.

15. Mary Travis, Houston Aphasia Recovery Center's "Let's Talk" Virtual Luncheon, March 31, 2021.

16. Cindy Watts, "CMA Fest: The Defining Themes for 2016 Event," *The Tennessean*, June 13, 2016.

17. "Randy Travis DWI Video Ruled Public Record," *Austin (TX) American-Statesman*, August 19, 2016; Travis and Abraham, *Forever and Ever*, 220.

18. Travis and Abraham, *Forever and Ever*, 267–68; Matt Arrowood, telephone interview with author, October 29, 2021; Harold Bruce Traywick, Certificate of Death, North Carolina Vital Records, BK 00130 PG 1046 INST # 01046, filed October 20, 2016; Dennis Traywick, interview with author, July 19, 2021.

19. Roger Brown, telephone interview with author, December 27, 2022; Travis and Abraham, *Forever and Ever*, 271.

20. Massengill interview.

21. Travis and Abraham, *Forever and Ever*, 150–51, 271–73; "Randy Travis Stuns by Singing after Stroke at Country Music Hall of Fame Induction," October 16, 2016; Conway interview; Nick Krewen, "Inspired Journey," *Country Music*, February/March 2001.

22. Randy Travis, comment to author, Travis ranch, Tioga, Texas, August 18, 2023.

# Epilogue

1. Randy Travis with Ken Abraham, *Forever and Ever, Amen: A Memoir of Music, Faith, and Braving the Storms of Life* (Nashville: Nelson Books, 2019), 286–88; Randy and Mary Travis, conversations with author, October 24, 2022, and August 18, 2023.

2. CMA Awards 50th Anniversary Opening Performance, November 2, 2016.

3. Travis and Abraham, *Forever and Ever*, 260–61; Gary Carter, telephone interview with author, November 1, 2019; Laura Brown, "Looking Back at the Rushed 1997 Closure of Opryland USA," *Nashville Scene*, December 29, 2022.

4. Scotty McCreery, telephone interview with author, February 1, 2022; Tracy Lawrence, telephone interview with author, September 21, 2021; Mo Pitney, telephone conversation with author, January 6, 2020.

5. Tony Conway, telephone interview with author, July 13, 2023; Cindy Watts, "Randy Travis Gets All-Star Salute," *The Tennessean*, February 9, 2017; Travis and Abraham, *Forever and Ever*, 278–80.

6. Mark Price, "Randy Travis Makes Rare Visit to Hometown Near Charlotte," *Charlotte Observer*, September 16, 2017; Mark Price, "Randy Travis Said Only 4 Words, but Hometown Crowd Roared in Reply," *Charlotte Observer*, September 19, 2017.

7. Barrett Hobbs, telephone interview with author, May 11, 2022.

8. Travis and Abraham, *Forever and Ever*, 286; Cindy Watts and Adam Tamburin, "CMA Fest Closes with Superstar Surprises," *The Tennessean*, June 12, 2018.

9. James Dupré, email to author, September 8, 2023; Matthew Leimkuehler, "Brooks and Underwood Honor Travis at ASCAPs," *The Tennessean*, November 13, 2019.

10. Travis and Abraham, *Forever and Ever*, vii; Terry Tyson, telephone interview with author, August 26, 2023.

11. Kyle Lehning, telephone interview with author, July 17, 2024; Cris Lacy on *CBS Sunday Morning*, May 5, 2024.

12. "Radio, Music, and Copyrights: 100 Years of Inequity for Recording Artists," hearing by House Judiciary Subcommittee on Courts, Intellectual Property, and the Internet, June 26, 2024, https://judiciary.house.gov/committee-activity/hearings/radio-music-and-copyrights-100-years-inequity-recording-artists-0 (accessed August 24, 2024).

13. James Dupré, telephone interview with author, October 24, 2020; Conway interview.

# INDEX

"1982," 32–34, 37

Abraham, Ken, 226
"A Few Ole Country Boys," 98, 100, 110, 112, 177, 179
Alabama (band), 48, 63, 10, 106
"All Night Long," 98
*Always and Forever*, 49, 51, 53–54, 56, 61, 63, 67, 92, 118
*A Man Ain't Made of Stone*, 150
"A Man Ain't Made of Stone," 152
"Amazing Grace," 153, 196, 212–13, 218, 222, 225, 228
"American Trilogy," 127, 162
*America Will Always Stand*, 162
"America Will Always Stand," 162, 167
Anderson, Bill, 224
Anderson, John, 16, 117, 125–26, 177, 205
"Angels," 168
*Annabelle's Wish* (movie), 143
*An Old Time Christmas*, 84–85
"Are We in Trouble Now?" 142
*Around the Bend*, 165–66
Arrowood, Matthew, 220, 248
Arrowood, Rose Marie, 134, 205, 248
Atkins, Chet, 97
*At Risk* (movie), 120

Azrak, Janice, 26–29, 32, 35–36, 51–53, 146

Ball, David, 38, 125
Bandy, Moe, 12, 16, 23
"Baptism," 153, 155
Barnett, David, 208–9
Barton, Dave, 16
"Before You Kill Us All," 123–25
Benton, Brook, 26, 85
Beougher, Cavanaugh, 138, 172, 221
Beougher, Mary. *See* Travis, Mary Davis
Beougher, Raleigh, 138, 172, 221
Beougher, Ritchie, 172–73
"Better Class of Losers," 104, 110, 113–14, 177
"Big Butter and Egg Man," 192
"Birth of the Blues, 98
Bishop, Charles, 32–33, 39, 93, 133
Black, Clint, 94–96, 101–2
*Black Dog* (movie), 145
Blackmon, Buddy, 31
Blythe, Bill, 206, 208, 216
Bourke, Rory, 177
Bowen, Jimmy, 26
"Box, The," 124–25
Bradley, Owen and Harold, 17
Bright, Mark, 169

Brooks, Garth, 73, 101,103,167, 221–22, 225–26
Brown, Joe, 193–94
Brown, Roger, 122–23, 221
Brown, T. Graham, 31, 34, 130
Brown, Zac, 176–77
Bryan, Luke, 225–26
Bryant, Clifford "Sammy," 185–87
Burke, L. D., 167
Bush, George H. W., 72, 77, 93–95, 106–8, 133, 167
Buttram, Terry, 21–4, 43

"Can't Hurt a Man," 179
Carter, Gary, 22, 24, 33–34, 39, 43, 55, 72, 76, 80, 114, 116–17, 245
Carter, Jimmy, 22, 24
Cash, Johnny, 56, 67, 159
Cash, Rosanne, 56
Casstevens, Mark, 49, 105, 112, 124–27, 141, 154, 178, 246
Cates, Mickey, 155
Chesney, Kenny, 177
*Christmas on the Bayou* (movie), 197
Collie, Mark, 84
Collins, Jay, 86
Colter, Jessi, 153
Conway, Tony, 214, 216–18, 221–22, 224–25, 228, 248
Cook, Bill, 198, 245
Corley, Gary, 135, 187–88
"Cowboy Boogie," 123
Crowell, Rodney, 56, 94
Cryer, Sherwood, 14, 43
Curb, Mike, 158, 170
Curtis, Michael, 156

Dalton, Webb. *See* Jones, David
Dary, Lance, 75, 154–55, 162–63, 189, 192, 198, 246
Davis (Blauw), Jeff: promoting Travis's career (1986–92), 46–47, 55, 57, 62, 66, 71–72, 93, 96–97, 109, 113, 116, 119; promoting Travis's career (1994–2013), 124, 133, 159–60, 174, 180–81, 198; promoting Travis's career, later years, 202–5, 219, 225, 228, 248
Davis, Mary. *See* Travis, Mary Davis

Davis, Ray, 208
Davis, Stubbs, 172
*Dead Man's Revenge* (movie), 120
Dean, Billy, 86
"Deeper Than the Holler," 68, 75, 92
de Wet, Pierre, 190–92, 217
Dickens, Little Jimmy, 23, 45, 98, 130
"Didn't We Shine," 178
"Diggin' Up Bones," 43–45, 47, 75, 155, 165, 177, 226
"Doctor Jesus," 154
"Do I Ever Cross Your Mind?" 97
"Don't Ever Sell Your Saddle," 153
*Down Home* (TV show), 119
Doyle, Major Bob, 73
Drillen, Dan, 33, 245
Dunn, Holly, 96
Dupré, James, 138, 195–96, 217, 226–28

Earle, Steve, 47–48
Eastwood, Clint, 99
Emery, Ralph, 16, 22, 24–25, 30–31, 51–52, 61, 81, 98, 101, 104, 121–23
Erwin, Gary, 205–6
Esposito, John, 214–15
"Everything That I Own (Has Got a Dent)," 166

"Faith in You," 166
Farnum, Zach, 226, 228, 246
*Fire Down Below* (movie), 143
Fisk, Elvin, 184–85
Forester Sisters, 31, 33, 37–38, 41
"Forever and Ever, Amen," 50–53, 56, 61, 63, 110, 142, 151, 156, 161, 165, 176–77, 216, 221, 223–25
"Forever Together," 110
Fortenberry, Jim, 185, 187
*Frank and Jesse* (movie), 120, 124, 141, 143
Friedman, Larry, 192
Frizzell, Lefty, 5, 10, 25, 111, 127
Fulbright, Paul, 126, 245
*Full Circle*, 141–42, 178
Fulton, Richard, 49

Gallimore, Byron, 143, 150
Gattis, Keith, 196
Gibson, Steve, 122, 225

Gill, Vince, 143, 159
*Glory Train: Songs of Faith, Worship, and Praise*, 164
Gosdin, Vern, 97–98, 101, 104–5
Graham, Billy, 158
Gray, Michael, 166
Gray, William, 202–3
*Greatest Hits, Volume I*, 115, 118, 141
*Greatest Hits, Volume II*, 115, 118
Greenwood, Lee, 17, 77
Griffin, Tim, 4
Griffith, Andy, 30, 120, 133
Grisham, Doyle, 29, 33
Grissom, Rich, 45

Haber, Gary, 99–100, 146, 175, 179–80, 215
Haggard, Merle, 5, 10–11, 15, 25, 29, 35, 47–48, 63, 98–99, 111, 127, 192, 221
Hampton, George, 200, 203
"Happy Trails," 81, 96–97
Hardison, Randy, 33, 246
"Hard Rock Bottom of Your Heart," 85, 92, 104
Harless, Dan Jr., 111
Harper, Carol, 55
Harper, John, 2, 7, 9–10
Harris, Emmylou, 56
Hatcher, Frank, 2, 9–10, 13–14
Hatcher, Lib: at Country City USA, 2, 8–14, 16–17; at Nashville Palace, 19–21, 23–25, 27; as Travis's manager, 29, 31–35, 37–40, 42–44, 46–47, 49–50, 52, 54–56, 59–60, 62, 64–66, 68–72, 76–79, 81–83, 85–87, 90, 92–94, 97–100, 105; as Travis's wife, 108–11, 114, 116–17, 119, 121, 124, 126, 128–29, 133, 140–42, 149, 214, 219, 225. *See also* Travis, Elizabeth
Helms, Jerry, 3, 6–7
Henderson, James Corley, 192–94, 197
Henley, Don, 177–78, 192
*Heroes and Friends*, 97, 100, 104, 176, 179, 225
"Heroes and Friends," 99, 101
"He Walked on Water," 85, 95, 125
Higdon, Pat, 29
*High Lonesome*, 110, 112, 114, 123
Hill, John W., 206
Hill, Steve, 24

Hinson, Steve, 28, 126–27, 198, 245
Hobbs, Barrett, 81, 136, 225
Hobbs, John A., 18–19, 21, 24, 32–33, 69, 81–82, 136, 225
Hogan, Ron, 30
"Hole, The," 143, 148
Honeycutt, Kenneth, 8, 131, 147
"Honky Tonk Moon," 68
Houston, Robb, 154–55, 163, 192, 198, 246
"How Do I Wrap My Heart Up for Christmas?" 84
Hughes, Kent, 195, 208–9
Hughes, Kim, 195–96, 209, 216–17
"Human Race, The," 98, 104
Hunt, James B., Jr., 147
Hunter, Nick, 28, 34, 61

"I'd Surrender All," 110
"If I Didn't Have You," 115
*Influence Vol. 1: The Man I Am*, 192, 198, 209
*Influence Vol. 2: The Man I Am*, 192, 213
*Inspirational Journey*, 152, 154–56, 158
"Is It Still Over?" 68, 78
"I Told You So," 25, 63, 67, 70, 168–69
*I Told You So: The Ultimate Hits of Randy Travis*, 169
"It's Just a Matter of Time," 85, 91, 155
"I Won't Need You Anymore," 63

Jackson, Alan, 101–4, 106, 110, 112, 114, 123, 167, 177, 221
Jay (Blauw), Jimmy, 46–47, 55
Jennings, Waylon, 27, 153, 192
Johnson, David, 40, 43, 72, 124, 126, 198, 246
Johnson, Doug, 157
Johnson, Jamey, 177, 189
Jonas, Kevin, Sr., 7–8, 38
Jones, David (Webb Dalton), 28, 63
Jones, George, 5, 7, 10–11, 15–16, 25, 32, 35, 41, 47, 56, 62, 79, 115, 167, 196, 198, 209; performing with Travis, 44–45, 58, 97–98, 101, 110–12, 162, 178
Judd, Naomi and Wynonna, 48, 53, 55–57, 61–63, 144

Kalbfeld, Mark, 121
King, B. B., 95, 99, 104
"King of the Road, 141

Knopfler, Mark, 142
Kristofferson, Kris, 177, 192, 214

Lacy, Cris, 176, 196, 214–15, 226–27
Landis, Barry, 152, 156–58
Lawrence, Tracy, 224
Ledford, Susan, 17
Lee, Brenda, 22, 218–19
Lee, Johnny, 43
Lehning, Kyle, 27, 34, 43, 60–63, 65, 81, 103, 106, 109, 112, 115, 122–25, 127, 140–42, 152, 161, 168–69, 171, 174, 217, 219, 225, 247–48; AI recording, 226–27; final Travis recording session, 196–97; recording *25th Anniversary Celebration*, 176–79; recording *Always & Forever*, 48–50; recording *An Old Time Christmas* and *No Holdin' Back*, 84–86; recording *Around the Bend*, 165–66; recording *Heroes and Friends*, 97–99; recording *Influence*, 190–92; recording initial Travis songs, 29, 31–32; recording *Old 8×10*, 68–70; recording *Rise and Shine*, 155–58; recording *Storms of Life*, 36–38; Travis's stroke, 203–4
Leim, Paul, 125–26, 142, 246
Lewis, Stan, 11
Lindley, John, 68
"Look Heart, No Hands," 115, 118
Louvin, Kathy, 84
Loveless, Patty, 58, 73–75, 95, 162, 214
Lynn, Loretta, 9, 11, 46, 51–52, 57, 59, 77, 97–98, 198
Lynne, Shelby, 178

Mack, Michael, 202–5, 208
Mandile, Steve, 126, 154, 246
Mandrell, Barbara, 24, 27, 101, 107
Mangum, Kate, 5
Markley, Dan, 59–60, 73–75, 89–90, 95, 102, 132
Massengill, Tim, 210–12, 221
*Matlock* (TV show), 120, 133
Mattea, Kathy, 41, 44, 63, 67, 88, 101
*Maverick* (movie), 120
Mayne, Bill, 105, 109, 142
McBride, Martina, 170
McCarter, Jennifer, 60
McCoy, Neal, 212

McCreery, Scotty, 224
McCrystal, Eamonn, 170–74, 176, 178–89
McEntire, Reba, 31, 55, 62, 79, 100–101, 115, 125
McGraw, Tim, 144, 179
McGuirt, Frank, 147
McMillan, Terry, 111
"Memories of Old Santa Fe," 122
Miller, Roger, 141
Miller, Tracy, 212
Milsap, Ronnie, 17, 48, 68, 170
Money, Rick L D Wayne, 21–22, 24, 33, 43, 72, 125–27, 174, 192, 198, 206, 245, 247
Monk, Charlie, 23, 25, 27, 42–43, 71, 128
Montgomery, Melba, 143
Moore, Buck, 124
"More Life," 177, 192, 207, 228
Morgan, Lorrie, 101, 144, 178, 214
Morris, Gary, 41, 107
Mote, Gordon, 157–58
Murphey, Michael Martin, 96, 122–23
Murray, Anne, 17, 88

Nelson, Robert Lyn and Uilani, 108
Nelson, Tommy, 216
Nelson, Willie, 22, 61–62, 84, 97–98, 105, 177, 191, 214
Nichols, Joe, 196–97, 209, 213
Nix, John, 192–93
*No Holdin' Back*, 85, 91, 95, 118, 155
"No Place Like Home," 45
Norman, Jim Ed, 28–29, 45, 49, 54, 92, 99, 121–22, 142
Norris, Chuck, 121, 172, 211

"Oh, What a Silent Night," 84
*Old 8×10*, 66–67, 78, 81, 92, 94, 118
"Old 8×10," 68
O'Neill, Tom, 93–94, 133
"On the Other Hand," 29–31, 34–35, 37–38, 40–42, 46, 48, 50–52, 56, 111–12, 125, 161, 221, 226, 247
Oslin, K. T., 61, 63, 70, 78, 162
*Outlaws: The Legend of O. B. Taggart* (movie), 120
"Out of My Bones," 144
Overstreet, Paul, 31, 41–43, 45, 50–51, 56, 61, 68, 84, 123

Paisley, Brad, 167, 176, 221–23
Parkey, Monty, 62, 71–72, 114, 213, 245
Parton, Dolly, 48, 60, 62, 70–71, 88, 97, 115, 161, 212–13
*Passing Through*, 164
Paxton, Bill, 120, 141
Pearl, Minnie, 56
"Pennies from Heaven," 192
Peoples, Rick, 122
Perry, Richard, 83
Peterson, Michael, 157
Phifer, Pruitt, 6–7
Pillow, Daryl, 19–21
Pillow, Ray, 19–20
Pitney, Mo, 224
Plyler, Janice, 10
Plyler, Larke, 10, 13–15, 44, 145–46
"Point of Light," 106–8, 110, 162
"Pray for the Fish," 159
Price, Ray, 178
*Price, The* (movie), 216–17, 226
"Promises," 68–69, 79, 83–84, 178
Propst, John, 24
Pruett, Jeanne, 25
Pyle, Denver, 96

Radford, Ronald, 15, 72, 74, 76, 113, 117, 245
*Rainmaker, The* (movie), 143
"Raise Him Up," 159–60, 162
*Randy Ray Live at the Nashville Palace*, 20, 24, 29, 33, 68
*Randy Travis: Christmas on the Pecos*, 167
*Randy Travis 25th Anniversary Celebration*, 176, 179, 192, 200
Ray, Randy, 19–20, 23–25, 27–28, 155. *See also* Traywick, Randy Bruce
"Reasons I Cheat," 12, 29, 32
Ree, Terry, 89–90, 102
Reed, Luke, 122
Reid, Mike, 177
*Rise and Shine*, 156, 158, 159
"Rise and Shine," 156
Rivelli, Tommy, 43, 75–76, 116–17, 126, 205, 246
Robbins, Marty, 18, 85, 122, 192, 247
Robertson, Mary Elizabeth. *See* Hatcher, Lib
Rodman, Judy, 43

Rogers, Kenny, 17, 31, 56, 169, 212
Rogers, Neil Patton, 45
Rogers, Roy, 81, 83, 96–97, 101, 131
Rooney, Mickey, 120
Rosen, Johnny, 24
Ross, Alan, 66
Russell, Johnny, 30, 58
*Rustlers' Raphsody* (movie), 29–30
Rutledge, Tom, 71–72, 75–76, 80, 91, 102, 114, 117, 125, 213, 246

Sawyer Brown (band), 41
Sax, Doug, 84–85
Schadt, Paul, 44, 147–48
Schlitz, Don, 31, 41–42, 50, 56, 61, 68, 92, 97, 106, 114, 123, 178
Schuyler, Thom, 106
Schwarzenegger, Arnold, 78, 94
Seals, Dan, 27, 41
Seals, Troy, 98
Sears, Kenny, 24–25, 28
Seely, Jeannie, 22–23, 25, 223
"Send My Body," 13, 24
Sexton, Drew, 21, 24, 32–34, 43, 55, 62, 116, 125–26, 155, 161–62, 245
"Shallow Water," 155
Shamblin, Allen, 85–86, 125
Sharp, Martha, 26–29, 31–32, 35–36, 38, 41, 49–50, 60, 68, 81, 84–85, 115, 122, 219
Shea, Jim, 121
Sheehan, Steve, 154, 246
Shelton, Ricky Van, 63, 73, 79, 88, 95, 101, 115, 214
"She's My Woman," 11
"Shopping for Dresses," 98
Shriver, Evelyn, 69–70, 87, 99, 110, 118
Shucher, Herb, 142, 246
"Singing the Blues," 85
Singletary, Daryle, 141–43, 157
Skaggs, Ricky, 27, 37, 41, 45, 56, 62
Skepner, David, 59, 73
Smith, Connie, 170, 178
"Smokin' the Hive," 99
Soderstrom, Kenny, 21–22
"Someone You Never Knew," 178
"Somewhere in My Broken Heart," 86
*Songs of the Season*, 165
"Spirit of a Boy, Wisdom of a Man," 148

Stampley, Joe, 11–12, 16, 178
Statler Brothers, 37, 79, 106
*Steel Chariots* (movie), 143
Stegall, Keith, 23–24, 27, 29, 31, 49, 103
Stoner, George, 10
*Storms of Life*, 36–37, 41, 43, 45, 47–49, 51–52, 54, 118, 124, 129, 141, 157, 165, 176, 179, 196, 213, 247
"Storms of Life," 41, 67
Strait, George, 27, 35, 41, 48, 55–56, 61–62, 63, 79, 88, 94–95, 101–2, 125
"Stranger in My Mirror," 148
Stroud, James, 141–45, 150
Stuart, Marty, 34
Sturm, Richard, 124
Swayze, Patrick, 145
Sweeney, Bill, 71, 82, 146–47, 166

Tant, Ann, 12
Thacker, Rocky, 33, 41–44, 58, 76, 80, 83, 87, 89, 91, 116–17, 126, 205, 245
*This Is Me*, 123–26
"Three Wooden Crosses," 157–59, 161–62, 164, 170, 181, 221
*Three Wooden Crosses: The Inspirational Hits of Randy Travis*, 169
Tillis, Pam, 33
*T.N.T.* (movie), 143
Tomberlin, Bobby, 37, 224
"Tonight I'm Playin' Possum," 196, 198, 209, 213
"Too Gone Too Long," 63
Trahern, Sarah, 218
Trask, David, 76
Travis, Elizabeth (first wife), 109–11, 121, 146, 150–51, 154–55, 163, 165–67, 170–76, 178–80, 182, 186, 190, 197, 215, 248. *See also* Hatcher, Lib
Travis, Mary Davis (second wife), 138–39, 172–75, 179, 181, 183, 187, 189, 191, 195–96, 200–9, 211–24, 226–28, 248
Travis, Merle, 40
Travis, Randy Bruce: Country Music Hall of Fame, 18–19, 115, 167, 215–16, 218, 220–22; court cases and arrests, 1–2, 6–7, 135, 181–82, 185–88, 190, 192–94, 197; marriage, Mary, 216; marriage and divorce, Elizabeth, 109, 146, 171–76, 179–80; movie making, 119–21, 143, 145, 151–52, 197; *Nashville Now* appearances, 22, 25, 30, 45–46, 51–52, 58, 62, 81, 98, 101–2, 104, 131; overseas tours, 58–60, 66–67, 72–76, 80, 88–90, 110, 132, 154, 162, 170, 183; recording sessions, 11, 18, 23–24, 27–29, 31, 36, 42–43, 49–50, 63, 68, 81, 84–86, 91–92, 97–99, 103, 106, 110, 115, 122–25, 141–44, 150–57, 161, 167, 169, 171, 176–78, 190–92, 197; stroke and recovery, 200–201, 204–14; as Randy Bruce Traywick, 3, 9–12, 15–17, 19–23, 25, 27–29, 38, 42, 64–65, 100, 109, 126, 134, 146–47, 223, 225
—award shows: Academy of Country Music, 34–35, 50–51, 61, 79, 88, 108, 126, 130, 142, 157, 169, 216; Country Music Association, 41–42, 55–57, 67, 70, 87, 94, 100, 103, 106, 112, 115, 157–59, 161–62, 197; Grammy Awards, 47–48, 61, 78, 156, 161, 165; *Music City News*/TNN Viewers' Choice, 37, 52, 61, 63, 79, 88, 94, 110, 131, 157; others, 61, 79, 92, 158–59, 161, 164–65
—concerts: (1985–1992), 32–33, 44, 47–48, 50, 54, 62–63, 72–73, 77–79, 102, 115–16; (1994–1999), 125–26; (2000–2013), 152, 154–56, 167–68, 174, 181, 189, 191, 198–99
Traweek, Robarde (seventh great-grandfather), 2
Traywick, (Alexander) Bruce (grandfather), 3, 30, 86
Traywick, Berryman (fourth great-grandfather), 2
Traywick, Betty (cousin), 3
Traywick, Bobbie Rose Tucker (mother), 6–7, 29–30, 39, 42, 44, 56, 64, 82, 134, 144–45, 153, 203, 221
Traywick, Curtis, Jr. (cousin), 3
Traywick, David Brownlow (brother), 3, 6, 134
Traywick, Dennis Erie (brother), 3, 5, 7, 29–30, 64, 109, 134, 139, 202–3, 208, 220, 248
Traywick, Harold Bruce (father), 3, 6–7, 13–14, 29–30, 39–40, 42, 44, 56, 64, 82, 134, 144–45, 150, 153, 220
Traywick, Linda Sue (sister), 3, 134
Traywick, Mary Elizabeth. *See* Travis, Elizabeth

Traywick, (Maud) Etta Davis (grandmother), 3
Traywick, Mike (cousin), 6, 16
Traywick, Randy Bruce. *See* Travis, Randy Bruce
Traywick, Ricky Harold (brother), 2–3, 5–7, 39, 134, 203, 205
Traywick, Ronnie (cousin), 6, 16, 58, 139
Traywick, Rose Marie (sister). *See* Arrowood, Rose Marie
Traywick, (William) Brownlow (great-grandfather), 2, 3
*Trial of Old Drum, The* (movie), 151–52
Tubb, Ernest, 10, 137, 192, 226
Turner, Josh, 162, 165, 167, 176, 205, 212, 220
Twain, Shania, 53
Twitty, Conway, 46–47, 51–52, 55–57, 72, 78, 97
Tyson, Terry, 137, 226

Underwood, Carrie, 168–69, 176, 223, 226
*Urban Cowboy* (movie), 14, 43

Van Dyke, Joe, 161–62, 180, 192, 198, 245
*Very Best of Randy Travis, The*, 164
Vipperman, Carl "Vip," 31
*Virtuoso, The* (short film), 195, 208, 217

"Waiting on the Light to Change," 99
Wariner, Steve, 35
Watson, Gene, 10–12, 16, 30, 58, 71, 178
Watson, Leon, 21–22, 247

Wayne, L D. *See* Money, Rick L D Wayne
Weinberg, Barry, 61, 73, 91, 109
Weir, Al, 187–89, 191, 201–4, 206, 208
Wenner, Gerry, 121
"We're Strangers Again," 98, 104
West, Dottie, 9
West, Shelly, 22
"Whisper My Name," 124, 158
Whitcomb, Allen, 37, 42, 46, 55, 71
Whitley, Keith, 34, 130
Williams, Bruce, 89–90, 102
Williams, Hank, 5, 10, 25, 45, 67, 111–12, 127
Williams, Hank, Jr., 33, 41, 48, 55–56, 61–62, 79, 94, 169
Williams, Mentor, 98
*Wind in the Wire*, 121, 123
"Wind in the Wire," 123
*Wind in the Wire* (movie), 121, 149
Wootten, Penny, 216
*Worship & Faith*, 161, 164
Wynette, Tammy, 62, 78, 97–98, 101, 104–6, 110, 144, 196, 214

Yearwood, Trisha, 112
Yoakum, Dwight, 37, 41, 47–48
York, Peter, 156
*You and You Alone*, 148
"You and You Alone," 143, 145
Young, Faron, 16, 52, 102, 247
Young, Kyle, 221
Youngblood, Jill, 38, 52, 66, 78, 128
*Young Guns* (movie), 119

**Diane Diekman** is the author of *Twentieth Century Drifter: The Life of Marty Robbins*, winner of the Belmont Country Music Book of the Year Award, and *Live Fast, Love Hard: The Faron Young Story*.

The University of Illinois Press
is a founding member of the
Association of University Presses.
———————————————

Composed in 10.25/14 Chaparral Pro
with Bauer Bodoni Std 1 display
by Lisa Connery
at the University of Illinois Press
Manufactured by Versa Press, Inc.

University of Illinois Press
1325 South Oak Street
Champaign, IL 61820–6903
www.press.uillinois.edu